Service Life Cycle Tools and Technologies:

Methods, Trends, and Advances

Jonathan Lee
National Central University, Taiwan

Shang-Pin Ma
National Taiwan Ocean University, Taiwan

Alan Liu
National Chung Cheng University, Taiwan

Information Science
REFERENCE

Managing Director:	Lindsay Johnston
Book Production Manager:	Sean Woznicki
Development Manager:	Joel Gamon
Development Editor:	Hannah Abelbeck
Acquisitions Editor:	Erika Carter
Typesetters:	Deanna Zombro, Chris Shearer
Print Coordinator:	Jamie Snavely
Cover Design:	Nick Newcomer

Published in the United States of America by
Information Science Reference (an imprint of IGI Global)
701 E. Chocolate Avenue
Hershey PA 17033
Tel: 717-533-8845
Fax: 717-533-8661
E-mail: cust@igi-global.com
Web site: http://www.igi-global.com

Library of Congress Cataloging-in-Publication Data

Service life cycle tools and technologies: methods, trends, and advances / Jonathan Lee, Shang-pin Ma, and Alan Liu, editors.
      p. cm.
  Includes bibliographical references and index.
   ISBN 978-1-61350-159-7 (hardcover) -- ISBN 978-1-61350-160-3 (ebook) -- ISBN 978-1-61350-161-0 (print & perpetual access) 1. Service-oriented architecture (Computer science) 2. Application software--Development. I. Lee, Jonathan, 1960- II. Ma, Shang-pin, 1977- III. Liu, Alan, 1964-
   TK5105.5828.S47 2011
   004.6'54--dc23
                              2011022621

British Cataloguing in Publication Data
A Cataloguing in Publication record for this book is available from the British Library.

All work contributed to this book is new, previously-unpublished material. The views expressed in this book are those of the authors, but not necessarily of the publisher.

Table of Contents

Section 3
Service Delivery

Section 4
Service Search and Selection

Section 5
Service Composition

Section 6
Service Verification and Validation

Preface

As service-oriented computing (SOC) gains wide acceptance, the need to understand the lifecycle of SOC-based software becomes inevitable, not only for developers, but also for users. SOC exploits both web services and service-oriented architectures (SOA) as fundamental elements for developing applications. Web services are autonomous, platform-independent computational elements that can be described, published, discovered, and composed using standard protocols to build applications across various platforms and organizations. SOA is a software architecture that identifies relevant participants and interactions that facilitate service publication, service discovery, service binding, and service composition. Currently, SOA technology is commonly treated as "implementing SOA with web services," which realizes SOC. Similar to the object-oriented paradigm, where software engineering has played a significant role both in describing software lifecycles and in providing fundamental and advanced technologies, SOC has become a new paradigm that is required of software engineering technologies. The development of service-oriented applications does not only depend on constructing service providers, but also considers service composition and delivery. Both service requesters and service providers, along with developers, will benefit from understanding the SOA lifecycle.

At present, research is ongoing in both industry and academia to address issues associated with the SOC domain, including service discovery, service composition, and service management. SOC fundamentally changes the way software applications are designed, constructed, delivered, and consumed, and it supports the development of interoperable, configurable and evolvable composite applications. It has emerged as a major trend of the computing paradigm in the past few years.

To apply service-oriented computing, we indentified high-level requirements for service-oriented environments that are realized by a service bus or a service engine to integrate and link all necessary components and services together. We have accomplished this by consolidating and summarizing extant industrial products and academic research:

- **Compatible with industrial standards:** service-oriented environments should be established based on standard specifications such as SOAP, WSDL, UDDI, BPEL, WS-policy, WS-security, OWL, et cetera. Standardization can enable the technology neutrality and interoperability that are very critical concerns for service-oriented computing.
- **Ease of integration with resources:** service-oriented environments should be capable of integrating data, applications, and processes. An important mission of the SOA is to enable multiple organizations or multiple departments in an enterprise to collaborate consistently. This inter- or intra-integration should be achievable as a result of technology neutrality and standards.

- **Service utility:** end users should be able to consume services on multiple devices (such as desktop computers, notebooks, handheld devices and cellular telephones), at any time, in any place. Thus, services should be hosted in the cloud (public or private) and exposed as standardized interfaces that allow various remote accesses via adequate authentication and authorization.
- **Context awareness and pluggability:** services delivered to the user should meet the user's personal needs, and services should be easily plugged into or out of the current working space that the service consumer is using. Accordingly, dynamic context and service selection, binding and re-binding should be considered during service delivery to achieve better adaptability.

For realizing above high-level requirements, we identified six research themes related to the concepts, issues, and methodology of service-oriented computing, including:

- **Service design and provision:** to build an SOA-based business solution, we need to first identify, design, and build services. In this phase, identifying business services and corresponding IT services is a critical concern. Next, we must design and build service implementations based on the IT service specifications. Choosing extant service components, wrapping or adapting existing software components into services, and establishing new services from the scratch are all common development strategies. Accordingly, a set of service components (with the same or different interfaces) will be prepared while above development strategies are performed well. The primary issues that should be addressed in the service design and provision phase include the following:
  - What are the service-oriented development processes and methods to be used? Should any new design patterns be specified to assist with building service-based/service- oriented software?
  - How should one develop service components in a more systematic manner? We should consider a means to model services from various viewpoints and explore the usage of formal specification for services and their integration with ontology.
  - How can we uncover the services embedded in legacy systems, databases, and web sites? What are the necessary service wrapping tools and procedures?
- **Service delivery:** most services, though varied in type and possessing different capabilities, need to be delivered to the requester's site. There are several requirements that should be addressed in the service delivery phase, including negotiating service contracts or service-level agreements, fulfilling the client's requests based on the contract, and rendering service results via appropriate channels (for software agents) or user interfaces (for end users). The main issues that would be addressed in service delivery phase include the following:
  - How to negotiate and establish Web Services Level Agreements and contracts?
  - How to compose remote services, local services, and UI components at the same time?
  - How to infuse user interactions into SOA and provide on-demand service user interfaces?
- **Service search and selection:** usually, multiple published services offer seemingly similar features but with some variations (e.g., different service interfaces, different attributes, different quality-level). A service requester can search, select, and bind services that satisfy his or her intensions. A service discovery facility can enhance the effectiveness of other activities (e.g., service design and provision, as well as service composition). Main issues that would be addressed in service search and selection phase include the following:

- How to transfer the original Web services into semantic Web services? How to annotate and interpret semantic information?
- How to capture the users' intension for making appropriate service requests? The query process should include refining users' query, generating query forms, and building users' personal ontology. Techniques such as goal formulation, ontological reasoning, case-base reasoning will be involved in this process.
- How to locate suitable services according to the user's request? Issues of semantics, uncertainty, and quality of web services should be addressed in the matchmaking process.

- **Service composition:** to fulfill a business solution or a user's request, combining multiple existing service components into a composite service is always beneficial. These composite services can be, in turn, recursively combined with other services into higher level solutions. Techniques for dynamic service composition and semi-automatic service composition can be applied in this phase. The main issues that should be addressed in the service composition phase include the following:
  - How should one fulfill the service transaction, rollback and compensation tasks in a complicated service flow? Service composition causes transactions to span in multiple web services. A service flow engine should be integrated with transaction-related functionalities to ensure safety in real business operation.
  - How should one efficiently realize QoWS-aware composition? Quality of web services is always an important concern when composing services. QoWS will affect the activities of selecting services, binding services, and re-planning composition paths. Challenges include how to provide an adequate model to define QoWS metrics, how to measure or calculate QoWS at runtime, and how to consolidate QoWS information to allow real-time alerts or offline process improvement.
  - How should one compose service dynamically per user request? Dynamic service composition focuses on translating users' needs into a service composition plan based on rule-based reasoning, state machine, and service patterns. The composition should include details about how service-to-service communications, collaborations, and flows are performed.

- **Service management:** services are monitored and controlled by configuring and collecting metrics, detecting failures at service levels and recovering the operational state of the malfunctioning service, as well as tuning service performance automatically or semi-automatically. One important goal in this phase is to ensure high reliability or high availability of the target system. The main issues that should be addressed in the service management phase include the following challenging questions.
  - How does one acquire and compute the quality of service, react appropriately to an abnormal status, and induce a common cause of performance decay for process improvement?
  - How can one increase and maintain service reliability and availability?
  - How should one mine service patterns through the analysis of users' behavior to adjust composite service dynamically and adaptively according to context changes or requirement changes?

- **Service verification and validation:** verification and validation (so-called "V&V") are important concepts in software engineering that aim to improve the quality of software products. Both dynamic testing and static checking mechanisms are common means to perform verification, which focuses on "building the product right," and to perform validation, which focuses on "producing the right product." V&V is also significant for developing SOA-based applications since we need to confirm that the service (either an atomic service or composite service) can offer the functionality and quality-levels it declares, and that it can satisfy the requester's demands. Main issues that would be addressed in service verification and validation include:

- The lack of source code about the service implementation makes it difficult to use white-box testing techniques and code-based test coverage criteria to test atomic web services.
- The lack of control over the services being composed happens when a service provider may change the services without notifying the service requester.
- The dynamic service binding can pose challenges in testing service compositions. Integration testing of service compositions needs to test all possible bindings in order to ensure that the dynamic behavior of service compositions is correct.
- The cost of testing service compositions can be a concern since service providers may charge a fee for each service invocation.
- The notions of concurrency, synchronization, and compensation also make service compositions difficult to understand and test. Currently, the supporting tools for testing these notions are still inadequate.

Above six research themes can be also treated as main activities or steps in the SOA lifecycle for developing and operating SOA-based systems. Firstly, service design and provision will be performed. Secondly, services will be delivered to the service requester. Thirdly, service management mechanism will be applied to ensure the success of service delivery. These three activities are the elementary tasks in the lifecycle. Service composition can be treated as an advanced service provision style to allow developers combine multiple component services at design time, or as an advanced service delivery style to search and select appropriate component services as well as to generate composite services dynamically at run time. Service verification and validation techniques can be embedded into both service design and service composition activities to improve the quality of either atomic services or composite services.

To provide a clear and consolidated view for current academic and industrial efforts in SOC, this book features fourteen chapters in eight parts to detail extant and promising methods, tools, and technologies along with the lifecycle of web services. The eight parts include introduction and foundation, service provision and design, service delivery, service search and selection, service composition, service management, service validation and verification, and SOA-based applications. In addition, this book provides a glossary section that includes definitions or descriptions of more than ninety terms in SOC domain.

SECTION 1: INTRODUCTION AND FOUNDATION

Chapter 1: Service-Oriented Computing: From Web Services to Service-Oriented Components

In this chapter, Chollet *et al.* present the different technologies implementing the new paradigm of SOA: Web Services, UPnP (Universal Plug And Play), DPWS (Devices Profile for Web Services), as well as service-oriented component OSGi (Open Service Gateway Initiative) and iPOJO. These technologies have been developed and adapted to multiple domains: application integration, pervasive computing, and dynamic application integration. Authors provide comprehensive analysis on these technologies and also propose in-depth summary and strong comparison.

SECTION 2: SERVICE PROVISION AND DESIGN

Chapter 2: Semi-Automated Lifecycles for Eliciting Requirements for Service-Oriented Environments

From a process and workflow point of view, Blake addresses the evolution of traditional software engineering approaches to support the conceptualization of abstract services that overlap multiple organizations. He stresses that traditional software engineering lifecycles must be enhanced with emerging processes related to the development applications for service-oriented environments. This chapter also discusses state-of-the-art approaches that elicit information about the requirements for service-oriented architectures. These approaches tend to leverage existing requirements engineering approaches to suggest aggregate service-based capabilities that are most effective for a particular environment.

Chapter 3: Quality of Service and Extra-Functional Properties for Web Services: A Model-Driven Approach

Stressing the importance of requirements specifications, Ortiz presents a model-based approach to deal with specifications and implementations of Quality of Service (QoS) and extra-functional properties (EPF) in a loosely coupled manner. The presented approach draws on two main software techniques, Model-Driven Architecture (MDA), which transforms models of QoS and EPF into code, and Aspect-Oriented Programming (AOP), which systematically handles scattered and tangled code of QoS and EPF. The chapter provides a case study to show results in increasing the system's modularity and thus reducing implementation and maintenance costs.

Chapter 4: The Foundations of Service Eco-Systems

In this chapter, Ghose seeks to design the formal basis for practical tools to support the design and maintenance of service eco-systems. He proposes a high-level Business Service Modeling Language (BSRL) that supports the modeling of the full spectrum of services, spanning from web services on the one extreme to abstractly defined business services on the other. Based on this language, the chapter describes a taxonomy of relationships between services in an eco-system. Besides, the author particularly addresses the question of which combination of functionalities might be packaged as a service, thus leading to a set of inter-related components constituting a service eco-system.

SECTION 3: SERVICE DELIVERY

Chapter 5: A QoS-Aware Service Bus with WSLA-Based Monitor for Media Production Systems

Due to enormously increasing distribution channels, media companies need to distribute their (television) programs through a variety of media, such as TV broadcasts, DVDs, the Internet, and mobile phones. Based on their industrial participations, Chen *et al.* describe a solution that was developed to address issues caused by multiple delivery pathways. It offers a media asset management system that is used to support media content production and distribution. Notably, this work implements service oriented architecture (SOA) that relies on an enhanced enterprise service bus (ESB). The enhanced ESB, referred to here as a QoS-Aware service bus (QASB), makes it possible to designate which of the available transcoding servers will perform a required task, thus providing a service selection scheme that improves the efficiency of media content production and distribution processes. This system was built for Taiwan's Public Television Service (PTS) in January 2010 and is currently providing complete support to the company's daily operations.

SECTION 4: SERVICE SEARCH AND SELECTION

Chapter 6: A Goal-Driven Approach for Service-Oriented Systems Design

This chapter introduces a goal-driven approach for modeling service requests in service-oriented systems. This approach is proposed to solve three research issues: how to represent a service request, how to map the request to predefined models, and how to generate a series of actions to satisfy these models. A goal model is used for user requirements elicitation, analysis, and representation. The service request from users is extracted and mapped to these goal models by a case-based method. A planning mechanism is designed to produce a sequence of activities to satisfy the extracted goals. A general architecture for an intention-aware service-oriented system is proposed for demonstrating how to apply the proposed approach.

SECTION 5: SERVICE COMPOSITION

Chapter 7: Bridging the Gap between Business Process Models and Service Composition Specifications

This chapter presents a flexible approach for aligning business process models with workflow specifications. Buchwald *et al.* propose an additional model layer, namely Business-IT-Mapping Model (BIMM), to maintain the complex dependencies that exist between high-level business process models (as used by domain experts) and technical workflow specifications (i.e., service composition schemas). Examples from practical settings illustrate the high effectiveness of this approach with respect to the maintenance of service-oriented applications.

Chapter 8: A Model-Driven Approach to Service Composition with Security Properties

Producing secure composite services is always a technical challenge that is difficult to tackle. With the emphasis in security problems, Chollet and Lalanda present a model-driven approach to service composition dealing with nonfunctional aspects. They propose a model-driven approach to facilitate the composition of heterogeneous and secured services. Authors also provide strong background work on security and model-driven topics for readers' reference.

Chapter 9: Adaptive and Dynamic Service Compositions in the OSGi Service Platform

Toward the challenges raised in dynamic service composition, Touseau *et al.* provide an overview on dynamic service oriented platforms, giving special focus on the OSGi service platform. Authors present principles and mechanisms that can help to handle "dynamicity", and supply information on the dynamic service-based component models targeting the OSGi platform. These models allow the realization of applications that are adaptive upon dynamic scenarios where service availability is uncertain.

SECTION 6: SERVICE VERIFICATION AND VALIDATION

Chapter 10: Service Composition Validation and Verification

Verification and validation techniques that can find defects to increase quality of software systems attract enormous interest and attention both in industry and academia. Palomo-Duarte analyzes plenty of approaches to web service and web service composition verification and validation. According to his full survey and in-depth analysis, there is a long way ahead to provide good support for testing techniques in WS-BPEL, the *de facto* service composition specification. Industrial tools include very limited testing support (mainly basic functional testing) whereas academia is taking the right steps in most directions, adapting techniques and facing trends. However, automatic tools supporting for V&V of service composition are remaining as a challenge in mainstream development tools.

SECTION 7: SERVICE MANAGEMENT

Chapter 11: Towards a High-Availability-Driven Service Composition Framework

Although availability of Web services plays a crucial role in building robust service-oriented applications, it has been largely neglected, especially for service composition. In this chapter, Lee *et al.* propose a service composition framework that integrates a set of composition-based service discovery mechanisms, a user-oriented service delivery approach, as well as a service management mechanism for composite services. Authors also conduct well-covered literature surveys for web service availability.

SECTION 8: SOA APPLICATIONS

Chapter 12: SOA Designed Health Care System for Taiwan Government

In Taiwan, the government agencies have promoted SOA proactively for a long period and have developed e-Government service platform for integrating a variety of government e-services. The Information and Communications Research Laboratories (ICL) of the Industrial Technology Research Institute (ITRI) is also committed in SOA research and has emphasized on the establishment of SOA service system regarding medical information and health care. Based on their successful experiences, Shi *et al.* describe how to construct health care applications based on SOA and Web services technology and propose a web service converged management platform, namely Web Services Security Gateway (WSSG), to decrease the complexity of various security policy management by separating the security control and system development.

Chapter 13: Case Study on SOA Implementation Framework and Applications

The Enterprise Service Bus (ESB) is an important middleware technology that provides a set of infrastructure capabilities that enable the integration of services in SOA, such as event-driven processing, content-based routing and filtering, as well as complex data transmission. Innovative Digitech-Enabled Applications & Services Institute (IDEAS) of Institute for Information Industry (III) in Taiwan has implemented an ESB that comprises four modules, including Event-Service, Message-Service, Data-Service, and Process-Service. From a practitioner's point of view, Weng *et al.* depict how to design and implement the ESB in depth and also discuss three industrial applications atop the ESB, including an e-learning system, a smart store system and a medical system.

Chapter 14: Abstract Service for Cyber Physical Service Composition

In this chapter, Zhao *et al.* propose an approach that models cyber physical system functionalities as services to solve the collaboration problem using semantic web services. The approach extends the existing OWL-S framework to address the natures of the cyber physical systems and their functionalities, which are different from software systems and their functionalities. The extension addresses the abstract service, resource contention, physical constraint, and context requirement issues. A case study is also provided to illustrate the proposed approach.

With a brief introduction to the outline of this book, the readers should be able to see the goals of this book, which are: to quickly inform the readers to grasp the current research status of SOC from the software engineering point of view, and also to lead the user to be aware of the importance of practicing software engineering in this new paradigm. Finally, we would like to express our sincere gratitude to everyone who has contributed to this book, including the authors and the reviewers.

Jonathan Lee
National Central University, Taiwan

Shang-Pin Ma
National Taiwan Ocean University, Taiwan

Alan Liu
National Chung Cheng University, Taiwan

Section 1
Introduction and Foundation

Chapter 1
Service–Oriented Computing:
From Web Services to Service–Oriented Components

Stéphanie Chollet
Laboratoire d'Informatique de Grenoble, France

Philippe Lalanda
Laboratoire d'Informatique de Grenoble, France

Jonathan Bardin
Laboratoire d'Informatique de Grenoble, France

ABSTRACT

The visionary promise of Service-Oriented Computing (SOC) is a world-scale network of loosely coupled services that can be assembled with little effort in agile applications that may span organizations and computing platforms. In practice, services are assembled in a Service-Oriented Architecture (SOA) that provides mechanisms and rules to specify, publish, discover and compose available services. The aim of this chapter is to present the different technologies implementing the new paradigm of SOA: Web Services, UPnP, DPWS, and service-oriented component OSGi and iPOJO. These technologies have been developed and adapted to multiple domains: application integration, pervasive computing and dynamic application integration.

INTRODUCTION

The Service-Oriented Computing (SOC) represents today a solution of choice to deal with integration issues. SOC promotes the use of well-defined composition units – services – to support the rapid development of applications. The central objective

of this approach is to reduce dependencies among composition units, where a unit is typically some remote functionality accessed by clients. By reducing such dependencies, each element can evolve separately, so the application is more flexible than monolithic applications (Papazoglou & Georgakopoulos, 2003), (Escoffier, 2007). Services are assembled in a Service-Oriented Architecture (SOA) that provides mechanisms and rules to

DOI: 10.4018/978-1-61350-159-7.ch001

specify, publish, discover and compose available services. Depending on the target application domain, different protocols and mechanisms are used to implement SOA. For instance, Web Services (www.w3c.org) are dominant to integrate IT applications. UPnP (UPnP Forum, 2008) or DPWS (Microsoft, 2006) are preferred in small area networks for devices. OSGi (OSGi Alliance, 2007) and iPOJO (Escoffier & Hall, 2007) are often used in centralized, embedded equipments.

The service-oriented approach has been implemented in many domains. Figure 1 illustrates the use of service technologies in different application domains.

This chapter is organized as follows. First, we present the Web Services technology and the requirements of application integration which are solved by Web Services. The second section deals with the pervasive computing and the technologies adapted to this domain: UPnP and DPWS. The third section introduces the Service-Oriented Computing in dynamic environment and the technologies implementing this new paradigm: OSGi and iPOJO. Before the conclusion, the fourth section proposes a comparison of the service technologies presented in the previous sections.

Figure 1. Service technologies and application domains

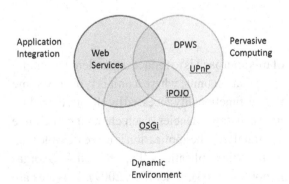

APPLICATION INTEGRATION

Web Services are the most popular and well-known technology for implementing Service-Oriented Architecture, both in the industry and the academia. In this section, we will present the main Web Services principles. Then, we will describe the three standards this technology uses: WSDL, UDDI and SOAP.

Web Services

The main purpose of Web Services was to render applications available via the Internet or from within an Intranet. Web Services comply with the service-oriented approach, meaning they can be described, published and discovered. A service provider can describe their service's functional and non-functional characteristics in a WSDL (W3C, 2001) file and then registers the service description in an UDDI (OASIS, 2004) service registry. A client, or consumer, can search the UDDI registry for services that meet their requirements.

From the consumer perspective, a Web Service is a black box that provides no technical details on its implementation. The only available information includes the Web Service functionalities, certain properties, location and invocation instructions.

Consumers use the SOAP protocol (W3C, 2000) to communicate with Web Services. The Web Services architecture is illustrated by Figure 2.

This architecture hides the Web Services implementation complexity from the user. Hence, a Web Service may use other services (*i.e.* Web Services, or of other types) in order to provide its functionalities. The Web Service's users remain completely unaware of such aspects. Certain coordination is required among the different service calls.

Web Services are a successful technology because of the loose-coupling it ensures between service consumers and service providers. As service providers describe offered service functionalities in a standard language, service consumers

Figure 2. Web service architecture

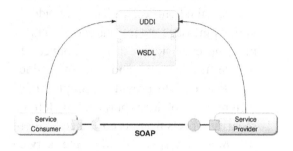

do not need to know the programming languages of the services they use. Service descriptions only specify the service functionalities, while the provider-specific technical details remain hidden from consumers.

Web Services are described in WSDL (*Web Services Description Language*) (W3C, 2001). A WSDL file comprises a functional service description and contains no information on the service implementation. In Addition, the WSDL description provides information on the service location and on the data and protocols to use for calling the service. In practice, this the WSDL file is an XML file divided into two parts:

- An abstract definition of the service interface, including the supported Web Service operations, parameters and data types.
- A concrete definition for accessing the service, including the service location (*i.e.* the service provider's network address) and the specific service access protocols.

A WSDL file describes a Web Service's functionalities. Nonetheless, it does not currently provide information on non-functional properties, such as security and transactions. New WSDL extensions have been proposed to deal with non-functional specifications, including WS-Security (OASIS, 2006) for security, WS-Transaction (IBM, 2004) for transactions and others named

WS-* (Weerawarana, 2005). Still, these new specifications are progressing slowly and evolving regularly.

A detailed WSDL description of a Web Service's interface does not suffice for clients to use that Web Service. In order to use a Web Service, a client must first find the Web Service and ensure that it corresponds to their requirements. For this purpose, the Web Services architecture proposes the use of an UDDI (*Universal Description Discovery and Integration*) service registry.

One of the main advantages of adopting the Web Services technology within an enterprise is the sharing of services via the Internet or in an Intranet. Sharing Web Services speeds up application development and thus allows reducing the enterprise's costs and delays. The UDDI service registry is the key element for service sharing, as it enables service referencing and functionality classification.

UDDI is a service registry specification that proposes Web Service description file registration and searching facilities, corresponding to client expectations. UDDI was initially designed by and for the industry for having an implementation platform-independent standard, in order to:

- **know** the enterprises that provide Web Services;
- **discover** the available Web Services that satisfy client requirements.

To simplify service searching operations, the UDDI standard proposes three different kinds of service registry:

- **White pages** that offer enterprise related information;
- **Yellow pages** that present services according to their functionalities, by using the standard industry taxonomy;

- **Green pages** that describe the services provided by enterprises. The Green pages contain location references for the Web Services WSDL description files.

Nevertheless, at present, UDDI registries are hardly used in practice. In fact, the simplified search techniques offered by the UDDI will make it impractical to assume that it can be very useful for Web Services' discovery or composition (Al-Masri, 2008). It seems that enterprises prefer to build Web Services architectures by developing their own service registries (*e.g.* The German Post – Deutsche Post). While this is an expensive solution, it is currently comprehensible, since registry technologies are presently rather incomplete and lacking in robustness.

WSDL and UDDI are two Web Services standards. WSDL enables the description of service functionalities and the manner they should be used. UDDI enables the registration of services that can subsequently be referenced and used by service consumers. Another important aspect of the Web Services architecture consists of the communication between the various parties involved. Web Services communication is implemented via with SOAP protocol.

SOAP (W3C, 2000) was initially an acronym for *Simple Object Access Protocol* and is a protocol whose syntax is based on XML. The goal of the SOAP protocol is the standardized exchange of data in distributed environments. SOAP provides access to remote services regardless of their run-time platforms. Initially proposed by Microsoft and IBM, the SOAP specification is currently a W3C Recommendation. Notably, since version 1.2, SOAP is no longer an acronym, as the notion of object has become obsolete.

A SOAP message is represented in a XML file, and contains a compulsory envelope, an optional header, and a mandatory body:

- the **header** element contains child elements, called entries, which allow adding various message extensions. For example, message extensions can be introduced to handle transactions and security. Since SOAP wanted to provide a simple, lightweight protocol, it has purposefully left out security aspects from its core specification.
- the **body** element contains the service method to invoke, as well as the method's invocation parameters.

The SOAP protocol relies on a communication standard such as HTTP (*HyperText Transfer Protocol*), but can also use other protocols, such as SMTP (*Simple Mail Transfer Protocol*). The advantage of using SOAP over HTTP is that it facilitates the communication by being able to pass through proxies and fire-walls. Hence, SOAP is easily adaptable to previous technologies, while remaining simple and extensible. SOAP provides the advantage of being platform-independent and programming language-independent. However the SOAP protocol is limited by its poor latency performance (Davis, 2002). This limitation is principally due to the cost of parsing the XML (SOAP calls). Some effort has been done in order to improve SOAP performance (Elfwing, 2002) and several alternatives have been proposed (*e.g.* JSON-RPC[1]).

Web Service and Application Integration

In recent years, application integration has become one of the most important domains in computer science. The main purpose is to provide the necessary methods and infrastructures to build new applications from existing applications, also known as legacy applications. This is a recurrent activity; it becomes inevitable when a company wants to expand its information system in order to provide new services, either internal or external.

These new services must generally interoperate with the existing applications, in order to rely on the enterprise data and to comply with the internal enterprise processes.

Application integration is a complex activity for one simple reason: the applications to be used by a new service were never designed for this, and in general, not even for communicating with each other. It results in strong differences in: the way of representing data; the absence of appropriate interfaces; different communication protocols used; access to shared data without synchronization; and applications evolving at different paces.

Today, Web Services provide significant technical support for integrating applications. Namely, they can partly solve the problems related to communication protocols by providing a unifying protocol based on Internet technologies. Certainly, this represents a limited part of the problems related to the integration of applications, but nevertheless advances towards uniformity in the description and communication of enterprise applications.

To conclude, we can note that Web Services represent a widespread technology for enterprise applications integration. Web Services will be increasingly used for inter-enterprise communications, based on distributed service registries (*Business to Business* [B2B]). Meanwhile, services available on Web remain more of a theoretical possibility than an actual reality. Microsoft has announced his intention to release to release *Windows Cloud*, based on the *Cloud Computing* concept, involving applications available from a Web server and accessible via the Internet, rather than installed on client machines. This concept is part of what is commonly called Software as a Service (SaaS), while Microsoft refers to it as *software plus service*. In case it successes, it could ease significantly Web Service adoption in desktop computing.

DEVICES

Pervasive Computing

Pervasive or ubiquitous computing corresponds to an information processing model where the user interacts naturally with their environment. The model proposed by pervasive computing consists of using the objects in the environment as a means of interaction between users and computer systems. This model was introduced for the first time in 1991 by Mark Weiser (Weiser, 1991) in an article presenting his vision of 21st century computing.

The appearance of this new information processing model was possible due to the evolution of physical devices for handling information. Devices involved in pervasive computing systems must have the following characteristics:

- **Miniature:** The devices must be able to naturally blend with the environment. For that purpose, the miniaturization of devices is necessary.
- **Communication:** The devices must be able to communicate and to interact with other equipment that is present in the environment.
- **Autonomy:** The devices must have their own source of energy in order to be autonomous.

The evolution of computer equipment in recent years appears to have contributed to the creation of devices that are coherent with the vision of pervasive computing.

Since the invention of computing and of the first computer, we have witnessed a race to miniaturize and continually increase the processing power of equipment. In the 1950's, computers occupied entire rooms and were only able to perform simple calculations. In contrast, devices today measure sometimes only a few millimeters and are capable of performing much more complex calculations. This physical evolution has allowed the popularization of computers and modified the way computers are used. In the 1950's, a single computer was utilized by hundreds of users. In the 1980's the personal computers appear. An individual has his own computer and can be considered the unique user. The evolution of devices continues, they multiply and now each user has several of them. The trend is the inverse of the beginning of computing. Before, there was one machine for multiple users; now we have multiple machines per user.

Another important point is the emergence of communication technologies between computers in the 1970's. Initially these technologies required costly communication infrastructures that carried little information. Today communication technologies have become widespread. The advent of the Internet in the 1990's created a network connecting devices from all over the world. This network uses low-cost communication technologies, which largely contributed to its widespread adoption by the general public. In more recent years, new communication technologies have been developed allowing wireless communication (*e.g.* WiFi, GSM, Bluetooth and RFID). These technologies are now embedded in devices allowing them to communicate with each other and augmenting their mobility.

Finally, the progress achieved in energy autonomy plays an important role in the emergence of this computing domain. Such evolution allowed the construction of computing devices capable of functioning for years (*e.g.* RFID sensors) using a simple battery. The evolution of the devices' energy autonomy currently triggers the other advancements in computing.

These advancements have lead to the creation of computing devices offering several modes of interaction to users. Such modes impact on the utilization of mobile devices such as PDAs or portable phones, which are both results of the previously described advancements. Current research efforts target techniques for increasing the devices' autonomy, as it represents a key factor. If this autonomy proved insufficient, the domain of pervasive computing would not move forward because its main actors (*i.e.* the mobile devices) would not have the required features.

Challenges of Pervasive Computing

This domain of computing encompasses a large number of applications particularly useful to help people in their everyday life. A pervasive computing system typically consists of a series of hardware and software capable of interacting with each other. A wide variety of electronic equipment is currently available to perform various functions, such as interacting with the real environment, providing control and display support to users, or making available data and services offered by applications to other equipment. The main challenge of pervasive computing is to provide a coherent pervasive environment, providing useful services and applications, involving a set of heterogeneous, distributed and dynamic equipment and software, communicating across different protocols. In this context, several characteristics specific to the field of pervasive computing make this area attractive in terms of industry and users, while raising difficult research problems for the development and management of these systems.

- **Distribution.** The devices are an integral part of the environment. They are scattered across the physical environment and are accessible through different protocols that can use cable or wireless technologies. Applications using the capabilities of such equipment do not necessarily run on the same equipments and are therefore distributed.
- **Heterogeneity.** There are currently a large number of software technologies and communication protocols for the field of pervasive computing. Today there are no plans on how to reach a consensus on a

common and uniform communication protocol. More than fifty protocols, working groups and specification efforts are already available for home networks. The standardization of communication protocols is not possible because the devices can be of very different natures, having an impact on the communication protocols used. For example, a lamp that has little resources communicates through a very simple protocol, while a PDA or a media server can use more complex communication protocols, for example protocols that consider security. In addition, manufacturers supplying equipment and protocols have no strategic interest in this type of uniform protocol, since they would lose control of their equipment.

- **Dynamism.** The availability of equipment in a pervasive environment is much more volatile than in other areas of computing. This problem is caused by several factors including:

  1. users can move freely and frequently change their location, hence having an impact on the position of equipment they carry;
  2. users can voluntarily turn on and off the devices or they may inadvertently run out of energy/battery;
  3. users and providers may periodically update the deployed services.

- **Multiple providers.** The devices in a pervasive environment generally come from different vendors. In addition, applications deployed and running on such equipment can be delivered by other suppliers. In this context, some applications will be established through collaborations between different providers involving the creation of applications with several administration authorities. It is envisaged that the equipment vendors and service providers want to keep some control over their devices and software and thus limit the access to external entities.

- **Scalability.** The number of devices present in a pervasive environment can be very important. This creates a problem of scalability in applications running in this type of environment. Thus pervasive systems must be capable of handling a large number of equipments that are also dynamic.

- **Security.** Security is a key role in building pervasive environments. Indeed, such open systems allow people in the environment to have access to the computing system. However, access to certain devices or personal data must be highly secured. The applications running on this type of system should guarantee the confidentiality of data. Access to private pervasive systems such as automated homes or cars must also include access control to ensure, for example, that a thief will not be able to disconnect the alarm system by connecting to the pervasive system.

- **Auto-adaption.** In addition to the dynamism of software and equipment, pervasive systems are constantly faced with the evolution in their execution context. These evolutions may include changes in behavior, location, mood and habits of users, as well as changes in behavior or availability of other software. The applications running on this type of environment must be able to adapt to these changes and develop strategies to address the various events that may occur during their execution.

- **Simplicity of use.** Finally, an essential characteristic of a pervasive system is the simplicity of use and management. Indeed, this type of system is intended to be used by users who have no knowledge in informatics. As a consequence, pervasive environments must be accessible and even transparent to anyone. The purpose of pervasive computing is to make the devices disappear from the environment. This means that the access interface to pervasive systems must be easy to use and the applications running in these systems must be capable of adapting to different events that can intervene to maintain services usable in all circumstances.

All of the presented features and properties of the pervasive applications and environments must be taken into consideration during the design and development of pervasive services. One of the important parts is to allow a pervasive system to continually adapt to changes in the environment. These evolutions may come from changes in the application and the runtime platform as well as from the changes on the physical environment and context of the user (*e.g.* resource availability, user location, preferences, or habits). In the context of pervasive computing, targeted users have no knowledge of computer systems. Therefore, the adaptations of the system must remain transparent to the user, while taking into account the difficulties previously mentioned, such as resource heterogeneity, distribution and multiple authorities.

Dynamic Service-Oriented Computing

The commonly accepted vision of the Service-Oriented Computing (SOC) is the Papazoglou's definition: "Services are self-describing, platform agnostic computational elements" (Papazoglou, 2003).

However, certain definitions introduce additional interactions that are specific to what we call the dynamic service approach. This approach is concerned with the modifications that occur in the service execution environment. Therefore, two primitives were added to the service-oriented approach:

- The service withdrawal (Figure 3), which informs consumers when a service provider becomes unavailable;
- The service notification (Figure 4), which informs consumers of the arrival of service providers that correspond to their requirements.

If the two primitives were included into the SOA, then consumers may choose and possibly exchange their service providers during runtime. Hence, we add a new SOA advantage by managing the environment's dynamic evolution.

The use of the service-oriented paradigm for building pervasive applications proves judicious because it provides low-coupling, late-binding, dynamism and support for multi-provider applications.

Figure 3. Service withdrawal

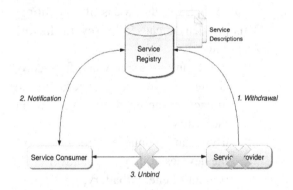

Figure 4. Service notification

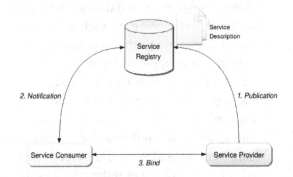

The service-oriented approach provides loose-coupling between application entities. This allows them to evolve separately. This feature is especially useful when building pervasive applications. Indeed, it allows an application to depend on a feature that is useful to its operation without worrying about the device that performs it. For example, an application could need a display, which could be provided by a television, a computer monitor or a PDA display. The application does not need to know how the image rendering service is implemented. This is an important feature for hiding device heterogeneity that is so common in the pervasive environment. The large variety of devices and their mode of operation and communication make it extremely difficult to implement applications involving these devices. Hiding the heterogeneity of communication protocols and devices simplifies the development of pervasive applications. This is possible due to the loose-coupling property provided by the service-oriented approach.

The service-oriented approach provides a late-binding feature. This allows to bind services when they will be used. This binding is made at runtime and not when services are deployed. Pervasive applications can greatly benefit from this property for dynamically binding the services available in the environment. For example, this enables a service that depends on a display service to only bind to an actual display service when it needs to execute. This feature notably permits the creation of applications that are compatible with multiple execution environments. For example, in the home automation domain, an application with this feature can be developed for all the targeted houses; the application will dynamically bind to the services available on each home environment. Without this feature, a different application should be specifically developed for each environment. This feature allows the development of applications that are generic with respect to the providers of their required services. Consequently, when implementing a home automation application,

developers have no control over the execution environment(s) where the application will be deployed. However, developers must make use of services provided by the execution environment. The use of late binding allows the developer to design their application on the assumption that a service will be present on the execution environment. At runtime, the application will automatically bind to the service available in the environment.

The dynamic service-oriented approach provides support for monitoring the availability of third party services. Moreover, this approach provides the opportunity to monitor the availability of dynamic devices in the environment. This property is especially useful when developing pervasive applications. Indeed, the availability of certain devices and software services may fluctuate on the execution platform. The dynamic service approach provides support for applications that can monitor the availability of these devices. The applications are then able to react to the departure or arrival of required devices and functionalities. In addition, service-oriented components approaches, such as iPOJO, automatically manage service dependencies and life-cycles, depending on the dynamic availability of required services. This approach enables the creation of pervasive applications that can automatically monitor the availability of functionalities offered by mobile devices. For example, an application requiring the use of an SMS service will be activated only when a mobile phone is present in the environment. This feature allows to create applications based on the assumption that a service will be present in the environment. The life cycle of the application will be managed automatically (*e.g.* the application becomes active when the required services are available). Dynamism is also extremely important when the middleware (*i.e.* the platform) runs on a mobile device. The reason is that when the platform is running on a PDA or SmartPhone, the user moves and discovers devices with which they can dynamically interact. In this case, the availability of devices becomes volatile and the ability to automatically follow dynamic changes is important.

The service-oriented approach offers support for the execution of multi-provider applications. This means that applications can be built using services from different providers. As a result, a single application can have multiple administrative authorities. This feature is notably useful for building applications that use devices from different suppliers. For example, an application may involve multimedia devices, such as television sets and other equipment, such as shutters, which are supplied by different vendors. This type of application makes use of services provided by different vendors. Each service is separately administered by a different entity. The service-oriented approach makes it possible for a single application to integrate the two services. In addition, supporting this kind of applications is useful because it is not always possible to know in advance which services provider will be available. The application could have been initially designed to work with services from a single provider, but for availability reasons finally configured to use a service from a different provider.

In conclusion, using the service-oriented approach facilitates the development of pervasive applications, as it addresses some of the challenges raised by this application type. Hence, the challenges of distribution, heterogeneity, dynamisms and multiple authorities are resolved by certain features of the dynamic service-oriented approach. Service-oriented component approaches address some of the complexity of self-adaptation, as a component automatically becomes invalid when one of its required services is unavailable.

UPnP and DPWS

UPnP and DPWS are two standards commonly used in pervasive environment. These specifications are based on the dynamic service-oriented architecture principles. Service provider publishes its device description on the network with a multicast protocol. Service consumer subscribes to the topic of the device. The service registry is not an entity of the UPnP and DPWS architecture; it is a logical view of the multicast mechanism, as illustrated by Figure 5.

UPnP (UPnP Forum, 2008) is the acronym for *Universal Plug and Play*. It is a specification defined from an industrial initiative and is currently run by the UPnP Forum. The goal of this specification is to simplify connections between heterogeneous communicating devices and the construction of home networks. UPnP was inspired and eventually derived from the Plug and Play technology, which allows dynamically connecting peripherals to a computer.

In details, the service registry is based on a discovery protocol, named SSDP (*Simple Service Discovery Protocol*), and an event protocol, named GENA (*Generic Event Notification Architecture*). The device description is defined with an XML file. The binding between the service producer and the service consumer is done through the SOAP protocol.

Nowadays, UPnP is widely used in SOHO hardware (*e.g.* routers, firewall) as a mean to administrate those devices in a seamless way. UPnP has also been adopted as a standard for media devices (*e.g.* TV, Hifi...) and software (*e.g.* media player).

However, the lack of default authentication as well as the use of HTTP over UDP has often been criticized. Similar initiatives, such as DPWS

Figure 5. UPnP and DPWS architecture

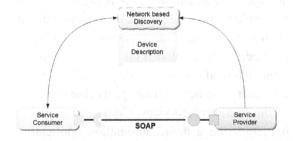

have been created as an answer to these criticisms. Indeed, the specification introduced by DPWS in addition to UPnP is fully aligned with Web Services technology. This alignment is done to enable a secure Web Service description, discovery and communication between networking devices.

DPWS is the acronym for *Device Profile for Web Services*. It is a specification (Microsoft, 2006) proposed and maintained by Microsoft. Windows Vista and Windows 7 natively integrate this specification. This simplifies integrating devices into a home or office network. DPWS is thus presented by Microsoft as a replacement for UPnP, although it is part of a monopolistic strategy.

DYNAMIC APPLICATION INTEGRATION

Service-Oriented Component

The component approach is older than the service approach and recommends the usage of components for constructing applications (Heineman, 2001). A component can be seen as a software block that is constructed to be assembled with other components (Wuyts, 2001). Components have two clear objectives:

- **Megaprogramming**, that is, module-based programming. Using large grain software blocks is intended to improve software reuse and productivity, and is favored in view of the ever growing size of software.
- **Improving software modularity**, which is not sufficient if only using, for example, object oriented programming techniques.

Components have been conceived to be re-used in different applications without requiring knowledge about how a component has been implemented. It suffices to know the functionality of a component and how to assemble it with others. In this section, we will explain the main characteristics of components and the benefits obtained from the component-oriented programming and service-oriented programming approaches.

No consensus can be found on the definition of component. However, one of the most cited definitions is that of Szyperski:

"A software component is a unit of composition which contractually specified interfaces and explicit context dependencies only. A software component can be deployed independently and is subject to composition by third parties." (Szyperski, 2002)

This definition mentions the most important concepts that characterize components:

- **Interface specification:** components expose their functionality through interfaces;
- **Explicit dependencies:** components present their requirements. There are two types of dependencies:
  - "logical" dependencies towards other components functionalities;
  - "physical" dependencies towards code, for example, software libraries.
- **Instantiation:** components provide a type and can be instantiated more than once;
- **Deployment independence:** a component is the default unit of deployment, although this characteristic has been controversial (Oreizy, 1998).

Components, being created in order to be assembled, require a composition mechanism which can be seen in Figure 6. As a matter of fact, most component approaches have defined a component based *Architecture Description Language*, called ADL, to define an application. ADL, which was not initially created, but later conceived, is based on two elements:

- **Instances:** component instances form the application's business logic. Instances are required for the applications functionality;

Figure 6. Example of component assembly

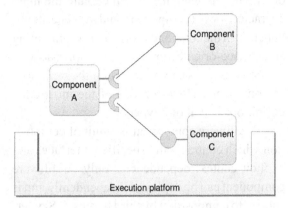

- **Connectors:** bindings between different component instances that are determined according to the properties provided and required by the different component types.

An execution environment is associated to the component oriented approach. Its purpose is to construct the final application and it is sometimes compared to a mini operating system (Bachmann, 2000) because it takes care of various aspects of the lifecycle of instances and/or of non-functional properties.

Analyzing the main concepts of the component oriented approach previously explained we can see that one of the strong points is the component lifecycle management: particularly, deployment and instantiation are only lightly covered by the service-oriented approach. Regarding the implementation method, this is not at all covered in the component-oriented approach.

It is interesting to note that, in the scientific community regarding the component-oriented approach, namely Component-Based Software Engineering (CBSE), an interesting approach has been proposed based on the concept of separation of concerns. The structure of components follow this principle, that is, the functional code of a component is clearly separated from the non-functional code, as for example is the case regarding transactions, persistence or security.

One of the most used methods for applying the separation of concerns principle is using containers. A container is illustrated in Figure 7.

The business logic code of a component is wrapped in a container that is in charge of certain non-functional aspects according to the specifications given by the user and the component's lifecycle management. There are many implementations of component models detailed and compared in (Cervantes, 2004a). These implementations focus, in general, on a unique non-functional aspect. For example, event-based communication in JavaBeans (Sun), or transactions and data persistence managed by Enterprise JavaBeans (EJB). Since many non-functional aspects are recurring, there are standard libraries of non-functional code. However, some approaches give the user the liberty to define their own non-functional aspects. These are called extensible component approaches. Fractal (ObjectWeb, 2004) is an example of extensible component model.

The Service-Oriented Component approach was proposed in 2004 in (Cervantes, 2004b). It combines the advantages of components and services. The concepts that exist in Service-Oriented Computing enrich the component model. This

Figure 7. Component structure

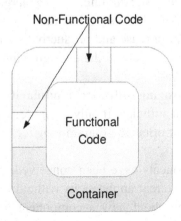

provides components with the capability of supporting dynamic availability of components at execution time.

This approach is based on the following principles:

- **A service provides functionality.** Services provide reusable operations.
- **A service is described by a service specification** which contains syntactic information and, eventually, behavioral and semantic information. This specification is useful for service composition, interaction and discovery. Dependencies with other services are expressed in the syntactic part of the specification.
- **A component implements a service specification.** Components must respect restrictions defined in the specification. Specifications imposed by the implementation must also be expressed.
- **The service-oriented interaction model is used for resolving all dependencies.** Services are implemented as component instances and registered in a service registry. This registry is used at execution time to locate the instances, which resolve the service's dependencies.
- **Service compositions are described as service specifications.** Composition is a specification of services that allow to choose the components to be instantiated. Composition is performed at the time components are found and instantiated. Bindings are not defined explicitly; they are inferred from service dependencies.
- **Service specifications are the foundation for substitutability.** In a composition, a component can be replaced by whichever component that respects the same service specification.

It is clear that with the service-oriented component approach, we benefit from the best of both worlds. From components we obtain a development model that is simple and a clear description of composition. From services, we obtain weak-coupling and dynamism. In the next sections, we will present two technologies, OSGi and iPOJO, that make possible a dynamic service-oriented component framework.

OSGi

OSGi (OSGi Alliance, 2007) is a service platform that was proposed by the OSGi Alliance formed by numerous companies such as IBM, Motorola and Nokia. The OSGi specification was originally proposed for home and network gateways. These gateways are commonly limited in memory and execution capacity. They also have high constraints regarding software components lifecycles because, in this domain, new software components must be deployable and assembled dynamically on the gateway without interrupting the execution of other components installed. Today, with the emergence of new application domains for embedded systems, such as the automotive or telecommunications industries, the OSGi platform is becoming the *de facto* standard for the development of dynamically reconfigurable applications. OSGi becoming a standard also because it is used in application servers such as the JOnAS 5 (ObjectWeb, 2007) application server hosted by OW2 or the Sun Glassfish v3 (Sun) application server from Sun Microsystems, or even for plug-in frameworks such as the Eclipse IDE (Gruber, 2005).

One of the strong points of the OSGi specification is the complete lifecycle management of components. The lifecycle considers the conditioning and packaging of software components, all the way to its uninstallation. To achieve this, OSGi proposes a specific deployment system. This system permits independently deploying different parts of an application. The unit of deployment being a bundle, they can be deployed and administered at runtime. Thus, it is possible to install, start, stop, update or remove bundles at runtime without interrupting the platform. The lifecycle of bundles is presented in Figure 8. One characteristic of bundles is that they specify dependencies with other deployment units at the Java package level. Packages are either provided or required. This permits ensuring at runtime that an application's code dependencies are resolved at runtime.

OSGi specifies a dynamic Service-Oriented Architecture. OSGi uses the Java platform and an implementation of the previously presented deployment layer. OSGi is a centralized platform with a service registry. Services are described using Java interfaces and semantic properties that users are free to specify. The invocation of a service is done by Java method calls. Figure 9 illustrates the Service-Oriented Architecture approach of the OSGi specification.

The principle of operation of the service-oriented architecture proposed by the specification is as follows:

- A service provider publishes a service in the OSGi registry. The service is described by a Java interface that defines the functional and syntactical parts for using the service. The service is completed with a set of properties that are freely specified by the provider.
- A service consumer uses the service registry to locate the services that satisfy its functional requirements and the complementary properties specified. The service registry responds giving the service consumer the list of services that satisfy the requirements.
- Consumers directly invoke services proposed by one of the providers proposed by the registry.

The OSGi specification provides a centralized Service-Oriented Architecture. The dynamism of this architecture is supported, in large part, by the service registry that permits locating all the service providers available. It maintains a relationship between the service descriptions and service providers. The OSGi platform provides a series of primitives and mechanisms so applications can be dynamically informed of the availability of services. A service provider can thus be removed, causing all its provided services to become unavailable, making them unusable by service consumers.

Figure 8. OSGi bundle lifecycle

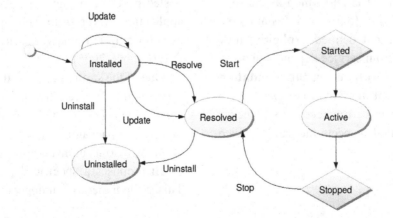

Figure 9. OSGi architecture

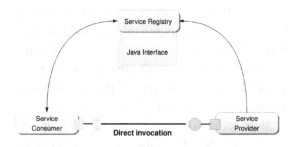

There are various implementations of the OSGi specification, both commercial (privative) and open source. Of these implementations, the most active communities are around the Apache Felix (http://felix.apache.org/site/index.html) project from the Apache Software Foundation, Equinox (http://www.eclipse.org/equinox/) from IBM and Knopflerfish (http://www.knopflerfish.org/) maintained by Makewave.

OSGi provides a dynamic service-oriented platform, but much of this dynamic interaction is left for developers to manually handle. This task has proven to be delicate and difficult, requiring an inherent knowledge of the OSGi mechanisms in order to avoid errors. To reduce the problem, iPOJO, a dynamic service-oriented component framework for automatically administering dynamism has been developed. We will present iPOJO in the next section.

iPOJO

The Apache iPOJO (Escoffier, Hall, 2007), (Escoffier, 2007) technology is an implementation of the service-oriented components approach. iPOJO stands for *injected Plain Old Java Object*. It was developed within the ADELE Computer Science team which is part of the *Laboratoire d'Informatique de Grenoble* (LIG). It is a sub-project of Apache Felix (http://felix.apache.org/site/index.html), which is itself an open source implementation of the OSGi R4 specification.

The main objective of iPOJO is to provide a runtime platform facilitating the development of applications based on the principle of dynamic architecture services. This platform (Figure 10) is based on the OSGi specification, and therefore it inherits some of its characteristics: it is in Java, and supports centralized leadership. In order to simplify dynamic application development using services, iPOJO proposes applying the principle of component-oriented approach to service, *i.e.* that services are located in the form of components.

iPOJO proposes:

- **Strongly linked model and execution machine:** all elements of the model exist at execution time, making more understandable the application's structure.
- **Dynamic service architecture with isolation:** the dynamic service interactions come from the OSGi architecture. iPOJO also offers a service isolation principle so certain services of an application can remain private.
- **Simple development model:** it can hide the complexity of dynamic SOA using the iPOJO development ideas (Fowler, 2000), and more specifically, it hides the complexity of OSGi dynamism. For this, the iPOJO runtime provides an injection machine and introspection to transparently manage these concerns.

Figure 10. iPOJO architecture

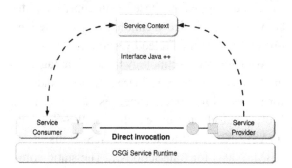

- **Structural composition language:** iPOJO can build applications from a structural composition of services. The composition is modeled using service specifications regardless of their implementation. This decoupling is a strong point of iPOJO because the execution infrastructure chooses an available implementation. Applications are dynamically designed and managed.
- **Introspection and dynamic reconfiguration features:** these mechanisms provide insight on the structure of the system that changes because of the inherent dynamism.
- **Extension mechanisms:** non-functional properties such as persistence, security or quality of service can be easily added.

Using these mechanisms, iPOJO eases the construction of dynamic service-oriented applications while respecting the principles of Service-Oriented Architecture. The simplification of handling dynamism is an important contribution that considerably helps development. Another contribution is the possibility to handle any non-functional property desired by the user.

iPOJO is used in a growing number of software products, such as, the Java EE application server JOnAS (*Java Open Application Server*) (http://jonas.objectweb.org) hosted by the OW2 consortium, and domestic gateway projects.

COMPARISON OF SERVICE TECHNOLOGIES

In this section, we propose to summarize and to compare the service technologies presented in this chapter, as illustrated by Table 1.

Web Services technology takes advantages of the dynamic community. There are many standards for the non-functional properties, named WS-*. More precisely, there are standards WS-Security (OASIS, 2006) for security, WS-Transaction (IBM, 2004) for transactions… The static com-

position of Web Services has been also standardized with WS-BPEL to orchestrate a set of Web Services. Several companies (IBM, Oracle, SAP…) have published the BPEL4People (Agrawal, 2007a) and WS-HumanTask (Agrawal, 2007b) specifications proposing how to include human interaction in WS-BPEL processes.

Both technologies, UPnP and DPWS, are becoming standards for home automation. They are based on the dynamic service-oriented architecture principles. Devices are described and available for use by clients. UPnP and DPWS, are very similar. The DPWS specification showed a standardization effort in the file description. The establishment of a common standard to all devices facilitates their use. Another very important asset in DPWS is the management of secure messages. Restrict access to certain devices can be enforced and thus makes applications more secure.

The most important aspect of these technologies is the dynamism that comes from dynamic service-oriented architectures. Dynamism makes it possible to envision applications that are responsive to the addition or removal of devices in a home or office network. For example, in a house, it is possible to create an application that uses a television and a PDA. It is clear that the television will remain in the house while the personal assistant may track the movements of its owner outside home, hence the need for dynamism.

Finally, there is a lack of maturity in these two software technologies. Experience shows that the development of applications using UPnP and/or DPWS requires a phase of software development and, above all, a test and robustness phase which is shown to be very expensive. There is also doubt that these technologies scale well. UPnP, for example, is very verbose and generates numerous messages on the network.

Both technologies, OSGi and iPOJO, are implementations of the principles of the service-oriented component approach. These two technologies use the mechanisms of the component approach, but also those of the service approach.

Table 1. Comparison of service technologies

	Web Service	UPnP	DPWS	OSGi	iPOJO
Specification	• WSDL interface • WS-* non-functional properties	• Description of UPnP devices • No non-functional properties	• Extended WSDL • Non-functional properties	• Java • No non-functional properties	• Java • Non-functional properties • Extensions possible
Implementation	• Many languages • Generation of client stubs	• Numerous languages • Device-side HTTP server • Proxy generated client-side	• Numerous languages • Device-side HTTP server • Proxy generated client-side	• Java • Packaged as bundles • Two dependency levels	• Java, composite • Packaged as bundles • Three dependency levels
Discovery	• UDDI • Active discovery	• Multicast declaration • Active and passive discovery	• Multicast declaration • Active and passive discovery	• OSGi service registry • Active and passive discovery	• Contextual, no global registry • Active and passive discovery
Communication	• SOAP over HTTP • Synchronous	• SOAP • Synchronous, event-based	• SOAP • Synchronous, event-based	• Java • Synchronous, centralized	• Java • Synchronous, centralized
Binding	• Type: direct • Static	• Type: direct • Dynamic	• Type: direct • Dynamic	• Type: indirect • Autonomic	• Type: indirect • Dynamic
Composition	• Orchestration • WS-BPEL	• Client/Server	• Client/Server	• Structural • No ADL	• Structural • Implicit ADL

Table 1 summarizes the main features of these two technologies.

iPOJO inherits all the benefits of OSGi, like dynamism, but also extends other features. For example, it is possible to manage non-functional properties. The main advantage of iPOJO is automating the management of dynamism, which is a very difficult task for developers to achieve. However, OSGi and iPOJO are centralized technologies that only support the Java language.

OSGi and service-oriented components such as iPOJO are becoming very popular. OSGi is now essential for example in the field of application servers (JOnAS, Websphere, Glassfish...) and iPOJO is now integrated into JOnAS, and will soon be integrated into Glassfish.

CONCLUSION

Service-oriented computing has appeared quite recently. The very purpose of this reuse-based approach is to build applications through the late composition of independent software elements, called services. Services are described and published by service providers; they are chosen and invoked by service consumers. This is achieved within a service-oriented architecture, providing the supporting mechanisms.

Service composition turns out to be complex. A major reason is that there are today many technologies for describing, publishing and composing services. Depending on the target application domain, different protocols and mechanisms are used to implement SOA. For instance, Web Services are dominant to integrate IT applications. UPnP or DPWS are preferred in small area networks.

OSGi and iPOJO are often used in centralized, embedded equipments. These technologies require deep expertise and cross-technology applications require almost unavailable skills.

We believe that the various technologies have to be perfectly understood in order to be mixed correctly. In this paper, we have described the different service-oriented approaches, understand their advantages and limits, and see how they can be combined. We also believe that tools will be needed to abstract away part of the differences between technologies. Ongoing works have shown promising model-based approaches (Chollet, 2009), (Pedraza, 2009).

REFERENCES

W3C. (2000). *Simple object access protocol (SOAP) 1.1.* May, 2000, from http://www.w3.org/TR/soap.

W3C. (2001). *Web services description language* (WSDL) 1.1. Retrieved from http://www.w3.org/TR/wsdl

Agrawal, A., Amen, M., Das, M., Ford, M., Keller, C., & Kloppmann, M. ... Zeller, M. (2007a). *WS-BPEL extension for people (BPEL4People), version 1.0.* Retrieved June, 2007, from http://download.boulder.ibm.com/ibmdl/pub/software/dw/specs/ws-bpel4people/BPEL4People_v1.pdf

Agrawal, A., Amen, M., Das, M., Ford, M., Keller, C., & Kloppmann, M. ... Zeller, M. (2007b). *Web services human task (WSHumanTask), version 1.0.* Retrieved June, 2007, from http://download.boulder.ibm.com/ibmdl/pub/software/dw/specs/ws-bpel4people/WS-HumanTask_v1.pdf

Al-Masri, E., & Mahmoud, Q. H. (2008). Investigating Web services on the World Wide Web. In *Proceedings of the 17th International Conference on World Wide Web (WWW'08).* (pp. 795-804). New York, NY: ACM.

Bachmann, F., Bass, L., Buhman, C., Comella-Dorda, S., Long, F., & Robert, J. ... Wallnau, K. (2000). *Volume II: Technical concepts of component-based software engineering*, 2nd ed. Software Engineering Institute.

Cervantes, H., & Hall, R. (2004a). A framework for constructing adaptive component-based applications: Concepts and experiences. In *Proceedings of the 7th Symposium on Component-Based Software Engineering* [Springer.]. *Lecture Notes in Computer Science, 3054*, 130–137. doi:10.1007/978-3-540-24774-6_13

Cervantes, H., & Hall, R. S. (2004b). Autonomous adaptation to dynamic availability using a service-oriented component model. In *ICSE'04: Proceedings of the 26th International Conference on Software Engineering* (pp. 614-623). Washington, DC: IEEE Computer Society.

Chollet, S., & Lalanda, P. (2009). An extensible abstract service orchestration framework. In *Proceedings of the 2009 IEEE International Conference on Web Services.* (pp. 831-838). Washington, DC: IEEE Computer Society.

Davis, D., & Parashar, M. (2002). Latency performance of SOAP implementations. In *Proceedings of the 2nd IEEE/ACM International Symposium on Cluster Computing and the Grid* (pp. 407-412). Washington, DC: IEEE Computer Society.

Elfwing, R., Paulsson, U., & Lundberg, L. (2002). Performance of SOAP in Web service environment compared to CORBA. In *Proceedings of Ninth Asia-Pasicific Software Engineering Conference (APSEC'2002)* (pp. 84-93). Washington, DC: IEEE Computer Society.

Escoffier, C., Hall, R., & Lalanda, P. (2007). iPOJO: An extensible service-oriented component framework. In *IEEE Conference on Services Computing (SCC 2007).* (pp. 474-481). Washington, DC: IEEE Computer Society.

Escoffier, C., & Hall, R. S. (2007). Dynamically adaptable applications with iPOJO service components. In *6th International Symposium on Software Composition* [Springer.]. *Lecture Notes in Computer Science, 4829,* 113–128. doi:10.1007/978-3-540-77351-1_9

Fowler, M. (2000). *POJO: Plain Old Java Object.* Retrieved from http://www.martinfowler.com/bliki/POJO.html

Gruber, O., Hargrave, B. J., McAffer, J., Rapicault, P., & Watson, T. (2005). The Eclipse 3.0 platform: Adopting OSGi technology. *IBM Systems Journal, 44*(2), 289–299. doi:10.1147/sj.442.0289

Heineman, G. T., & Councill, W. T. (2001). *Component-based software engineering: Putting the pieces together.* ACM Press, Addison-Wesley Professional.

IBM. (2004). *Web services atomic transaction* (WS-AtomicTransaction). Retrieved from http://download.boulder.ibm.com/ibmdl/pub/software/dw/library/ ws-atomictransaction200411.pdf

Microsoft Corporation. (2006). *Devices profile for Web services.* Retrieved from http://specs.xmlsoap.org/ws/2006/02/devprof/devicesprofile.pdf.

OASIS. (2004). *Universal description discovery and integration specification* (UDDI), version 3.0.2. Retrieved from http://www.oasis-open.org/committees /uddi-spec/doc/spec/v3 /uddi-v3.0.2-20041019.htm

OASIS. (2006). *Services security: SOAP message security 1.1* (WS-Security 2004). February, 2006, from http://www.oasis-open.org/committees /download.php/16790/ wss-v1.1-spec-os-SOAPMessageSecurity.pdf.

ObjectWeb. (2004). *The Fractal Project.* Retrieved from http://fractal.objectweb.org/

ObjectWeb. (2007). JOnAS: Java open application server. Retrieved from http://wiki.jonas.objectweb.org/xwiki/ bin/view/Main/WebHome

Oreizy, P., Medvidovic, N., Taylor, R. N., & Rosenblum, D. S. (1998). Software architecture and component technologies: Bridging the gap. In *Proceedings of the Workshop on Compositional Software Architectures.*

OSGi Alliance. (2007). *OSGi service platform core specification, release 4, version 4.1.* Retrieved from http://www.osgi.org/download / r4v41/r4.core.pdf.

Papazoglou, M. P. (2003). Service-oriented computing: Concepts, characteristics and directions. In *WISE'03: Proceedings of the Fourth International Conference on Web Information Systems Engineering* (pp. 3-12). Washington, DC: IEEE Computer Society.

Papazoglou, M. P., & Georgakopoulos, D. (2003). Introduction. *Communications of the ACM, 46*(10), 24–28. doi:10.1145/944217.944233

Pedraza, G., & Estublier, J. (2009). Distributed orchestration versus choreography: The FOCAS approach. In *Trustworthy Software Development Processes* [Springer.]. *Lecture Notes in Computer Science, 5543,* 75–86. doi:10.1007/978-3-642-01680-6_9

Sun Microsystems. (n.d.). *Java SE desktop technologies.* Retrieved from http://java.sun.com/javase/technologies/desktop/javabeans/index.jsp

Sun Microsystems. (n.d.). *Glassfish: Open source application server.* Retrieved from https://glassfish.dev.java.net/

Szyperski, C. (2002). *Component software: Beyond object-oriented programming* (2nd ed.). Addison-Wesley Longman Publishing Co.

UPnP Forum. (2008). *UPnPTM device architecture 1.1.* Retrieved from http://www.upnp.org/specs/arch/ UPnP-arch-DeviceArchitecture-v1.1.pdf

Weerawarana, S., Curbera, F., Leymann, F., Storey, T., & Ferguson, D. (2005). *Web services platform architecture: SOAP, WSDL, WS-Policy, WS-Addressing, WS-BPEL, WS-Reliable Messaging, and more*. Prentice Hall PTR.

Weiser, M. (1991). The computer for the 21st century. *Scientific American, 265*(3), 66–75. doi:10.1038/scientificamerican0991-94

Wuyts, R., & Ducasse, S. (2001). Composition languages for black-box components. In *Proceedings of the First OOPSLA Workshop on Language Mechanisms for Programming Software Components* (pp. 33-36).

ENDNOTE

[1]   http://json-rpc.org/wiki/specification

Section 2
Service Provision and Design

Chapter 2
Semi–Automated Lifecycles for Eliciting Requirements for Service–Oriented Environments

M. Brian Blake
University of Notre Dame, USA

ABSTRACT

Service-based tools are beginning to mature, but there is a cognitive gap between the understanding of what currently exists within an organization and how to use that knowledge in planning an overall enterprise modernization effort that realizes a service-oriented architecture. Traditional and contemporary software engineering lifecycles use incremental approaches to extract business information from stakeholders in developing features and constraints in a future application. In traditional environments, this information is captured as requirements specifications, use cases, or storyboards. Here, we address the evolution of traditional software engineering approaches to support the conceptualization of abstract services that overlap multiple organizations. Traditional software engineering lifecycles must be enhanced with emerging processes related to the development applications for service-oriented environments. The chapter discusses state-of-the-art approaches that elicit information about the requirements for service-oriented architectures. These approaches tend to leverage existing requirements engineering approaches to suggest aggregate service-based capabilities that might be most effective for a particular environment.

DOI: 10.4018/978-1-61350-159-7.ch002

INTRODUCTION: THE BACKGROUND OF SERVICE LIFECYCLES THAT SUPPORT NEW REQUIREMENTS ENGINEERING PRACTICES

Since the term software engineering was coined in the 1960s, one of the primary thrusts has been toward software modularity. A goal of software modularity is the development of packaged software mechanisms that perform concise domain-specific tasks. Such an application can be clearly understood by adjacent stakeholders and seamlessly integrated and consumed into new systems. A significant thrust towards software modularity was the introduction of object-oriented analysis and development. *Object-oriented programming* was first introduced in the early 1960's as a part of the development of SIMULA 67 (Nygard, 1986). Interestingly enough, the impact of object-oriented systems was not fully realized until the mid 1980's with the establishment and acceptance of methodologies introduced by Ivar Jacobsen, Grady Booch, and James Rumbaugh. This represented a gap of approximately 20 years before object-oriented programming experienced large-scale acceptance in application. Similarly, while *component-based programming* (i.e. a higher-level abstraction of object-oriented design) was introduced in late 1960's as a part of the NATO conference on the software *crisis* (Naur & Randell, 1969), it was not until the mid 1990's that large-scale component –based applications became apparent.

The combination of components and the World-Wide Web has led to the emergence of Web services: components with URIs that can be invoked according to standard protocols. Web services underlie the general notion of a *System of Systems* where the underlying computations and interactions follow the principles of *service-oriented computing* (Bichler & Lin, 2006)(Rao & Su, 2004). Unlike the above two approaches for building systems, service-oriented computing has experienced a relatively short horizon from conceptualization to application. While Gartner has been credited for the first mention of service-oriented architecture in 1996 (SSA, 1996), just 5 years later research labs, industrial organizations, and federal government facilities have all adopted a paradigm shift to create these types of architectures within their domains (see Figure 1).

Service-oriented architecture (SOA) is made possible by the existence of services both inside and outside of an enterprise. Within such an environment, independent tasks can be referred to as organizational *capabilities. Web services* provide the implementations of the capabilities and represent the building blocks. Properly-developed web services should execute well-defined tasks as supported by concise, openly accessible interfaces. As such, it is apparent that the first step in the development of any SOA is the acceptance of a service-based development approach (Blake, 2007) and the population of an array of services that represent capabilities across a wide variety of domains.

Figure 1. The evolution of software modularity

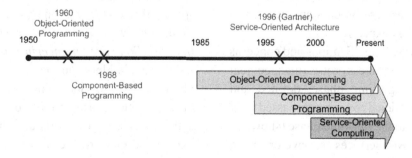

In prior work (Blake, 2007), two key activities were introduced for software engineers that develop service-centic software systems (SCSS), *service development* and *service-centric system management*. Service development is similar to the traditional notion of software engineering. Since Web services are the backbone for SCSS environments, software engineers must be skilled in developing modular software services that decompose business processes into manageable sub-capabilities. By decomposing capabilities into modular services, organizations can share their offerings at multiple levels of granularity while also creating unique access points for their peer organizations. Although software engineers must intimately understand business process details, the software development lifecycle for developing the individual Web services will resemble traditional iterative processes such as the Rational Unified Process (Krutchen, 1998). The general phases in this lifecycle are *Conceptualization*, *Analysis*, *Design*, *Development*, *Testing*, *Deployment*, and *Retirement*. In the Conceptualization and Analysis phases, the software engineer manages the elicitation of requirements that clarify the business needs. Design, Development, and Testing is an iterative set of phases where services are designed, created, and evaluated through testing. Results of the testing phase are used as feedback to the design phase. Services are then deployed for universal access and, at some time in the future when the business offering changes, the services are removed and retired. This notion of software lifecycle, also illustrated in Figure 2, is generally managed by software engineers from beginning to end while also engaging subject matter experts, business process engineers, and application domain experts.

Just as functional specifications and concerns are passed from the business process management phase to the design-time phase, defined and simulated nonfunctional concerns are passed from the design phase to the run-time phase (shown in Figure 2). Once Web services are developed and deployed, software engineers must engage in service-centric system management lifecycles to allow on-demand services to be discovered, analyzed, and composed/consumed. This environment is far more dynamic than the traditional operations associated with component and/or library-oriented software systems. Since service-based capabilities are managed in distributed locations outside of the consumers' control, this environment requires more specialized development lifecycles for maintaining predictable operations. Furthermore, the insertion of agreements between consumers and producers will require the intervention of service-oriented software engineering professionals. This new lifecycle resembles the previously mentioned development lifecycle; however the focus is on managing available services in real-time. In addition, the seven phases are slightly different, *Business Process Conceptualization*, *Domain Analysis*, *Discovery*, *Composition*, *Evaluation*, *On-Demand Composition*, and *Rebinding*. Although Business Process Conceptualization and Domain Analysis are phases that also attempt to capture the business needs, these phases must take into account the fact that the solution services already exist. Discovery, Composition, and Evaluation are phases that represent the core of the service-oriented computing paradigm (Papazoglou, 2003) of finding, blueprinting, and analyzing candidate services at design-time. Finally at run-time, On-Demand Composition and Rebinding allows composite service-oriented business processes to be constructed and evolved over time.

The service-centric system management lifecycle is modular, by nature. The lifecycle can be split into three aggregate phases, *Business Process Management*, *Software Engineering at Design-time*, and *Software Engineering at Run-time*. Different stakeholders can manage these aggregate phases. Since services will already exist with open specifications, business process engineers and subject matter experts are able to evaluate existing services to see if they meet their busi-

Figure 2. Various SCSS lifecycles

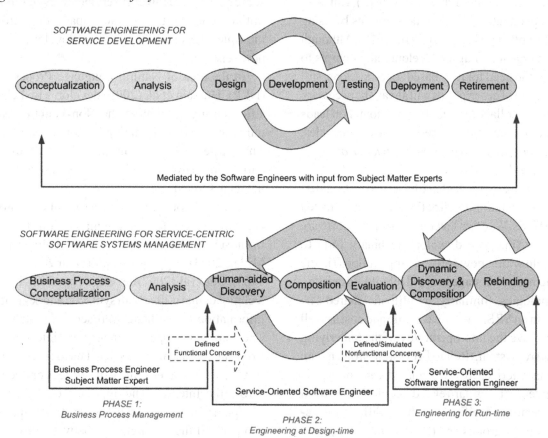

ness needs. *Service-oriented software engineers*, at design-time, must understand the implications of establishing long-standing business processes considering the candidate services. Subsequently, *service-oriented software integration engineers* must develop and monitor approaches for automated software to manage service integration in real-time.

An open problem in the *Phase 1: Business Process Management*, which has not been addressed in current literature, is how to define the requirements for capabilities appropriate for transformation into service environments. Typically, this transformation enhances existing, more traditional software environments into new SOA-based systems. This chapter describes the

state-of-the-art and proposed approaches for the creation of new semi-automated lifecycles for service-based requirements engineering.

BACKGROUND: RELEVANT REQUIREMENTS ENGINEERING APPROACHES

A significant and early step in software development processes (Fuggetta & Wolf, 1996) is to identify and describe system features and boundaries. Traditionally, such descriptions are usually captured in text-based documents, known as Software Requirement Specifications (SRSs) (IEEE 1998). Other visual approaches like the

Unified Modeling Language (UML) can also be mapped into text-based descriptions by using XML or other techniques (XML, 2010). Although the emergence of agile development attempts to reduce the need for text-based specifications, still some form of descriptions will always be necessary for group collaborations. This phenomenon leads to a natural question for service-based lifecycles, that is, *how to discover shared services from SRSs that already exist?*

Software lifecycles have benefited from understanding shared and well defined services extracted from SRSs. We often leverage third-party software libraries (that you download in binary form to compile within new software applications) in the implementation stage to avoid rebuilding existing technologies. Similarly, by utilizing shared services in an SRS, we can save time and cost as well as improve the interoperability of the underlying software system. Related research projects can be characterized by two related categories, (1) discovery of similar/related requirements from requirement specifications from different organizations or groups and (2) automatic extraction of meta- or semantic information that can be used to define open services.

With regards to (1), Spanoudakis et al. (1999) has developed elegant formal approaches for discovering overlaps across requirement specifications. Their intention is to find overlaps between different specifications to reveal inconsistencies while our purpose is to utilize requirement overlaps to extract shared services from different requirement specifications. They formally decompose a specification into symbols that can have relations to other symbols, while symbols in our approach are directly related to aspects of the specification documents and the underlying sentence structure.

Zachos et al. (2006) developed a service recovery tool that can be integrated with RUP and UML to generate service queries. Their research focuses on assisting users to find the most suitable software service from a service database. Their approach is effective for reusing open source services. However service lifecycles must initially uncover the abstract capabilities across multiple SRSs that may be later developed into new services.

In the area of Natural Language Processing (NLP), Hussain et al. (2008) develop a text classifier aiming at splitting the Non-Function Requirements (NFR) from requirement documents. This is a general clustering approach where direct correlation between different requirement documents is limited.

As to category (2), there are a number of projects that attempt to derive semantic information from service-based specifications (Mukerji & Miller, 2003) (Nygaard, 1986) (Naur & Randell, 1969). Guo et al. (2007) developed ontology-based techniques that utilize both syntactic and semantic information to facilitate web service matching. Their approach operates interprets information from one service then uses that data to find similar services within a repository of services or openly across the Internet. The approach described in this paper differs in so much as it attempts to compare all the requirements between different SRSs. Also, this approach operations on requirements specifications and not on software interface specifications.

Hayes et al. (2006) use techniques from information retrieval area to facilitate requirement processing and comparison. They use information retrieval to trace requirements from specification to implementation. While their approach focuses on requirement tracing during different stages of the software lifecycle, there is a need for conceptualizing potential functional overlap early in the software development lifecycle.

In preliminary work (Yale-Loehr et al., 2010), web services are derived from requirements documents. The notion of sentence structure is used to compare specifications considering nouns and verbs only. An overarching, semi-automated requirements elicitation process and lifecycle is required to address the need for transformation of service-based systems.

SEMI-AUTOMATED SERVICE-ORIENTED REQUIREMENTS ENGINEERING

Requirements engineering in this environment must operate on many types of artifacts currently existing in traditional organizations. In order to develop a hierarchy of information describing a SOA, it is important to understand what types of information are available. In our experiences, we have found that business processes and preliminary service development efforts have multiple document types that further describe their functions and capabilities. Figure 3 shows a subset of all documents that exist in an inter-organizational business environment. Ultimately, a hierarchy of unstructured documents must be developed that can be used to derive capabilities from existing textual artifacts.

To understand the connections between unstructured textual artifacts, it is important to study the internal information. Prior work (Yale-Loehr et al., 2010), to be discussed in more detail in later sections, investigated automatic approaches for correlating multiple SRS documents. The first step was to decompose the specification into its underlying components. As an example, SRS documents can be decomposed into parts as shown

Figure 3. Hierarchy of operational documents appropriate for requirements extraction

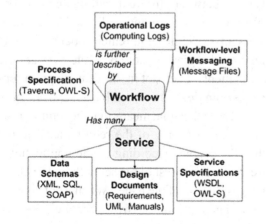

in Figure 4. By converting the document into lower-level parts, locations for information such as input/output data, nonfunctional concerns, and interface information can be isolated. *This is just one example, but a generic lifecycle must incorporate all documents inFigure 3and others*. In Yale-Loehr et al., software specifications, such as requirement documents, from multiple organizations were scanned and integrated. Consequently, potential shared services among collaborating organizations were interpreted and recommended. The human-naming tendencies underlying the requirement documents have certain rules that can be exploited to search for similarity across disparate organizations. This was a significant finding, because it suggests that, within particular document types, underlying behaviors of the creators of the documentation can be leveraged to isolate relevant information in a consistent, perhaps repeatable manner. This approach will be central to the automatic generation of cross-domain semantic networks.

In the absence of explicit semantic meta-data, a key technique in real-world will be the emergence of enhanced syntactical matching approaches (Yale-Loehr et al., 2010) informed by the characteristics extracted from existing documents within the repository. This approach combines several natural language processing approaches with data structures that define naming tendencies of document authors. Consequently, systems can learn how the service providers articulate their meaning into words by examining many sample documents inside the scientific computing environment. Thresholds from existing documents are applied in natural language comparison algorithms to find equivalent words and phrases between document types from different service providers across multiple domains.

Figure 4. Decomposing an SRS into sub-parts to support service-based requirements re-engineering

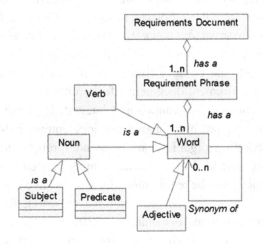

A GENERAL PROCESS FOR EXTRACTING ABSTRACT REQUIREMENTS FROM GENERAL DOCUMENTS

The biggest barrier to software intended to reason about "human-created" data is the variation in the way functions are described. Often, software fails to identify capabilities that have the same meaning when they use different words or assumes different sentence structures. To overcome this problem, new requirements engineering processes must leverage less tightly-constrained approaches to reason about equivalence in descriptions. Synonyms of the words in a description in addition to the original word may offer flexibility when calculating the similarity degree of two requirements. Among others, new approaches in this domain should have two general features:

1. Correlating requirements that differ only by the change of descriptive words into their synonyms.
2. Identifying requirements that do not share the same sentence structure but the underlying meaning is the same.

Consequently, the overall process of discovering service-based requirements from textual documents can be generalized into three steps. First, each document subsections can be parsed into a set of words. This provides a list of sets of words for each document or artifact. These word sets are presumed to describe capabilities. Then by using the extracted words, multiple documents are compared against each other to determine overlapping requirements. The third and last step is to construct abstract software services based on these overlapping requirements. This high-level process is also illustrated in Figure 5.

PROOF OF CONCEPT SYSTEM: DERIVING REQUIREMENTS FROM SRSS

In previous work (Yale-Loehr et al., 2010), an application was developed that implemented the semi-automated requirements process particularly for SRS documents. The application is divided into 6 tabs. The *File* tab allows the user to select up to three requirement specification documents. The application assumes that these documents will have requirement numbers, text, and a line break. As such, the application can process most standard SRS documents. With the File tab, the user can initiate the requirements aggregation process.

In Figure 6, the *Visual* tab is illustrated. This tab uses a Venn diagram to directly showing the overlaps between different requirements across different SRS documents. Each Venn circle represents a single requirement document. The intersected regions denote possible overlapping requirements. Each dot in the Venn diagram represents a single requirement. If a dot appears only in one circle then that means that the requirement is not similar to any of the requirements in the other documents according to the application's threshold. The threshold is set with by the slider on the right side of the panel. When a dot appears in the shared region of two or three circles that

Figure 5. A generic process for deriving service-based requirements

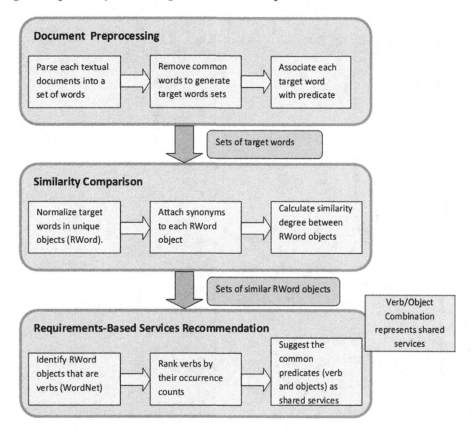

that means a pair of similar requirements was determined among the various documents. When the user *mouses over* a dot in the shared area, an information tab will show up displaying the actual pair of similar requirements as well as the similar words found within them.

The *Yes/No* tab and *Percentage* tab show a matrix that contains the similarity information for every pair of requirements. The *Yes/No* tab shows yes or no depending on whether two requirements are deemed to be similar. The Percentage tab shows the similarity score for the pair of requirements. When a pair of similar requirements meets the user-specified threshold then the text within the cell is set to bold. The *WordSize* tab mimics the creation of a *Word Cloud* (http://www.wordle.net/). Verbs are visualized on one panel where frequently occurring words are shown in bigger font consisting of various colors.

The rightmost tab, *Services*, shows the suggested services. Also within Figure 6, the bottom left corner shows the *Services* tab. Verbs are extracted from similar requirements and converted into service names. For example, the requirement, "The system must store latitude/longitude data within a persistent database", might be shown as "Data Management Service (latitude)". The verbs from the overlapping requirements with the highest occurrence count are converted into services in the *Services* tab. The occurrence count is used as a label for each recommended service.

PRELIMINARY EXPERIMENTATION

In order to evaluate the performance of this approach, it was tested on 3 real-world software requirement specifications from on-going software

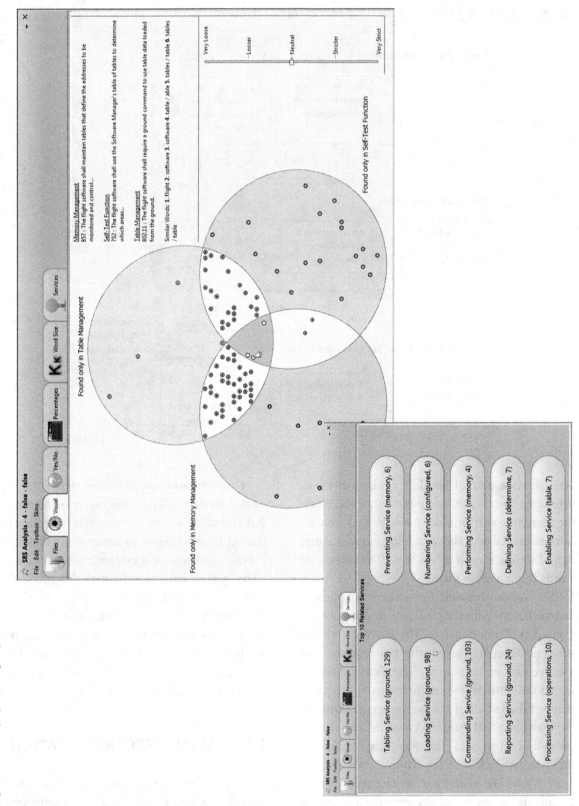

Figure 6. Proof of concept system

development projects for 3 separate data-centric applications within the same branch of the federal government. The first application is a data sharing environment for information engineers. The second application is an automated search and discovery application for a tagged data catalog. The final application is a message transfer and document sharing module. During the lifecycle of this project, 6 human software architects met to discuss shared services. Although the requirements documents were not explicitly used to develop the shared requirements, it was these software architects that led the earlier development of the requirements. As such, their respective knowledge of the systems is implicitly derived from the requirements documents. The three requirements documents have a sum of approximately 1200 requirements. Precision and recall results from the studies were shared in previous work (Yale-Loehr et al., 2010). The results are summarized (for completeness) the original studies.

In the previous study, the software suggested 81 shared services versus the 46 services suggested by the human software architects. Neither the group of software architects nor our prototype was constrained by a maximum number of recommendations. The prototype made 8 recommendations that matched the human recommendations verbatim and 5 other recommendations which have synonymous meanings with other human recommendations. As such, there were a total of 13 services that accurately matched human recommendations. An interesting result was the recommendation of 7 additional shared services that the human software architects did not initially suggest. Considering these statistics and with respect to the approach emulating human behavior, the prototype has a precision of 16.05% (13 out of 81) and a recall of 28.26% (13 out of 46). Although the precision and recall for emulating human results was low, the authors are encouraged by overall results. The most promising result was that the prototype suggested 7 other services that several of the software architects

agreed were perhaps missed during their own discussions. Furthermore, the software made the service recommendations within minutes while it took human architects about 9 hours to develop with their suggestions. The timely manner of this approach suggests that it can serve as an efficient first pass tool to scan the requirement documents and generate a candidate list of shared service. These candidates can save the time used by human architects during their analysis and thus improve the overall software lifecycle.

A second experiment was executed on over 10 random SRS documents downloaded from the Internet (SRSR, n.d.). This experiment attempted to develop recommended software services from a heterogeneous set of requirements. The experiment was executed on pairs of SRS documents. In Table 1, several overlapping requirements from one particular experiment are shown. The leftmost column shows requirements from one SRS document. The middle column shows requirements from a SRS document from an entirely different organization that the prototype suggests overlap the requirements in the same row from the leftmost column. The rightmost column shows the automatically generated service recommendations that correspond to the overlapping requirements. It is clear that the requirements are not exactly the same. However, the underlying capabilities to fulfill the requirements are generally consistent. This approach seeks to discern the shared capabilities and suggest the development of services would fulfill both requirements. As such, it is not necessary for the requirements to completely overlap.

DISCUSSION AND FUTURE WORK

The set of experiments summarized in the previous section had two purposes. The first experiment evaluated the prototypes ability to discovered shared requirements as compared to human-directed interventions. The second experiment evaluated the approach to aggregating the requirements from

Table 1. Sample overlapping requirements and recommended services

Requirements with Meaningful Overlap		Representative Service Recommendations Nomenclature: Service Name (Object)
The TCS shall support a LOS data link and SATCOM data link capability.	Each significant event message shall be routed for downlink and to data storage as a CCSDS packet.	Reporting Service (status) Receiving Service (data) Initiating Service (restart) Detecting Service (flight)
TCS shall provide the capability to monitor the status of all AV subsystems reporting status.	Time maintenance status shall be provided to the ground as housekeeping.	
The TCS shall be capable of interfacing with the specified data terminal and issuing data link terminal commands.	A Generic request is one where the requester must explicitly provide all the data required by the flight software.	

documents randomly selected from the Internet (SRSR, n.d.). As expected, variations in the human language are a barrier to precision. However, with minimal use of semantic markings the results have some promising features. This approach has the ability to evaluate SRS documents rapidly without data preparation. Furthermore, the approach can amplify human efforts in service-centric software lifecycles. Other insights are derived directly from preliminary experimentation.

- *Requirement documents from the same domain or closely related domains tend to have more meaningful overlapping requirements than requirements randomly selected from different domains.* The reason for this observation is that requirement documents from the same domain often have similar or highly overlapping vocabularies which can be leveraged during the similarity comparison process.
- *Non-Functional Requirements (NFRs) tend to receive more meaningful matches than Functional Requirements (FRs) during the similarity comparison.* Although different aspects of existing software systems may have different jobs, they often share some common non-functional requirements such as usability, scalability, security, availability and so on. This requirements

engineer process can easily match these requirements. This is implicitly supported by related work as most related projects concentrate on nonfunctional concerns in requirements engineering.

- *The systematic comparison of documents (as implemented in this approach) is capable of revealing requirements that are missed in the human-driven process.* The most promising result was the discovery of services that software engineers missed when manually looking for abstract capabilities. In addition, the engineers agree that the recommended services were important. The performance of this semi-automated toolset suggests that the approach is positioned favorably to act as a first pass tool when scanning requirement-oriented documents and generating lists of shared service candidates. These candidates can reduce the efforts of human software engineers during their analysis and improve their accuracy.

Studies in this chapter have introduced the need for contemporary requirements engineering approaches. In future work, the process must be evolved to more extensively leverage the *sections* within the specification. Commonality of the types of information contained within specific document sections across a variety documents might increase the overall precision. Existing development environments (such as Eclipse) might be extended with these contemporary requirements engineering approaches. In this way, existing and new requirements engineering practices can be aligned in real time.

ACKNOWLEDGMENT

This work was enhanced by discussions with Dr. Michael Huhns of the University of South Carolina and by Mr. Yi "David" Wei of the University of Notre Dame.

REFERENCES

W3. (2011). *Web Services description.* Retrieved from http://www.w3.org/2002/ws/desc/

Bichler, M., & Lin, K. J. (2006). Service-oriented computing. *IEEE Computer, 39*(3), 99–101.

Blake, M. B. (2007). Decomposing composition: Service-oriented software engineers. *IEEE Software, 24*(6), 68–77. doi:10.1109/MS.2007.162

Faatz, A., & Steinmetz, R. (2002). *Ontology enrichment with texts from the WWW.* In Semantic Web Mining 2nd Workshop at ECML/PKDD'02. (Helsinki, Finland, Aug 2002).

Fuggetta, A., & Wolf, A. (Eds.). (1996). *Software process.* England: Wiley.

Guo, H., Ivan, A., Akkiraju, R., & Goodwin, R. (2007). Learning ontologies to improve the quality of automatic web service matching. In *Proceedings of the International Conference on Web Services*, (pp. 118-125).

Hayes, J. H., Dekhtyar, A., & Osborne, J. (2003). Improving requirements tracing via information retrieval. In *Proceedings of the 11ᵗʰ IEEE International Requirements Engineering Conference*, (pp. 138-147).

Hess, A., & Kushmerick, N. (2003). Learning to attach semantic metadata to web services. In *Proceedings of, ISWC2003, 258*–273.

Huhns, M. H., & Singh, M. P. (2005). Research directions for service-oriented multi-agent systems. *IEEE Internet Computing, 9*(6), 65–70. doi:10.1109/MIC.2005.132

Hussain, I., Kosseim, L., & Ormandjieva, O. (2008). Using linguistic knowledge to classify non-functional requirements in SRS documents. *NLDB '08*(London, UK, June 2008), (pp. 287-298).

IEEE. (1998). *Std 830-1998: IEEE recommended practice for software requirements specifications description.* Retrieved from http://ieeexplore.ieee.org/xpls/ abs_all.jsp?arnumber=392555

Krutchen, P. (1998). *The rational unified process: An introduction.* Addison-Wesley.

Mittal, K. (2007). *SOA unified process.* Retrieved from http://www.kunalmittal.com/ html/soup.shtml

Mukerji, J., & Miller, J. (2003). *MDA guide version 1.0.1* (Tech. Report OMG/2003-06-01), Object Management Group. Retrieved from www.omg.org/docs /omg/03-06-01.pdf

Naur, P., & Randell, B. (1969). *Software engineering. Report on a conference sponsored by the NATO Science Committee, Garmisch, Germany, 7th to 11th October 1968 Scientific Affairs Division* (pp. 138–155). Brussels: NATO.

Nygaard, K. (1986). Basic concepts in object oriented programming. *Proceedings of the 1986 SIGPLAN Workshop on Object-Oriented Programming*, (pp 128-132), Yorktown Heights, NY.

OWL-S. (2008). *Home.* Retrieved from http://www.daml.org/owl-s/

Papazoglou, M. (2003). Service-oriented computing: Concepts, characteristics and directions. In *Proceedings of WISE '03.*

Rao, J., & Su, X. (2004). A survey of automated Web Service composition methods. In *Proceedings of the First International Workshop on Semantic Web Services and Web Process Composition, SWSWPC 2004*, San Diego, California, USA, July 6th.

Sirin, E., Hendler, J., & Parsia, B. (2002). Semi-automatic composition of Web services using semantic descriptions. In *Proceedings of Web Services: Modeling, Architecture and Infrastructure workshop in conjunction with ICEIS2003.*

Spanoudakis, G., Finklestein, A., & Till, D. (1999). Overlaps in requirements engineering. *Automated Software Engineering, 6*, 171–198. doi:10.1023/A:1008718614166

SRSR. (n.d.). *Software requirement specification repository*. Retrieved from http://www.nd.edu/~soseg /requirement_software/

SSA. *(1996)*. Research Note SPA-401-068/9, 12 April 1996: Service Oriented Architectures, Part 1 and 2.

XML. (2010). *UML to XML design rules*. Retrieved from http://xml.coverpages.org/ uml2xmlDesignRules.html

Yale-Loehr, A., Schlesinger, I., Rembert, A., & Blake, M. B. (2010). *Discovering shared services from cross-organization software specifications.* IEEE SCC 2010 (Miami, Florida, July 5-10, 2010).

Zachos, K., Zhu, X., Maiden, N., & Jones, S. (2006) Seamlessly integrating service discovery into UML requirements processes. *IW-SOSE '06* (May 27-28, Shanghai, China), (pp. 60-66).

Zeng, L. (2004). QoS-aware middleware for Web services composition. *IEEE Transactions on Software Engineering, 30*(5), 311–327. doi:10.1109/TSE.2004.11

Chapter 3
Quality of Service and Extra–Functional Properties for Web Services:
A Model–Driven Approach

Guadalupe Ortiz
University of Cádiz, Spain

Behzad Bordbar
University of Birmingham, UK

ABSTRACT

Service-Oriented Architecture and Web services aim at producing loosely coupled applications which are easier to scale and manage. In addition, loosely coupled systems are less susceptible to errors when modifications and maintenance activities are required. Extending Web services to implement Quality of Service or Extra-functional properties often result in the code that is scattered and tangled in different parts of the main functionality code. This violates decoupleness of the application. In this chapter, we shall present a model-based approach to deal with specification and implementation of Quality of Service and extra-functional properties in a loosely coupled manner.

The presented approach draws on two main software techniques: Model-Driven Architecture, and aspect-oriented programming. The method involves modeling of the Quality of Service and Extra-functional properties in a platform-independent fashion. Then applying model transformation, the platform-independent models are transformed into platform-specific models, and finally into code. The code for Quality of Service and Extra-functional properties are integrated into the system relying on aspect-oriented techniques in a decoupled manner. The presented approach is evaluated with the help of a case study to establish that the approach results in increasing the system's modularity and thus reducing implementation and maintenance costs.

DOI: 10.4018/978-1-61350-159-7.ch003

INTRODUCTION

Service-Oriented Architecture (SOA) aims at letting distributed applications to communicate, in a platform-independent and loosely coupled manner, providing systems with great flexibility and easier maintenance. Web services have become the best known implementation of SOA, in which various development aspects of the system are maintained based on the use of a wide range of WS standards. Applications developed following Web service standards are loosely coupled; loosely coupled applications are normally easier to scale, manage and extend and less susceptible to errors when modifications are required. Two other significant advantages of adopting Web services are *interoperability* and the *use of Internet standard protocols* for communication. Interoperability is achieved via using XML for capturing message and description of the service. Adopting XML allows combining services which are developed on different platforms by different groups of developers. The use of Internet standard protocols, such as *http*, will permit easier communication through the net a vast infrastructure. Thus, Web services provide a unique suite of technologies for the integration of business, which allows companies to integrate internal applications, to publish active applications for other companies and to use third-party applications.

On the other hand, the software engineering community is currently moving on to application development based on models rather than technologies. Model-driven development allows us to focus on essential aspects of the system, delaying the decision on which technologies to use in the implementation for later steps of the development. Models may be used in multiple phases of development, from the initial system specification to its testing. Each model will address one or more concerns, independently of the remaining issues involved in the system's development, thus allowing the separation of the final implementation technology from the business logic achieved by the system. In addition, Model-driven development advocates automated model transformation by using software to create new models from the existing models. Transformations between models enable the automated development of the system from the models themselves; therefore, model definition and transformation become key parts of the process.

Although Web service implementation is properly achieved by development middlewares, *Quality of Service* (QoS) and *Extra-functional Properties* (EFP) have not been given due consideration. In particular, in Web services the implementation of QoS *–criteria that match the needs of service requestors with those of the service provider's* - and EFP *-functionality which does not perform main but added value system objective-* is not carried out in a loosely coupled manner; the functionality related to QoS and EFP is scattered and tangled all over the main functionality code. Consequently, there is a lack of tools for earlier stages of Web service development in which QoS, EFP and WS-* standards integration are considered. The same problem has been studied by component-based and object-oriented communities which are also interested in the separation of concerns. One solution adopted by such communities is to use aspect-oriented techniques, which allow us to encapsulate and modularize transversal concerns in the systems. Using aspects result in improving the decoupleness of software systems and reducing maintenance costs. In our approach we advocate the use of aspect-oriented programming in the implementation of QoS and EFP to create loosely coupled services. So, in a sense our approach brings together Model-Driven Architecture and Aspect-Oriented Software Development (AOSD) to provide good support for software evolution through an appropriate separation of concerns; AOSD has focused on modeling crosscutting concerns whereas MDA concentrates on the explicit separation of platform-independent from platform-specific concerns and the model-driven generation of processes.

This chapter describes a methodology that integrates Quality of Service and Extra-functional properties into Web service model-driven development, where services and properties remain separated during all stages of development– from platform-independent models to code- and property traceability across all these phases is maintained.

For this purpose, two UML profiles for QoS and Extra-functional properties will be presented. These profiles are used to specify different characteristics and properties through the use of stereotypes at a platform-independent level. In this sense, QoS and EFP are defined as model elements, thus allowing them to be added to services during the modelling phase. Then, these platform-independent models can be converted into platform-specific models and the latter into code, automatically, through the application of a set of predefined transformation rules.

Concerning platform-specific models, we have defined and implemented suitable metamodels for QoS and EFP within service-oriented applications. In this case the service-oriented scope will limit, on the one hand, the amount of ways in which characteristics and properties can be integrated into the developed services: given the nature of Web services, property functionality and measurement code can only be injected on service operations' execution or invocation. On the other hand, additional attributes will be required in order to provide a description of the properties or the QoS characteristics, so that the essential Web service characteristic of auto-description be maintained. In this regard we propose an aspect-oriented metamodel on the one hand; on the other, a policy description and a QoS description-based one, respectively.

Finally, this chapter will show how an aspect-oriented implementation of the QoS and EFP functionality, automatically generated from platform-specific models, provides us with a decoupled development appropriate for such properties and characteristics, which can be perfectly integrated

with the services' implementation. Furthermore, an XML-based description of the properties and characteristics will also be automatically obtained from these models and attached to the corresponding services so that they can be used to complement the WSDL description and to make the client aware of the requirements and limitations of the offered service.

To conclude the chapter we will analyze the benefits of the generated code on the system, which will contribute to its optimum implementation and maintenance, thus reducing development costs and maintaining property traceability at all stages of development, whilst reducing development workload.

BACKGROUND

In this section we provide a background to the two main types of technology we are using in this paper; first of all we provide an introduction to *Model-Driven Development* (MDD) and secondly to *Aspect-Oriented Programming* (AOP).

Model-Driven Development

The software engineering community is currently moving on to application development based on models rather than technologies (http://www.omg. org/mda/). Model-driven development allows us to focus on the essential aspects of the system, delaying the decision of which technology to use in the implementation for a later step. Models may be used from the initial system specification to its testing. Each model will address one concern, independently of the remaining issues involved in the system's development, thus allowing the separation of the final implementation technology from the business logic achieved by the system. Transformations between models enable the automated system development from the models themselves; therefore, model definition and transformation become the key parts of the process.

In this concern the programming task for developers is usually divided into three different phases (see Figure 1):

- First of all, a *Platform-Independent Model* (PIM) is proposed with the purpose of representing our system without coupling it to any specific platform or implementation language.
- Secondly, a *Platform-Specific Model* (PSM) represents our system based on a specific target platform. In fact, we may have different platform-specific models for different technologies so that we can reuse the PIM of our systems in several environments.
- Finally, *Code Layer* provides our final application code, which may be generated automatically from the platform-specific model.

Aspect-Oriented Techniques

AOP arises due to the problems detected in *Object-Oriented Programming* (OOP). OOP is supposed to permit the encapsulation and modularity of related data and methods. This should imply code organized into meaningful units and not blended at all. However, we may find it impossible to model several concerns into a unique and structured decomposition of units. We could have

Figure 1. Model-driven process

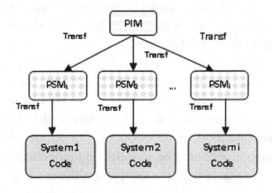

transversal concerns, which cannot be included in the logical code structure by functionality. As a result of these crosscutting concerns, code is scattered and tangled all over our application (Elrad et al., 2001).

AOP describes five types of element to modularise crosscutting concerns: firstly, we have to define the *join point* model which indicates the points where we could include new behaviours. Secondly, we have to define a way to indicate the specific join points to specify in which points of the implementation the new code is to be inserted. Next, we ought to determine how we are going to specify the new behaviour to be included in the join point referred to. We would then encapsulate the specified join points and their corresponding behaviours into independent units. Finally, a method to weave the new code with the original one has to be applied. Thus, aspects will allow us to consider the device model and user preferences in a decoupled way with respect to the main functionality of the client.

LITERATURE REVIEW

Web Service Model-Driven Development

We can find several approaches focused on model-driven development of Web services, some of them based on the development of the services themselves such as the one from Gronmo et al. In this work a model-driven Web service development process in which Web service descriptions are converted into UML models, and vice versa, is described (Gronmo et al., 2004). Other representative approaches focus on the model-driven development of Web service compositions, an example of which could be the work from Baïna et al. who present a framework in which the starting point is an external specification of a Web service (e.g., interface and protocol specifications); they support the generation of service implementation templates and their specifications (Baïna et al., 2004). The work from Staikopoulos et al. focuses on a model-driven approach which starts from a BPEL system and provides a platform-independent model represented by Petri nets (Staikopoulos et al., 2006). Pedraza et al. (Pedraza et al., 2009) deal with business process modelling differentiating functional and non-functional concerns in the system and using annotation on the process model elements for the latter. Chollet et al. (Chollet et al., 2009) also present a generative environment in which non-functional properties are taken into account, specially focusing on orchestration of abstract services. Nevertheless, in this chapter we are going to deal with a wider and more general purpose top-down model-driven development of services, which do not necessarily have to be composed, since the properties and QoS characteristics considered to be later integrated will be included for the initial phases of development.

The research presented by J. Bézivin et al. (Bézivin et al., 2004) deserves special attention: it covers Web service modeling from PIM to PSM and then to code, providing several alternatives. Among these alternatives, we can point out the one in which the PIM is decorated with Jaxrpc (https://jax-rpc.dev.java.net/) configuration elements, then converted into WSDL format and configuration files and finally Java and Jaxrpc implementations are obtained. They use UML in order to model services, which are represented as classes. Then, Java, WSDL and JWSDP (*Java Web Services Developer Pack* – http://jwsdp.dev.java.net/) metamodels are provided as platform-specific metamodels. The transformation rules from PIM to PSM are also provided.

What is most remarkable of all these approaches in relation to this chapter is that most of them do neither consider QoS nor EFP in their model-driven approaches and if they do, do not make use of standard modeling languages or do not generate implementation code.

Describing and Implementing Quality of Service and Extra-Functional Properties for Web Services

In recent years, research on Web services QoS has received considerable attention: in particular, Ludwig (Ludwig, 2003) describes QoS characteristics of Web services and lists open issues related to the possibility of flexible implementation of QoS-aware systems. The same author presents an XML-based language for specifying Service Level Agreements in (Ludwig et al., 2003), -WSLA. WSLA can be used by both service provider and customer to describe the Quality of Service provided and or required by their services or clients. Regarding Extra-functional properties it has been the XML-based standard WS-Policy (Bajaj, 2006), the one preferred for property description. Our approach is architecture-independent, we aim to provide a classification of QoS criteria and EFP properties which are relevant to Web Services –as suggested by Ludwig in (Ludwig, 2003), - and to implement and monitor them in a non-intrusive way, thus respecting Web service decoupleness. Besides, WSLA and WS-Policy can be integrated into our method. Therefore, our proposal supplies a flexible implementation for QoS which is complementary to the WSLA and WS-Policy-based description.

Therefore, Web service standards such as WSDL and UDDI do not support Extra-functional aspects nor QoS; there are several proposals which deal with this problem: Xu et al. (Xu et al., 2007) propose an extension of UDDI to include QoS information; in particular, they consider a reputation management mechanism to keep a track on the services reputations as a part of the discovery process. They also provide algorithms for matching and selecting services. In this line, Ran (Ran, 2003) suggests a method of QoS discovery by extending the UDDI, which requires human involvement. Such methods are suitable for small number of services, but will not scale. As a result, the task of comparison is often delegated to a QoS broker and is be carried out by a specific software.

There are various QoS brokers in the literature for Web services, among them (D'Mello et al., 2008), (Chen et al., 2006), (Menascé et al., 2002), (Serhani et al., 2005), (Tian et al.,2003) and (Tian et al.,2004). For example, in (D'Mello et al., 2008) services are ranked on the basis of the level satisfaction of the clients. In this area, some papers extend existing standards to present methods of ranking ((Tian et al.,2003) and (Tian et al.,2004)). In this sense, a typical approach is to match the requested QoS characteristic with the existing services for example by averaging on the QoS values by the requesters (Hu et al., 2005); other approaches introduce QoS Metrics for the ranking (AI-Masri et al., 2007). Another example is the one from Gouscos et al. (Gouscos et al., 2003), who advocate using a pricing mechanism along with other QoS attributes such as provided response time and probability of failure. They propose modifying WSDL and UDDI document to include such characteristics to be used by the brokers.

The task of discover can inflict extra computation and communication burden on the involved services, which may hamper scalability. One of the popular methods for dealing with this issue is to use P2P architectures: Fatih Emekci et al. (Emekci et al, 2004) proposed a Web service discovery which includes QoS attributes related to reputation and Farnoush Banaei-Kashani et al. (Banaei-Kashani et al., 2004) introduce WSPDS (Web Services Peer-to-peer Discovery Service), which is a decentralized discovery service with semantic-level matching capabilities. Other approaches that use P2P for this purpose are (Hunaity, 2008) and (Weifeng et al., 2007).

Discovery is out of the scope of this chapter, however we will see how our proposal provides the possibility of considering EFP and QoS from the system models and generate the appropriate description and implementation code, should it be necessary, avoiding the necessity of a specific broker.

Modeling Quality of Service and Extra-Functional Properties for Web Services

As previously said, research on Web services QoS and EFP has received considerable attention in the last years, also in the scope of model-driven development, such as the research of (Cardoso et al., 2002), (Schmit et al., 2005), (Weis et al., 2004), (Zeng et al., 2004) and (Zhou et al., 2004).

Cardoso et al (Cardoso et al., 2002) deal with QoS for workflows, tasks and processes in the scope of Web services. They provide a collection of task measurements and implementations guidelines depending on the type of workflow. Their approach relies on QoS measurements for specific workflow tasks, which compared to our platform-independent modeling approach is at a lower level of abstraction. As well as the previous work, this research is aimed at tasks and workflows QoS and not on higher level modelling constructs. Zeng (Zeng et al., 2004) focuses on QoS in Web service compositions aiming at matching the best composition among services based on QoS criteria measurements. Finally, the approach from Zhou et al (Zhou et al., 2004) provides a QoS ontology for Web services, which may be useful, again, at a different level of the application lifecycle, but not when the software engineer is modeling the system's main PIM. We are using models which describe QoS characteristics at any level of abstraction, from platform-independent models to code.

Weis et al. (Weis et al., 2004) apply a similar model-driven approach to our approach to QoS focusing on the components' interaction from the middlewares point of view. A major difference between our approach and the approach presented in (Weis et al., 2004) is the separation of concerns between QoS and systems, which results in easier maintenance and a less cluttered implementation.

Regarding Extra-functional properties, in the Web Service Modeling Framework–WSMF- (Fensel et al., 2002) ontologies are utilized to define the terminology to be used by other elements of WSMF specifications. A *goal* specification consists of two elements: pre-conditions describe what a Web service expects to receive in order to provide its functionality and post-conditions describe what a Web service returns in response to its invocation. Since Web Service Modeling Ontology (WSMO) is used in this framework to define services, Extra-functional properties can be described by the XML syntax provided by WSMO for this purpose. They also may be modeled as pre or post conditions, following the goal syntax. Both alternatives are possible, but none of them follows the UML syntax. However, based on this initial semantic description it is possible to define modelling constructs for properties.

Adaptive Services Grid (ASG) (Toma et al., 2006) are particularly related to our approach as services are specially characterized by their interfaces and operations and the corresponding parameters in the models. Pre and post conditions are also included in the model, as well as service metadata that provide additional service information. In this approach, the developer has to define the desired Extra-functional property in this system by using the WSMO syntax (Lausen et al., 2005). Then the required Extra-functional property may be automatically converted into a UML representation.

In the scope of SOA, we note that most suggested approaches where Extra-functional properties or Quality of Service characteristics are considered are not based on modeling standards such as UML. In fact, most of the approaches which consider Extra-functional properties in their models are mainly based on XML-based standard proposals (such as WS-Policy (Bajaj et al., 2004) and Web Service Level Agreement (WSLA) (Ludwig et al., 2003)) or on semantic expressions. Although they are useful property description proposals for other stages of development, none of these approaches

can be considered as a standard graphical way to model Extra-functional and implementation in accordance to description is not provided at all.

DEFINING QUALITY OF SERVICE AND EXTRA-FUNCTIONAL PROPERTY FOR WEB SERVICES

In the following lines we summarize what we mean by the terms Quality of Service and Extra-functional property in this chapter.

Quality of Service

In recent years the study of QoS in Web services has received considerable attention ((Ran, 2003), (Zeng et al., 2004), (Zeng et al., 2003)), (KangChan et al., 2003). We have classified QoS criteria described in the literature into three main categories:

- **Execution Criteria:** These QoS criteria can be measured on every invocation to the service.
  - **Execution Price (Zeng, 2004):** the execution price of invoking a service operation is the price the client has to pay when requesting the invocation.
  - **Execution Duration (Zeng, 2004) / Response Time (Ran, 2003):** average time needed to fulfil a service operation request, measured from the instant the client makes the request to the time the reply arrives.
  - **Processing Time (Zeng, 2004) / Latency (Ran, 2003):** average time required to process a message.
  - **Reliability (Zeng, 2004) / Throughput (Ran, 2003):** percentage of successfully completed requests of a service in a unit of time.
- **Service Provider Criteria**: These QoS criteria are often measured by an external entity, such as a service provider.

○ **Availability (Ran, 2003), (Zeng, 2004):** it is the probability for a service to be available, often calculated as the average time a service is accessible within a unit of time.

○ **Reputation (Zeng, 2004):** it measures how much customers trust a service. Such measurement is often carried out by conducting a customer satisfaction survey.

○ **Scalability (Ran, 2003):** scalability is the capacity of the service provider to supply an increase in computational power to process a higher number of requests in the same amount of time.

○ **Capacity (Ran, 2003):** it measures the number of requests the provider can handle without degrading performance criteria such as response time.

• **Exception-Related Criteria:** these criteria depend on the behaviour of the service under special situations or errors, which have to be measured externally.

○ **Robustness (Ran, 2003).** It measures how well the service behaves when invalid inputs are provided.

○ **Exception Handling (Ran, 2003).** It measures how well the service behaves when exceptions occur.

○ **Accuracy (Ran, 2003).** It measures the average number of errors produced by the service.

This chapter will focus on execution criteria since they are the set which is needed at first stages of Web service development and those which are more related to EFPs.

Additionally, it is important to take into account two important characteristics of the measurement of QoS in Web services, which are as follows (Ludwig, 2003):

• Firstly, those invocations to Web services are mainly done through the Internet. Hence, there is currently no global supervisor to oversee the measurement process. As a result, even though QoS certification could be partly done by third parties, at present such measurements must be carried out either at server side or at client side.

• Secondly, Web services are auto-descriptive, for example they are represented by their interface WSDL files. To describe QoS as part of a Web service description, one should provide a representation of QoS which can be integrated to such descriptions. An example of such an approach is an XML-based description of QoS criteria: WSLA (Ludwig et al., 2003). Throughout this chapter we will see how a WSLA-based description for QoS will be easily integrated into our approach.

Extra-Functional Property Classification

The term Extra-functional property can be found in the literature with different uses and meanings and the same could be said about the term non-functional property. We can sometimes find both terms being used with the same meaning, or we find communities which defend both to have completely different meanings ((Bajaj et al., 2004), (Baresi et al., 2005), (Duclos et al., 2002), (Rottger et al., 2004)). For this reason we are going to clarify more in depth what we mean by Extra-functional property in this chapter.

Extra-functional properties are pieces of code which provide additional functionality to the system, where this functionality is not part of the main one or of the main concern approached by the system. A typical example is a bank system Website, whose main functionality is to provide a portal in which customers can make transactions with their money and accounts. An Extra-functional property is, in this case, providing security to the operations performed by the customer.

There are some Extra-functional properties which commonly appear in systems such as authentication, confidentiality, audit, timing…, whereas others are more domain specific such as getting realtime results which may be important, for instance in a stock market or a weather forecast system.

We find this concept sometimes referred to as functional aspects; however in order to avoid a possible misunderstanding between the functional aspect (the property itself) and aspect implementation (an option for the property implementation) we avoid using this term and prefer to use Extra-functional property. It is also sometimes referred to as policies, however we do not want to use this term to avoid confusion between the whole property and the property description by using WS-Policy.

Regarding the categorization of properties, we can find several distinct classifications depending on the community, as for instance the one presented by Gleason et al. (Gleason et al., 2005), where they define properties designed to encourage use (data protection), those devised to constrain access (authentication), policies on availability (QoS), etc. Other classifications simply differentiate between properties which specify traditional requirements and capabilities, namely authentication or encryption, and those which are more related to service use or selection, such as Quality of Service characteristics (Real Time) or privacy policies (Log) (Weerewarana et al., 2005).

We neither provide a new classification based on the properties' functionality nor follow any of the previously mentioned above, since this is not relevant in our development. We just differentiate EFP from QoS characteristics, since there is a clear difference between injecting new behaviour for an extra functionality in our system and measuring a QoS criteria in our system (the latest is not providing new functionality to the system itself)

FILLING THE GAP OF EXTRA-FUNCTIONAL PROPERTY AND QUALITY OF SERVICE IN THE SCOPE OF WEB SERVICES

As we have mentioned before, simplicity and a loosely coupled environment are remarked by many approaches to be important characteristics models should follow. We have seen how there are several approaches which intend to include Extra-functional properties or Quality of Service characteristics in Web services, mainly based on textual description, whether based on XML-based description standards or semantic-based ones. Emerging XML or semantic-based standards are appropriate for a different level of service description, but not for a platform-independent model for which it is desirable to have a graphical notation to be integrated into the general system model, even particularly positive if based in UML.

There is not a determined and fixed defined standard for modeling Web services, however there are several approaches in which UML is used in different ways to model them. Thus, we could say that the tendency is to evolve towards a standard based in software modeling standards, such as UML. There are two main trends in UML Web service modeling, one which defends that UML Web service modeling is to be done by representing each element in the WSDL file in the UML model (Bezivin et al, 2004), specifically by creating a stereotype for these elements, and another one which claims that interface and operations are the core of Web service modeling and there is no need to include such a large amount of elements in the model which could induce to confusion (Grønmo et al., 2004). We cannot infer which will be the standard for Web service modeling in the future, however we can affirm that, whichever is the preferred option interfaces and operations will be an important part of these models, which is the relevant information for the approach presented in this chapter. As a conclusion, we can say that a graphical notation for EFP and QoS in the sphere of Web service development is necessary and it should be easily used in conjunction with Web service model-driven development approaches.

In this chapter we will provide a model-driven approach which allows introducing Extra-functional properties and Quality of Service characteristics into Web service development without impairing the loosely coupled environment ([Ortiz et al., 2005], [Ortiz et al., 2007]). In this sense, first of all, two UML profiles are provided to facilitate loosely coupled Extra-functional property and Quality of Service modeling at PIM level. Then, using a set of transformation rules, the platform-independent model turns into platform-specific ones. Finally, the appropriate code is obtained by applying the corresponding transformation rules to the platform-specific models. This code consists of an aspect-oriented implementation for property functionality and Quality of Service

measurement development and a policy based one and a QoS description based one for property and QoS description.

MODELING QUALITY OF SERVICE AND EXTRA-FUNCTIONAL PROPERTIES AT A PLATFORM-INDEPENDENT LEVEL

Our method for QoS is motivated by the approach adopted by (OMG, 2008) and similar approaches which are based on Meta-Object Facility (MOF) (OMG, 2006). However for illustration purposes we shall present a simpler profile, in which, additionally, we have considered the main characteristics of Web services.

In order to model the different QoS criteria, we propose the use of the profile in Figure 2.

Figure 2. Quality of service profile

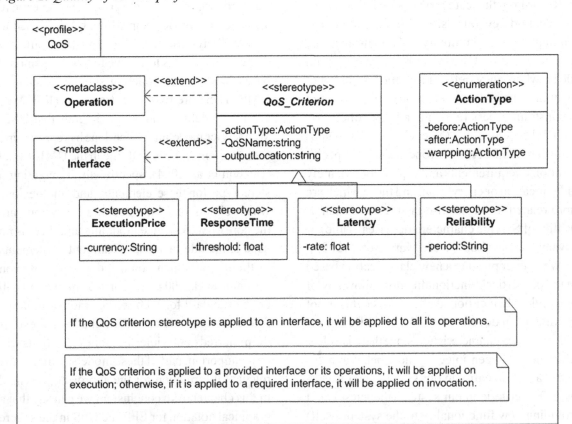

Whenever necessary, additional attributes can be added to the profile criteria to deal with extra capabilities such as Constraint Control or Actions. The profile elements are described as follows:

- We define the abstract stereotype *QoS_Criterion*, which will extend operation or interface metaclasses. The QoS criterion provides three attributes: the first one is *actionType*, which indicates whether the measurement will be performed before, after or wrapping the stereotyped operation's execution. Secondly, *name* contains the criterion name and, finally, *outputLocation* indicates where the measurement result will be recorded.

- To define *actionType*, an enumeration is provided with three alternative values: before, after, wrapping: the quality criterion may be measured before executing the stereotyped operation, after it or both before and after the operation's functionality.

In order to illustrate the proposal we have developed a real case-study based on a course administration system used in a typical University by students and members of staff (specifically the one used in the *Centro Universitario de Mérida –CUM–* in Mérida -Spain-). The system consists of several Web services (*PreregistrationService, RegistrationService, ExamOpportunityService, AcademicResultsService* and *TeacherService* -for further details see (Ortiz, 2007)). Our case study aims to consider the following QoS criteria in the named services: latency and response time will be measured to check if the service really saves students time and if the university server is working properly, respectively.

- **Latency:** latency will be measured over the selected *PreregistrationService* operation and the interface offered by *RegistrationService*. These operations handle the University system database,

therefore it is important to know how long every performed registration takes, of less importance being how long delivering the answer to the student takes. This criterion is measured from the moment the execution starts in the service side and therefore is considered in the service model.

- **Response Time:** response Time will be measured for bringForwardExam and cancelExam in *ExamOpportunityService*, for teacherSearch in TeachersService and the AcademicResults interface. Let us assume that the three services are widely used by the students. Moroever suppose that *AcademicResultsService* requires a confirmation from the invoked operations, therefore it is important to check how long the student has to wait to receive the response. Since this criterion is measured from the moment the invocation is done in the client side, it is considered in the client model.

Figure 3 depicts how these Quality of Service criteria are included in the case study system platform-independent model.

Let us start with the service side. In Figure 3 we can see the PIM of the Web service-based system representing the case study. *NewPreregistration* in the interface offered by *PreregistrationService* and the interface offered by *RegistrationService* are stereotyped with the stereotype Latency. It can also be seen that the *outputLocation* value varies from one stereotype instance to another. It may also be noted that the rate value has been set to 1; it will be used to compare the measured latency with the appropriate rate established by the developer. Then we will log the result obtained from comparing both values.

In the same figure we can see the client-side model, where we have included the corresponding QoS stereotypes. It is shown that the required interface *AcademicResultsServiceIF* is stereotyped with *ResponseTime*. Also, *bringForwardExam* and *CancelExam* are stereotyped in the required

Figure 3. Platform-independent model with QoS stereotypes

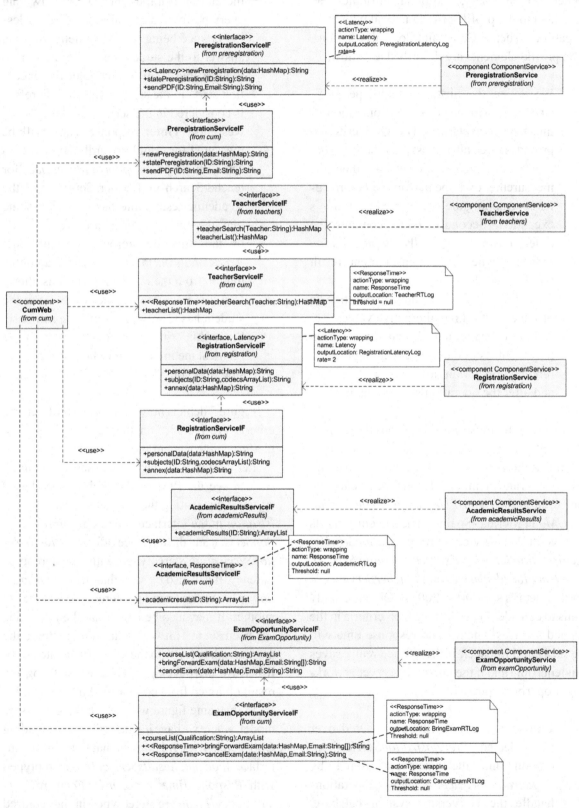

interface *ExamOpportunityServiceIF*, as well as *teacherSearch* in *TeacherServiceIF*. Different values for *outputLocation* can be discerned. In this case the threshold value has been left as null; the threshold value may be set in order to check whether or not response time is below this value and record it or take action accordingly; however; this case study only measures and records the latency of the operations.

Platform-Independent Metamodel for Extra-Functional Properties

In order to maintain our system loosely coupled when adding Extra-functional properties to the model at platform-independent level, we propose the profile in Figure 4, whose elements will be explained as follows.

To start with, we define the abstract stereotype called Extra-functional property in order to reflect that Extra-functional properties are parts of the system which do not constitute the main service functionality, but provide additional value to it. The Extra-functional property provides five attributes: the first one is actionType, which indicates whether the property functionality will be performed before, after or instead of the stereotyped operation's execution – or if no additional functionality is needed it will have the value none, only possible in the client side. Secondly, the attribute optional will allow us to indicate whether the property is performed optionally – the client may decide if it is to be applied or not – or compulsorily –it is applied whenever the operation is invoked. Then, a third attribute, ack, is included: when false it means that it is a domain-specific property and so only the skeleton code can be generated, otherwise it will have the value true indicating it is a well-known property whose full functionality code can be generated. Next, we have one more attribute, policyID, which will contain the name to be assigned to the created policy. Finally, the attribute priority will let us establish which properties have to be considered

Figure 4. Extra-functional property profile

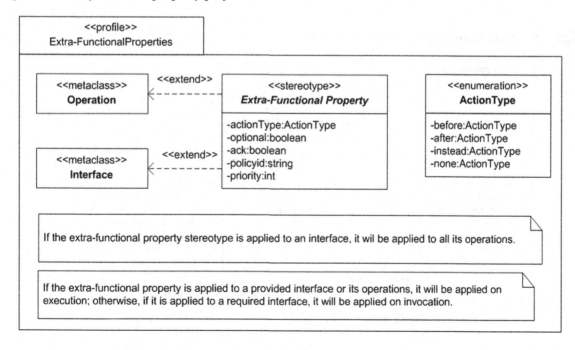

first at execution time, when more than one are affecting the same operation. This is necessary in order to be able to compose several properties which might be applied to the same operation in the service, which is definitely a relevant issue in this scope.

In order to define actionType, an enumeration is provided with four alternative values: before, after, instead or none. These different values relate to the different options available to perform the properties at implementation time, as they may include new behaviour before the stereotyped operation execution, after it or they can even replace the operation's functionality by a different one. The none value, as mentioned before, is only used at the client side. We can mark here the difference in relation to the QoS profile: in the QoS profile we always measure the QoS criterion, this mean that the client do not have nothing to do with the QoS measurement and therefore we do not have to add any additional value in this profile to take this into account. Besides, QoS criterion proposed are all well known, they do not depend on the specific domain, so the full code is always

generated for them and therefore there is no need for additional attributes in the stereotype such as ack or priorities.

The Extra-functional property stereotype will be specialized into different stereotypes related to well-known properties or to domain-specific ones in the particular systems modeled. Each property may have additional attributes, represented as tagged values, related to their specific functionality, as shown in Figure 5. The properties added in the profile are the ones required by the case study as explained later on.

It is important to mention that the usefulness of the stereotype in Figure 2 and the one in Figure 4, is the same, even though in Figure 2 specific QoS characteristics are defined from the initial definition of the profile and profile in Figure 4 is extended in a later stage (Figure 5). We did it this way due to, as previously mentioned, we assumed that available QoS characteristics were known in advance, meanwhile Extra-functional properties might be more domain-specific and therefore it might be more appropriate to extend the profile with them for the system in question that we are

Figure 5. Extra-functional property profile extended with specific property

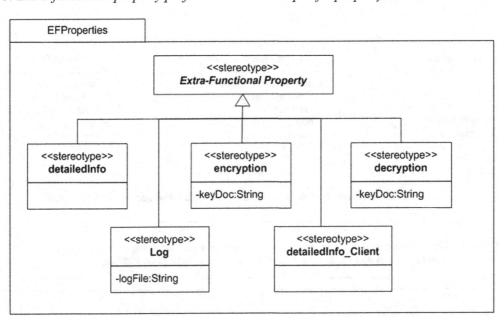

modeling. However, this does not affect at all to the final models of the systems.

If we consider again the real case study presented in the previous section, three properties are added in the case study services: *log*, *detailedInfo* and *decryption*:

- **Log:** it has been applied to the interface offered by the registration service.
- **detailedInfo:** when bringing forward an opportunity exam by the use of the exam opportunity service, the client may decide not only to change the exam opportunity but also to get additional information on the date and room in which the exam will be taken. Considering the importance of this process, we also added a log property to this operation, thus priorities among properties will also be considered.
- **decryption:** when the client requests the pdf file with the preregistration information to be sent to him in the preregistration service, the invocation parameters will have to be encrypted, since the service will decrypt them at reception; the system would fail if no encryption took place.

These properties have been integrated in the service model as shown in Figure 6, where we can see that they stereotype the corresponding service operations or interfaces.

In the top of the figure we can see how decryption stereotypes operation *sendPDF* in interface *PreregistrationServiceIF*. In general, stereotype attributes are defined as tagged values; in order to show their values in the model picture, we have also included them as notes. Decryption attribute values indicate that the property functionality will replace the operation execution (*actionType=instead*), the property is always carried out (*optional=false*), it is not a well-known property in the sense that the full functionality code cannot be generated (*ack=false*), the policy

is identified with the name decryption_ao4ws (*policyId=decryption_ao4ws*), the document containing the decryption key is named myPrivateKey (*KeyDoc=myPrivateKey*) and finally no priority is specified.

Around the centre of the figure we can see how the log has been used to stereotype interface *registrationServiceIF*. The property values indicate that the log is going to be realized after the execution of the operations in the interface (*actionType=after*), it is not an optional property (*optional=false*), the full code can be generated for this property (*ack=true*), the identifier for the policy is log_ao4ws (*policyID=log_ao4ws*), the file where the data is going to be recorded is myLogFile (*logFile = myLogFile*) and no priority is established.

Finally, in the bottom side of the figure we can see that two properties, detailedInfo and log, which stereotype the operation *bringForwardExam* in interface *ExamOpportunityServiceIF*. On the one hand, *detailedInfo* attributes show us that the property-related functionality is going to be executed instead of the *bringforwardExam* operation one (*actionType=instead*), the client may choose for the property to be applied or not (*optional=true*), the full functionality cannot be generated (*ack=false*), the policy identifier is detailedInfo_ao4ws (*policyId=detailedInfo_ao4ws*) and it will be the first functionality to be developed if more functionalities are carried out by other properties (*priority=1*). On the other hand, log values indicate that the log is going to be realized after the execution of the operation (*actionType=after*), it is not an optional property (*optional=false*), the full code can be generated for this property (*ack=true*), the identifier for the policy is log_ao4ws (*policyID=log_ao4ws*), the file where the data is going to be recorded is bringForwardFile (*logFile = bringForwardFile*) and it will be the second functionality to be developed if more functionalities are carried out by other properties for this operation (*priority=2*).

Figure 6. Platform-independent model with EFP stereotypes

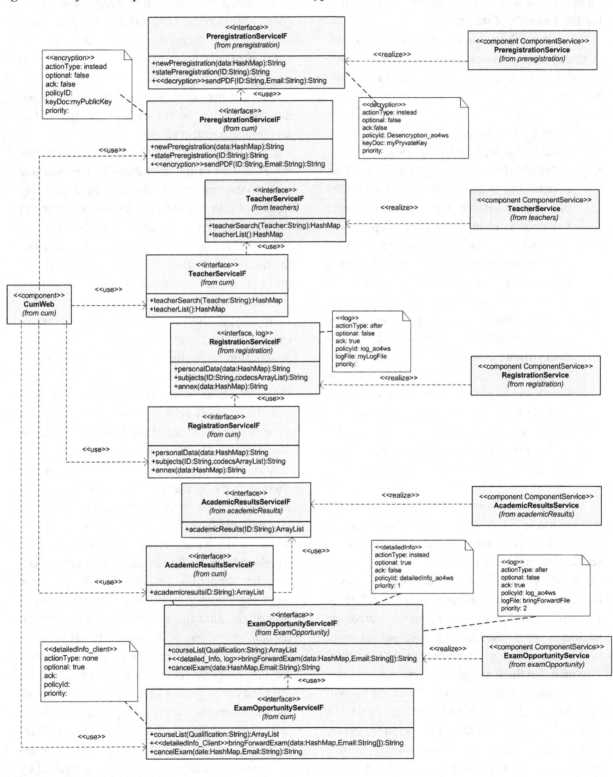

Finally, once the client knows the properties provided by the service, he may add those which are optional and of interest to him and he will have to take mandatory ones into account. If we analyze the properties being used by the service, we can depict the following scene:

- log is not optional and does not require any additional information, nor additional functionality from the client side. Therefore, it is not considered in the client side.
- The decryption done in the service requires an encryption in the client side; thus, we have to take into account that invocations to *sendPDF* have to be encrypted. This leads us to adding the property encryption in *sendPDF*, in the client required interface.
- Finally, *detailedInfo* is an optional property. Our client decided to make use of it, thus providing the students with additional information when they change exam opportunities. In this regard, *detailedInfo_ Client* will have to stereotype *bringforwardExam* in the required interface.

Consequently, we have added encryption and detailedInfo_client properties to the model, as shown in Figure 6.

Property encryption stereotypes *sendPDF* in the required interface *PreregistrationServiceIF*. Its attribute values indicate that the property functionality will replace the operation call (*actionType=instead*), the property functionality is always carried out (*optional=false*), it is not a well-known property in the sense that the full functionality code cannot be generated (*ack=false*), and the document containing the decryption key is named myPrivateKey (*KeyDoc=myPrivateKey*).

The property *detailedInfo_Client* has been applied to the operation *bringForwardExam* in the required interface *ExamOpportunityServiceIF*. Its attributes show us that the property implies no functionality to be added (*actionType=none*) and

it is an optional property which we are choosing (*optional=true*). In this case no value is indicated for ack since functionality code cannot be well-known or unknown if no functionality has to be developed.

No policyId has to be specified in the client side, since policy description is to be shown by the service. No priorities are necessary in this case. As a result, both fields are empty for both properties.

Please notice that EFP and QoS stereotypes would normally be included in the same platform-independent model; we did it separately in this chapter for facilitating the understanding of the models.

MODELING QUALITY OF SERVICE AND EXTRA-FUNCTIONAL PROPERTIES AT PLATFORM-SPECIFIC LEVEL

There are two fundamental aspects of properties which may be dealt with in a different manner depending on the final platform used or even according to the desired final results, which are implementation and description; this is the reason why we provide different specific metamodels.

In regard to implementation, QoS requires code for its measurement and Extra-functional properties imply certain functionality which has to be provided, be it by the host where the property or characteristic is deployed, be it by the code implementation itself. Due to the fact that only a few middlewares currently deal with some of these types of property and characteristics, we consider it appropriate to create this functionality code as part of the service itself. However, in order to maintain the main functionality decoupled from the property and QoS-related one and to avoid intrusive code in the main service functionality we propose an aspect-oriented approach. Consequently, this decision delimits our first metamodel to an aspect one.

Secondly, Web services are self-descriptive by definition: the Web service description language provides us with the way to describe services in such a way that the clients have entire information to invoke them. When adding QoS or Extra-functional properties it is essential to provide a description of them. The WSDL document is not the most appropriate means to describe properties if we wish to maintain main and property functionality decoupled; the WS-Policy document is a suitable option for Extra-functional properties, as well as the WSLA specification is suitable for QoS. As a result, we conclude that we need a metamodel for Quality of Service and Extra-functional property description to be modelled; the proposed metamodels will therefore be QoS description-based and policy-based, respectively.

Aspect-Oriented Metamodel

As we said before, AOP establishes aspects as the way to model crosscutting concerns. Aspects are units of encapsulation which incorporate two principal elements: pointcuts and advices (Elrad, 2001). On the one hand, through pointcuts we determine in which specific points of the implementation we wish to insert the new functionality; on the other, advices identify the new code to be injected, thus reflecting the desired new behaviour in the application.

The aspect metamodel is shown in Figure 7. The elements that constitute the Aspect package, which contains the necessary elements for the definition of the aspect metamodel, and their attributes are described in the following lines considering the elements in the figure from top

Figure 7. Aspect-oriented metamodel

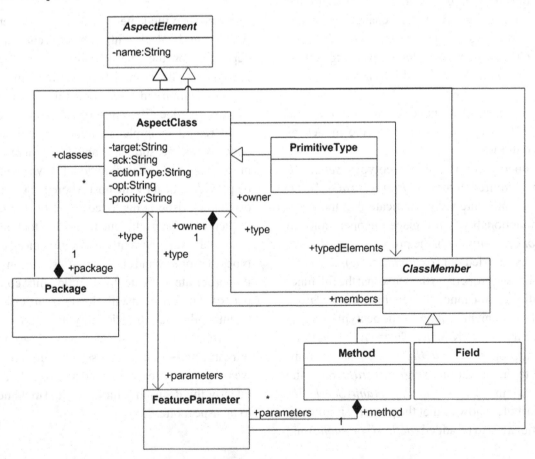

down and from left to right, that is, with the following order: *AspectElement, AspectClass, PrimitiveType, Package, ClassMember, Method, Field* and *FeatureParameter.*

Abstract Class AspectElement

This class comprises the main base element in the aspect metamodel. In this sense, many of the elements later defined will extend this class. It provides the following attribute:

- **Attribute name (String):** it contains the name of the element.

Class AspectClass

This class provides a way to define an aspect class, extending the AspectElement element. It provides the following references and attributes:

- **Reference parameters (Feature Parameter [ ]):** it consists on a sequence of parameters, this is, the class parameters. Each of them will have a name and a type, as defined later on.
- **Reference members (ClassMember [ ]):** it supplies a sequence of class members, namely the fields and methods which are defined in this class.
- **Reference typedElements (ClassMember [ ]):** it supplies a sequence of class members, namely the fields and methods which are defined in this class.
- **Reference "package" (Package [ ]):** it supplies the package in which this class is contained.
- **Attribute target (String):** it indicates the point in the execution of the program where the aspect functionality is going to be injected.
- **Attribute ack (String):** it indicates the key name of the property if the aspect is

well-known or it has the value false when domain-specific.

- **Attribute actionType (String):** it indicates if the extra functionality is going to be added before, after or instead the original method execution.
- **Attribute opt (String):** it indicates if the property application is optional for the client invocations or not.
- **Attribute priority (String):** it indicates the priority of the property among others which are applied to the same operation.

Class PrimitiveType

This class provides the primitive types which may be used in the models, extending the AspectClass element.

Class Package

This class provides a way to define a package containing AspectElements and it itself extends AspectElement. It provides the following reference:

- **Reference classes (AspectClass [ ]):** it supplies a sequence of java classes which belong to this package.

Abstract Class ClassMember

This class provides a way to define the members of a class, this is, its fields and methods, and it is also extending the class AspectElement. It provides the following references:

- **Reference type (JavaClass):** it supplies the type of member: the Field type or the type returned by the Method, respectively.
- **Reference owner (JavaClass):** it supplies the owner of the member, namely the class which contains this member.

Class Method

This class provides a way to define a method, extending the ClassMember element. It provides the following reference:

- **Reference parameters (Feature Parameter [ ]):** it consists in a sequence of parameters, this is, the method parameters. Each of them will have a name and a type, as defined later on.

Class Field

This class extends ClassMember and provides a way to define the Fields in the classes.

Class FeatureParameter

This class provides a way to define the parameters in the methods, extending the JaxrpcElement element. It provides the following references:

- **Reference type (AspectClass):** it provides the type of parameter.
- **Reference method (Method):** it provides the method which the parameter belongs to.

Policy-Based Metamodel

The policy metamodel is shown in Figure 8. The elements which constitute the Policy package, which contain the necessary elements for the definition of the Policy metamodel, and their attributes are described in the following lines, analysing the figure from top to bottom and from left to right:

Abstract Class PolicyElement

This class comprises the main base element in the policy metamodel. In this sense, many of the elements later defined will extend this class. It provides the following attribute:

- **Attribute name (String):** it contains the name of the element.

Class Package

This class provides a way to define a package containing PolicyElements and it itself extends PolicyElement. It provides the following reference:

- **Reference classes (PolicyClass [ ]):** it supplies a sequence of PolicyClass which belong to this package.

Figure 8. Policy-based metamodel

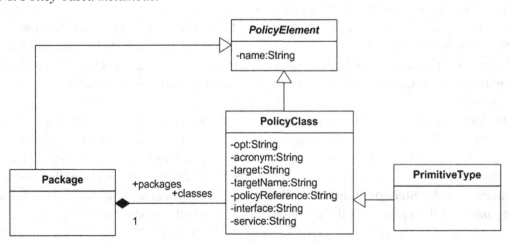

Class PolicyClass

This class provides a way to define a policy class, extending the PolicyElement element. It provides the following reference and attributes:

- **Reference "package" (Package [ ]):** it supplies the package in which this class is contained.
- Attribute opt (String): it indicates if the property application is optional for the client invocations or not.
- **Attribute acronym (String):** it provides the acronym used for the property description.
- **Attribute targetType (String):** it indicates the type of element for the property to be applied.
- **Attribute targetName (String):** it provides the name of the element for the property to be applied.
- **Attribute policyReference (String):** it provides the reference where the policy will be deployed.
- **Attribute interface (String):** it provides the name of the interface where the property has been included.
- **Attribute service (String):** it provides the name of the service which offers the interface which contains properties.

Class PrimitiveTypes

This class provides the primitive types which may be used in the models, extending the PolicyClass element.

QoS Description-Based Metamodel

The QoS description metamodel is shown in Figure 9. The elements which constitute the QoS description package, which contain the necessary elements for the definition of the QoS description metamodel, and their attributes are described in the following lines, analysing the figure from top to bottom and from left to right:

Abstract Class QoSDescription

This class comprises the main base element in the policy metamodel. In this sense, many of the elements later defined will extend this class. It provides the following attribute:

- **Attribute name (String):** it contains the name of the element.

Class Package

This class provides a way to define a package containing QoSDescriptions and it itself extends

Figure 9. QoS description-based metamodel

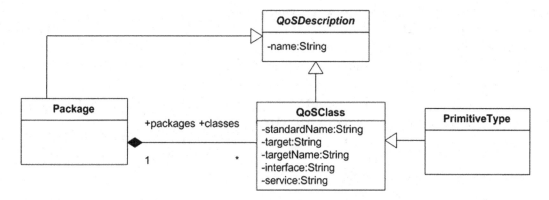

QoSDescription. It provides the following reference:

- **Reference classes (QoSClass [ ]):** it supplies a sequence of QoSClass which belong to this package.

Class QoSClass

This class provides a way to define a QoS description class, extending the QoSDescription element. It provides the following reference and attributes:

- **Reference "package" (Package [ ]):** it supplies the package in which this class is contained.
- **Attribute standardName (String):** it contains the name of the QoS criterion.
- **Attribute target (String):** it indicates the type of element for the QoS criterion to be measured.
- **Attribute targetName (String):** it provides the name of the element for the QoS criterion to be measured.
- **Attribute interface (String):** it provides the name of the interface where the QoS criterion has been included.

- **Attribute service (String):** it provides the name of the service which offers the interface which contains QoS criteria.

Class PrimitiveTypes

This class provides the primitive types which may be used in the models, extending the QoSClass element.

GENERATING CODE FOR QUALITY OF SERVICE AND EXTRA-FUNCTIONAL PROPERTIES

From the aspect, policy and QoS description specific models, where additional attribute values can be added or modified, we will generate the code motivated below:

- From the aspect metamodel we will generate an AspectJ (www.eclipse.org/aspectj) implementation; that is, an AspectJ aspect will be generated for each aspect class in our model. AspectJ pointcuts will be determined by the target element. Concerning the advice, depending on the actionType attribute value, the advice type will be before, after or around.

Algorithm 1. Log property aspect for bringForwardExam operation in examOpportunity

```
package examOpportunity;
public aspect examOpportunity_bringForwardExam_log {
pointcut examOpportunity_bringForwardExam_log_P():execution (public examOppor-
tunity ExamOpportunityServiceIF.bringForwardExam(..));
after ():examOpportunity_bringForwardExam_log_P(){
        try{
                        PrintWriter out1 = new PrintWriter  (new Buffered-
Writer (new FileWriter ("bringForwardFile", true)));
                        out1.println(thisJoinPoint.toLongString());
                        out1.close();
        }catch(Exception e){System.out.println(e)}
```

- With regard to the Quality of Service description, it is proposed to generate an XML document using WSLA syntax. In this sense, an XML file where the QoS criterion described will be generated.
- With regard to property description, it is proposed to generate a document which encapsulates the WS-Policy and WS-PolicyAttachment elements for each property. In this sense, an XML file where the policy is described and attached to the service is generated.

AspectJ Code

We show two examples of aspect code, one for an Extra-functional property application and the other one for a QoS criterion measurement.

Algorithm 1 shows the *log* property aspect for *bringForwardExam* operation in *examOpportunity*. We can see how the functionality provided by the aspect is realized after the execution of the said operation.

Algorithm 2 shows the *responseTime* criterion for *teacherSearch* operation in *teacherService*. We can see how the criterion measurement code is realized around (before and after) the execution of the said operation.

WS-Policy Code

The policy generated for log property for *bringForwardExam* operation in *examOpportunity* is shown in Algorithm 3, where we can see how it is attached to *ExamOpportunityService*, port type to *ExamOpportunityServiceIF* and operation *bringForwardExam*. The address where the service is deployed could be supplied. The policy description is also provided, where the namespaces to use are still to be included, depending on the specific policy; finally, the policy name is added.

WSLA Code

The Web Service Level Agreement code generated for response time criterion for *teacherSearch*

Algorithm 2. ResponseTime criterion for teacherSearch operation in teacherService

```
public aspect teacherService_teacherSearch _responseTime{
pointcut teacherSearch_responseTime():
 execution(public teacherService.teacherSearch (..));
 String around ():teacherSearch_responseTime (){
    float responseTime = 0;
    String result=null;
    try {
        long initialTime= System.currentTimeMillis();
        result=proceed();
        long finalTime= System.currentTimeMillis();
        responseTime = finalTime-initialTime;
        PrintWriter rT = new PrintWriter  (new BufferedWriter (new FileWriter
("C:/TeacherRTLog", true)));
        rT.println(thisJoinPoint.toLongString()+" "+responseTime+" ms");
        rT.close();
    }catch (IOException e)
return result;}
```

Algorithm 3. Policy generate fro log property for bringForwardExam operation in examOpportunity

```
<wsp:PolicyAttachment >
        <wsp:AppliesTo>
                <wsp:EndpointReference>
                <wsp:ServiceName>ExamOpportunityService</wsp:ServiceName>
                <wsp:PortType>ExamOpportunityServiceIF</wsp:PortType>
                <wsp:Operation>bringForwardExam</wsp:Operation>
                <wsp:Address>...</wsp:Address>
        </wsp:EndpointReference>
        </wsp:AppliesTo>
        <wsp:Policy xmlns:wsp="..." xmlns:wsl="...">
        <wsl:examOpportunity_bringForwardExam_log />
        </wsp:Policy>
</wsp:PolicyAttachment>
```

operation in *teacherService* is shown in Algorithm 4, where we can see how it is attached to port type *TeacherServiceIF* and operation *teacherSearch*. The address where the service is deployed could be supplied. The metric name and type returned are provided. The uri with the location of the metric information is added to the generated code.

EVALUATION

In regards with QoS we can say that the use of AOP ensures that the implementation of the QoS monitor remains modularized during the process, from the modeling stage to the generation of code that implements the monitor. Same can be said in relation to Extra-functional property, which thanks to the use of AOP their Extra-functionality remains completely decoupled. As a consequence of the

Algorithm 4. Web service level agreement code for response time criterion for teacherSearch operation in teacherService

```
<Operation xsi:type="wsla:WSDLSOAPOperationDescriptionType"
name="teacherSearch">
<SLAParameter name="responseTime"
        type="float">
<Metric name="responseTime" type="float">
 <MetricURI>http://ao4QoS/testResponse
 </MetricURI>
</Metric>
<WSDLFile> […]</WSDLFile>
<SoapBindingName>teacherServiceIF </SoapBindingName>
<SoapOperationName>teacherSearch </SoapOperationName>
</Operation>
```

system's modularity, QoS and EFP implementation and description are completely encapsulated into units.

In our approach, traceability is perfectly maintained from the platform-independent models at design stage to code. This is because every Quality of Service criterion and Extra-functional property are represented as a stereotype, respectively, in the platform-independent model. Then the transformation maps the criterion or property into the platform-specific representation. Finally, the same criterion and property are mapped into the AspectJ aspect and WSLA and WS-Policy description, respectively. The path can also be followed in the opposite direction, from code to PIM. Consequently, a QoS criterion will be traceable during the process of transformation, as well as an EFP will.

Our method improves maintainability of the developed system. Since the code of the QoS monitor and Extra-functional property implementation remains separated from the main functionality, it is easier to add, delete or modify QoS criteria and EFP without affecting the main service functionality of the system. The traceability described above also contributed to better maintenance of the system. The combination of separation of concerns and traceability ensures better system maintenance.

Having a profile with a predefined set of models for QoS criteria and EFP and automatic code generation allows us to reuse the criteria and property in different systems without the need of re-implementing them over and over again. Moreover, portability of the PIM across middleware vendors is increased thanks to the predefined profiles. Besides, the profile can be extended with any property specific to the system in question.

Applying MDA results in faster development cycles. Automatic code generation produces well structured systems with fewer human-induced bugs. Our experiments have shown that the amount of automatically generated code can vary considerably. At least, it is possible to generate the skeleton code for every QoS criterion and Extra-functional property. Moreover, if the criterion or property has been specifically described in our system and we have created specific transformation rules for it, it is possible to generate the full code. Additional information on the evaluation conducted to the method can be consulted in (Ortiz et al., 2008).

It is often argued that AOP results in extra overhead in terms of performance. However, modern AOP weavers have evolved considerably. In particular, the AspectJ community has recently devoted considerable effort to address their compiler performance. Modern implementations of AspectJ are claimed to match the functionality of non-aspect oriented implementations, while providing all advantages associated to the use of aspects (García, 2006), (Ortiz, 2007)) and (Ortiz et al., 2008).

FUTURE RESEARCH DIRECTIONS

Several directions could be considered for future work, which will be traced in the following lines. In near future we shall create a repository of predefined Extra-functional properties for which the full code template can be generated automatically. The repository will include well-known properties in the Web service domain, such as a digital signature or login. Web services are a relatively new area of computer science, as a result there is not a wide set of well-known and well characterized Extra-functional properties other than security-related ones. However, some additional properties could be considered too, such as *real time*, *accuracy*, etc.

Another direction for future research includes an extension to deal with service provider and exception-related criteria, some of which can be monitored adopting similar methods to the one discussed in this chapter. For example, availability can be diagnosed by creating a monitor which constantly checks services accessibility. This may impose further load on the system, which may have adverse effects on its availability, so the issue requires further research to strike a correct balance by doing right level of monitoring to identify problems with the performance. Other criteria, such as Reputation, require user involvement. These criteria demand conducting surveys and arranging for virtual user groups to provide feedback; this is also a direction for future research. Another possible direction for future research is to integrate constrains checking and their corresponding actions on the QoS profile for them to be considered from platform-independent models and to obtain the necessary code automatically.

Bringing MDA into focus, it is important to remember reusability of platform-independent models for various platform-specific implementations is one of the main purposes of a model-driven approach. In this respect, additional work can be pursued on this topic; in particular, we remark platform-specific models and implementations' development for mobile devices. We have already starting working on this topic and preliminary results can be found at (Ortiz et al., 2009).

To conclude, the dynamic addition of software artefacts is a subject whose importance has increased in the last years in various disciplines. In this concern, future work could also consider the generation of a dynamic aspect-oriented implementation from Extra-functional property models and Quality of Service criteria in order to inject new behaviours and measurements even if services are already deployed.

CONCLUSION

Some clear benefits of the contributions of this proposal are analysed below:

- It can be widely found in different discipline environments that Extra-functional properties and Quality of Service criteria should be decoupled from the main system functionality. In addition, producing a loosely coupled environment is one of the main pillars of the Web service development. The present proposal allows us to maintain EFP and QoS in Web service development completely decoupled from the main functionality entities at all stages of development.

- In general, it is also widely known that model-driven development facilitates the development of applications from a platform-independent model until the final code implementation. Furthermore, Web services may be modelled in a platform-independent manner and later transformed into a model specific to the platform in question, and finally into code. In this regard, properties and characteristics are integrated in this development from a platform-independent model, through a platform-specific model in which implementation and description remain separated and finishing with a final code implementation for each of these types of model. It is often argued that adopting Model-Driven Architecture results in simplicity and traceability. Transformations between models are even simpler when the different parts of the models remain decoupled, as is the case in our approach; traceability allows the exact location of every model element in other level models or in the code and vice versa; this is also achieved by our approach.

- Aspect-oriented techniques are also widely known by several disciplines as a good alternative when decoupling Extra-functional properties. We have demonstrated that this is also a good option for Extra-functional property implementation and Quality of Service measurements in the Web services scope and we have avoided the learning curve of using an additional programming language in development by automatically generating their code. Furthermore, Web services are inherently self-descriptive elements; this is the reason why we have also generated the standard WS-Policy description for the implemented properties and WSLA description for measured criteria.

ACKNOWLEDGMENT

The first author acknowledges the support from *Ministerio de Ciencia e Innovación* (TIN2008-02985) and from *Fondo Europeo de Desarrollo Regional* (FEDER).

REFERENCES

Baïna, K., Benatallah, B., Casati, F., & Toumani, F. (June, 2004). Model-driven web service development. In A. Persson, J. Stirna (Eds.), *International Conference on Advanced Information Systems Engineering, Lecture Notes in Computer Science: Vol 3084* (pp. 290-306). Latvia.

Bajaj, S., Box, D., Chappeli, D., et al. (2006). *Web services policy 1.2 framework (WS-Policy)*. IBM Research. Retrieved April 2010, from http://www.w3.org/Submission /WS-Policy/

Banaei-Kashani, F., Chen, C., & Shahabi, C. (June 2004). WSPDS: web services peer-to-peer discovery service. *Proceedings of the International Conference on Internet Computing,* (pp. 733-743). CSREA Press.

Baresi, L., Guinea, S., & Plebani, P. (September, 2005). WS-policy for service monitoring development. In A. C. Bussler, M. Shan (Eds.) *VLDB Workshop on Technologies for E-Services, Lecture Notes in Computer Science: Vol. 3811* (pp. 72-83). Norway.

Bézivin, J., Hammoudi, S., Lopes, D., & Joault, F. (2004). *An experiment in mapping web services to implementation platforms.* (Tech. Rep. No. 04.01). LINA: Université de Nantes.

Cardoso, J., & Miller, J. (2002). *Modeling quality of service for workflows and web service processes. (Technical Report UGACS -TR-02-002).* University of Georgia.

Chollet, S., & Lalanda, P. (2009). An extensible abstract service orchestration framework. In *Proceedings of the IEEE International Conference on Web Services(ICWS 2009).* IEEE Computer Society Press.

D'Mello, D., & Ananthanarayana, V. S. (December 2008). A qos model and selection mechanism for qos-aware web services. *Proceedings of the International Conference on Data Management.*

Duclos, F., Estublier, J., & Morat, P. (2002). Describing and using non functional aspects in component based applications. In *ACM Proceedings 1st International Conference on Aspect-oriented Software Development,* (pp. 65-75), The Netherlands. ACM Press

Elrad, T., Aksit, M., Kitzales, G., Lieberherr, K., & Ossher, H. (2001). Discussing aspects of AOP. *Communications of the ACM, 44*(10), 33–38. doi:10.1145/383845.383854

Emekci, F., Sahin, O. D., Agrawal, D., & ElAbbadi, A. (June 2004). A peer-to-peer framework for web service discovery with ranking. *Proceedings of the IEEE International Conference on Web Services* (pp. 192). IEEE Computer Society. AI-Masri, E., & Mahmoud, Q. H. (2007). Discovering the best web service. *Proceedings International World Wide Web Conference* (pp. 1257-1258). ACM.

Fensel, D., & Bussler, C. (2002). *WSMF in a nutshell.* Retrieved April 2009 from http://www1-c703.uibk.ac.at/ ~c70385/wese/wsmf.iswc.pdf

García, A. Sant 'Anna, C., Figuereido, E., Uirá, K., Lucena, C., & von Sta, A. (2006). Modularizing design patterns with aspects: A quantitative study. In P. Tarr (Ed.), *Transactions on Aspect-Oriented Software Development, Lecture Notes in Computer Science.*

Gleason, T., Minder, K., & Pavlik, G. (2005). Policy management and web services. At L. Cagal, T. Finin, & J. Hendler (Eds.), *Procedings of Policy Management For the Web Workshop at the IWWW Conference*, (pp. 57-60). Japan.

Gouscos, D., Kalikakis, M., & Georgiadis, P. (December 2003). An approach to modeling web service QoS and provision price. *Proceedings of the International Conference on Web Information Systems Engineering Workshops* (pp.121-130). IEEE Computer Society.

Grønmo, R., & Skogan, D. Solheim, & I. Oldevik, J. (2004). Model-driven web services development. In S. Yuan & J. Lu (Eds.), *International Conference on e-Technology, e-Commerce and e-Service 2004* (pp. 42-45). IEEE Computer Society. Chen, H., Yu, T. Lin, k. (July 2006). QCWS: An implementation of QoS-capable multimedia Web services. *IEEE Fifth International Symposium on Multimedia Software Engineering* (pp. 165-187). Springer.

Hu, J., Guo, C., Wang, H., & Zou, P. (October 2005). Quality driven web services selection. *Proceedings of the IEEE International Conference on e-Business Engineering* (pp. 681-688), IEEE Computer Society.

Hunaity, M. A. R. (September, 2008). Towards an efficient quality based web service discovery framework. *Proceedings IEEE Congress on Services* (pp. 261-264). IEEE Computer Society.

Kang Chan, L., Jong Hong, J., Won Seok, L., Seong-Ho, J., & Sang-Won Park, H. (2003). *QoS for Web services: Requirements and possible approaches*. W3C Working Group Note. Retrieved October 2010 from http://www.w3c.or.kr/ kr-office/TR/2003/ws-qos/

Lausen, H., Polleres, A., & Roman, D. (2005). *Web service modeling ontology*. Retrieved April 2010 from http://www.w3.org/ Submission/WSMO/

Ludwig, H. (2003). Web services QoS: External SLAs and internal policies or: How do we deliver what we promise? In *IEEE Computer Society Proceedings International Conference Web Information Systems (*pp 43-59), Italy.

Ludwig, H., Keller, A., Dan, A., King, R. P., & Franck, R. (2003). *Web service level agreement (WSLA) language specification*. Retrieved April 2010 from http://www.research.ibm.com/wsla / WSLASpecV1-20030128.pdf

Menascé, D. A. (2002, November). QoS issues in web services. [IEEE.]. *IEEE Internet Computing, 6*(6), 72–75. doi:10.1109/MIC.2002.1067740

OMG. (2006). *Meta-object facility (MOF) core specification*. Retrieved April 2010 from http://www.omg.org/ spec/MOF/2.0/PDF/

OMG. (2008). *OMG UML profile for modeling quality of service and fault tolerance, v 1.1*. Retrieved April 2010 from http://www.omg.org/ spec/QFTP/1.1/PDF/

Ortiz, G. (2007*) Integrating extra-functional properties in Web Service model-driven development*. Unpublished doctoral dissertation, University of Extremadura, Spain. Retrived from http://Webs. ono.com/gobellot/documents/PhDThesis_Guadalupe Ortiz.pdf

Ortiz, G., Bordbar, B., & Hernández, J. (2008). Evaluating the use of AOP and MDA in web service development. *IEEE International Conference on Web Services (ICWS 2008)* (pp. 78-83). IEEE Computer Society.

Ortiz, G., & García de Prado, A. (2009) Adapting Web services for multiple devices: A model-driven, aspect-oriented approach. *IEEE Computer Society Proceedings International SERVICES Conference* (pp. 754-761), USA.

Ortiz, G., Hernández, J., & Clemente, P. J. (2005). How to deal with non-functional properties in web service development. In Lowe, D., & Gaedke, M. (Eds.), *Web engineering* (pp. 98–103). Springer. doi:10.1007/11531371_15

Ortiz, G., & Leymann, F. (2006). Combining WS-policy and aspect-oriented programming. In P. Dini, P. Lorenz, D. Roman, & M. Freire (Eds.), *IEEE Advanced International Conference on Telecommunications and International Conference on Internet and Web Applications and Services (AICT-ICIW'06)* (pp. 143-148). IEEE Computer Society.

Pedraza, G., Dieng, I. A., & Estublier, J. (2009). FOCAS: An engineering environment for service-based applications. In *Proceedings of the 4th International Conference on Evaluation of Novel Approaches to Software Engineering (ENASE)*.

Ran, S. (2003). A model for web services discovery with QoS. *ACM SIGecom Exchanges, 4*(1), 1–10. doi:10.1145/844357.844360

Röttger, S., & Zschaler, S. (2004). Model-driven development for non-functional properties: Refinement through model transformation. *Lecture Notes in Computer Science, 3273*, 275–289. doi:10.1007/978-3-540-30187-5_20

Schmit, B., & Dustdar, S. (2005). Model-driven development of web service transactions. *International Journal of Enterprise Modeling and Information Systems Architecture, 1*(1), 46–65.

Serhani, M. A., Dssouli, R., Hafid, A., & Sahraoui, H. (July 2005). A QoS broker based architecture for efficient Web service selection. *Proceedings of the IEEE International Conference on Web Services* (pp. 113-120). IEEE Computer Society.

Staikopoulos, A., & Bordbar B. (2006). Bridging technical spaces with a metamodel refinement approach. A BPEL to PN case study. *Electronic Notes in Theoretical Computer Science*.

Tian, M., Gramm, A., Naumowicz, T., Ritter, H., & Schiller, J. (December 2003). A concept for QoS integration in Web services. *Proceedings International Conference on Web Information Systems Engineering* (pp. 149-155). IEEE Computer Society.

Tian, M., Gramm, A., Ritter, H., & Schiller, J. (September 2004). Efficient selection and monitoring of QoS-aware Web services with the WS-QoS framework. *Proceedings IEEE/WIC/ACM International Conference on Web Intelligence* (pp. 152-158). IEEE Computer Society.

Toma, I. Roman, D. Fensel, D. (2006). Modeling Semantic Web services in ASG: The WSMO-based approach. *Springer Verlag Semantic Content Engineering Proceedings*, Linz.

Weerawarana, S., Curbera, F., Leymann, F., Storey, T., & Ferguson, D. F. (2005). *Web services platform architecture: SOAP, WSDL, WS-Policy, WS-Addressing, WS-BPEL, WS-Reliable Messaging, and more*. Prentice Hall.

Weifeng, L., & Jianjun, Y. (August 2007). pService: Peer-to-peer based Web services discovery and matching. *Proceedings International Conference on Systems and Networks Communications* (p. 54). IEEE Computer Society.

Weis, T., Ulbrich, A., & Geihs, K. (2004). Quality of service in middleware and applications: A model-driven approach. *IEEE Enterprise Distributed Object Computing Conference* (pp 160-171).

Zeng, L., Benatallah, B., Dumas, M., Kalagnanam, J., & Sheng, Q. (2003) Quality driven web service composition. *Proceedings International Conference on World Wide Web* (pp. 411-421). Hungary. Xu, Z., Martin, P., Powley, W., & Zulkernine, F. (July 2007). Reputation enhanced QoS-based Web services discovery. *Proceedings IEEE International Conference on Web Services* (pp. 249-256). IEEE Computer Society.

Zeng, L., Benatallah, B., Ngu, A. H. H., Dumas, M., Kalagnanam, J., & Chang, H. (2004). QoS-aware middleware for web services composition. *IEEE Transactions on Software Engineering, 30*(5), 311–327. doi:10.1109/TSE.2004.11

Zhou, C., Chia, L., & Lee, B. (2004) DAML-QoS ontology for Web services. *Proceedings of the IEEE International Conference on Web Services.*

KEY TERMS AND DEFINITIONS

Aspect-Oriented Programming: A programming paradigm which complement object-oriented programming, in which transversal functions are isolated from the main program's business logic.

Extra-Functional Properties: They are properties of the system which provide additional functionality to the system, which is not part of the main functionality of the system.

Model-Driven Development: A software development methodology which focuses on creating models of the systems, leaving implementation technologies for a later stage.

Model-Driven Engineering: A software development methodology which focuses on creating domain models, rather than on the computing concepts.

Quality of Service: Quality of Service is a set of quantifiable quality properties of a service.

Service-Oriented Architecture: Service-Oriented Architecture is an architectural style, based on services.

Web Service: Modular application that can be invoked through the Internet following some established standards.

Chapter 4
The Foundations of Service Eco–Systems

Aditya Ghose
University of Wollongong, Australia

ABSTRACT

The literature on services is replete with references to service eco-systems, yet no attempt has been made to develop a set of principled conceptual underpinnings for these. This chapter aims to address this gap. This chapter also seeks to design the formal basis for practical tools to support the design and maintenance of service eco-systems. It describes a high-level Business Service Modeling Language (BSRL) that is general enough to support the modeling the full spectrum of services, spanning from web services on the one extreme to abstractly defined business services on the other. Based on this language, it describes a taxonomy of relationships that might hold between services in an eco-system. These relationships are then leveraged to formally define a notion of equilibrium in a service eco-system. The chapter then extends the analysis to a deeper level of detail, by considering inter-operation relationships between the process designs that realize services. The chapter briefly considers the challenge of service-oriented analysis and design, and in particular, addresses the question of which combination of functionalities might be packaged as a service, thus leading to the set of inter-related components constituting a service eco-system.

DOI: 10.4018/978-1-61350-159-7.ch004

INTRODUCTION

Most large-scale service delivery settings involve complex collections of inter-dependent services. Consider an airport, where the services on offer include passenger check-in, baggage handling, passenger security screening, customs, cargo handling, food courts, lounges, aircraft refuelling, aircraft maintenance and air traffic control (to name just a few). There are several interesting features of service delivery settings such as these. First, the number, scale and complexity of the services on offer are large. Second, most of these services are inter-dependent (both in terms of design and execution). For instance, the design of the passenger check-in service is determined in critical ways by the design of the passenger security screening service (should visas be checked at check-in or at the security screening stage?). Third, changes to any one of these services are likely to impact several other services. Fourth, there are multiple alternative ways in which changes might be implemented. For instance, a change to aviation authority regulations requiring that all passengers must be checked against a national "watch-list" could be implemented by requiring airlines to perform this check, or by having this check performed by the customs service at emigration checkpoints. Fifth, some of these services exist to realise component functionalities of other services. For instance, a small airport supporting short-hop flights might offer a catering service only because some of the airlines using the airport would like to offer a lounge service to their premium passengers. Sixth, there are multiple design alternatives for determining a service landscape that realizes the required functionalities (some of the preceding examples have illustrated this on a smaller scale). Finally, these collections of services must operate under complex constraints imposed by the domain (including compliance constraints).

There are no easy ways of dealing with the design, maintenance and full life-cycle management of such complex collections of services. In this chapter, we argue that a *formal service eco-systems* view can provide a particularly useful solution to the problem. *Our intention is to leverage the eco-systems metaphor by using mathematical characterisations of such eco-systems – in particular of equilibria.* In our conception of service eco-systems, service designs will play a role analogous to that of biological entities in a biological eco-system. As in biological eco-systems, service designs are created (or discovered, using automated toolkits (Ghose et al., 2007)), modified during their lifetimes, and eventually discarded. Like biological eco-systems, service designs undergo constant change, driven by changing requirements or changes in the operating context. Like biological eco-systems, perturbations in a service eco-system propagate across its constituent services, driven by the need to maintain a range of critical *inter-service* relationships. These include:

- **Functional dependencies:** These exist between a pair of services when one of the services depends on the other for *realizing* some of its functionality. We may interchangeably describe these as *realization links*. In many settings, these links provide the *existential rationale* for a service, i.e., the reason why a service exists (these are critical in any account of *servitization*).
- **Consistency links:** In many cases, service designs might be related via consistency constraints. These are distinct from realization links in the sense that the services might not depend on each other for realizing their functionality, but might have intersecting *functional signatures* (the set of objects/artefacts impacted by the service).

As in biological systems, service eco-systems are characterized by competing forces (such as the competing pulls of alternative ways of realizing a given service functionality, or alternative resolutions to inconsistency between a pair of service designs). Finally, like biological eco-systems, service eco-systems settle into equilibria after being perturbed. An equilibrium in an eco-system is a "steady state", where the competing forces balance each other out. Changes to an eco-system perturb these equilibria, but the system eventually settles into a new equilibrium that accommodates these changes. We will deem a service eco-system to be in an equilibrium if all inter-service realization and consistency links are satisfied, and there is no alternative equilibrium that further minimizes change to the prior state of the service eco-system. Several key tasks in services engineering, including the implementation, deployment and life-cycle management of services require the computation of service eco-system equilibria.

The recent interest in services science has led to research in *business service management*, using a multi-disciplinary synthesis of thinking from the disciplines of computing, management, marketing and potentially several others. Business services can be of many different kinds. The notion includes within in its ambit business process outsourcing services, clinical services, customer contact services as well as IT-enabled services, to name a few representative examples. Our objective in this chapter is develop techniques that can apply to the full spectrum of services from web services on the one extreme to business services on the other.

We shall formally view a service as: (1) a set of processes (described via process models), (2) a set of resources (described via resource models), (3) a set of *utilization links* correlating process models with resource models and (4) a high-level service description (this component is modeled in the BSRL language described in the next section). Given the need for modeling and analyzing service

functionality, we shall annotate process models with *semantic effect annotations*. In particular, we shall leverage the ProcessSEER (Hinge, Ghose & Koliadis, 2009) approach to semantic effect annotation. The ProcessSEER framework permits us to determine, at design time, the answer to the following question that can be posed for any point in the process design: what would the effects of the process be if it were to execute up to this point? The answer is necessarily non-deterministic, since a process might have taken one of many possible alternative paths through a process design to get to that point. The non-determinism also arises from the fact that the effects of certain process steps might "undo" the effects of prior steps – the inconsistencies that result in the "snapshot" of the domain that we seek to maintain might be resolved in multiple alternative ways (a large body of work in the reasoning about action community addresses this problem). The answer to the question is therefore provided via a set of *effect scenarios*, any one of which might eventuate in a process instance. The ProcessSEER approach simplifies the task of *semantic effect annotation* by only requiring that tasks (populating a *capability library*) be annotated with context-independent *immediate effects*. The ProcessSEER tool then contextualizes these effects by propagating them through a process model (specified in BPMN in the current instance) to determine the *cumulative effect scenarios* at the end of each task. ProcessSEER uses formal machinery (theorem-provers) to compute cumulative effects, but provides an analyst-friendly Controlled Natural Language (CNL) interface, coupled with a domain ontology, that permits the immediate effects of tasks to be specified in natural language (but with a restricted set of sentence formats). The use of CNL permits us to translate these natural language specifications into underlying formal representation, which in turn makes the use of theorem-provers possible. ProcessSEER also makes provision for local (task-specific) non-functional annotations to be propagated through a process design, so that we are able to determine the cumulative non-functional scenarios for each task in a process design as well.

The notion of *minimal change* in our informal definition of equilibrium in a service eco-system is important, since we wish to ensure that information is discarded (by modifying service designs, or discarding them, to satisfy functional dependencies and consistency links) only if there is a strong justification for doing so. In a similar vein, we may generate new service designs, but only when there is adequate justification for doing so. Measuring and minimizing the extent of change to service designs is a complex task.

Parts of this framework leverage intuitions from earlier work on *model eco-systems* (Ghose & Koliadis, 2008). We shall show that the service eco-systems approach provides the holistic view that helps us avoid several problems associated with implementing changes to services in isolation. We believe that the service eco-systems framework leads to an adequate methodological basis for service life-cycle management.

SERVICE REPRESENTATION

In this section, we present the design of the Business Service Representation Language (BSRL) and summarize results from (Ghose, et al., 2010). A key component of any service management framework is a service modeling language. We also need a language that is general enough to model any kind of service, including web services or services in an SOA on the one extreme and business services on the other. This would make it possible to seamlessly apply the same toolkit to develop and manage the full spectrum of services.

The design of such a language poses several challenges. Unlike web service modeling, business service modeling requires that we view human activity and human-mediated functionality through the lens of computing and systems engi-

neering (and building a framework that is general enough to include both notions of services within its ambit). This clearly requires an enhanced set of modeling constructs that go beyond those that have been used for web service modeling. This also requires a modeling notation at a higher level of abstraction - one that supports the description of complex business functionality using abstract modeling constructs that offer a natural fit with concepts used to describe these services in everyday discourse. In the course of our research, we have found a close correlation between the notions of *services* and *contracts* (although the two notions are quite distinct). Our study of real-life business service descriptions, in domains as diverse as government services, IT services and consulting services, suggests that some contractual concerns appear routinely in service descriptions, and are part of the discourse on service design and re-design. Our survey of existing service modeling frameworks also suggests that while these are interesting and worthwhile, none come with the complete set of required features. The development of the Business Service Representation Language (BSRL) described in this section was motivated by these concerns.

BSRL was developed as part of a project to develop a framework and supporting toolkit for strategic service alignment. The Strategy Modeling Language (SML) developed in this project provides the value modeling component to BSRL service models (discussed in detail later).

The BSRL Meta-Model

A service model in BSRL consists of the following components:

- **Service ID**
- **Preconditions**
- **Post-conditions**
- **Inputs**
- **Outputs**

- **Goals:** These are the *intended effects (post-conditions)* of a service (note that not all post-conditions are intended - e.g., it might not be my goal to debit my account with a certain amount of money, but that might be the effect of seeking to achieve the goal of purchasing an airline ticket using an online ticket booking service).

- **Assumptions:** These are conditions on whose validity the execution of a service is contingent, but whose validity might not be verifiable when a service is invoked or during its execution. Assumptions need to be monitored during the execution of a service - if a violation is detected (once the truth status of the condition is revealed), the service may have to be aborted. Assumptions are common in informal service descriptions, but might not be identified as such. In our work modeling business services offered by government agencies, we have found references (in textual service descriptions) to lists of "`client responsibilities'". These are statements of what service clients are responsible for doing, in order to enable the provider to fulfil the relevant service. These are clearly not pre-conditions, since they cannot be evaluated when a service is invoked. Indeed, checking to ensure that a client has fulfilled all client responsibilities is impractical in general. Instead, one can use the non-fulfilment of these responsibilities as a trigger for aborting the execution of a service, or for abrogating the contractual obligations of the service provider. "Force Majeure" clauses in contracts are also examples of assumptions (i.e., the provider commits to delivering a service provided no natural disaster intervenes etc.).

- **QoS specifications:** Quality-of-Service (QoS) factors are described as a set of <QoS-factor, range> pairs, where the range provides the upper and lower bounds of QoS factors with quantitative evaluations (note that upper and lower bounds might be equal), or is a qualitative value.

- **Delivery schedules:** These are specified as a set of <functionality, deadline> pairs. Arguably, a delivery schedule is part of a QoS specification, but these require special handling during service decomposition - hence the special status accorded to them.

- **Payment schedules:** These are represented in a manner similar to delivery schedules. These are not ontologically part of a service QoS specification, but are arguably part of the set of assumptions. Like delivery schedules, these require special handling during service decomposition - hence the special status accorded to them.

- **Penalties:** These are specified as a set of < condition, amount > pairs, such that *amount* is the penalty paid if *condition* becomes true. Arguably, penalties are part of the QoS specification, but these require special handling.

- **Value model:** For each stakeholder in the service, a distinct value model is included in the service description. A value model represents how a service delivers value to a given stakeholder. A value model can serve as the basis for service design, and for redesign in the face of change (where the impact on value models of alternative redesigns provides the basis for deliberation on how best to implement change).

- **Resource model:** The ability to understand how a service needs to be provisioned is a critical component of service design. This understanding also underpins any attempt at service optmization. A resource model describes available resources in a manner as expressive as a UML class diagram, with the usual part-whole and generalization-specialization relationships. In addition, a special *uses* relationship is required to describe how a given resource might use another. In general, a set of BSRL service models might share a common *resource ontology* - the resource model for a service is then a reference to a set of resource classes/instances in this ontology. These might be at different levels of abstraction. For instance, a service might be described as using a "printer" resource, or more specifically an "inkjet printer" resource or even more specifically an "HP inkjet printer resource". Note that the notion of a resource is general, and might include in its ambit people, tools, energy, other operating inputs and so on.

We note that not all service models will populate every component of the template described above. We do not commit to a specific language for representing pre- and post-conditions, goals and assumptions. These could be described informally in natural language, or formally (such as in temporal logic, as used in goal-oriented requirements engineering [Yu, 1997; van Lamsweerde, et al., 1998]).

The Service Value Model

A value model, as mentioned earlier, is a critical component of a service model. It provides the basis for service design (in very much the same way that a requirements model provides the basis for system design - arguably, requirements modeling is a special kind of value modeling). Value models support service re-design, with alternative re-design assessed in terms of their impact on the value model. Traditionally, value modeling has been considered in economics and decision theory, with utilities being used as value measures. Utilities are inadequate for our purposes for many well-understood reasons (which we shall not elaborate here for brevity) including the difficulties associated with obtaining numeric measures of the utility to a given stakeholder from a service. More recently, Gordijn et al have proposed

the e3 Value framework (2001) which provides conceptual modeling constructs to describe how actors exchange *value objects*. We believe that the notion of value objects can be generalized, and that ultimately a service or system delivers value to a stakeholder by helping achieve the goals or objectives of the stakeholder. In an enterprise setting, *enterprise strategies* provide the goals/ objectives of the enterprise stakeholder. We have developed the *Strategy Modeling Language (SML)* to provide a formal basis for representing enterprise strategy, and have evaluated its expressive adequacy over a range of real-life organizational strategy documents (SML turns out be adequate). SML provides a useful value modeling framework and is outlined below.

An SML *strategy model* is a set of *strategy statements* of the following three kinds:

- **A goal:** Goals are descriptions of conditions that an organization seeks to achieve. Goals admit boolean evaluation, i.e., an organization is able to clearly determine whether it has achieved a goal or not (consider the following example: {\em "Our corporate strategy is to be the market leader in mobile handsets"}). This notion of a goal closely corresponds to that used in goal-oriented requirements engineering.

- **An objective function:** An objective function is a construct used in operations research techniques to define what the *preferred* or *optimal* solution to an optimization problem might be. These are typically articulated as *maximize f* or *minimize f*, where f is a function defined on the *decision variables* (using which the constraints that *feasible solutions* are required to satisfy are also written). Our analysis of a large number of actual corporate strategy documents, as well as the management literature, suggests that strategies involving *corporate performance measures* or *key performance indicators* (KPIs) are articulated in the form of maximization or min-imzation objectives. Consider the following statements of strategy: "Our strategy is to minimize order lead times", or, "Our strategy is to maximize customer satisfaction". In the first of these, the intent is to minimize a function encoding order lead time while in the second, a funcion encoding some definition of customer satisfaction (for instance, using average customer wait times at the customer contact centre, the number of escalations, the number of product returns etc.) is maximized.

- **A plan:** A plan is a set of goals together with a set of sequencing and related co-ordination constraints. In the most general sense, a plan can be as complex as a process model. Here, we will view plans only as linear sequences of goals. This is because SML is designed to be used by senior management, i.e., individuals within an organization who might be involved in strategy formulation. Also, our analysis of a large number of actual corporate strategy documents suggests that strategies are typically articulated at a very high level of abstraction, where control structures more complex than linear sequencing is never required. A typical example is the following anonymized but actual strategy statement: "Our strategy is to first gain market acceptance in NZ, then position ourselves in the UK market, then use the UK market credibility to enter the Australian market". There are three steps (goals) in this strategy, connected via a linear sequencing relation.

In the following, we will use the terms *strategy model* and *value model* interchangeably.

Leveraging the Value Model for Service Evolution

Value models underpin the analysis required for *service evolution*. We shall use the notion of service evolution to denote situations in which service models need to be modified. Drivers for such modifications might be:

- Service re-purposing, necessitated by altered requirements/goals/strategies that the service was designed to realize.
- Service improvement, i.e., improving the performance of the service relative to one or more QoS factors.
- Operational drivers, such as changes to service delivery platforms.
- Compliance, i.e., service re-design triggered by a finding of non-compliance.

We are interested in two different kinds of analysis to support service evolution: impact analysis and trade-off analysis. In impact analysis, we aim to understand the impact of a proposed change on the value model of a service. For instance, which strategies in a given stakeholder's value model will become unrealized as a consequence of the change? Which stakeholders' value models will be impacted by the proposed change? In trade-off analysis, we seek to identify the best amongst alternative service designs (in terms of their impact on the value model) implementing the required change.

A given change constraint (e.g., re-purpose the service in a given manner, make a service design compliant, or improve a QoS factor to meet a given threshold) can be implemented in multiple different ways. Trade-off analysis will be required to identify which of these alternative realizations of the change request we would choose to adopt. One way this could be done is to seek the alternative which minimizes impact (either with respect to set inclusion or with respect to set cardinality). A deeper discussion of service evolution is out of the scope of this chapter.

SERVICE EQUILIBRIA

It is useful to make a distinction between *basic* and *derived* services in an eco-system. A *basic service* is one that is designed to realize user goals, requirements or strategies. A baggage-handling service in an airport is an example of a basic service. A derived service is one that is designed to execute some of the functionality of a basic service. Outsourced services are the most common examples of derived services. An airport may, for instance, choose to outsource the baggage lifting and trucking service to an external service provider and the security screening service to another external provider, while keeping the baggage tagging and automated sorting services in-house. In this example, the basic service of baggage handling can be viewed as being offered by the airport to meet an obvious client need. While baggage handling appears as a distinct service in the eco-system, parts of its functionality appears in the service descriptions of the security screening and the baggage lifting/trucking services respectively. These latter two are *derived services* in this scenario. Formally, the parent *basic service* will be viewed as being *functionally dependent* (and related by *functional dependency links*) to the derived services. Derived services may, on occasion, further outsource their functionality to other derived services (and thus be functionally dependent on these).

Services in an eco-system may be found to be inconsistent for a variety of reasons. We present a taxonomy of these below:

- **Effect inconsistency:** Services with inconsistent *effects* (or *post-conditions*) may appear in flawed service eco-system designs. For instance, a service that offers food and beverage plus duty free shopping outlets has the effect of slowing passenger transit time between security screening points and departure gates. An usher service has the opposite effect of speeding up passenger transit time between security screening points and departure gates. Clearly both services should not exist in the same eco-system, except if the services are invoked under mutually exclusive conditions (i.e., the service pre-conditions are mutually exclusive). Thus, if the preconditions of the usher service specify that the service is invoked only under conditions of heavy passenger load, then it is reasonable for the usher service to co-exist with the food/beverage and duty-free shopping service (whose preconditions specify that the service is to be offered during periods of normal passenger load). Formally, an effect inconsistency is deemed to occur in a service eco-system if it contains services whose post-conditions are inconsistent, but whose preconditions are consistent.

- **Assumption inconsistency:** An assumption inconsistency occurs in a service eco-system if there exists a set of services related via functional dependency links whose assumptions are inconsistent. In other words, derived services should not be based on assumptions that are inconsistent with the assumptions of the services they are derived from. For instance, the design of the passenger check-in service might be based on the assumption that the checking of passengers against a national security "watch-list" is conducted by the customs services at a point further downstream in the passenger handling workflow deployed at the airport. Note that this is an assumption, as opposed to a precondition since it is impossible to verify whether the checking has been completed prior to the invocation of the check-in service – the service *assumes* that it will be performed by another service at a later point in time (recall that assumptions are conditions that ought to hold for a service to execute, but whose truth or falsity cannot always be reliably established before or during the execution of the service). If the same eco-system contains a customs processing service that assumes that the "watch-list" based checking is performed by the airline passenger check-in service, then we have an instance of assumption inconsistency.

- **QoS inconsistency:** The definition of QoS inconsistency will leverage a notion of *constraint entailment* defined below. We will say that a set of constraints is satisfiable if and only if there exists an assignment of values to the decision variables such that all of the constraints in the set are satisfied. We will assume access to a *constraint negation operator* $(\neg)$ which asserts the negation of the associated constraint predicate. Thus, $\neg (x < 20)$ is $x \geq 20$, and so on. A constraint c is said to *entail* a constraint c' if and only if $\{c\} \cup \{\neg c'\}$ is unsatisfiable. A Quality-of-Service inconsistency occurs in a service eco-system if there exists a pair of services $S1$ and $S2$ where $S1$ depends on $S2$, and there exist QoS constraints $c1$ (associated with service $S1$) and $c2$ (associated with service $S2$), where both $c1$ and $c2$ have intersecting signatures (i.e., they refer to at least one common QoS variable) and $c2$ does not entail $c1$. Consider, for instance, the baggage handling service, which offers a guarantee of baggage processing within 25 minutes (encoded, say, by the constraint $PT < 25$, where PT refers to processing time). Consider, further, a situation where the baggage lifting/trucking service which guarantees a maximum processing time of 35 minutes ($PT < 35$). Intuitively, we have a problem because the outsourced service might potentially lead to the violation of the QoS guarantee offered by the baggage handling service. This is also captured by the QoS inconsistency condition since the constraint $c2$ ($PT < 35$) does not entail the constraint $c1$ ($PT < 25$).

- **Resource inconsistency:** Resource inconsistency captures a very obvious and pragmatic dimension to reasoning about service designs. We assume that every service eco-system is associated with a set of resource constraints (specifying, for instance, the total budget available). Resource consistency stipulates that the resource requirements of individual services in an eco-system do not exceed the maximum available for a given resource type. It is important to flag to designers of service eco-systems situations where the current design is likely to violate what are often fairly hard resource constraints.

A key requirement for a well-designed service eco-system is that there should be no redundant replication of functionality across services. One way of capturing this requirement is to ensure that there do not exist services $S1$ and $S2$ in the eco-system such that the post-condition of S2 is entailed by the post-condition of S1 (if this were to be the case, then S2 would be entirely redundant, since all of its functionality would be achieved by S1). However, we need to allow for the possibility of both the service that outsources part of its functionality (S1) and the derived service (S2) that executes this outsourced functionality to co-exist in the eco-system. In such situations, the post-conditions of S2 would be entailed by the post-conditions of S1.

Formally, a service eco-system will be deemed to be *non-redundant* if and only if there do not exist services $S1$ and $S2$ in the eco-system such that the post-condition of S2 is entailed by the post-condition of S1, except if S1 is functionally dependent on S2.

Formally, an *equilibrium* in a service eco-system represents a *design* of a collection of services which is *consistent* and *non-redundant*.

THE SEVA METHODOLOGY

In this section we outline the SEVA ("service" in Sanskrit) methodology for the analysis and design of service eco-systems. SEVA differs from analysis and design methodologies for SOAs such as SOMA (Zhang et al., 2008). in its ability to offer a more general notion of service than that of a web service. As is clear from the preceding discussion, the notion of service adopted in this chapter integrates both business services and services in the sense of service-oriented computing, and views these as part of the same continuum. At this level of abstraction, the differences between the possible execution engines for a service (often human in the case of business services, and IT-based in the case of service-oriented computing) ceases to matter. The material in this section is largely based on (Ghose, 2010).

Table 1 summarizes some important aspects of why modeling and analysis for services must differ from traditional modeling and analysis (one would also include SOMA [Zhang et al.] in this category).

SEVA includes the following key steps:

1. *Servitization analysis*, where we decide what functionalities need to be packaged into a service.
2. *Service interdependency identification*, where we identify the functional dependencies and consistency links between the constituent services in a service eco-system.
3. *Service provisioning*, where we correlate services to resource models to understand what resources would be made available to each service.

In the following, we outline the first step, which is arguably the most complex.

Servitization Analysis

A key question that we need to answer is the following: given the range of functionalities within an organizational context, how should these be partitioned into a set of services? It might be argued that any subset of the set of functionalities (including singleton subsets) can be viewed as a valid set to be packaged into a service. Ultimately, the notion of a service is useful (1) as the finest level of granularity at which functionality is associated with service providers, (2) as the basis for pricing and (3) as a unit of analysis for performance monitoring (via non-functional requirements or QoS factors). It is clear from practice that some combinations of functionalities "make

Table 1. Summary of why modeling and analysis for services must differ from traditional modeling and analysis

Traditional: Modeling/specifying the target system (may include a domain model) **Services:** Modeling/specifying the enterprise services architecture (i.e., a sophisticated domain model is all we need)
Traditional: Specifying functionality (plus some NFR) **Services:** Optimal provisioning
Traditional: Usage context is a given **Services:** Usage context must be anticipated
Traditional: Design driven by user requirements/goals **Services:** Design driven by value models and predicted contract profiles

more sense" packaged as a service than others. We posit that there are two dimensions to this intuitive notion of servitization:

- **Manageabiliy:** A service must be manageable, in terms of being able to measure its performance relative to its (performance) requirements. Some services have intangible or difficult-to-assess outputs. A consultancy service that offers advice on how to improve client experience in an airport is a difficult service for an airport to manage, since its performance (in this instance, the quality of its advice) cannot immediately be assessed (the impact of deploying such advice might only be apparent many months later). This can lead to problems in appropriately formulating contractual guidelines on what conditions must be met for full payment for the service rendered. It is no surprise, then, that the business model of consulting service providers is heavily reliant on reputation and trust, as opposed to directly assessable quality or performance measures. *A pre-condition for packaging a set of functionalities into a service is the ability to identify a set of performance measures that can be directly correlated to payment in a contractual sense.* At this point, there is no obvious means of automating this analysis, and this must remain a methodological guideline.
- **Utility:** Some combinations of functionalities are infeasible or impractical. Consider the following example from cooperative game theory: a service that manufactures left-foot shoes is infeasible in isolation (as is a service that manufactures right-foot shoes). However, a service that manufactures both is meaningful, since the pair (a left-foot shoe and a right-foot shoe) constitutes a saleable unit. This forms the basis for the study of *coalition formation* (Sandholm et al., 1999; Sombattheera &

Ghose, 2008). In this class of techniques, we assume the existence of a *characteristic function,* which, given any subset of a set of services (or agents), generates a numeric utility value associated with that subset. The *optimal coalition structure problem* seeks to identify the optimal partitioning of a set of agents (or services), i.e., the partitioning that maximizes the total utility across all the partitions (as determined by the characteristic function). Clearly, servitization requires the identification of optimal ways to partition the set of available functionalities, with each partition being packaged into a service.

SERVICE ECO-SYSTEMS AT THE PROCESS LEVEL

Our discussion thus far has focussed on looking at inconsistencies within service descriptions in a service eco-system. In this section we extend this account to the process level. We consider the problem of detecting inconsistencies within inter-operating processes. We assume here that the process level account is a refinement of the service level account (i.e., that service descriptions get refined to process descriptions). We acknowledge that this is not always the case, i.e., the reverse can also be true (where process models refer to lower-level services). This section describes a framework originally developed in (Koliadis & Ghose, 2007).

Our focus is on semantic inconsistencies between inter-operating process specifications. We evaluate inconsistency between effects (as evaluated by the ProcessSEER framework outlined earlier) in order to ensure that the properties required of objects (messages) transferred between inter-operating processes are met. We define inconsistency in inter-operating business process models as a contradiction between the effect scenarios of the two synchronizing tasks.

In other words, each message sent by an inter-operating process to another must correspond to the message that is expected by the receiving process. Consider the predicate *Knows (Agent, Object, Property, Value)*, which describes how a process participant's knowledge is updated via the enactment of an activity. By using this predicate, we can define a general rule for identifying inconsistencies during synchronization. This rule states that agents (i.e. process participants) must agree on the values of all properties of objects that form the basis for message transfer. We enforce this rule only at synchronization points, and only objects involved in message exchange.

Formally:

$$\forall \text{ o: Object, p: Property, v1, v2: Value}$$
$$Knows(a_i, o, p, v1) \wedge \neg equal(v1, v2)) \rightarrow$$
$$\neg Knows(a_j, o, p, v2).$$

Let Pi and Pj be two inter-operating processes, and let ti in Pi and tj in Pj be two corresponding tasks involved in message exchange. In the rule above, a_i and a_j represent the roles identified as owners of processes Pi and Pj respectively. Let D represent the background knowledge base that also includes domain constraints. An inconsistency exists between Pi and Pj, if for some effect scenarios es_i associated with ti and some effect scenario es_j associated with tj, $es_i \cup es_j \cup D \models \perp$ holds.

In order to resolve an inconsistency, analyst involvement will be required. Negotiation between the participants will need to occur, conceivably with reference to some agreed upon contract. In order to guide negotiations, an identification of the possible causes would be desirable. Specifically, inconsistencies between inter-operating processes have unique causes that can be identified via regression analysis. This involves backtracking through a process involved in an inconsistency to a point where the inconsistency is identified. As a result, the preceding activity is identified as responsible for introducing the inconsistency. In some cases, the cause may be traced across

synchronization points to other inter-operating processes. The decision at this point as to how the activity might be modified is left to the analyst.

RELATED WORK

The existing literature on service eco-systems does not address the problem of formal modeling of services and service dependencies, nor does it explore the notion equilibrium. In 2006, Barros and Dumas use the eco-system metaphor to describe large collections of web services, their architecture in terms of the roles of broker, mediator and provider and aspects of the web service lifecycle. In 2009, Riedl et al offer a reference model (and case study of its application) for quality management in service eco-systems. In 2007, Sawatani discusses service value chains, contrasts these with product value chains and argues for ways in which research might contribute to this conception of service eco-systems. In 2008, Zambonelli and Viroli discuss how the natural eco-system metaphors might contribute to the design of service eco-systems. Their approach is similar to ours in seeking inspiration from natural eco-system metaphors, but their contributions are considerably more abstract. In 2009, Scheithauer et al introduce a detailed approach to service modeling from a range of different perspectives, inspired in part by the Zachman framework for enterprise architectures.

CONCLUSION

Much of the current practice in the design and analysis of service-oriented architectures, as well as business service architectures, is ad-hoc in nature. Services are often not modeled in adequate detail, and inter-service dependencies are typically ignored. There is a clear need for systematizing these activities. This chapter offers a set of techniques to address this need. It makes five key contributions. First, it offers a sophisticated service modeling language (in the form of BSRL). Second, it offers a detailed taxonomy of inter-service dependencies. Third, it offers a formal notion of equilibrium in service eco-system. Fourth, it describes the SEVA methodology for the analysis and design of service eco-systems, with particular emphasis on servitization analysis. Fifth, it describes how dependencies and consistency at the process level can be analysed.

REFERENCES

Barros, A. P., & Dumas, M. (2006). The rise of Web Service ecosystems. *IT Professional, 8*(5). doi:10.1109/MITP.2006.123

Ghose, A. K. (2010). *The SEVA approach to service modeling and analysis*. Decision Systems Lab, University of Wollongong Technical Report 2010-TR-01.

Ghose, A. K., & Koliadis, G. (2007). Auditing business process compliance. In *Proc. of ICSOC-2007, Lecture Notes in Computer Science*. Springer.

Ghose, A. K., & Koliadis, G. (2008). Model eco-systems: Preliminary report. Invited talk in *Proceedings of the Fifth Asia-Pacific Conference on Conceptual Modelling (APCCM 2008)*.

Ghose, A. K., Koliadis, G., & Cheung, A. (2007). Rapid process discovery. In *Proc. of ER-2007, Lecture Notes in Computer Science*. Springer.

Ghose, A. K., Le, L. S., Hoesch-Klohe, K., & Morrison, E. (2010). The business service representation language: A preliminary report. In *Proceedings of SMART-2010, Lecture Notes in Computer Science*. Springer.

Gordijn, J., & Akkermans, H. (2001). E3-value: Design and evaluation of e-business models. *IEEE Intelligent Systems, 16*(4), 11–17. doi:10.1109/5254.941353

Hinge, K., Ghose, A. K., & Koliadis, G. (2009). Process SEER: A tool for semantic effect annotation of business process models. In *Proc. of the 13th IEEE International EDOC Conference (EDOC-2009)*, IEEE Computer Society Press.

Koliadis, G., & Ghose, A. K. (2008). Verifying semantic business process models in inter-operation. In *Proceedings of the SCC-2007*. IEEE Computer Society Press.

Riedl, C., Böhmann, T., Rosemann, M., & Krcmar, H. (2009). Quality management in service ecosystems. *Information Systems and E-Business Management, 7*(2), 199–222. doi:10.1007/s10257-008-0080-6

Sandholm, T., Larson, K., Andersson, M., Shehory, O., & Tohmé, F. (1999). Coalition structure generation with worst case guarantees. *Artificial Intelligence, 111*(1-2), 209–238. doi:10.1016/S0004-3702(99)00036-3

Sawatani, Y. (2007). Research in service ecosystems. In *Proceedings of Portland International Center for Management of Engineering and Technology (PICMET'07)*.

Scheithauer, G., Augustin, S., & Wirtz, G. (2009). Describing services for service ecosystems. In G. Feuerlicht & W. Lamersdorf (Eds.), *Proc. of ICOSOC-2008 Workshops, Lecture Notes in Computer Science: Vol. 5472*, (pp. 242-255). Springer.

Sombattheera, C., & Ghose, A. K. (2008). A best-first anytime search algorithm for coalition structure generation. In *Proceedings of the 7th International Conference on Autonomous Agents and Multi-Agent Systems*.

van Lamsweerde, A., Darimont, R., & Letier, E. (1998). Managing conflicts in goal-driven requirements engineering. *IEEE Transactions on Software Engineering*, (November): 1998.

Yu, E. S. K. (1997). Towards modeling and reasoning support for early-phase requirements engineering. In *Proceedings of the Int'l Conf. on Requirements Engineering*, (pp. 226-235).

Zambonelli, F., & Viroli, M. (2008). Architectures and metaphors for eternally adaptive service ecosystems. In Badica, C. (Eds.), *Intelligent Distributed Computing Systems and Applications* (pp. 23–32). Springer-Verlag. doi:10.1007/978-3-540-85257-5_3

Zhang, L.-J., Zhou, N., Chee, Y.-M., Jalaldeen, A., Ponnalagu, K., & Sindhgatta, R. (2008). SOMA-ME: A platform for the model-driven design of SOA solutions. *IBM Systems Journal*, *47*(3), 397–413. doi:10.1147/sj.473.0397

Section 3
Service Delivery

Chapter 5
A QoS-Aware Service Bus with WSLA-Based Monitor for Media Production Systems

Ing-Yi Chen
National Taipei University of Technology, Taiwan

Guo-Kai Ni
National Taipei University of Technology, Taiwan

Rich C. Lee
National Taipei University of Technology, Taiwan

ABSTRACT

The past few years have seen a dramatic rise in the distribution channels available to media companies. While media companies once distributed their programming through one or two mediums, such as TV broadcasts and video tapes, the same programming is now also distributed through additional mediums such as the Internet and mobile phones. In consequence, media companies are faced with increasingly complex problems associated with translating one piece of programming into multiple formats for distribution. As a result, the IT systems of these companies are now required to handle both new content formats and to ensure that content is simultaneously and successfully prepared in order to meet scheduling and distribution requirements for multiple delivery pathways. This paper describes a solution that was developed to address this problem. It consists of a media asset management system that is used to support media content production and distribution. In addition, this work implements service oriented architecture (SOA) that relies on an enhanced enterprise service bus (ESB). This enhanced ESB, referred to here as a QoS-Aware service bus (QASB), makes it possible to designate which of the available transcoding servers will perform a required task, thus providing a service selection scheme that improves the efficiency of media content production and distribution processes. This system was implemented at Taiwan's Public Television Service (PTS) in January 2010 and is currently providing complete support to the company's daily operations. Since implementation, this automated process has i

DOI: 10.4018/978-1-61350-159-7.ch005

increase the average number of transcoding jobs completed daily from 500 to 700 – and increase of 40 percent. This increased productivity has in turn resulted in a decrease in the amount of time staff must wait for jobs to be completed to 3-5 days from a pre-QASB time of 7-10 days.

INTRODUCTION

As the number of content formats and distribution channels used by media companies has grown, IT systems have had to adapt to the rapidly growing need for improved data management and transcoding services (Footen & Faust 2008). Unfortunately, many of these systems are limited in this regard because they are built on heterogeneous platforms that are distributed throughout various business units such as production, programming acquisition and broadcasting (Dettori, Nogima, Schaffa, & Banks 2009). Typically, issues associated with heterogeneity have required manual integration. This approach is time consuming, not only in terms of labor inputs, but also in terms of increased time required to prepare programming for distribution.

To alleviate these problems, and improve the efficiency of daily operations, an automated integration of these diverse business processes is necessary. In many industries, Service-Oriented Architecture (SOA) has become the de rigueur paradigm for system integration and business process management (Liegl 2007). There are many successful examples of SOA use in industries as diverse as telecommunications (Chen, Ni & Lin 2008), healthcare (Yin, Chen, Wu & Pu 2009), government (Lee 2009) and so on.

Figure 1 presents the media production and distribution environment of a typical television station. The media content – both analog tapes and digital files – is acquired from different sources in multiple formats. This content must then be processed and transcoded into formats suitable for broadcast or delivery through other pathways. Note that when media is being distributed through different mediums, it must first be translated into target application-specific formats. An increase in the volume of required transcoding, then, results in a performance bottleneck in media production and distribution.

To alleviate this strain on the production process, transcoding service centers contain numerous servers to allow for increased work comple-

Figure 1. Media production and distribution environment

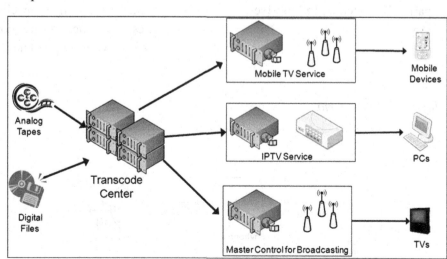

tion. Work assigned to these servers is balanced through the introduction of middleware that dispatches tasks and balances the task load undertaken by each server.

In such sophisticated heterogeneous critical systems integration design, we need to consider more about the design not just for identifying the requirements of the application, developing software that implements the requirements, and for allocating appropriate resources (processors and communication networks); the overall perspectives about the system must be taken into account before actual design process, such as reusability, performance, security, dependability, and others. We used software quality model as a framework to examine our design by giving specific quality attributes to see if the design met the non-functional requirements as flows:

- **System Qualities:** availability, modifiability, performance, security, testability, usability, and others.
- **Business Qualities:** time-to-market, cost-and-benefit, product lifetime, target market, roll-out schedule, integration, and others.
- **Architectural Qualities:** conceptual integrity, correctness and completeness.

In general, the quality attribute scenario consists of six parts, illustrated as follows (see Figure 2):

- **Source of Stimulus:** the entity generating the stimulus that affects the artifact.
- **Stimulus:** A state of concern has changed and imposed against the artifact.
- **Environment:** the affected container of the stimulated artifact.
- **Artifact:** the part or parts of the system stimulated.
- **Response:** how the system should respond to the stimulus.
- **Response Measure:** how the response can be measured and test.

Assuring the to-be architecture meets the quality attribute requirements is very important prior to actual design stage. During the quality attribute examination process, the alternative solutions of trade-offs must be well documented and become the decision view (Dueñas & Capilla 2005) of the development. To assure our design will reliably meet its quality attribute requirements, our method abides by the following criterion (Bachmann et al. 2005):

- Our quality attribute examining process follows ISO 9126-1 of software product evaluation standard, it lists six primary quality attributes as follows:
  - **Functionality** is the set of attributes that bear on the existence of a set of functions and their specified properties. The functions are those that satisfy stated or implied needs.

Figure 2. Quality attribute scenario

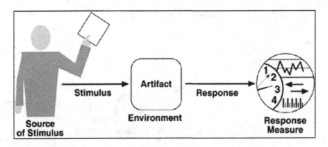

○ **Reliability** is the set of attributes that bear on the capability of software to maintain its level of performance under stated conditions for a stated period of time.

○ **Usability** is the set of attributes that bear on the effort needed for use, and on the individual assessment of such use, by a stated or implied set of users.

○ **Efficiency** is the set of attributes that bear on the relationship between the level of performance of the software and the amount of resources used, under stated conditions.

○ **Maintainability** is the set of attributes that bear on the effort needed to make specified modifications.

○ **Portability** is the set of attributes that bear on the ability of software to be transferred from one environment.

A quality attribute requirement can affect any attribute whether on the list or not and so a method to achieve all quality attribute requirements must embody great breadth in reasoning about quality attributes.

• Our quality attribute examining process has a mechanism to manage the design trade-offs, so that the latter implementation can be easily enhanced when former quality attribute constraint is relieved.

• Our quality attributes cover hardware/software elements in addition to behavioral descriptions. In our design, we specially focused on the modifiability which considers dependencies among modules, probabilities of change propagating and cost of modification.

By considering the quality attributes of non-functional requirement, our design takes advantage of ESB of SOA. The ESB plays a choreographic role orchestrates those exposed losely-coupled services via rich connectivity layer between services. A service is a software component that is described by meta-data, which can be understood by a program. The meta-data is published to enable reuse of the service by components that may be remote from it and that need no knowledge of the service implementation beyond its published meta-data. The ESB, as the name revealed, is a message bus where connected services exchange information, a service is triggered when expected data is arrived. The ESB virtualizes the services that are made available through the bus. The service requestor, both in its application logic and in its deployment, does not need to have any awareness of the physical realization of the service provider. The requestor does not need to be concerned about the programming language, runtime environment, hardware platform, network address, or current availability of the service provider's implementation (Schmidt et al. 2005).

A performance quality attribute must be seriously evaluated; it determines the feasibility of design in the real world wide application. The overall performance modeling approach follows the general capacity planning process (Liu et al. 2007):

• Mapping our design at the software architecture level to analytical model elements.

• Characterizing the workload pattern against the components of our design as the input for the performance model.

• Calibrating the performance model by populating the parameter values of our design.

• Validating the performance model and predicting the performance through simulation.

A strong reason that we chose ESB as the building block of our design was to meet the following critical quality attributes (Papazoglou et al. 2007):

- **Service Enablement: Modifiability.** Each discrete application adapted to our design needs to be exposed as a service as well to make the maximum integration result.
- **Service Orchestration: Configurability.** The adapted distributed services need to be configured and orchestrated in a unified way through ESB configuration module.
- **Deployment Emphasis: Reliability.** The solution service mechanism should be shifted from test to the production environment, addressing security, reliability, and scalability concerns.
- **Management Services: Manageability.** The solution service mechanism must be audited, maintained and reconfigured. The latter requirement requires that corresponding changes in processes must be made without rewriting the services or underlying application.

For adapted discrete services, our design is hidden from the callers behind the abstract service interface that can be also annotated with policies to cover non-functional requirements via Quality of Services (QoS). Our design interacts with adapted services in a loosely-coupled manner through the service bus: (1) the service needs not know the caller that is interacting with, (2) the service uses message bus provided by ESB giving the functionality for message routing among the services, (3) the adapted services need not share a common data format by means of data transformation scheme (Dimka et al. 2007).

Based on the above discussed quality attributes to meet the solution goal, the ESB of SOA provides a mature platform for our solution. In an SOA solution, this core middleware function is performed by an Enterprise Service Bus. An ESB typically provides message routing and trans-formation capabilities that integrate distributed heterogeneous systems. Although vendors such as IBM, BEA, and Oracle provide ESB products for service routing and message transformation, these solutions don't provide a QoS-Based service selection capability (Wu, Liu, & Wu 2008). The limitation of this conventional approach is that while an ESB provides service routing capabilities to balance the loading of each transcoding server, it cannot necessarily meet service level agreements (SLA) that are dictated by users. For example, a conventional ESB could be used to complete transcoding, but could not be guaranteed to complete the transcoding by a pre-defined deadline if additional requests are made upon the server. Satisfying service level agreements would require intelligent service routing that can respond to changes by altering work queues and reassigning tasks as necessary.

The work presented here employs intelligent service routing as solution by utilizing a SOA that relies on an enhanced Enterprise Service Bus. This enhanced ESB, referred to here as a Qos-Aware Service Bus, (QASB) constitutes a significant improvement over conventional ESBs because it supports QoS service selection during runtime, thus coordinating existing service components in order to improve work efficiency. The QASB presented here also provides administrators with the ability to define specific selection algorithms to cope with specific business situations.

The QASB's intelligent service routing assigns and reschedules tasks with a service selection algorithm that performs execution time predictions by means of historical performance data that is collected during runtime. This mechanism is used to ensure that transcoding requests are completed on time.

Public Television Service (PTS)

The Public Television Service (PTS) is a publicly-owned broadcasting company in Taiwan. With approximately 1,200 employees, the company broadcasts on five television channels. In January 2010 PTS implemented the QASB system discussed here in order to facilitate media asset management, automatic production and distribution of its video and audio content. Like other major media providers, such as the Corporation for Public Broadcasting (CPB) in the United States and the Japan Broadcasting Corporation (NHK) in Japan, PTS seeks to produce high quality media content and to deliver that content through different kinds of distribution channels. These include Mobile TV, IPTV and are intended to allow users to receive multimedia content in an ever increasing range of environments.

The new system integrates PTS's existing IT systems – including program production, transcoding servers and broadcasting systems – and establishes an automatic business process that improves productivity. More specifically, it provides PTS with the ability to capture, reuse and share its digital files, and to convert them into multiple formats – opening up even more opportunities to reach new customers.

The rest of this paper is organized as follows. The next section is composed of a literature review of quality-based service selection research. This is followed by description of the QoS-Aware Service Bus and its main components. Next the chapter presents experimental results derived from the evaluation of the QASB's effectiveness during its implementation at PTS. The evaluation contrasted QASB's algorithm with the performance of a conventional enterprise service bus and illustrated that the QoS approach presented here allows for significant gains in function with only minimal impact on processing time. In addition, we evaluated the accuracy of the proposed prediction methodology used to support the QoS-Aware Service Bus in deciding which service provider is most suitable. This paper also discusses the efficiency of each of the algorithms used over the course of experimentation. Finally, the chapter presents a summary of system performance and a conclusion.

LITERATURE REVIEWS

At the moment, SOA is receiving some attention in the media industry. Weken et al., for example, presented an automated workflow infrastructure for a professional media production environment based on SOA (Weken, Assche, & Clabaut et al. 2009). Additionally, Sur et al. presented a media enabled service bus that integrates a heterogeneous IPTV production environment (Sur, Schaffa, & McIntyre et al. 2008). Although Weken (2009) and Sur (2008) both illustrate practical experiences in building service oriented media application, they do not discuss how to coordinate existing service components in order to meet service level agreements (SLA).

While not yet presented in connection to the media industry, QoS-based service selection has become a popular research topic in service oriented computing. Essentially, QoS seeks to ensure that those services that are invoked, meet certain criteria of quality criteria – such as on-time completion – as defined by users. Most research (Hwang, Lim, Lee et al. 2008) (Dimitrios & Michael, 2008) (Kritikos & Plexousakis, 2009) in this area relies on quality attributes, such as response time, cost, reliability and availability, of the candidate services for comparing and selecting appropriate services to complete specific work requirements. The difficulties associated with selecting the most suitable service from a set of equivalent services are aptly illustrated by through the Multiple Choice Knapsack Problem (MCKP) which demonstrates that such selection is a non-deterministic polynomial (NP) complete problem (Yu & Lin, 2005).

Gao and Wu (Gao & Wu, 2005) proposed and developed a dynamic QoS evaluation mechanism that was based on performance prediction technology and constructed on a Neural Network, service selection framework. This paper emphasized that current QoS models are generally composed of static parameters and haven't taken the dynamic nature of service performance into consideration.

Another approach was presented by Ding et al. This work proposed a Greedy Service Selection (GSS) algorithm that chose and executed service instances which had the greatest "benefit/cost" ratios. (Kun, Bom & Xiaoyi et al. 2009)

The work of Yu and Lin (Yu & Lin 2004) expanded on the Enterprise Service Bus by introducing a QoS broker module between service clients and providers (servers). The broker was responsible for collecting QoS information, making selection decisions, and negotiating with servers to get QoS commitments. Their work proposed two algorithms – Homogeneous Resource Allocation Algorithm and Non-homogeneous Resource Allocation – and compares the efficiency of them. The work illustrated the difficulty of developing an algorithm that is suitable for all situations. As a result of these findings the QASB presented here uses a selection strategy that is based on business requirements.

While this body of research provides service selection algorithms and frameworks for establishing criteria that best meet user needs, it does not provide an adequate solution to the needs of the media industry. The research presented in this literature review only focus on services operating for short periods of time. The nature of work undertaken by the media industry necessitates that service components be able to undergo long periods of operation in fulfilling service requests.

The research presented here attempted to develop a more robust approach that was suitable to fulfill this requirement.

Table 1 documents the differences between five different Enterprise Service Bus approaches: this paper, Yu and Lin, Ding et al., Gao et al and a conventional ESB. Five criteria are used for comparing the five approaches. The first criterion is used to describe the support of QoS Service Selection. The second documents whether the quality of service information is collected dynamically in runtime or statically. The third criterion assesses the approaches use of a standardized interface that allows for the application of alternative service selection algorithms. The fourth criterion assesses the approaches' ability to conduct dynamic task rescheduling during operation. The final criterion identifies the deployment level (laboratory or commercially) at which the approach was tested.

QoS-Aware Service Bus

The QoS-Aware Service Bus (QASB) is composed of a number of different components. These components, along with the overall system architecture are illustrated in Figure 3.

Table 1. Comparison of ESB approaches

	QASB	Yu and Lin	Ding et al.	Gao et al.	ESB
QoS Service Selection	Y	Y	Y	Y	N
QoS Information Collection	Dynamic	Dynamic	Static	Dynamic	Dynamic
Alternative Selection Algorithms	Y	Y	N	N	N
Dynamic Task Rescheduling	Support	No support	No support	No support	No support
Deployment Level	Commercially	Laboratory	Laboratory	Laboratory	Commercially

Media Production Process

The media production process refers to media produced and controlled by PTS. This media is derived from a number of different sources, and as such exists in a number of different formats. These formats are typically not interoperable.

QoS Computation

Broadcasting is the primary business of PTS and media files need to be prepared before their scheduled broadcasting time. Preparation of media files is impacted by both transcoding requirements and time until broadcasting deadlines. The QoS computation component is used to estimate the time required by each of the available services to complete a given task – provided the service is able to complete the task before its broadcast deadline. The component is designed to execute prediction estimates for the time required by each of the available servers to complete a specific task.

This estimated time is calculated by means of historical data that are collected through service monitoring. There are many factors that can impact transcoding times, such as hardware and software configurations, file sizes, and formats. Research presented here relied exclusively upon the criteria of file size and file format because the hardware and software configurations were stable in the PTS computing environment.

The file size can be calculated by bit rate and the duration of the file's media. Equation 1 shows the calculation of media file size.

$$S(M) = M_{br} * M_{time} \qquad (1)$$

Where:

$S(M)$: the size of media file
M: media file
M_{br}: bit rate of the media file
M_{time}: the length of the media file

Tasks associated with file format and transcoding can be separated into two major parts – source file decoding and target file encoding. The time required for decoding and encoding depends on the media file format. Time required for decoding and encoding is established through the calculations illustrated in Equations 2 and 3.

$$\text{Decode}(M_f) = \sum_{i=1}^{n} \frac{S_i/T_i}{n} \qquad (2)$$

Figure 3. Architecture components of the QoS-aware service bus (QASB)

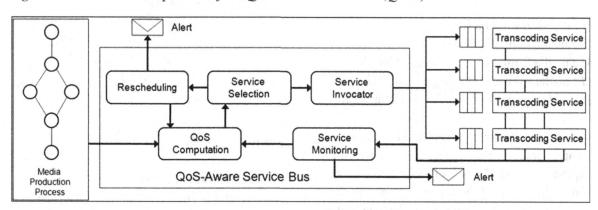

Where:

M_f: Media Format
Decode(M_f): the average decoding time of specific
   file format
n: the number of records in the historical data
S_i: media file size of the i_{th} record
   T_i: decoding time of the i_{th} record

$$\text{Encode}(M_f) = \sum_{i=1}^{n} \frac{S_i/T_i}{n} \qquad (3)$$

Where:

Encode(M_f): the average encoding time of specific
   file format
n: the number of record in historical data
S_i: media file size of the i_{th} record
T_i: encoding time of the i_{th} record

Equation 4 shows the calculation of the total transcoding time. The calculation incorporates the results of calculations made in Equations 2 and 3.

$$T(M_s, M_t) = \frac{S(M_s)}{Decode(M_{sf})} + \frac{S(M_t)}{Encode(M_{tf})} \qquad (4)$$

Where:

M_s: the source media file
M_t: the target media file
M_{sf}: media format of the source media file
M_{tf}: media format of the target media file
$T(M_s, M_t)$: the required time for translating M_s to M_t

Equation 5 shows the calculation of the estimated time of completion for a transcoding request. The calculation is based upon both the transcoding time of the target task, and the cumulative transcoding times for tasks with higher priority in the server queue.

$$\text{Estimate}_t = T(M_s, M_t) + \sum_{i=1}^{m} T(M_{si}, M_{ti}) \qquad (5)$$

Where:

Estimate$_t$: the estimated execution time
$T(M_s, M_t)$: the required time for translating M_s to M_t
m: the number of jobs that in queue
$\Sigma T(M_{si}, M_{ti})$: the time spent in queue before a job
   will begin transcoding

In order to establish the accuracy of this approach as a prediction methodology, a correlation calculation was used to explore the relationship between the actual execution times and the estimated execution times. Correlation is a measure of the degree to which two variables – actual values and estimated values – are related. If the two are highly correlated, the value of one of the variables can be predicted if the other variable is known. The degree to which the two variables are correlated is measured by means of covariance and variance. The covariance is a measure of how much two variables change together. The variance is a measure of how far a given set of variables lie from the mean for those variables. The equation used for this correlation calculation is presented as follows:

Variance of actual value:

$$V_{actual} = \frac{\sum_{i=1}^{n} actual_i^2}{n} - \frac{\left(\sum_{i=1}^{n} actual_i\right)^2}{n^2} \qquad (6)$$

Where:

V_{actual}: the variance of actual values
n: the number of actual values in the historical data
$actual_i$: the i_{th} actual historical values

Variance of estimated value:

$$V_{estimate} = \frac{\sum\limits_{i=1}^{n} estimate_i^2}{n} - \frac{\left(\sum\limits_{i=1}^{n} estimate_i\right)^2}{n^2} \tag{7}$$

Where:

$V_{estimate}$: the variance of estimated values
n: the number of estimated values in the historical data
$estimate_i$: the i_{th} historical estimated value

Covariance of actual and estimated value:

$$Cov(actual, estimate) = \frac{\sum\limits_{i=1}^{n} (actual_i * estimate_i)}{n} -$$
$$\frac{\sum\limits_{i=1}^{n} actual_i * \sum\limits_{i=1}^{n} estimate_i}{n^2} \tag{8}$$

Where:

$Cov(actual, estimate)$: the covariance of actual and estimated values
n: the number of actual and estimated values in the historical data
$actual_i$: the i_{th} actual historical value
$estimate_i$: the i_{th} historical estimated value

Correlation between actual and estimated values:

$$r(actual, estimate) = \frac{Cov(actual, estimate)}{\sqrt{V_{actual} * V_{estimat}}} \tag{9}$$

Where:

$r(actual, estimate)$: the correlation between actual and estimated values
$Cov(actual, estimate)$: the covariance of actual and estimated values
V_{actual}: the variance of actual values
$V_{estimate}$: the variance of estimated values

The significance of the results can be described using the four different levels defined as follow:

- When $0.9 \leq r^2$, the relationship is considered predictive and you can use it with high confidence.
- When $0.7 \leq r^2 < 0.9$, there is a strong correlation. The relationship is adequate for planning purposes.
- When $0.5 \leq r^2 < 0.7$, there is an adequate correlation for many purposes. Use the relationship for planning, but with caution.
- When $r^2 < 0.5$, the relationship is not reliable for planning purposes.

If the r^2 value represents a strong correlation between the actual and estimated values, it implies the two sets of historical data – the estimated and actual results – can be used to plan the transcoding job scheduling (Humphery 1995). This relationship is expressed in Equation 10.

$$Actual_k = \beta_0 + \beta_1 Estimate_k \tag{10}$$

Equation 10 employs two parameters, β_0 and β_1. The following formulas are used to calculate the β_0 and β_1 for the historical data.

$$\beta_1 = \frac{\sum_{i=1}^{n} actual_i * estimate_i - n * actual_{avg} * estimate_{avg}}{\sum_{i=1}^{n} estimate_i^2 - n * estimate_{avg}^2}$$

(11)

$$\beta_0 = actual_{avg} + \beta_1 * estimate_{avg}$$ (12)

Although the estimated completion time was calculated using the most important factors, file size and file format, the accuracy of the estimation cannot be guaranteed because of other, less common, occurrences that are not included in the calculation. These other factors, which include occurrences such as server shutdowns and disk errors, are difficult to predict. In consequence, the use of linear regression provides additional data, β_0 and β_1, that can be used in a recalculation of Equation 10 in order to attain a more robust and accurate estimate. The recalculation of Equation 10 is illustrated in Equation 13.

$$\text{RE} = \beta_0 + \beta_1 Estimate$$ (13)

Where:

RE: the revised estimation value

β_0 and β_1: the parameters that are calculated by Equation 11 and 12

Estimate: the initial estimate determined through Equation 5

Figure 3 illustrates the comparative accuracy of estimates determined both with and without using linear regression. Note that Figure 4 organizes media files into five categories based on the duration of each media file – under 10 minutes, 10-30 minutes, 30-60 minutes, 60-90 minutes and more than 90 minutes.

The estimated value without linear regression is based exclusively on file size and format and uses an optimistic prediction algorithm (shown in Equation 5). The principle consequence of using estimations that do not employ linear regression is the occurrence of an increased number of runtime alerts as a result of service monitoring. When linear regression is used in calculating an estimation (Equation 13), additional variables, like server shutdown and disk error, are considered in addition to the primary variables of file size and format. The improved accuracy of the linear regression method provides a sort of buffer that minimizes the number of alerts generated by the

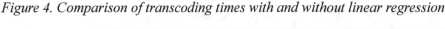

Figure 4. Comparison of transcoding times with and without linear regression

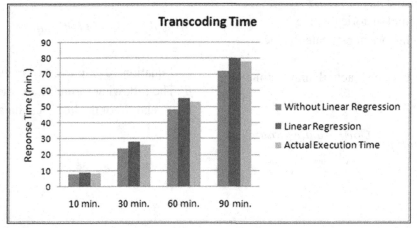

system. With the use of linear regression the relationship between actual and estimated values (determined in Equation 9) has an r2 value of 0.907, indicating that estimated values can be used in prediction with a high degree of confidence.

Service Selection

The service selection module is responsible for choosing which of the available services – that can meet the required service level agreement – will be assigned to complete a task. In this context, the service level agreement is simply a specific task that must be completed by a service provider in the required way by a requested deadline. The QoS computation module provides the information about the estimated execution time for each of the candidate service providers so that the service selection module can select the most suitable service provider and establish a service level agreement by assigning a given task to that service provider. The QoS-Aware Service Bus is capable of supporting different selection strategies for dealing with different situations such as cost consideration, reliability issues and so on. The QASB discussed here employed the earliest node first algorithm in order to ensure a high number of jobs were completed in keeping with their respective service level agreements.

The pseudo-code of the earliest node first selection algorithm is listed in Algorithm 1.

Considerable research has approached the topic of QoS service selection schemes that are able to meet user requirements, but none of the work has addressed the problem of ensuring service quality when a service becomes unavailable. The QASB addressed this problem through the use of a job rescheduling mechanism that reassigns jobs in order to achieve the highest possible rate of SLA achievement.

Task Rescheduling

In a non-QASB approach, employees reconfigure the job queue when a priority work request is made. Unfortunately, employees are poorly positioned to consider the impact of a priority request on other jobs waiting in queue.

In a system that employs multiple services there are many different ways of addressing a priority job request. The QASB ensures that when a priority job is assigned, as many queued job requests as possible are still able to meet their SLAs. This is the task of the rescheduling algorithm which identifies the job management option that will have the least impact on the system as a whole. In essence, the algorithm will select the option that will allow the priority job to be completed while causing the lowest possible number of disruptions to other jobs waiting in queue.

Figure 5 illustrates a possible scenario in which the inclusion of a priority job request (1) in a queue, adversely impacts a second job (2) in the

Algorithm 1. Pseudo-code of the earliest node first selection algorithm

```
Transcoder serviceSelection(Collection qualityResult, Request job){
        qualityResult.sortbyPredictedValue();
            if (job.isSatisfied(qualityResult[0].predictedValue)){
                return qualityResult[0].getServiceInstance();
            }else{
                return null;
            }
}
```

same queue. When any new request is added to a queue, the QASB uses a rescheduling algorithm that estimates the impact of scheduling changes on other jobs waiting in queue. If the inclusion of the priority job is found to impact other jobs, the rescheduling algorithm utilizes information generated by the QoS computation to initiate the service selection/invocation process to reschedule the impacted job(s).

In the Figure 4 scenario, the reassignment of the affected job (2), negatively impacts another job (3) when it is rescheduled. Job 3 is in turn assigned a new position in queue. This reassignment negatively impacts job 4, which is also rescheduled in a new queue.

If a job cannot be successfully rescheduled, an alert is triggered by the rescheduling algorithm that notifies system administrators that the job cannot achieve its SLA. Administrators can then formulate an alternative strategy for completing the required job.

In order to ensure that the initial scheduling of a priority job has a minimal impact on the various service provider queues, the rescheduling algorithm conducts an impact assessment on all of the jobs in available queues before the priority job is assigned a place. This assessment is made in to determine both the number and the priority of the jobs affected in each queue by the inclusion of the priority job. This impact analysis can be graphically represented by a tree diagram like

that seen in Figure 6. In Figure 6 the root of the tree diagram represents the priority transcoding request. The leaf nodes represent the transcoding jobs that are affected by the parent node. The example in Figure 6 represents the scenario illustrated in Figure 5. Since this scenario was selected by the QASB, it represents the option which had the lowest impact on queued jobs.

The pseudo-code of the reschedule algorithm is listed in Algorithm 2.

In measuring the impact of any rescheduling option, two important factors are considered by the algorithm: depth and width. The depth of the tree refers to the number of queues that will be impacted by the introduction of the new job order. The width of the tree refers to the number of jobs in effected queues that will be affected by the introduction of the new job order. The option that has the least depth and width will be selected for implementation.

Pluggable Design

Although the QASB provides a QoS-Based Service Selection mechanism, this solution may not meet user needs in all situations. In its current form, QASB service level agreements only consider time of completion. Changing business requirements could conceivably require the inclusion of additional variables such as cost. In order to provide the system with a sufficient flexibility to adapt to

Figure 5. The impact of a priority job request on other jobs in queue

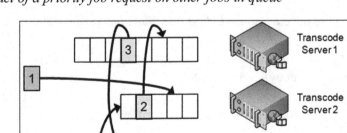

Figure 6. A tree diagram illustrating an impact analysis for the example outlined in Figure 4

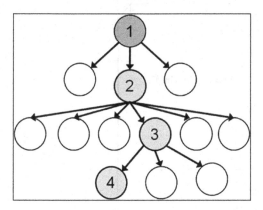

– doQoSComption, doServiceSelection, doRescheduling and so on – in accordance with the servicerouting method. In addition, the program skeleton constructed by researchers provides hook operations – doQoSComption, doService-Selection, and doRescheduling – that allow for future implementation of alternative algorithms to complete each of these tasks. In essence, the system is built around a pluggable capability that allows developers to use different algorithms in order to deal with a complex and changing business environment.

Service Monitoring

Service Monitoring system is widely used to track of service behavior and discover whether anomalies occurred in service-oriented community (Hershey & Runyon 2007) (Baresi, Guinea & Nano et al. 2010). The service monitoring component that presents here is responsible for collecting data on the behavior and execution results of the transcoding services in runtime. The component consists of three elements – a monitoring database, a service monitor and a monitoring agent. The monitoring database is used to store the data collected, including informa-

changing needs, the QASB was implemented by following the template method pattern (Gamma, Helm, Johnson & Vlissides 1995), meaning the system only uses a defined program skeleton of an algorithm. The system's algorithms – QoS computation, service selection, and rescheduling – can all be overridden by other components to allow differing behaviors in the QASB. Figure 7 illustrates this capability.

To use a QASB, developers must first design the concrete algorithms used by the system. The program skeleton of algorithms provides a service routing capability and defines the algorithm steps

Algorithm 2. Pseudo-code of the reschedule algorithm

```
Transcoder reschedule(Request job){
       Transcoder[ ] instances = getAllTranscoderInstances();
       Transcoder[ ] candidates = checkReschedulable(job, instances);
       if (candidates.size() == 0) {
             return NULL;
          }
       IAResult[ ] resultset = new IAResult[ candidates.size() ];
       for (int i = 0; i < candidates.size(); i++){
             resultset[ i ] = impact_analysis (job, candidates[ i ]);
       }
       sort(resultset);
       return result[ 0 ].getTranscodingService();
}
```

Figure 7. The pluggable design of the QASB

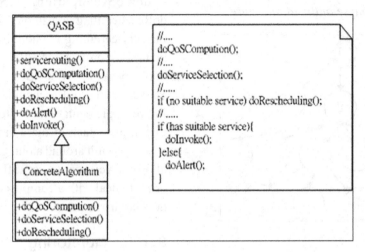

tion on service execution times, data inputs and outputs. The service monitor captures and filters data based on the monitoring model designed by developers. The service monitor provides the required information for QoS-Aware Service Bus to decide which service is providing the best quality of service at that time. The monitoring agent is installed on each service provider and is used to capture and forward the service execution data to the service monitor. In addition, the service monitoring module also provides alert capability that is triggered when active monitoring of service providers reveals that a job will not be completed in keeping with its SLA. The alert message would trigger a proactive problem management process to deal with it (Chen, Ni & Lin et al. 2010).

Transcoding Service

The transcoding services provide the capability of translating one media format into another. Conventional web services have long accomplished this through use of a request-response communication mechanism that keeps the connection between service consumer and providers until the service consumer receives a response message. Given the large size of media files handled by the QASB, it is difficult to keep stable connections

for sufficiently long periods of time to allow for execution. In consequence the QASB cannot rely on a request-response communication mechanism. Rather, an asynchronous web service invocation mechanism is used for invoking transcoding services. An abstract service definition of the transcoding service (Monson, Dettori & Nguyen et al. 2009) is applied to design the adapter of exist transcoding system.

EXPERIMENTAL RESULTS

Experimental results presented in the section were attained through the implementation of a QASB at Taiwan's Public Television Service (PTS). The PTS experimental environment is described in Table 2. With the new QASB, PTS now employs 2 IBM WebSphere Business Process Servers, 25 AnyStream Agility transcoding servers and 2 IBM WebSphere Enterprise Service Buses in its media transcoding system.

In this environment, the transcoding servers are tasked with dealing with all media format translation requests. Example requests might include such things as translating a video tape into both a digital video file and a different digital media format. The number of jobs these serv-

Table 2. Hardware and software configuration

	CPU	Memory	OS	Software	Number
Transcoding Servers	Intel X5650	16GB	Windows Server 2008	*AnyStream Agility* 2G (Telestream Corporation)	*25*
Business Process Server	Intel X5460	8GB	Windows Server 2008	WebSphere Business Process Server (IBM Corporation)	2
Qos-Aware Service Bus	Intel X5460	8GB	Windows Server 2008	WebSphere Enterprise Service Bus (IBM Corporation)	2

ers were able to complete, at the intended service level, with and without employing the linear regression-based estimations, formed the basis for evaluating of the effectiveness of the QASB.

On average, the transcoder servers were required to perform more than 700 media file transformations per day. These media files can be organized into five categories – under 10 minutes (18.18%), 10-30 minutes (18.18%), 30-60 minutes (27.27%), 60-90 minutes (33.33%) and more than 90 minutes (3.03%). Of the total number of translations, 45% were media files translated for broadcasting. An additional 20% of the files were translated for sale to other media users. The remaining 35% of media files were translated for PTS's digital asset management system. Each job request has a service level agreement that defined the deadline by which the job had to be completed.

In evaluating the performance of the QoS Aware Service Bus, a performance comparison was first made between the QASB and a conventional Enterprise Service Bus. Identical sets of data were run through identical operation sequences on both the QASB and the conventional ESB, IBM WebSphere Enterprise Service Bus. Figure 8 illustrates the comparative results of this evaluation. Note that the increased time required by the QASB was only within the range of a few seconds regardless of load conditions.

Despite the small increase in processing time required by the QASB, the system managed to achieve impression improvements in both number of jobs that could be processed per day, and the number of days required to ensure jobs in queue would be completed. Since PTS's previous system lacked an intelligent service selection algorithm,

Figure 8. Performance evaluation between conventional ESB and QASB

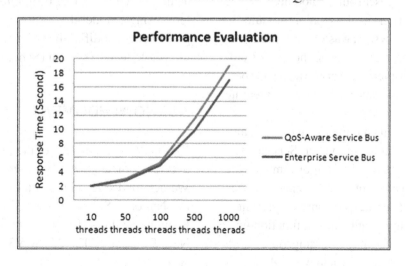

it was only able to complete an average of about 500 transcoding jobs each day. In consequence, staff requesting transcoding services needed to request those services an average of 7-10 days before they were needed.

With the implementation of the QASB and its intelligent service selection algorithm, PTS's system has increased its daily transcoding load to an average of 700 jobs. The increase volume of jobs that can be completed daily has, in turn, resulted in a reduction in the average number of days staff must wait for requests to be completed. With the QASB, PTS's current production and distribution process only requires jobs to be requested an average of 3-5 days before they are needed. The introduction of the QASB has resulted in a 40 percent increase in the number of jobs that can be accomplished each day and a 50 percent decrease in the amount of time required to ensure jobs are completed.

CONCLUSION

In this chapter, a QoS-Aware Service Bus was developed to perform QoS service routing based on execution time prediction. To achieve this task the QASB, which is a modified Enterprise Service Bus, was built around a series of modules. These included a QoS computation module, a service selection module, a rescheduling module, a service monitoring and a service invocation module. In order to ensure the system was flexible enough to adapt to changing requirements, the QASB employs a pluggable interface that allows developers to override the program skeleton and integrate alternative algorithms.

The QASB was then implemented and evaluated at Taiwan's Public Television Service. The evaluation contrasted QASB's algorithm with the performance of a conventional enterprise service bus and illustrated that the QoS approach presented here allows for significant gains in function with only minimal impact on processing time. With the QASB, PTS was able to achieve a 40 percent

increase in the number of jobs that could be transcoded daily, and a 50 percent reduction in the amount of time required to ensure jobs were completed before they were needed.

In addition to implementing the QASB in transcoding services, PTS is exploring a number of target areas in which the technology could provide potential value. Future work in this area will be directed at using this QoS-Aware Service Bus to deal with other business areas at the company. It is hoped that this chapter will serve as a reference point for further research on this subject.

Modern enterprise consists of complicate business systems. The enterprise service-oriented architecture becomes more and more mainstream for designing and implementing enterprise business systems. Our design takes advantage of the benefit of SOA, and it follows the generic and abstract model of enterprise service-oriented architecture (Tang et al. 2008). The model consists of seven sets: services, service consumers, service data, service infrastructure, service processes, service management and service quality attributes. A great challenge for enterprises is the improvement of the utilization of their landscape of heterogeneous applications in complex EAI (Enterprise Application Integration) scenarios. Enterprise Application Integration Patterns help to address this challenge by describing recurring EAI problems and proposing possible solutions at an abstract level. Our design follows EAI patterns using a model-driven architecture approach gives better modifiability of quality attribute to the whole service system (Scheibler et al. 2008).

ACKNOWLEDGMENT

We thank the employees of the Public Television Service Company who contributed to this project. We acknowledge with gratitude the support of the National Science Council and Ministry of Economic Affairs, Taiwan, R.O.C., under Grants NSC 99-2221-E-027-041-MY3 and 99-EC-17-A-02-S1-135.

REFERENCES

Al-naeem, T., Gorton, I., Ali Babar, M., Rabhi, F., & Benatallah, B. (2005). *A quality-driven systematic approach for architecting distributed software applications*. 27th International Conference on Software Engineering.

Bachmann, F., Bass, L., Klein, M., & Shelton, C. (2005). Designing software architectures to achieve quality attribute requirements. *IEE Proceedings. Software*, *152*(4). doi:10.1049/ip-sen:20045037

Baresi, L., Guinea, S., Nano, O., & Spanoudakis, G. (2010). Comprehensive monitoring of BPEL processes. *IEEE Internet Computing*, *14*(3), 50–57. doi:10.1109/MIC.2010.66

Behkamal, B., Kahani, M., & Akbari, M. K. (2009). Customizing ISO 9126 quality model for evaluation of B2B applications. *Information and Software Technology*, *51*(3), 599–609. doi:10.1016/j.infsof.2008.08.001

Chen, I. Y., Ni, G. K., Kuo, C. H., & Lin, C. Y. (2010). A service-oriented management framework for telecom operation support systems. *IEEE International Conference Service System and Service Management* (pp. 1-5).

Chen, I. Y., Ni, G. K., & Lin, C. Y. (2008). A runtime adaptive service bus design for telecom operations support systems. *IBM Systems Journal*, *47*(3), 445–456. doi:10.1147/sj.473.0445

Dettori, P., Nogima, K., Schaffa, F., & Banks, T. (2009). *Solution for the media and entertainment industry: Media Extensions for SOA*. IBM While Paper. Retrieved March 1, 2010, from http://www-01.ibm.com/common /ssi/cgi-bin/ssialias?infotype=SA &subtype=WH&htmlfid=MEW03004USEN

Dimitrios, G., & Michael, P. P. (2008). *Service-oriented computing*. The MIT Press.

Dueñas, J. C., & Capilla, R. (2005). *The decision view of software architecture*. Software Architecture Lecture Notes in Computer Science.

Footen, J., & Faust, J. (2008). *The service-oriented media enterprise: SOA, BPM, and Web Services in professional media systems*. Focal Press.

Gamma, E., Helm, R., Johnson, R., & Vlissides, J. (1995). *Design patterns: Elements of reusable object-oriented software*. Addison Wesley.

Gao, Z., & Wu, G. (2005). Combining Qos-based service selection with performance prediction. *IEEE International Conference on e-Business Engineering* (pp. 611-614).

Hershey, P., & Runyon, D. (2007). SOA monitoring for enterprise computing systems. *IEEE International Enterprise Distributed Object Computing Conference* (pp.443-443).

Humphery, W. S. (1995). *A discipline for software engineering*. Addison Wesley.

Hwang, S. Y., Lim, E. P., Lee, C. H., & Chen, C. H. (2008). Dynamic Web service selection for reliable web service composition. *IEEE Transaction on Services Computing*, *1*(2), 104–116. doi:10.1109/TSC.2008.2

IBM. (n.d.). *WebSphere enterprise service bus*. IBM Corporation, Retrieved December 17, 2010, from http://www.ibm.com/software/ integration/wsesb/

IBM. (n.d.). *WebSphere process server*. IBM Corporation. Retrieved December 17, 2010, from http://www-01.ibm.com/software/integration/wps/

Karastoyanova, K., Wetzstein, B., van Lessen, T., Wutke, D., Nitzsche, J., & Leymann, F. (2007). Semantic service bus: Architecture and implementation of a next generation middleware. *2007 IEEE 23rd International Conference Data Engineering Workshop*, (pp. 347-354).

Kritikos, K., & Plexousakis, D. (2009). Requirements for QoS-based Web Service description and discovery. *IEEE Transaction on Services Computing, 2*(4), 320–337. doi:10.1109/TSC.2009.26

Kun, D., Bo, D., Xiaoyi, Z., & Ge, L. (2009). Optimization of service selection algorithm for complex event processing in enterprise service bus platform. *International Conference on Computer Science & Education* (pp. 582-586).

Lee, Y. K. (2009). An implementation case study: Business oriented SOA execution test framework. *International Joint Conference on INC, IMS and IDC* (pp-435-430).

Liegl, P. (2007). The strategic impact of service oriented architectures. *IEEE International Conference and Workshops on the Engineering of Computer-Based Systems* (pp. 475-484).

Liu, Y., Gorton, I., & Zhu, L. (2007). Performance prediction of service-oriented applications based on an enterprise service bus. *31st Computer Software and Applications Conference*, (pp. 327-334).

Monson, P., Dettori, P., Guglielmino, P., Nguyen, C. T., Nguyen, T. N. C., Nogima, J., & Schaffa, F. A. (2009). *Abstract service definition for media services.* IBM Redpaper, Retrieved February 20, 2010, from http://www.redbooks.ibm.com/

Papazoglou, M. P., & van den Heuvel, W.-J. (2007). Service oriented architectures: Approaches, technologies and research issues. *The International Journal on Very Large Data Bases, 16*(3). doi:10.1007/s00778-007-0044-3

Scheibler, T., & Leymann, F. (2008). A framework for executable enterprise application integration patterns. *Enterprise Interoperability, 3*(4), 485–497. doi:10.1007/978-1-84800-221-0_38

Schmidt, M. T., Hutchison, B., Lambros, P., & Phippen, R. (2005). The enterprise service bus: Making service-oriented architecture real. *IBM Systems Journal, 44*(4). doi:10.1147/sj.444.0781

Sur, A., Schaffa, F., McIntyre, J., Nogima, J., Alexander, M. E., & Dettori, P. (2008). Extending the service bus for successful and sustainable IPTV services. *IEEE Communications Magazine, 46*(8), 96–103. doi:10.1109/MCOM.2008.4597111

Tang, L., Dong, J., & Peng, T. (2008). A generic model of enterprise service-oriented architecture. *IEEE International Symposium Service-Oriented System Engineering*, (pp. 1-7).

Telestream Corporation. (n.d.). *AnyStream agility* Retrieved December 17, 2010, from http://www.telestream.net /telestream-products/anystream.htm

Weken, D. V., Assche, S. V., Clabaut, D., Desmet, S., & Volckaert, B. (2009). Automating workflows with service oriented media applications. *World Conference on Services-I* (pp. 507-514).

Wu, B., Liu, S., & Wu, L. (2008). Dynamic reliable service routing in enterprise service bus. *IEEE Asia-Pacific Services Computing Conference* (pp. 349-354).

Yin, J., Chen, H., Deng, S., Wu, Z., & Pu, C. (2009). A dependable ESB framework for service integration. *IEEE Internet Computing, 13*(2), 26–34. doi:10.1109/MIC.2009.26

Yu, T., & Lin, K. J. (2004). The design of QoS broker algorithms for QoS-capable Web services. *IEEE International Conference on e-Technology, e-Commerce and e-Service* (pp.17-24).

Yu, T., & Lin, K. J. (2005). Service selection algorithms for Web services with end-to-end QoS constraints. *Information Systems and E-Business Management, 3*(2), 103–126. doi:10.1007/s10257-005-0052-z

KEY TERMS AND DEFINITIONS

Enterprise Service Bus (ESB): A software architecture for middleware that provides fundamental services for more complex architectures. For example, an ESB incorporates the features required to implement a service-oriented architecture (SOA). In a general sense, an ESB can be thought of as a mechanism that manages access to applications and services (especially legacy versions) to present a single, simple, and consistent interface to end-users via Web- or forms-based client-side front ends.

Loosely-Coupled: Loosely coupled systems provide many advantages including support for late or dynamically binding to other components while running, and can mediate the difference in the component's structure, security model, protocols, and semantics, thus abstracting volatility. This is in contrast to compile-time or runtime binding, which requires that you bind the components at compile time or runtime (synchronous calls), respectively, and also requires that changes be designed into all components at the same time due to the dependencies. In brief, a loosely coupled architecture allows you to replace components, or change components, without having to make reflective changes to other components in the architecture/systems.

Publish/Scribe Messaging: Topic-based messaging. In a publish-subscribe system, senders label each message with the name of a topic ("publish"), rather than addressing it to specific recipients. The messaging system then sends the message to all eligible systems that have asked to receive messages on that topic ("subscribe"). This form of asynchronous messaging is a far more scalable architecture than point-to-point alternatives such as message queuing, since message senders need only concern themselves with creating the original message, and can leave the task of servicing recipients to the messaging infrastructure. It is a very loosely coupled architecture, in which senders often do not even know who their subscribers are.

Quality Attributes: Such as response time, accuracy, security, reliability, are properties that affect the system as a whole. Most approaches deal with quality attributes separately from the functional requirements of a system. This means that the integration is difficult to achieve and usually is accomplished only at the later stages of the software development process.

Quality of Service (QoS): A set of technologies for managing network traffic in a cost effective manner to enhance user experiences for home and enterprise environments. QoS technologies allow you to measure bandwidth, detect changing network conditions (such as congestion or availability of bandwidth), and prioritize or throttle traffic.

Server Load Balancing: In order to achieve web server scalability, more servers need to be added to distribute the load among the group of servers, which is also known as a *server cluster*. The load distribution among these servers is known as load balancing. Load balancing applies to all types of servers (application server, database server), however, we will be devoting this section for load balancing of web servers (HTTP server) only. When multiple web servers are present in a server group, the HTTP traffic needs to be evenly distributed among the servers. In the process, these servers must appear as one web server to the web client, for example an internet browser. The load balancing mechanism used for spreading HTTP requests is known as IP Spraying.

Section 4
Service Search and Selection

Chapter 6
A Goal–Driven Approach for Service–Oriented Systems Design

Chiung-Hon Leon Lee
Nanhua University, Taiwan

Alan Liu
National Chung Cheng University, Taiwan

Arthur Shr
Louisiana State University, USA

ABSTRACT

This chapter introduces a goal-driven approach for modeling service requests in service-oriented systems. There are three challenges to this approach: how to represent a service request, how to map the request to predefined models, and how to generate a series of actions to satisfy these models. A goal model is used for user requirements elicitation, analysis, and representation. The service request from users is extracted and mapped to these goal models by a case-based method. A planning mechanism is designed to produce a sequence of activities to satisfy the extracted goals. By these methods, a more convenient and efficient service for users can be provided. A general architecture for an intention-aware service-oriented system is proposed for demonstrating how to apply the proposed approach.

INTRODUCTION

In our daily lives, services may be provided by anybody, but the quality of services provided may differ from person to person. For those who have worked together for a long time, the desire of one person does not need to be expressed clearly or precisely, because they have mutual understanding. If a boss tells a capable assistant about attending a meeting on certain day in a certain city, the assistant may use the past experience about attending a meeting to arrange the business trip that the boss desires. The business trip may need services for arranging the transportation, booking a hotel, making appointments, etc. If a service-

DOI: 10.4018/978-1-61350-159-7.ch006

oriented system is to be used, the user needs to enter a set of clear and precise requests to get a service in return.

Several techniques and standards have been proposed to facilitate accessing web services, but it is still hard to let an ordinary user to enter a simple request and receive results directly returned from the service providers to satisfy the user's requirements, making it a challenging problem for a web service system. The requested system may have to interact with the user to elicit more information for acquiring the suitable web services, discovering services, selecting services, composing services, processing information returned from the services, and demonstrating the results to the user. For these purposes, how to integrate service providers, system's capabilities, and elicited user information becomes an important issue when developing an intelligent web services application. An interaction scenario among the system user, service requestor, service broker, and service provider is illustrated in Figure 1. The service requester interacts with the user and tries to complete the user's delegations. The service broker collects a list of web services advertisements from service providers, accepts the service request from the requester, and tries to discover, select, and access a web service to satisfy the service request from the user.

Because the service requester has no knowledge about the service providers, the initial query it sends to the service broker might not correspond exactly with the query input that a service provider might require in order to provide a suitable service. Such problem may be simple as a value missing for a parameter, or complicated as ambiguous keywords to process. The requester may have to interact with the user to elicit more information for accessing the web services.

A goal-driven approach is a widely used method for software requirements elicitation and representation (Lee, Xue, & Kuo, 2001). Requirements specifications are generated by a goal-based requirements analysis process in which the functional and nonfunctional requirements will be extended with goal models. A set of computable goal models that represents the user requirements can be selected and refined as the basis of defining services. The software designers can also design related system services based on these models. The user's vague and imprecise intention can be extracted and mapped to computer understandable and computable goal models.

Figure 2 shows a model to represent the problem discussed above. In the figure, software requirements are the source of what a user wants

Figure 1. An interaction scenario of the user, requester, broker, and provider

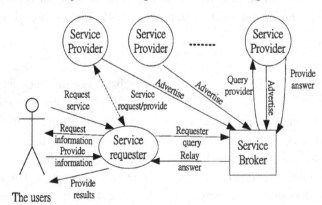

from a system and they may be further analyzed as the intention of what the user expects the system to do. For bridging requirements and intention, we use the goal model concept to analyze, extract, and record the needed information. This analysis is applied to enhance the service request construction, in which the request entered by the user may be vague. For such vague input, the system is still expected to be able to extract important terms from it. In such case, those terms may need to be expanded to contain more information to form a clearer user request. The goal model that is constructed based on requirements then will be used to support such expansion, and the service request may be designed as a vector which contains a set of terms extracted. All goal models are elicited from software requirements (Loucopoulos, & Karakostas, 1995) and also represent an abstract description of the capability which the system can perform.

After the goal model is constructed, we need a mechanism to carry out plans to meet the goal of a user. A plan consists of a series of actions which is the result of invoking external services and calling internal functions of the system interacting with the user. An external service is the service provided by external objects such as web service providers or other software agents (Gib-

bins, Harris, & Shadbolt, 2004). By laying out the plans to meet the goal of a user, the system is considered to fulfill the intention of the user and satisfy user requirements.

As with any goal-driven analysis, a goal may be a simple goal or an abstract goal consisting of sub-goals. When analyzing a service request, the intention of the user may be explicit or implicit. For the explicit intention, the goal model is obtained from the requirements presented above. The implicit intention, in turn, is obtained by further analyzing the system requirements and is represented as an extended goal model. When considering having the goals met by service providers, the service requests are like the requirements and the intention of the user to satisfy. The service request may include explicit and implicit intentions that are represented by goal models. An original set of goal models are elicited from user requirements, and system requirements can provide information needed for extended goal models. The relationships among the service request, user intention, goal models, and requirements are shown in Figure 3.

This chapter introduces a goal-driven approach to integrate software requirements, internal system functions, external web services, and user information to interpret and satisfy the user's service requests. The proposed approach is intended to be applied to service-oriented systems to accumulate knowledge about application domain, system capabilities, web services, and user information to satisfy extracted user requests. In other words, this approach draws attention to the parallelism concept between goal-driven requirements engineering and the process of service selection, composition, and execution. It should be noted that the term *service* used in this chapter means any service provided by a computer system, and web service is one of such services.

Figure 2. The concept of service request interpretation and satisfaction

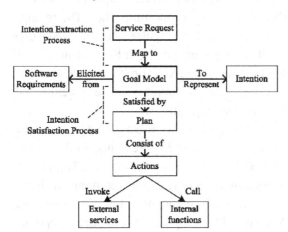

Figure 3. The relationships of the service request, user intention, goal models, and requirements

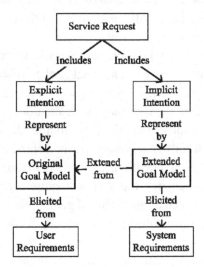

BACKGROUND

Service-oriented computing has gained popularity with its characteristics in platform independence, language independence, and other attractive characters (Singh, & Huhns, 2005). There are different approaches proposed to cope with the challenges of web services research (Wang, Huang, Qu, & Xie, 2004), and enhance the services provision such as service composition (Chan, & Lyu, 2008), service discovery (Sycara, et al. 2004), service selection (Hwang, et al, 2007), etc. However, how to understand the user's service request and how to deliver proper services to satisfy the request still remain as an important research topic for assisting the users to obtain their requirements through service-oriented systems. We try to use goal-driven analysis to capture user requirements along with user intention.

Research in detecting and understanding user intention is also important in Human-Computer Interaction (HCI) and Human-Robot Interaction (HRI) (Breazeal, 2004). The purpose of using intention as another source of information is to free the user from providing too many details and precise requirements. We can observe the domains

of HCI and HRI to see several ways to facilitate the context information gathering and user request identification, such as visual recognition of hand and body gestures, conversational interaction, force-feedback tactile gloves, or fusing the multi-modal input (Marsic, Medl, & Flanagan 2000)(Iba, Paredis, & Khosla, 2003). However, in many web applications, such as network search engines and web service systems, a keyboard and a mouse are widely expected input devices for user-computer interaction. For using a dialog-oriented input, a natural language based approach for on-demand service composition is reported (Pop, et al. 2010). Without relying on a complete natural language processing method, our research goal is to simplify interaction by using only a simple sentence or some keywords.

We have proposed a web services request tool to enhance the access of web services (Lee, & Liu, 2006), in which two main problems were identified: how to interpret the service request from the string entered by the user and how to integrate the internal services implemented in the system and external services on the Internet to satisfy the user's request. The approach is to model and interpret service requests from system users, and the extracted service request will be mapped to a set of goal models (Lee, & Liu, 2005a).

We perceive that acquiring precise requirements in software engineering is similar to acquiring the intention from a service request. The difference is that the service request provided by the user may be a 'one-time' shot. The requirements engineer for a regular software system may elicit the requirements from the user iteratively, but the user of a service-oriented system issuing a service request cannot bear the system to ask him too many questions.

In our research, we use a goal-driven method to analyze the user requirements. Rolland et al. (Rolland, Souveyet, & Achour, 1998) proposed a structure for analyzing the requirements based on a verb and its parameters. Lee et al. (Lee, Xue, & Kuo, 2001) proposed a systematic approach to handling the interaction among nonfunctional requirements and their impacts on the structuring of requirement specifications. Inspired by the Rolland's and Lee's researches, our method uses a goal model to represent the user's intention (Lee, & Liu, 2005b). The goal models can guide the system to generate a plan, and the execution of the plan will be expected to satisfy the user's intentions.

GUIDING SERVICE-ORIENTED SYSTEM DESIGN BY A GOAL-DRIVEN APPROACH

Three challenges are identified in designing a service-oriented system by a goal-driven approach: how to represent service request, how to map the request to predefined models, and how to generate a series of actions to satisfy these models. This section will introduce a goal model for user requirements elicitation, analysis, and representation. In our approach, a case-based method is used to record successful models and map the service request from users to goal models. Then, a planning mechanism is designed for the system to produce a sequence of activities to satisfy the extracted goals. By these approaches, the system can provide a more convenient and efficient service for users.

Goal Representation

In this research, we expect our goal model to express the requirements of the user and the intention of the user to help enhance the service request. Thus, the aim is to design a goal model that is able to express the user input which is bound to explicit and implicit requirements. The process is similar to building ontology for domain knowledge and other information related to the user usage. The content must be defined clearly for system to use as attributes. When analyzing goal models, there will be more sub-goal models

produced, and the analysis between related goal models produces important implicit information and constraints especially for nonfunctional requirements. For this reason, we extend the work in the goal-driven use case (GDUC) method (Lee, & Xue, 1999) to find detail attributes that will be discussed later. Figure 4 depicts this idea by defining a goal model with three parts: *Contents*, *Properties*, and *Relationships*. The *Contents* part is to store the information extracted from the user input, the *Properties* part is to express the role of the goal model, and the *Relationship* part is to record the relationship among the goal model with other related goal models.

Contents

The *Contents* part consists of four fields to express the information extracted from the user input: *Action*, *Object*, *Constraint*, and *Parameters*. For analyzing a service request, the basic idea of this part is similar to analyzing a sentence with a subject, verb, object, and other modifiers. The *Action* field contains what the user expects the system to perform, and the verb in a sentence is usually treated as an action. The *Object* field is to store something that is affected by the action, and that

Figure 4. The goal model

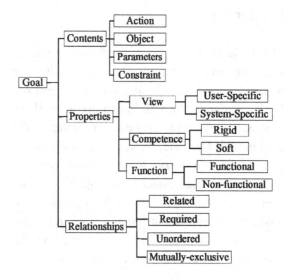

will be a noun. The *Parameter* field contains the information to aid the description of the object. The *Constraint* field is the nonfunctional requirements to describe the action to perform in a certain way, and it is like a modifier. As an example, a service request like "Schedule a meeting on June 20 in the afternoon" itself will be the *Contents*, the term "schedule" will be an *Action*, "meeting" is the *Object* of the *Action*, "June 20" is parameter of the *Object*, and "afternoon" is the *Constraint* of the meeting time selection.

For designing a system to extract more information from a service request entered by the user, simply parsing the request into terms is not enough. The produced terms are checked with a goal model to produce more information. The *Contents* part is the first information that the system is to check what goal models are most appropriate. Our aim is not to have the user enter a complete sentence, but a keyword or a verb phrase. We can use an existing natural language processing method to parse a sentence into terms, and we form a method to match this set of terms to an existing goal model if we have a collection of goal models available. If there is no existing goal model available, we can build up a collection of goal models with a learning mechanism. More discussion about the details will be presented in the goal discovery section.

Properties

The *Properties* part consists of three fields to specify extra information gathered from the user requirements: *View*, *Competence*, and *Function*. We have adapted the definition proposed in (Lee, Xue, & Kuo, 2001) to define the properties of the goal model. The field, *View*, concerns whether a goal model is *user-specific* or *system-specific*. A *user-specific* goal model is an objective of the user in using the system; a *system-specific* goal model is requirements on functions that the system provides to support the *user-specific* goal. The original goal derived from the user's request is always a *user-specific* goal because it reflects the intention that the user wants the system to do. It should be noted that there is a minor difference between our definition on *View* and the definition proposed in (Lee, Xue, & Kuo, 2001), in which the sub-fields, *View* as *actor-specific* and *system-specific*, are defined. Consider an example of a need for buying an airline ticket. A request like "schedule a flight" will be a *user-specific* goal and "select a proper flight" a *system-specific* goal to extend the user-specific goal.

The definition of the *Competence* field classifies the goal as rigid or soft. A rigid goal must always be satisfied, while a soft goal may be satisfied to a degree using an evaluation method. For example, "schedule a flight" is a rigid goal, because the system needs to schedule a flight for the user; otherwise the system needs to say to the user that the flight cannot be scheduled for some reason. The result of either satisfied or fail is expected for this goal. Consider a phrase, "arrange a convenient flight." It is a soft goal, because the term "convenient" is vague and may be interpreted in many ways. If the system wants to determine whether a flight is convenient or not, it needs to refer to a set of evaluation criteria such as the departure time, service class of the flight, price, etc.

The *Function* field consists of the *Functional* and *Nonfunctional* fields for holding the functional and nonfunctional requirements. A functional goal describes what function the system should have, and a nonfunctional goal defines the constraints to a functional goal. For a service request "schedule an afternoon flight on June 20," in which "schedule a flight" is a functional goal, "afternoon" and "June 20" will be a nonfunctional time constraint to the functional goal.

Consider a scenario that a person needs to go to a business trip. The main goal of this person is to schedule a flight, so that he is able to attend a meeting in another city. To achieve this main goal, the person needs to look up for a suitable flight and book for a selected flight. After arriving at the destination, he needs a car to attend a meeting which he has added to his schedule. Using the GDUC analysis method, we can analyze the need of a user who is going for a business trip. As shown in Figure 5, identifying the user, Passenger, as the actor, we can derive use cases: "Schedule a flight," "Query flight," "Book flight," and "Select flight." For each use case, we will obtain associated goals like *ScheduleFlight, QueryFlight, SelectFlight*, and *BookFlight* respectively. Because the system is supposed to provide the services to query flight, book flight, and schedule a train, bus, or taxi to somewhere, the goals *ScheduleFlight, QueryFlight*, and *BookFlight* will be functional, rigid, and user-specific goals. It should be noted that the GDUC analysis is iterative and the use cases and goals may be modified throughout as more information is revealed.

Imagine that we need a service-oriented system to satisfy the above requirements. It is obvious that it will be a composite service if we consider that each goal is satisfied by an atomic service. However, if we require a system to integrate these services together automatically based on a simple user input, then it will be difficult since we need more information. Thus, we need a reasoning mechanism to obtain and make use more information, in which usable goal models are reused.

Taking the use case, "select flight," for further analysis, we can obtain a result shown in Figure 6. Even if the user does not assign a specific flight number and the information extracted from the user's request is not enough to select a flight, the system is expected to still select a proper flight for the user. Because the action of selecting proper flight will constrain the action of selecting flight and "proper" is a fuzzy term, the goal *SelectProperFlight* will be nonfunctional, soft, and user-specific. In this example, four evaluation criteria are defined to extend the meaning of the term "proper": price, time, company, and cabin-class. There are three nonfunctional, soft, user-specific goals derived from their related use cases, *MinimumPrice, ArrangeAvaliableTime*, and *SelectHigherCabinClass* defined while a

Figure 5. A "schedule a flight" use cases and related goals

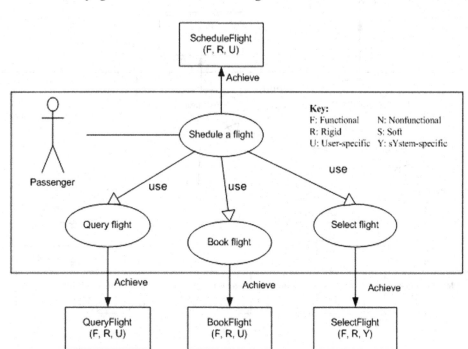

nonfunctional, soft, system-specifc goal, *SelectUserPreferredFlight*, is determined. These goals are nonfunctional because they will constrain the execution of "select proper flight" use case, they are soft because these goals will be allowed to satisfied to a degree.

Relationships

The role of the *Relationships* part is to keep the relevant goals together, and it consists of four fields, namely, *Related, Required, Unordered,* and *Mutual-exclusive*. The *Related* field stores the names of all possible related goal models, the *Required* field the required goal models for achieving the original goal model, the *Unordered* field the related goals which could be satisfied in any order, and the *Mutual-exclusive* field those related goals which could not be satisfied at the same time.

Considering the goals in Figure 5, *QueryFlight, SelectFlight, BookFlight,* and *AssertEvent* are required for completing the goal *ScheduleFlight*; *AssertEvent* and *BookFlight* are mutual-exclusive because if the system has booked a flight, it does not need to book a flight again. It should be noted that *Mutual-exclusive* has higher priority than *Required*. If both *Bookflight* and *AssertEvent* are recorded in the *Required* field but they also appear in the *Mutual-exclusive* field, the system will treat them as mutual exclusive and select one of them. In Figure 6, *SelectProperFlight* will be a *Related* goal of *SelectFlight* and there are four related goals for *SelectProperFlight*: *MinimumPrice, ArrangeAvaliableTime, SelectHigherCabinClass,* and *SelectUserPreferredFlight*. Because there is no need to restrict the achievement order of these goals, they will be assigned in the *Unordered* field.

Figure 6. Extended use cases and goals of the use case "select flight"

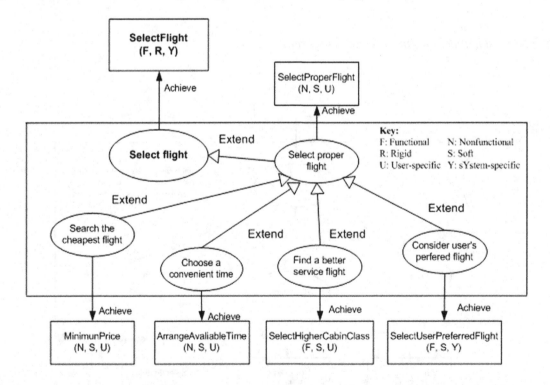

Goal Discovery

The goal discovery process adapted from the Goal-Driven Use Case (GDUC) approach in (Lee, & Xue, 1999) identifies goals through the following three steps: (1) identifying use cases, (2) extending use cases, and (3) refining use-case models. The first step is similar to finding the actors and use cases in any use-case approaches. Actors could be a human user, hardware, or virtual software programs, while the use cases should be those tasks in the system to meet the minimum requirements, i.e., to achieve actors' rigid and functional goals. However, we are more interested in those use cases associated with the human user rather than other actors, because the goal models extended from the human user's use cases are the basis for interpreting the user request. For example, the flight scheduling service system shown in Figure 5 is developed for servicing the passenger; therefore, it is obvious the passenger is an actor. The use case *Select flight* is the case for passenger to achieve the goal *SelectFlight*, which is functional, rigid, and system-specific. This use case represents a sequence of tasks starting from a passenger's request to select a flight until a desired flight is reserved for the user. The use case *Select flight* requires the steps to generate a schedule flight to achieve the goal *SelectFlight*: (1) sending a service request for querying possible flights; (2) having the passenger select a desired flight from the obtained flight list; (3) booking the flight for the passenger; and (4) presenting the result to the passenger.

The second step is to create extended use cases to take different types of goals into account. An extended use case is created to optimize or maintain the soft goals which are related to achieving a rigid goal. A soft goal is a desirable property for a system and can be partially satisfied. For example, in Figure 5, the use case, *Select proper flight*, is an extended use case from the *Select flight* use case, which is a soft goal. This use case is to select a flight to optimize or maintain the convenient of the passenger. An extended use case is also created to achieve this goal, such as *Get inexpensive Price*, *Arrange convenient Time*, *Arrange comfortable flight*, and *Arrange user preferred flight*. These use cases are designed to achieve the goals by considering different passenger's preference or service levels. Achieving a nonfunctional goal is another purpose that we create the extended use case. Nonfunctional goals usually define the constraints that the system needs to satisfy. Apparently, *Get inexpensive Price*, *Arrange convenient Time*, *Arrange comfortable flight*, and *Arrange user preferred flight* are the use cases to achieve the nonfunctional goals of *MinimumPrice*, *ArrangeAvaliableTime*, *SelectHigherCabinClass*, and *SelectUserPreferredFlight*, respectively. An original goal is functional, rigid, and user-specific. An extended goal is weakly dependent on its associated original goal because satisfying an original goal will not always guarantee that its associated use case can also be satisfied, unless it is soft. In our approach, the contents and properties of a goal model will be also filled in this step.

After finding suitable actors and use cases in the system and associating each use cases with a goal, the third step is to refine the use-case model derived. We review the common fragment among these use cases in the use-case model and group the similar parts into an abstract use case. We can use the *use* relation to refine the use-case model. We did not include abstract use cases in the example shown in Figure 5; however, searching or updating a flight in the database is a common behavior of the use cases, *Query flight*, *Book flight*, and *Select flight*. Thus, in Figure 7, we create an abstract *Search flight* use case which is formed based on the common fragment from these three use cases. We also create another abstract use case *Update flight*, which is produced based on the *Book flight* and *Select flight* use cases only. Furthermore, the new use-case goal model shown in Figure 7 is built by adding two abstract use cases, *Search flight* and *Update flight*.

To obtain desired goal models of a system is a gradual and iterative process. Through the use case driven requirements analysis, rough goal models identified are repeatedly refined. In our approach, we have restricted the use case derivation based on a verb and its parameters, and then it will be easier for the system designer to extract the content part of the goal model from the use case. In the GDUC approach, the properties of the goal model will be obtained and evaluated. The relationships between use cases and goals will be evaluated by investigating the effects on the goals after the functions associated with those use cases are performed. Possible relationships may also be found by exploring the interaction between goals in the use-case level as well as system level. Editing the relationship of the goal model needs more designer's effort, so that the information may aid reuse of the goal models.

When considering a scenario where a flight scheduling web services system is used, we can derive the *ScheduleFlight* goal model with a sequence of actions shown in Figure 8. First, a service request is made for querying a flight, and a service provider is located. A list of flight is generated by the service provider in charge, and the user makes a selection based on the result provided. Then a booking service is requested, the service is carried out, and the result is presented to the user. Instead of looking at the sequence of actions as a fixed flow, we see that the services are independent from each other and can be used alone or combined with other services. Users may only want to query a flight, so we can refined the goal model by combining Steps 1 to 5 into one abstract use case "query flight" to perform the query flight activity. In another case, users may want to buy an inexpensive ticket, and then the

Figure 7. Two abstract use cases: "search flight" and "update flight" in the new goal model

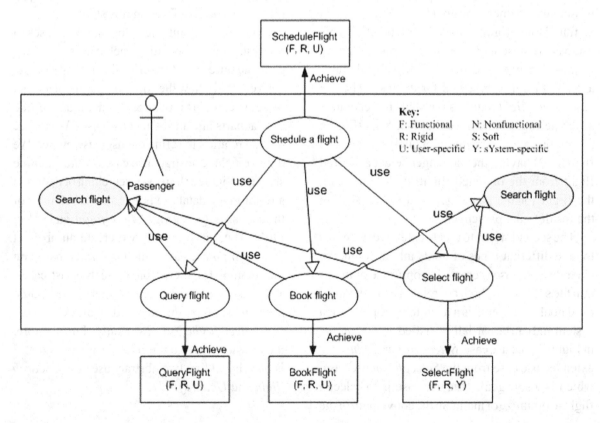

system will present the sorted flight list according to the ticket price to the users. This special requirement is a nonfunctional requirement and the goal model can be refined by extending the "book flight" use case to cover such scenario. The steps of goal discovery and scenario authoring are complementary activities. When a use case is found, a scenario can be authored and its related goals can be discovered from the original use case and also from its scenario.

Retaining and Reusing Goal Models

As discussed through goal-driven analysis, two main tasks are identified in the user intention extraction process: how to process keywords from a service request and how to map the extracted terms into a goal model. The former is to parse and interpret the keywords entered for finding

possible senses of the keywords. The latter is to map the interpreted keywords to the related goal models. As we study the intention of a user to enrich the understanding of user requirements, we see that this information is also beneficial in aiding personalization of a service request. If a services-oriented system is to provide personalized services to satisfy the user requests, the service requester is the first to be studied in system design since it is the place to interact with users and obtain more information from the users.

Following the goal construction method described in the previous sections, we are able to construct goal models to satisfy user requests. As the user accumulates the interaction with the system, a collection of goal models will be generated. If those goal models can be recorded as experiences for future use, the goal model construction process can be replaced by the process

Figure 8. A sequence of actions associated with scheduling a flight

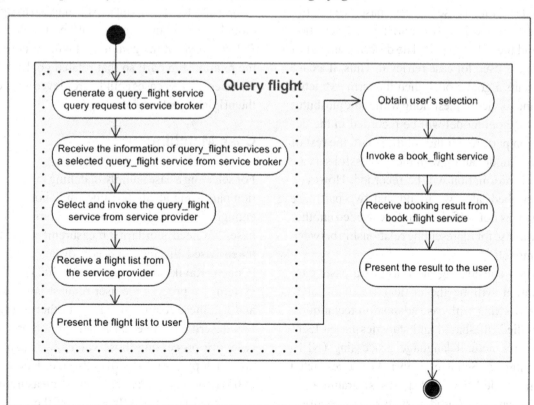

of finding a correct goal model from a set of goal models available. Based on this reason, we have used case-based reasoning (CBR) techniques in related research (Lee, Liu, & Huang, 2010) (Lee & Liu, 2010). By finding a similar goal model, some information including user intention can be derived from the past experience. The following describes Case-Based Service Request Interpretation (CBSRI) approach to interpret service requests from system users.

Case Design

The advantage of using the CBR approach is that the previous experience for request interpretation can be stored in a case base, and when the system encounters a new service request, the old interpretation of service request can be retrieved and adapted to interpret the new service request (Watson, 1997). If the new problem has been solved, the system can store the new solution to the case base for future usage.

In designing a case in a case base, we usually divide the case into two parts: the description part and the solution part. The description part of the case is used for case retrieval. Thus, if a case represents a goal model, then the term extracted from the service request along with some attributes from the goal model will be recorded in the description part. As for the solution part, the rest of the goal model along with the successful service request information will be recorded. However, as described later, we found that two-part case design was not sufficient, and we needed another part in a case for representing relationship between goal models.

When considering the reuse of a case, case adaptation will be the critical issue to solve. When working with case adaptation techniques, we studied rule-based and statistics-based techniques for natural language processing (NLP) (Manning, & Schutze, 1999). For a restricted domain, a rule-based approach uses a grammar for parsing sentences based on syntax and semantics.

A statistics-based approach, on the other hand, attempts to extract the semantics of a sentence by means of a stochastic model, using a learning mechanism, such as Hidden Markov Models (HMM) and probabilistic recursive transition networks. In CBSRI, we have applied a rule-based approach to CBR for interpreting service requests.

Beside the description part and the solution part, we use an additional part, called the relation part. As mentioned earlier, the description part consists of features or facts to identify the case, and the solution part contains a solution to apply to a problem. The relationships among the case base, case, problem domain, and solution domain are shown in Figure 9. The case A is a case in a case base, in which it has relationship with other cases, namely B, C, and D. This information is stored in the relation part.

For the case content, we use the information based on service request as the description part. The solution part contains the *Contents* and *Properties* of the goal model. Using the *Contents* and *Properties*, the user input can be mapped to a goal model for finding user intention. Finally, the *Relationships* of the goal model will be stored in the relationship part, so that related goal models recorded in other cases could be retrieved to extend the original goal model.

Case Matching

For selecting a case, simply matching the description part using attribute values may not be good enough. When selecting a case from the case base, we need similarity measurement such as token-based distance and edit-distance metrics (Cohen, Ravikumar, & Fienberg, 2003). In our system, we process the user request into tokens and use these tokens along with other information described above in the description part of a case. For processing those values, we adapt the approach proposed in (Michelson, & Knoblock, 2005) to build up a set of similarity measurement vectors (SMV) that reflect each of the different

Figure 9. The relationships among the case-base, case, problem domain, and solution domain

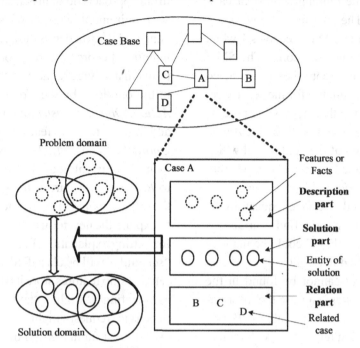

similarity types and use these vectors for similarity measurement. In our research, we use an approach consisting rescoring and testing, in which rescoring step recalculates each SMV to produce a new score for ranking candidate cases and the testing step evaluates whether the candidate cases match the service request. The rescoring process involves comparing the corresponding values in each SMV, and the values are changed to 1 or 0 according to a simple rule described next. Comparing all SMVs by its corresponding content, the rescoring rule is to change the maximum value to 1 and make other values 0. Assume we have m SMVs with n scores in each vector represented as $SMV_i = <S_{i1}, S_{i2}, ..., S_{in}>$, where $i = 1..m$. The rescoring process is as follows:

for $j=1$ to n do
$S_{ij} = 1$ if S_{ij} is maximum ($\{S_{1j}, ..., S_{mj}\}$) for $i=1..m$
else $S_{ij} = 0$

In our implementation, we choose different string distance measurement methods to evaluate the distance between a request and candidate cases. Each SMV contains 8 scores, and following the study in (Cohen, Ravikumar, & Fienberg, 2003) (Michelson, & Knoblock, 2005), we use different metrics to produce the content of an SMV. For an SMV with $n = 8$, S_{i1} to S_{i3} are calculated using the Levenstein distance, S_{i4} to S_{i6} Jaccard similarity, and S_{i7} to S_{i8} Soundex distance.

For illustration, assume we have a service request "arrange a flight from Chiayi to New York September 3 with alan before 9:00," and have two candidate cases "schedule a train from KaohSiung to Chiayi on October 6 with ken," and "planning a flight from Chiayi to NewYork on January 8 about 2 p.m." After scoring process, we have 2 SMVs for two candidate cases SMV1 and SMV2: <-51, 0.27, 0.70, 0.29, 0.25, 0.19, 0.70, 0.55> and <-33, 0.47, 0.75, 0.34, 0.29, 0.22, 0.68, 0.66>. With rescoring SMV1 becomes <0, 0, 0, 0, 0, 0, 1, 0> and SMV2 becomes <1, 1, 1, 1, 1, 1, 0, 1>.

After rescoring, the ranking scores for each SMV are produced. The ranking score is simply the sum of all 1's. Thus, SMV1 receives 1 while SMV2 has 7 as their ranking scores. The SMV with the highest ranking score then is evaluated to check whether it is suitable for the service request. When performing the case testing process for case selection, the system will use the *Action* and *Object* information of the goal model which is stored in the candidate case to check whether the synonyms of the *Action*, *Object*, or *Parameters* fields can be found in the service request. In the previous example, the system finds "arrange a flight" and "planning a flight" could be mapped to the same goal "ScheduleFlight."

If *Action* or *Object* cannot be found in the service request, the system can use the information of *Parameters* to "guess" possible *Action* or *Object*. For example, if a request is like "arrange a seat from Chiayi to New York September 3 with alan before 9:00," the system have no sense about "seat" but the goal "ScheduleFlight" still can be retrieved by using the information of *Parameters*. If the information of *Parameters* is not enough to "guess" and the *Action* and *Object* cannot be found in the service request, the case will fail the testing. If the testing fails, the rescoring process takes place with other cases (without the case that has been evaluated). When all candidate cases fail, the user will be asked to enter detail requirements.

Adaptation knowledge is required for making the retrieved case suitable for solving the given problem. When retrieving a case containing a goal model, whether that goal model representing the current requirements is an exact match or a similar match, the solution part needs to be evaluated. CBSRI assume that similar problems have similar solutions (Wilke, & Bergmann, 1998). In many case, null adaption is used (Watson, 1997), in which the users are responsible for modifying the case for the current usage. For pursuing automatic adaptation, the domain needs to be defined clearly.

In our approach, domain is already defined through the requirements analysis phase. The content of a goal model is filled in as the user requirements and intention become clearer. For adapting the new terms in a service request, we index the concepts in the ontology by the *Contents* of goal model: *Action*, *Object*, *Constraint*, and *Parameters*. We add four relationship features: *Related*, *Required*, *Unordered*, and *Mutual-exclusive* to the concepts in the domain ontology. These features are similar to *Relationships* part of the goal model. We use these features and identification rules as guideline to explain the new term or to interact with the user for getting explanation. For example, the concept "schedule" will be classified as an *Action* and the relationship features store its related *Objects* such as "meeting", "flight", "taxi", and "bus" because the service requests might be "schedule a meeting", "schedule a flight", etc. If the term "schedule" is identified in the service request but the system cannot find the predefined related *Object* "meeting", the system can determine whether the object of the action is "flight", "taxi", or "bus" by using the identification rules stored in the ontology. The features of *Object*, *Constraint*, and *Parameters* are defined in a similar way, but the *Object* field stores its related *Parameters*, the *Constraint* field its related *Actions,* and the *Parameters* field its related *Objects*.

Using this mechanism, the interpretation capability of the system can be extended by learning the new terms. For example, assume that the service request entered by the user is "Plan a meeting on March 3 at 3 p.m." After the case retrieval, there will be a case found. If the retrieved case contains the description part with "Schedule a meeting on January 31 at 9 a.m.", a new case will be learned with the information of "plan" being "schedule" after interacting with the user and confirming that the new service request can be represented by the retrieved case.

Experimental Results on Case Selection

How to separate, parse, and abstract the keywords entered to derive a set of annotated terms is an important step for retrieving related goal models. In general, accurately assigning correct morphological tags to input text is a challenge in Information Retrieval and NLP. One problem with assigning parts of speech is that a given word can be used in many ways like the word, Schedule, which could be a noun or a verb. For getting a suitable parsing approach for intention extraction, we implement three parsing approaches for comparison: an augmented transition networks (ATN) parser, an HMM parser, and a case-based parser. The ATN and HMM parser are adapted from (Mark, 2005).

The original work on ATN was used to address a shortcoming of context free grammars for NLP such as difficulty in dealing with different sentence structures that has similar meanings. An ATN parser is like a finite state machine for recognizing word sequences as specific words or different phrases, etc. In ATN, the grammar has to be expanded to handle many special cases such as handling number agreement between subjects and verbs or determining the "deep structure" of input texts. In this experiment, a set of parsing rule for ATN is designed in Java for parsing.

The basic word set used in parsing process is extracted from Wordnet 2.0. An experimental lexicon shown in Table 1 is also designed and used to expand the basic word set. The expanded lexicon contains some words and related part of speeches of these words. A training service request set is automatically generated by referring this lexicon as the training file for HMM and Case-based Parser.

Three variables are defined for evaluating the performance of different parsing approaches: the number of training service requests $N_{SR\_Training}$, the number of testing service requests $N_{SR\_Testing}$, and the parsing rate. Assume that the number of tokens in a service request string is N_{tokens} and the number

of correctly tagged tokens is N_{tagged_tokens}, the parsing rate $PR = N_{tokens} / N_{tagged\_tokens}$. The program is implemented by Java language and the platform used in this experiment is Windows XP Professional, Intel Core 2 2.0G, 2048M RAM.

First, we evaluate the recall performance of ATN, HMM, and Case Retrieval (CR) approaches. Ten input testing requests are generated by referring the predefined lexicon and without unknown words. The CR retrieves a similar previous service request for tagging the newly entered service request but without learning and reasoning. The evaluation result is shown in Figure 10. It is obvious that PR of HMM is best when using the words in predefined lexicon to generate service request strings. The PR of HMM and CR reached highest point when the number of training requests is increased to 200. The maximum PR of CR is about 0.8, because it only simply uses the synonym words of retrieved sentence to parse the sentence newly entered.

Table 1. Expended words for experimental lexicon

Tags	Related words
Action	schedule, scheduling, plan, planning, arrange, arranging, query, querying, show, showing, display, displaying, select, selecting, change, changing, book, booking, move, moving
Object	meeting, group_meeting, flight, airplane, vehicle, car, bus, taxi, train
Constraint	before, after, about, under, above, behind
Interval	from, to
Articles	A, an, the
Location	AILab, Room443, Room505, L.A., NewYork, Tokyo, Taipei, Chiayi, Tainai, Taichung, Kaohsiung
People	Leon, Alan, Ken, Long, Auther
Month	January, February, March, April, May, June, July, August, September, October, November, December
Time	pm, p.m., am, a.m.
Pronoun	he, she, me, it, you, I
Conjunction	And, or
Preposition	on, at, to, down, with

Next, we evaluate the parsers by inputting requests which contain unknown words. Because different users might use different words for service request, we randomly replace terms in the automatically generated service request to emulate this situation. The expected result of this experiment is that the PR of CBR parser should increase to a degree, because it can accumulate the parsing experience and use old parsing result to parse newly encountered requests.

It should be noted that in this experiment we do not apply any adaptation knowledge for parsing to simplify the problem, because different design of adaptation knowledge will lead to different parsing rate. The experiment results shown in Figure 11 are in accordance with our expectation. The experiment results show that the CBR parser approach has best parsing rate if the user requests contain unknown words for the system. The PR of the trained CBR parser is about 0.73. It means that there are about 30% of terms in a service request that cannot be correctly tagged.

How to increase PR is an important issue in this work. We consider this issue from two directions. First, if a service request contains unknown terms, the system can interact with the user to learn and store the unknown terms for future reuse.

By using adaptation knowledge of the CBR parser and the information stored in the retrieved cases, the PR will increase. Second, a new user enters a service request already stored in the system but the user expects the system to perform different activities. In other words, the request exceeds the scope of the current service. In our opinion, the system can show the user a service list that the system will perform after intention extraction and satisfaction process. If some services in the list cannot satisfy the user request, the system can provide a tool that let the user to edit the list. Because the editing processes are similar to the goal discovery process introduced in the previous section, we can reuse the semi-automatic goal discovery tool for editing the service list.

Application

In this Section, we sum up our approach from two aspects, the iterative use of goal-driven analysis to improve modeling and a prototype system based on this approach along with CBR and planning techniques. For illustration purpose, we adopted a meeting scheduling system described in (Lee & Xue, 1999), and then extended the system by

Figure 10. Evaluation results of ATN, HMM, and case retriever

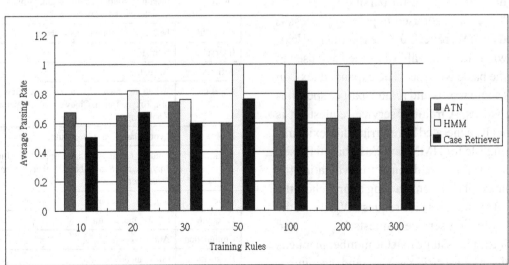

Figure 11. Evaluation results of ATN, HMM, case retriever, and CBR. ($N_{SR\_Training}$ =20)

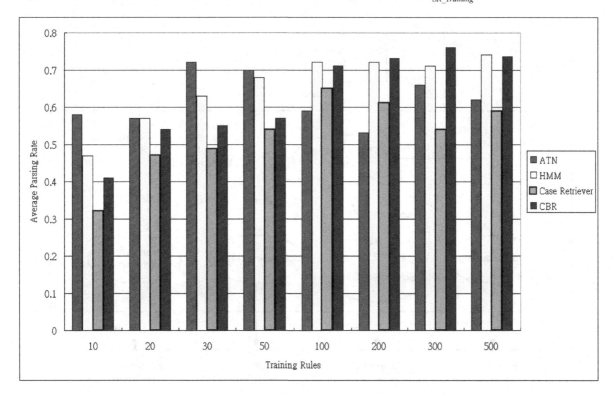

Iterative Goal Model Derivation

adding the flight scheduling system used as an example in this chapter to provide a service-based personal scheduling system. The meeting scheduling system is considered as an internal service; whereas the slight scheduling system is an external service. Therefore, the extended system does not only provide the internal service of planning a meeting, but also can cooperate with external web services providers to schedule a flight for the users. Finally, an intention-aware service-based personal scheduling system is constructed to apply our proposed approach.

Iterative Goal Model Derivation

Deriving goal models is one of the main tasks in an intention-aware service-oriented system. The goal discovery process introduced in previous sections helps us to identify goal models and stored in a structure shown in Figure 4. After the goal-driven requirement analysis process, we need to obtain

more suitable goal models for the composite services we are going to develop. The iterative nature of the analysis combined with goal models in the case base can be effective in deriving more goals that are not clearly specified. To illustrate this concept, consider a service request, "Plan a business trip". Building on the promises that we have a meeting planning system, this service request will be analyzed as a composition with the requirements of scheduling a flight in Figure 5. Thus, Figure 12 shows an extension to Figure 5, two more use cases, "Schedule a vehicle" and "Assert event to schedule" can be derived. For these use cases, we find associated goals like *ScheduleVehicle* and *AssertEvent* respectively. The goal *ScheduleVehicle* and *AssertEvent* will be functional, rigid, and user-specific goals.

As a result, we will have goal models developed for internal and external services. As a sample, Table 2 shows the structure of a goal model for an internal service named *PlanMeeting*, while the

Figure 12. "Plan a business trip" use cases and related goals

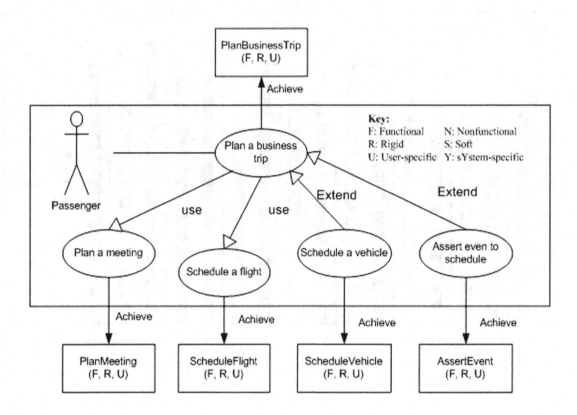

structure of a goal model for an external service named *ScheduleFlight* is shown in Table 3. We have already illustrated the goal model of *ScheduleFlight* with its goal-driven use case in Figure 5. During the service request process, the keywords entered by users and its related terms will be recorded in the *Content* field of Table 2 and Table 3. In Table 2, for example, the *Action* field of the goal *PlanMeeting* is *Plan* and its *Object* field is *Meeting*. The purpose of this special task in our approach is that the personal scheduling system can use the information to serve other requests by matching request strings entered by users with the goal models the system has collected, and then the system can quickly find a suitable goal model for new requests if the system has collected the goal models. Moreover, after analyzing the relationships among goal models, we will build up a more complicate but organized goal

model hierarchy structure for speeding up the mapping process in Case-Based Service Request Interpretation (CBSRI) approach.

Derived System Architecture

To realize the proposed approach, a prototype system for the intention-aware service-oriented system has been built and its architecture is shown in Figure 13. It contains five modules to lead the user in entering a service request, personalize the request, find the related goals, generate plans, and execute plans. The modules are namely, the communication module, the personalization module, the intention extraction module, the intention satisfaction module, and the plan execution module. These modules represent the following three concepts that are directly related to the content of this chapter:

Table 2. A goal model for internal service

Goal: PlanMeeting	
1. Content	
1.1. Action	Plan
1.2. Object	Meeting
1.3. Parameters	Location, Date, Time, Peoples
1.4. Constraint	TimeConstraint
2. Properties	
2.1. View	User-specific
2.2. Competence	Rigid
2.3. Function	Functional
3. Relationships	
3.1. Related	ReplanMeeting, IncreaseAttendance, MakeConvientSchedule, AccommodateImportantMeeting
3.2. Required	none
3.3. Unordered	none
3.4. Mutual-exclusive	none

Table 3. A goal model for external service

Goal: ScheduleFlight	
1. Content	
1.1. Action	Schedule
1.2. Object	Flight
1.3. Parameters	Location, Date, Time, Cabin, Company
1.4. Constraint	TimeConstraint, PriceConstraint
2. Properties	
2.1. View	User-specific
2.2. Competence	Rigid
2.3. Function	Functional
3. Relationships	
3.1. Related	QueryFlight, SelectFlight, BookFlight,
3.2. Required	QueryFlight, SelectFlight, BookFlight,
3.3. Unordered	none
3.4. Mutual-exclusive	ScheduleFlight, BookFlight

1. **Intention extraction.** The intention extraction module and the personalization module realize the work for extracting user intention by constructing goal models. The *Goal structure* is a database which stores goal models and relationships among goal models, the *Goal retriever* uses the case-based intention extraction approach to retrieve related goal models, and the *Goal reasoner* utilizes the information in the retrieved goal models and the goal selection algorithm for selecting and adapting candidate goal models to process the user requests.

2. **Intention satisfaction.** The intention satisfaction module is responsible to generate a plan of actions to meet the goal of the user. The basic technique realize also on CBR, and the *Plan library* contains the old goal-plan hierarchy for previous user intention satisfaction. The structure of goal-plan hierarchy is introduced in (Lee & Liu, 2005a). The *Plan retriever* uses the identified goal model and the description part of the goal-plan pair in the plan library to retrieve candidate plans for satisfying the newly goal model. The *Plan reasoner* uses its plan adaptation knowledge to modify the candidate plan into a new plan that could be used to satisfy the user request.

3. **Plan execution.** The plan execution module is the interface to carry out the sequence of actions detailed in a plan. The *Plan executor* executes plans generated and the *System function library* stores entries of concrete system functions.

The Communication module provides a set of function to communicate with users and the external services providers. The main purpose of our approach is to demonstrate how to produce a suitable plan for user intention satisfaction, the plan executor in our system is designed for testing the protocol of a plan. Thus, the feedback from the *Plan reasoner* is important to our research to know whether the derived plan is suitable.

Figure 13. A general architecture of the intention-aware service-oriented system

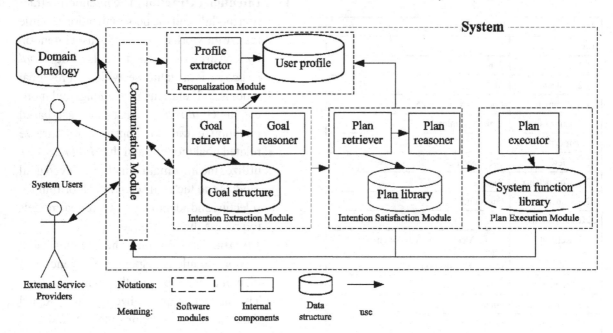

As for the *Plan executor*, it is the interface to the internal and external services. The feedback from it will be evaluated on how these service providers are capable in carrying out the plans. For such evaluation, there are studies done on the topic of service level agreements and quality of services (Comuzzi, & Pernici, 2009). The different approaches proposed to handle the problem of planning and acting in nondeterministic domain are found in (Russel, & Norvig, 2003). When a system designer wants to design and implement a new system, the main tasks are to design and implement the *Goal structure*, *Plan library*, *System function library*, and adaptation knowledge of the *Goal reasoner* and *Plan reasoner*. Most of the other parts of the system can be reused. A more detailed planning mechanism based on this concept is presented in (Lee, Liu, & Huang, 2010). With the goal models captured, more information can be given to the planner. Therefore, the attributes like *Actions*, *Objects*, *Constraints*, and *Parameters* are used in designing a plan. When using external or internal services, unexpected events like time out or execution failure during

the execution of a plan may occur. In order to solve this kind of nondeterministic problems, a monitoring mechanism is added to our planning mechanism, and re-planning is done if necessary.

CONCLUSION

This chapter introduced a goal-driven approach to requirements analysis for capturing the explicit and implicit requirements, nonfunctional requirements, and user intention. The main goal is to process the service request entered by the user to make the request more precise and effective. The approach uses the GDUC analysis method for creating goal models in which different kinds of requirements, user intention, and service-related information are recorded. In order to reuse the goal models, CBR is used for learning and adapting the goal models for future use. A planning mechanism is implemented to bridge goal and service for constructing a plan based on a sequence of services. Thus, a service request can be transformed to a precise and meaningful service request, so that a suitable service whether it is atomic or composite can be found. The main theme of the chapter focuses on the goal model construction and goal usage, but techniques in CBR and planning are also discussed.

REFERENCES

Breazeal, C. (2004). Social interactions in HRI: The robot view. *IEEE Transactions on Systems, Man, and Cybernetics*, 181–186.

Chan, P. P. W., & Lyu, M. R. (2008). Dynamic web service composition: A new approach in building reliable web service. In *Proc. of The IEEE Int. Conf. on Advanced Information Networking and Applications*, (pp. 20-25).

Cohen, W. W., Ravikumar, P., & Fienberg, S. E. (2003). A comparison of string metrics for matching names and records. In *Proc. IIWeb 2003* (IJCAI2003 Workshop), (pp. 73-78).

Comuzzi, M., & Pernici, B. (2009). A framework for QoS-based Web service contracting. *ACM Trans. Web*, *3*(3), 1–52. doi:10.1145/1541822.1541825

Gibbins, N., Harris, S., & Shadbolt, N. (2004). Agent-based Semantic Web services. *Elsevier J. Web Semantics*, *1*(2), 141–154. doi:10.1016/j.websem.2003.11.002

Hwang, S. Y., et al. (2007). On composing a reliable composite Web Service: A study of dynamic Web Service selection. In *Proc. of The IEEE Int. Conf. on Web Services*, (pp. 184-191).

Iba, S., Paredis, C. J. J., & Khosla, P. K. (2003). Intention aware interactive multi-modal robot programming. *Proc. of the IEEE RSJ Conf.* (pp. 3479-3484).

Lee, C. H. L., & Liu, A. (2005). Model the query intention with goals. In *Proc. of The IEEE Int. Workshop on Ubiquitous Smart Worlds,* (pp. 535-540).

Lee, C. H. L., & Liu, A. (2005). *User intention satisfaction for agent-based semantic Web services systems*. In Proc. of 12th Asia-Pacific Software Engineering Conference (APSEC'05), Taipei, Taiwan, Dec, 2005.

Lee, C. H. L., & Liu, A. (2006). Toward intention-aware interface for Web Services request enhancement. In *Proc. of The IEEE Int. Workshop on Ad Hoc and Ubiquitous Computing*, (pp. 52-57).

Lee, C. H. L., & Liu, A. (2010). A goal-driven approach for service request modeling. *International Journal of Intelligent Systems*, *25*(8), 733–756. doi:10.1002/int.20429

Lee, C. H. L., Liu, A., & Huang, K. H. (2010). A using planning and case-based reasoning for service composition. *Journal of Advanced Computational Intelligence and Intelligent Informatics*, *14*(5), 540–548.

Lee, J., & Xue, N. L. (1999). Analyzing user requirements by use cases: A goal-driven approach. *IEEE Software*, *16*(4), 92–101. doi:10.1109/52.776956

Lee, J., Xue, N. L., & Kuo, J. Y. (2001). Structuring requirement specifications with goals. *Information and Software Technology*, *43*, 121–135. doi:10.1016/S0950-5849(00)00144-0

Loucopoulos, P., & Karakostas, V. (1995). *System requirements engineering*. London, UK: McGraw-Hill.

Manning, C. D., & Schutze, H. (1999). *Foundations of statistical natural language processing*. Cambridge, MA: The MIT Press.

Mark, W. (2005). *Practical artificial intelligence programming in Java*. Retrieved from http://www.markwatson.com/opencontent/

Marsic, I., Medl, A., & Flanagan, J. (2000). Natural communication with information systems. *Proceedings of the IEEE*, *88*(8), 1354–1366. doi:10.1109/5.880088

Michelson, M., & Knoblock, C. A. (2005). Semantic annotation of unstructured and ungrammatical text. In *Proc. of IJCAI2005*, (pp. 1091-1098).

Pop, F. C., Cremene, M., Tigli, J. Y., Lavirotte, S., Riveill, M., & Vaida, M. (2010). Natural language based on-demand service composition. *International Journal of Computers, Communications & Control, 5*(5), 871–883.

Rolland, C., Souveyet, C., & Achour, C. B. (1998). Guilding goal modeling using scenarios. *IEEE Tran. On Software Engineering, 24*(2), 1055–1071. doi:10.1109/32.738339

Russel, S., & Norvig, P. (2003). *Artificial intelligence: A modern approach* (2nd ed.). London, UK: Prentice Hall.

Singh, M. P., & Huhns, M. N. (2005). *Service-oriented computing: Semantics, processes, agents*. New York, NY: John Wiley & Sons, Ltd.

Sycara, K. (2004). Dynamic discovery and coordination of agent-based semantic Web services. *IEEE Internet Computing, 8*(3), 66–73. doi:10.1109/MIC.2004.1297276

Wang, H., Huang, J. Z., Qu, Y., & Xie, J. (2004). Web services: Problem and future directions. *Elsevier J. Web Semantics, 1*(3), 309–320. doi:10.1016/j.websem.2004.02.001

Watson, I. (1997). *Applying case-based reasoning: Techniques for enterprise systems*. California: Morgan Kaufmann Publishers.

Wilke, W., & Bergmann, R. (1998). Techniques and knowledge used for adaptation during case-based problem solving. In *Proc. IEA/EIA Conference, Lecture Notes in Computer Science: Vol. 1416*(pp. 497-506).

Wu, L., Liu, L., Li, J., & Li, Z. (2005). Modeling user multiple interests by an improved GCS approach. *Expert Systems with Applications, 29*, 757–767. doi:10.1016/j.eswa.2005.06.003

Section 5
Service Composition

Chapter 7
Bridging the Gap between Business Process Models and Service Composition Specifications

Stephan Buchwald
Daimler AG, Germany

Thomas Bauer
Daimler AG, Germany

Manfred Reichert
University of Ulm, Germany

ABSTRACT

Fundamental goals of any Service Oriented Architecture (SOA) include the flexible support and adaptability of business processes as well as improved business-IT alignment. Existing approaches, however, have failed to fully meet these goals. One of the major reasons for this deficiency is the gap that exists between business process models on the one hand and workflow specifications and implementations (e.g., service composition schemes) on the other hand. In practice, each of these two perspectives has to be regarded separately. In addition, even simple changes to one perspective (e.g. due to new regulations or organizational change) require error-prone, manual re-editing of the other one. Over time, this leads to degeneration and divergence of the respective models and specifications. This aggravates maintenance and makes expensive refactoring inevitable. This chapter presents a flexible approach for aligning business process models with workflow specifications. In order to maintain the complex dependencies that exist between high-level business process models (as used by domain experts) and technical workflow specifications (i.e., service composition schemas), respectively, (as used in IT departments) we introduce an additional model layer – the so-called system model. Furthermore, we explicitly document the mappings between the different levels (e.g., between business process model and system model). This simplifies model adoptions by orders of magnitudes when compared to existing approaches.

DOI: 10.4018/978-1-61350-159-7.ch007

INTRODUCTION

Service Oriented Architecture (SOA) is a much discussed topic in companies (Barry, 2003; Erl, 2005; Erl, 2007; Josuttis, 2007; Mutschler, Reichert, & Bumiller, 2008). SOA was introduced to increase enterprise flexibility. Accordingly SOA is expected to support business requirements more quickly than conventional software technology. In this context, business processes and their IT implementation play a crucial role. In particular, there is a high need for quickly adaptable business process implementations, when considering the fact that process changes often become necessary in companies (Weber, Reichert, & Rinderle-Ma, 2008; Weber et al., 2009; Weber, Sadiq, & Reichert, 2009). We pursue the goal to design a SOA in a way that enables easily adaptable business process implementations when compared to contemporary software architectures.

Additionally, we obtain a traceable documentation of the dependencies that exist between high-level activities (i.e., process steps) of a business process model and the technical elements of its corresponding workflow specification (e.g., human tasks or service calls). Thus automated consistency checking across the different model layers becomes possible as part of the software development process. In particular, the effects late adaptations of a business process model have on its corresponding workflow specification and vice versa can be easily traced by utilizing the known dependencies between business process activities on the one hand and workflow activities on the other hand.

A major advantage of our approach is the straightforward creation of the Business-IT-Mapping Model (BIMM) to avoid an unnecessary definition of complex mapping rules. Instead, we maintain rather simple relationships between business processes and workflow activities. Examples from practical settings illustrate the high effectiveness of this approach with respect to the maintenance of service-oriented applications.

The chapter is structured as follows: We first provide some background information and introduce a basic method for defining service oriented information systems. Then, we describe how business processes can be transformed into a service composition specification. Following that, we discuss how dependencies can be transparently maintained by using an additional Business-IT Mapping Model. Then, we describe the usage of such model and a proof-of-concept prototype. Finally, we discuss related work and conclude with a summary.

BACKGROUND

A business process represents the documentation of business requirements of the desired service oriented information system (Weske, 2006). Business requirements are often identified by interviewing end users and process owners. These persons detail their own business processes graphically by modeling activities and control flow. Therefore, the main demand on a *business process model (short: business process)* is comprehensibility for end users and process owners (Bobrik, 2005). Moreover, their respective business department is normally responsible for modeling the business processes. Even if the operational implementation of this task is carried out by (external) consultants, the business departments still retain responsibility for the results, because only business users command the necessary expertise. During the design phase of business processes, it is primarily the structure of the process flow (control flow), its activities, and authorized users which are documented.

In the following, we first define a general process (Definition 1). Subsequently we define a business process model (Definition 2) as a derivation of a general process.

Definition 1 (Process)

Let P = (N, E, NT, ET, EC) be a Process with

- *N (Nodes) a set of Nodes,*
- *E (Edges) a set of directed Edges where (N, E) defines a coherent directed graph,*
- *NT: N → {Start, End, Activity, ANDSplit, ORSplit, XORSplit, ANDJoin, ORJoin, XORJoin, LoopEntry, LoopExit, DataObj} defines for each node n ∈ N a Node Type NT(n),*
- *ET (Edge Types) describes a set of Edge Types. ET: E → {ControlFlow, DataFlow, Loop} defines for each Edge e ∈ E a Edge Type ET(e),*
- *EC(e) defines for each Edge e with ET(e)∈ {ControlFlow, Loop} a transition condition cond respectively the value true (true means that the transaction condition always applies). For each Edge e with ET(e)∈ {DataFlow} EC(e) is undefined.*

A business process is defined as follows:

Definition 2 (Business Process)

A business process BP = (BN, BE, BNT, BET, BEC) is a Process that corresponds to Definition 1 with

- *Business Nodes BN = {bn$_1$, ..., bn$_m$} (e.g. activity or business service (Stein, 2009; Werth, 2008)),*
- *Business Edges BE = {be$_1$, ..., be$_n$},*
- *Business Node Types BNT, Business Edge Types BET and Business Edge Conditions BEC corresponding to Definition 1*

End users and process owners model business processes to document business requirements. Additionally, business processes are used for process analysis and process optimization. Process owners usually have little or no IT background. Therefore,

they do not describe the contents of a business process in a formal way. Instead, they use simple graphical notations and textual descriptions, such as offered by business process modeling tools (e.g. extended Event-driven Process Chains (eEPC) in ARIS (Scheer, Thomas, & Adam, 2005). Generally, not all aspects are detailed in a business process or shall be modeled at this early stage (e.g. in order to reduce complexity). Therefore, the business process is deliberately vague in some places. This incompleteness concerns the process structure itself (i.e. the control flow) as well as other aspects (e.g. no detailed definition of data structures).

Figure 1 shows an example of a business process (in BPMN2.0[1] notation, see OMG, 2009). It describes a simplified process for product changes in the automotive domain. This process ensures that change requests for components are verified and authorized before they are realized. A change request is created by completing a change request form. Since changes usually affect several parts, additional information on these parts must be gathered. Then, the change request will be detailed and evaluated by the responsible change manager. Depending on this evaluation, a decision is made whether or not the proposed change request will be implemented.

Based on this business process, a new service-oriented information system can be implemented. This software implementation, however, is executed by software engineers. They do not make business-relevant decisions during system implementation, but take over the information and requirements documented in the business process instead. For a platform-specific implementation of a service-oriented additional information beyond the respective business process become necessary: for instance, data objects, implemented services, user interfaces (such as mask design), business rules, and underlying organizational models. We refer to the corresponding technical description of a business process as *executable model process (short: executable process)* or

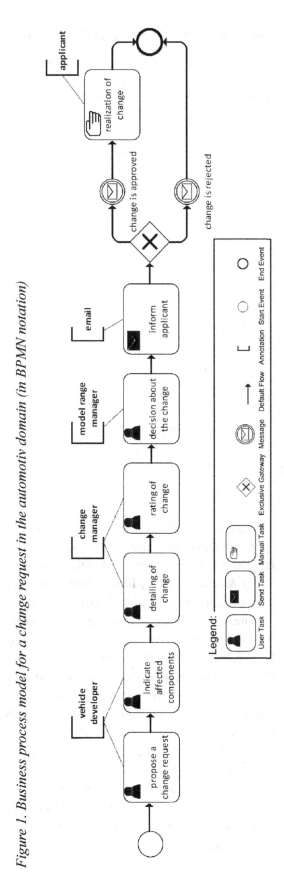

Figure 1. Business process model for a change request in the automotiv domain (in BPMN notation)

service composition schema. The executable process has to be complete and formal to be executable by a workflow engine. Moreover this technical description must meet all demands of the Meta Model used by the engine (e.g. BPEL [OASIS, 2007], BPMN 2.0 [OMG, 2009], ADEPT ADEPT ADEPT [Dadam & Reichert, 2009]). The concrete meta model that has to be used depends on the execution platform chosen. For example IBM WebSphere Process Server (WPS) is using an extension of BPEL in version 6.2, which is strongly oriented at BPMN (IBM, 2008b).

Specialists for designing a service composition schema are usually not present in business departments, but the respective responsibility lies with the IT department. In many companies, the required expertise is not available at all. Consequently, the implementation of the service composition schema is often outsourced to external software vendors. Figure 2 shows a part of the service composition schema of the business process we depict in Figure 1.

Closing the gap between business process management (cf. business process in Figure 1) and IT implementation (cf. service composition schema in Figure 2) is a fundamental challenge to be tackled for a SOA. The use of workflow technology is not sufficient to fulfill the requirements for a flexible SOA. When regarding current practice, the interaction between business and IT departments during the software development process need to be improved in particular. This aspect is usually referred to as business-IT alignment (Chen, 2008): Information systems should meet business requirements and needs more alternatively than present solutions. In addition to a strong process orientation, it becomes necessary that business requirements and business processes are documented comprehensively. Furthermore, loss of information and corruptions in the development process of the service-oriented information system must be avoided. If changes are made to the business requirements (e.g. as documented in Figure 1), they should be transferred

127

Figure 2. Service composition schema designed in WebSphere integration developer (in BPEL notation)

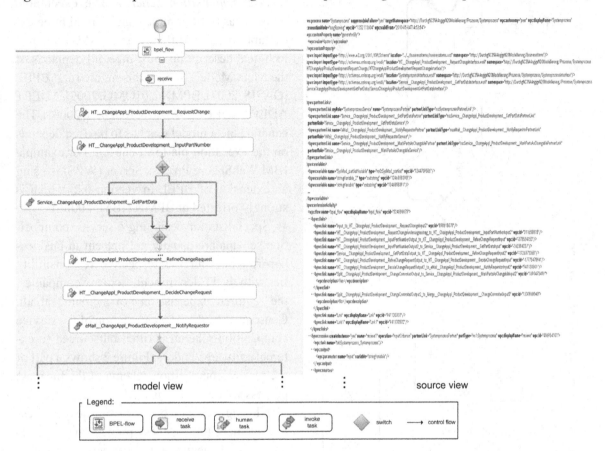

correctly into the implementation of a service-oriented information system (cf. Figure 2). This should be as quickly as possible. On the other hand, changes to the SOA environment may occur, e.g. when services are shut down or services migrate to a new version. A flexible reaction on such scenarios is important in any SOA to keep it viable.

To achieve this, an additional model layer is needed to transforming business requirements and processes (business processes) into a conceptual representation of the IT implementation (service composition schema).

There are several approaches using such intermediate model layer. Examples include MID M3 (Pera, & Rintelmann, 2005), IBM SOMA (Arsanjani et al., 2008; Arsanjani, 2004), IDS Scheer AVE (Yvanov, 2006) and Quasar Enterprise (Engels, & Voss, 2008). In the *Enhanced Process*

Management by Service Orientation (ENPROSO) approach we target of use an intermediate model layer, the so-called "System Model" (Buchwald, Bauer, & Reichert 2010). In the following sections we will detail the ENPROSO approach.

The responsibility for creating a *system model process (short: system process)* is located in the IT department. Changes to the system process should be confirmed by the concerned business department. The representation of the system process has to be understandable to business users. Its contents are the same as in a business process. However, it has to be defined in a complete and formal manner in order to achieve a platform independent IT specification (service composition schema). That means non-formal business process models have to be replaced and detailed in the system process:

Definition 3 (System Process)

A system process SP = (SN, SE, SNT, SET, SEC) is a process that corresponds to Definition 1 with

- *System Nodes SN = {sn$_1$, ..., sn$_k$} (e.g. a technical service call or a human task),*
- *System Edges SE = {se$_1$, ..., se$_l$}*
- *System Node Types SNT, System Edge Types SET and System Edge Conditions SEC corresponding to Definition 1*

In the ENPROSO project, we pursue a three-level modeling method to realize (and implement) process and service-oriented information systems in a SOA (cf. Figure 3). All three model layers include relevant process aspects like data objects, business rules, services, and organization model (Reichert, & Dadam, 2000; Weske, 2007). These will be refined in the different model layers (beginning with the business model). Changes to process aspects have to be confirmed by the business department and must be implemented by the IT department (Rinderle-Ma, & Reichert 2009). Therefore, storage of the dependencies between the different model layers is crucial. Different object types relate to each other: Business processes create different data objects, use business rules, and call services. As the restructuring of the control flow and activities in the business process presents the greatest challenge with respect to model transformations, we focus on this aspect in the following.

CONCEPTS FOR PROCESS TRANSFORMATION

This section describes the basic concept for transferring business processes into system processes. The transformation of a business process into a system process requires the adaptation of this process (i.e. restructuring and detailing of the business process). We introduce the different types of structural changes along our running example from Figure 1. In addition, we identify various approaches to realize the documentation of the relationship between the different layers of modeling (cf. Figure 3). Finally, we describe how a system process can be transferred into a service composition schema

Basic Types of Transformations

As discussed above, it is necessary to store all dependencies between business requirements and the corresponding IT realization. For each activity of the business model (and also the corresponding properties and requirements), the corresponding activity of the system model must be derivable (cf.

Figure 3. Levels of process modeling and other aspects

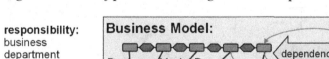

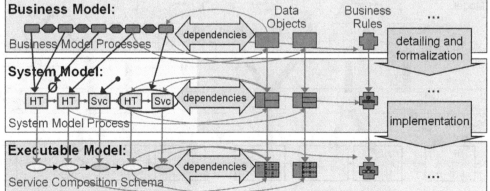

Figure 3). Normally, this is not easy to realize, since an IT department usually follows different goals and guidelines than the business department. An example of a simple transformation is the renaming of the business activity *[propose a change request]* into activity *[HT_ChangeAppl_ProductDevelopment_RequestChange]* of the system process as shown in Figure 4. Such simple change of labels is easy to handle. However, we often need a larger restructuring when transferring business process activities into system process activities. This is caused by the differences in modeling information and level of detail between the business departments and the IT departments. Further, manual activities which shall not be automated at all may be modeled in the business process. Their documentation is nonetheless important for process handbooks or activity accounting. Accordingly, manual activities are not copied one-to-one into the system process, but are rather grouped together or even omitted entirely. As our example, consider the activity *[realization of change]* in Figure 4. IT-based activities of the business process are often described roughly or not at all. Therefore, they have to be refined or added into the system process. Other *business process activities* are split in various IT-based activities of the system process (*system process activities*), for example

user interactions, Service Calls, or transformation of data objects. For instance, the activity *[indicate affected components]* is split into a Human Task (Agrawal et al., 2007a; Agrawal A. et al. 2007b) for user interaction (*HT_..._InputPartNumber*) and a Service Call (*Service_..._GetPartData*).

Taking account of such transformations, our approach enables transparency of relations between business process activities and their IT implementation. Similarly, transparency is supported in the opposite direction, since it is important for the execution of a service oriented information system that activities affected by changes in the environment can be identified in the business process. This allows for quick reactions to upcoming changes, like a service shut down.

In the following we describe different types of transformations that occur frequently in practice.

- **Type 1 (Rename Activities) (Figure 5):** In the simplest case, a business process activity is mapped to exactly one system process activity. For instance, filling out a form can be realized as a Human Task (Agrawal et al., 2007) in a BPEL process. Activities of the executable model are often subject to naming conventions. This results in different names for activities and data objects in the business

Figure 4. Transformation between the business model and the system model

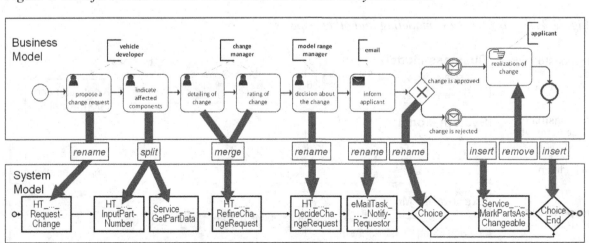

Figure 5. Type 1

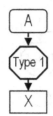

Figure 6. Type 2

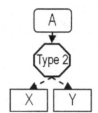

model and the system model. To ensure a comprehensible documentation between the different model layers, we have to manage such adaptations explicitly. For example, the business process activity *[propose a change request]* is realized by the Human Task *[HT_ ChangeAppl_ProductDevelopment_RequestChange]* in the system process (cf. Figure 4).

- **Type 2 (Split Activities) (Figure 6):** Service-oriented workflow engines require a strict distinction between activities with user interaction (Human Tasks) and Service Calls (BPEL invoke). This distinction has not been made in service-oriented workflow engines so far. Classical workflow engines, such as IBM WebSphere MQ Workflow (IBM, 2005), or AristaFlow BPM Suite (Dadam & Reichert, 2009; Reichert & Dadam 2009) consider activities as larger units. These units may interact with users and exchange data with backend systems. Since such units, however, are hardly reusable, they do not meet the basic philosophy of SOA (Erl, 2005; Erl, 2007; Josuttis, 2007; Mutschler, Reichert, Bumiller, 2008). In the example

shown in Figure 4, it is necessary to split activity *[indicate affected components]* into a user interaction (to input of the part numbers) and a service call (to determine the remaining part data from a product data management (PDM) system). There are also cases that require more than one service call. For example, data must be read from different backend systems before they can be displayed in a user form.

- **Type 3 (Merge Activities) (Figure 7):** During the analysis of business processes, logically related tasks are identified to be modeled by means of separate activities. If activities of a continuous sequence are always realized by the same person, it makes sense to merge them into one system process activity. Nevertheless, this activity can be described as a form flow; i.e. a sequence of forms. In our illustrating example, the business process activities *[detailing of change]* and *[rating of change]* are merged to one activity *[HT_..._RefineChangeRequest]* in the system process.

- **Type 4 (Insert Additional Activities into the system process) (Figure 8):** After the decision board has permitted the change and the requestor is informed accordingly, the change may be carried out. In order to actually implement it, the affected components have to be set into state *changeable* in the PDM-System. This is done by a service call *[Service_MarkPartsAsChangeble]*, which is inserted by a specific transformation type

Figure 7. Type 3

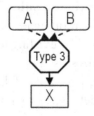

Figure 8. Type 4

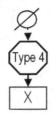

Figure 9. Type 5

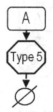

into the system process. Often, additional activities for the logging of relevant events or errors that occurred are necessary as well.

- **Type 5 (Remove Activities from the Business Process) (Figure 9):** A business process often contains activities whose execution should not be controlled and monitored by a workflow management system. In our example, activity *[realization of a change]* will be performed autonomously by an engineer. Consequently this activity shall not be to be implemented in a workflow management system, but is important at the business model level for calculating processing times and simulating process costs. Similar scenarios exist for activities that describe the "welcoming of a customer" or "conducting a sales conversation".

If required, additional types of transformations may be defined, for example, the transformation of *m* activities of the business process into *n* activities of the system process.

Generally, it is by far not trivial to identify the relations between business process activities and corresponding technical system process activities. Therefore, all transformations that were performed between business process activities and system process activities have to be stored explicitly. The way we suggest to realize such functionality is described in the following.

Dependencies between Business Process and System Process

A traceable documentation of dependencies is fundamental for closing the gap between business processes and their corresponding IT implementation. In this section, we examine fundamental approaches for transforming a business process into a system process:

- **Approach 1 (Copying Business Processes):** The business process is copied into the system process before it is restructured. System processes are typically created with another tool than the business process. In such case, a tool change must be carried out (e.g. from a business process modeling tool like ARIS into a CASE tool). This tool change makes it difficult to copy business processes directly into processes of the system model. To realize this, a special import functionality is necessary. Different meta models for business processes and processes of the system model (e.g. eEPCs and UML Activity Diagrams) and the limited import functionality of existing typically tools result in loss of information during the import. Often, it is even more appropriate to model the system process manually from scratch.
- **Approach 2 (Using Sub-Processes):** One possibility for refining process information also supported by existing tools is to introduce sub-processes. As shown in Figure 10a, for example, an activity of the business process can be detailed by a whole sub-process.

The relationship between the activity of the business process and the sub-process in the system model remains visible. For example, this can be realized in ARIS by referencing a sub-process through a so-called "assignment" of the original activity. If a tool change takes place in respect to the modeling of the business process and the system model, it is necessary to import the business process into the system model (cf. Approach 1).

In this variant only the renaming (cf. Basis Types of Transformation, Type 1), splitting (Type 2) and removal (Type 5) of activities can be realized. Merging of activities (Type 3) is not possible since Approach 2 is only applicable to single activities. Likewise, insertion of activities (Type 4) is not possible, since no object exists in the business process that can be refined in the system process. Moreover, the (overall) structure of the business process no longer exists on the system process level. The structure of the system process can only be reconstructed via the business process itself and the corresponding refinement relations. This is very confusing for the process designer and renders the derivation of a service composition scheme cumbersome.

- **Approach 3 (Business-IT-Mapping Model):** We now introduce a new type of model whose instances are called *Business-IT-Mapping Model (BIMM)*. BIMMs describe in which way activities from the business process are transferred into activities of the system process. Likewise, all system process activities can be traced backwards to the business process activities they originated from. With this new model we can define all required types of transformation.

Business processes are often modeled using business modeling tools whereas system processes are realized with CASE tools. The purpose of the BIMM is to document relationships between business processes and system processes. It describes no order (control flow) between the activities of the system process model. Thus, only individual activities have to be exported from the business modeling tool and have to be imported into the system process modeling tool (cf. Figure 10b). This is easy to realize, because there is no meta model change necessary for a process graph.

Approach 3 allows for the documentation of all types of transformation. It is expandable by adding additional types of transformation. All changes made in the business process or in the system model are immediately obvious. The dependencies between activities from the business process and system process activities are bidirectionally traceable. A disadvantage of this approach is the need to define the additional BIMM as well as the effort to define and manage this model by hand. Since all other approaches have serious disadvantages, we opt for Approach 3.

Figure 10. Variants for managing relationships between business process and system process

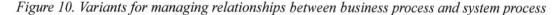

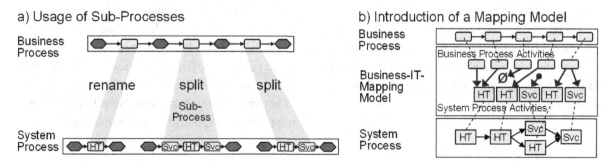

Transformation of the System Process into a Service Composition Schema

As mentioned above, the transformation of the system process into a service composition schema should be as simple as possible, since the executable model is often implemented by external service providers or IT departments, who do not have any knowledge about the corresponding business process.

The transformation between these models should be one-to-one. All aspects modeled in the system process are transferred to the service composition schema. These aspects are formalized and detailed depending on the necessities of the target platform: For example, a system process is documented as a UML Activity Diagram and should be implemented as a BPEL Process. In addition, manual activities are documented as Human Tasks in the system process (Agrawal et al., 2007). Moreover, it is necessary to use suitable BPEL constructs (e.g. While, Parallel-ForEach) to realize the control flow defined in the system process as a BPEL process.

The traceability between these models is straightforward, since every aspect of system process is directly transferred into the service composition schema. Identification of corresponding objects (e.g. activities) between the models is possible via their names. Only for the special case that the system process does not fulfill the naming conventions of the target platform, an additional table to map names is necessary. This table has a simple structure since a system process activity is always assigned to exactly one activity of the service composition schema.

There are no relevant challenges regarding the traceability between the system model and the executable model. Hence, this transformation will not be considered further in the following sections of this chapter.

DESIGN OF THE BUSINESS-IT-MAPPING MODEL

The business process modeling tools (e.g. ARIS or MID Innovator) and notations (e.g. eEPC [Scheer, Thomas, & Adam, 2005], BPMN [OMG, 2009] or UML-Activity Diagrams [OMG, 2004]) are usually selected by the respective business departments. Likewise, the implementation platform or language (e.g. IBM WebSphere Process Server and BPEL [OASIS, 2007]) normally can not be chosen freely by the software developers. On the other hand, the system model must meet certain requirements, like comprehensibility. In principle, an IT department can choose between several modeling languages (e.g. eEPC, BPMN), if there is no company policy for a specific notation or a modeling tool. Notations and tools have some impact on the quality of the BIMM, which will be discussed later.

The BIMM, as shown in Figure 10b, defines a connecting link between business processes and system processes. Currently, this link is not supported by business process modeling or CASE tools. In the following sections we will explain how a BIMM should be designed. This is important to ensure the traceability between a business process and system process. Finally, we show how the example scenario (cf. Figure 1) can be realized by selected notations.

Structure and Internal Consistency

The BIMM is defined during the development of the system process. The IT department has the responsibility for the BIMM as well as the system model. Therefore, the same modeling tools and the same notations should be used for designing of the BIMM and the system process.

In general, the BIMM defines a set of relations which map the activities of the business process to activities of the system process. Each of these relations corresponds to exactly one transformation type. A relation should be always realized by some unique object in the BIMM (and not only by edges). This object describes the type of the transformation and additional attributes like the name of the transformation, its description, or the contact from the business department who approved the transformation. We define a BIMM as follows:

Definition 4 (Business-IT-Mapping Model)

Let BIMM = {$Transf_1$, ..., $Transf_k$} be a Business-IT-Mapping Model for a business process BP = (BN, BE, BNT, BET, BEC) and a system process SP = (SN, SE, SNT, SET, SEC) with

- *the transformation $Transf_i$ = (N1, N2, OpType) with*
  N1 is a set of nodes,
  N2 is a set of nodes and
  OpType ∈ {Map, Split, Merge, Remove, Insert}
- *The following functions are defined:*
  $BNodes(Transf_i)$ provides the nodes N1
  $SNodes(Transf_i)$ provides the nodes N2
  $OpType(Transf_i)$ provides the corresponding Transformation Type OpType

To ensure internal consistency, it is necessary to define the types of transformation correctly:

Definition 5 (Internal Consistency of the Business-IT-Mapping Model)

BIMM = {$Transf_1$, ..., $Transf_n$} is a **consistent Business-IT-Mapping Model** if ∀ $Transf_i$ ∈ BIMM the following conditions are fulfilled:

- ¬∃ *($Transf_i$ and $Transf_j$) with:*
  ∃ n with n ∈ $BNodes(Transf_i)$ and
  ∃ s with s ∈ $SNodes(Transf_i)$
- *if $OpType(Transf_i)$ =**Map**then:*

$|BNodes(Transf_i)| = 1$, i.e. exactly one source node in N1 and
$|SNodes(Transf_i)| = 1$, i.e. exactly one target node in N2

- *if $OpType(Transf_i)$ =**Split**then:*
$|BNodes(Transf_i)| = 1$, i.e. exactly one source node in N1 and
$|SNodes(Transf_i)| > 1$, i.e. actually more than one target node in N2

- *if $OpType(Transf_i)$ =**Merge**then:*
$|BNodes(Transf_i)| > 1$, i.e. actually more than one source node in N1 and
$|SNodes(Transf_i)| = 1$, i.e. exactly one target node in N2

- *if $OpType(Transf_i)$ =**Remove**then:*
$|BNodes(Transf_i)| = 1$, i.e. exactly one source node in N1 and
$|SNodes(Transf_i)| = 0$, i.e. no target node in N2*

- *if $OpType(Transf_i)$ =**Insert**then*
$|BNodes(Transf_i)| = 0$, i.e. no source node in N1 and*
$|SNodes(Transf_i)| = 1$, i.e. exactly one target node in N2

Figure 11 shows our ENPROSO modeling approach including the previously established BIMM to document relationships between the business process and the system processes.

Current modeling tools do not support the concept of our BIMM. Therefore, we have to use and adapt an existing model type in order to realize the BIMM (e.g. as an eEPC, BPMN model or UML Activity Diagram). This model type must store business process activities, system process activities, and also dependencies between them. Depending on the notation and the tool, a special model type can be derived for BIMM. To realize the transformation between business process activities and system process activities, special types for nodes as well as edges are used.

Figure 12 shows a BIMM which correspond to the example introduced above (cf. Figure 4). This BIMM is designed in a "neutral" notation.

Figure 11. Business-IT-mapping model to document relationships

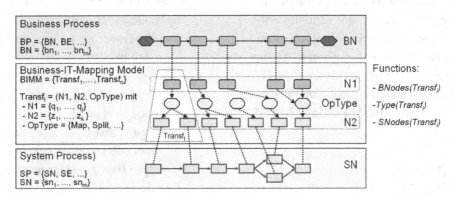

Transformation types are visualized by octagons to differentiate them from business process activities and system process activities. Transformation edges between activities and transformation types are shown with dashed directed edges.

Overcoming the Limitations of Existing Tools

A BIMM includes business process activities, system process activities and also relations between them. The meta model that is appropriate to realize a BIMM depends on the notations and the tools used for these two models. To document the dependencies between business process activities and system process activities in the BIMM, it is necessary to realize references to activities in both models. This can be achieved easily if both models are specified in the same tool. Frequently,

however, the BIMM is created with different tool than the business process. The gap between tools must thus be managed in referencing. For this purpose, there are basically the following options:

- **Option 1 (Exporting Activities):** The activities of the business process are exported by using a standardized interface (e.g. as XML file) and imported into the system process. Copies of activities from the business process are now available in the system process. They contain an identifier (ID) referencing the activity in the business process. Thus, an unambiguous identification of corresponding activities in the business process is possible. In addition, descriptive data on activities from the business process should be imported into the system process, e.g.

Figure 12. Business-IT-mapping model for the example scenario presented in Figure 1

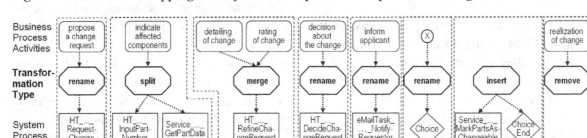

the name of the responsible person in the business department.

If there is no export and import functionality no appropriate exchange format between different tools, it is sufficient to read the ActivityID in the business process and store it in the system process activity manually.

- **Option 2 (Using a Repository):** Another option is the usage of a repository (Buchwald, Bauer, & Pryss, 2009). In this case, there is no need for bilateral interfaces between different tools, since Business Activities are stored directly in the repository. During the design of a system process stored business process activities can be imported. Subsequently, the IDs of the business process activities are explicitly managed by the repository (Buchwald, Tiedeken, Bauer, & Reichert, 2010).

The SOA repository can even play an additional role if it stores the whole Business-IT-Mapping Model. To achieve this, every object and relation between business processes and system processes must be stored and managed by the repository. It can thus be traced which system process activity relates to which business process activity. Furthermore, long-term storage of the BIMM and the corresponding dependencies (even if the modeling tools become unavailable) can be realized. Because of the tool-independent interface of a SOA repository, it can be used by different partners and various tools. This is important if there are tool changes in a later phase of the development process.

Tool Support for Generating the Business-IT-Mapping Model

The BIMM can be created and managed manually. However, a support tool would be helpful. Special tool functionality is required to generate the BIMM

(semi-) automatically. Figure 13 shows how to generate such a model: For instance, the business process activity *indicate affected components* (cf. Figure 4) is chosen for detailing (*1* in Figure 13). The tool should offer functionality to select the business process activity (*2*: source activity) and the desired transformation type (*2*: Type 2 split). Additionally, the number and the corresponding names for the system process activities (*2*: target activities) have to be defined. With this information, the corresponding BIMM fragment (*3a*) can be created automatically. Furthermore, the new system process activities are created in the system process (*3b*). They constitute the basis for the process definition (by drawing edges, etc.).

USAGE OF THE BUSINESS-IT-MAPPING MODEL

The BIMM enable traceability of performed transformations between business processes and system processes. Furthermore a fast mapping (and implementation) of altered business requirements to activities of the executable model (service composition schema) are provided. Likewise when changes in the environment of the executable model like the shut down of a service (cf. Figure 4, *Service_GetPartData*) occurs, the corresponding business activities can be identified easily (cf. Figure 4, *indicate affected components*). Thus, responsible business managers can be informed quickly in order to authorize such changes. Finally, BIMM information can be used at runtime to monitor activities (Business Activity Monitoring, BAM [Amnajmongkol et al., 2008]). This is useful, for example, to check whether the defined business requirements are met (e.g. processing time of a task).

In this section, we describe how to deal with changes to the business process or the service composition specification. As discussed above, it is important to ensure the consistency between the different model layers (cf. Figure 3).

Figure 13. Tool functionality, the example of the transformation type 2 (split)

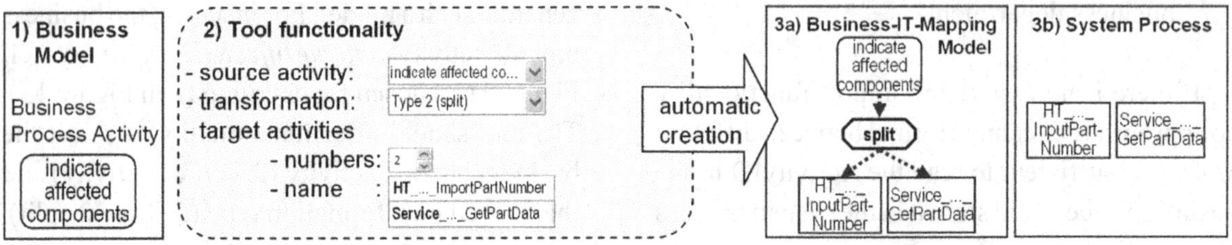

Ensuring Consistency between Model Layers

One advantage of the BIMM is that it allows to ensure consistency between the different model layers. Thus, errors in implementation can be avoided. In addition, changes at the business model level or at the executable model level can be identified via a consistency analysis. Below, we describe requirements concerning the consistency between the different model layers:

- **Consistency Requirement 1:** Changes are usually initiated by the business department. These business changes must be propagated into the other models (cf. Figure 14). Our BIMM approach offers the basis for automated analysis of consistency. For this purpose, after changing a business process all business process activities have to be imported into the BIMM (cf. Step 1 in Figure 14). The consistency analysis then compares the set of imported activities in the BIMM with the existing ones (Step 2). If source activities in the BIMM do no longer exist, they have been deleted from the business process (Step 2a). This information is communicated, for instance, in the form of a report to the business process modeler (Step 3). Therefore, a software developer adapts the BIMM and the system process appropriately by removing these activities. For this case we have defined an inconsistency rule (R1 in Definition 6-1).

This rule identifies the deletion of business process activities.

If business process activities are added to the business process, the consistency analysis will recognize identifies that source activities are missing in the BIMM (Step 2b). Then, if the activity has technical relevance the modeler has to update the BIMM and the system model suitably. For this case, we have defined another inconsistency rule (R2 in Definition 6-1).

Definition 6-1 (Structural Inconsistency)

Let $BP = (BN, BE, BNT, BET, BEC)$ be a business process, $SP = (SN, SE, SNT, SET, SEC)$ a system process and $BIMM = \{Transf_1, ..., Transf_n\}$ a Business-IT-Mapping Model. Then, there exists an inconsistency if one of the following rules is fulfilled:

- *Inconsistency Rule R1:* $\exists\ Transf_i \in BIMM$, $\exists\ bn \in BNodes(Transf_i)$ with: $bn \notin BN$
- *Inconsistency Rule R2:* $\exists\ bn \in BN$ and $\neg\exists\ Transf_i \in BIMM$ with $bn \in BNodes(Transf_i)$

- **Consistency Requirement 2:** If accessible timestamps for business process activity objects are supported by the business process modeling tool (e.g. the attribute "last modified" that is maintained by ARIS), changes on individual business process activities can be identified. The consistency analysis not only compares the updated with the existing set of business process activities, but also the time stamps of individual business process activity objects. For this purpose, the timestamp of the business process activity is exported. This timestamp is then saved in the corresponding object of the BIMM. After re-importing the business process activities into the BIMM, activities with modified timestamps can easily be detected (cf. Step 2c in Figure 14). If Inconsistency Rule R3 is applies, a business process activity of the business process has been changed (R3 in Definition 6-2).

Of course, there are changes which can be ignored by modelers of the system process because they are irrelevant to the IT implementation (e.g. changes in costs for execution of activities that are relevant only for a process simulation and analysis). An analysis of changes provides a superset of the actually necessary adaptations. Nevertheless, it is crucial to ensure that no changes remain undetected.

Definition 6-2 (Structural Inconsistency – Continuation Part 1)

- *Inconsistency Rule R3: $\exists\ bn\ \in\ BN$ with related $bn'\ \in\ BNodes(Transf_i)$ and Timestamp(bn) > Timestamp(bn')*

- **Consistency Requirement 3:** Not all changes are initiated by the business department (cf. Business Changes in Figure 14) in practice. Often, it is necessary to implement changes directly in the system process (or even in the service composition schema of the executable model) without adaption of the business process. For instance, this may be the once when quick reactions to changes in IT operations, like the sudden suspension of a service, become necessary. We call such

changes environment changes. They can be identified by consistency analysis based on the BIMM as well: If an activity is removed from the system process, the consistency analysis detects that the corresponding activity still exists in the BIMM (R4 in Definition 6-3). Together with the business department, a decision is made whether only the BIMM should be modified (so that the inconsistency is resolved), or if the proposed change also affects the business process.

Additionally, our consistency analysis detects the absence of newly added system process activities in the BIMM (R5 in Definition 6-3). A frequently occurring case is that already existing system process activities are changed, e.g. a new service version is called or a staff assignment rule was modified (Erl et al., 2009). Such changes can be identified by comparing the timestamps (analogous to consistency requirement 2): If Inconsistency Rule R6 (Definition 6-3) is fulfilled, an activity of the system process has been changed. Subsequently, the timestamp of the corresponding activity in the BIMM is updated. The change should also be propagated to the business process, if it is relevant from the business perspective.

Definition 6-3 (Structual Inconsistency –Continuation Part 2)

- *Inconsistency Rule R4: $\exists\ Transf_i \in BIMM$, $\exists\ sn \in SNodes(Transf_i)$ with: $sn \notin SN$*
- *Inconsistency Rule R5: $\exists\ sn \in SN$ and $\neg\exists\ Transf_i \in MM$ with $sn \in SNodes(Transf_i)$*
- *Inconsistency Rule R6: $\exists\ sn \in SN$ with related $sn' \in SNodes(Transf_i)$ and Timestamp(sn) > Timestamp(sn')*
  If R1 ... R6 is not fulfilled, BIMM is consistent to BP and SP.

To quickly identify changes, modelers have to be informed actively. Therefore, a visualization of information about changes directly in the system process is useful (cf. Step 3 in Figure 14): A task list integrated in the corresponding modeling tool can help to visualize all changes to be implemented. Subsequently, the modeler marks changes in the task list which he has already considered (cf. Step 4). Alternatively or additionally affected system process activities can be highlighted until the modeler has confirmed the elimination of the inconsistency. Both variants prevent changes from avoiding notice. For the realization of these variants, it is a prerequisite that the modeling tool offers a (expandable) functionality for task list management and for marking activities.

Application Scenarios and Enhancements

A further usage of the BIMM is possible if its information set is expanded. In the following we describe two potential enhancements for the BIMM:

- **Enhancement 1:** The control flow (sequence, loops, etc.) between business process activities could be included into the BIMM in order to detect changes automatically after a re-import (for instance, switched order of activities). As mentioned above, the transfer of business processes into another modeling language is difficult. Changes in the control flow can easily be detected by comparing the two model versions of the business process (which is supported by conventional modeling tools directly). Therefore, we do not suggest storing the control flow in the BIMM. The resulting efforts should be avoided.

- **Enhancement 2:** Similarly, we can use information about the control flow of the system process stored in the BIMM: If we know in which order system process activities are executed (for example, after a split transformation in the BIMM), it is possible to generate parts of the system process automatically. Together with the information about the control flow of the changed business process, the whole system process can be generated anew. This means that the previous version of the system process will be discarded. However, an automatic generation of the entire system process is hardly realizable in practice. Due to the vague and informal description of the business processes, it is extremely difficult to formally specify the resulting (complex) transformation rules. For instance, cases

Figure 14. Consistency analysis for business changes

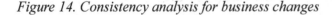
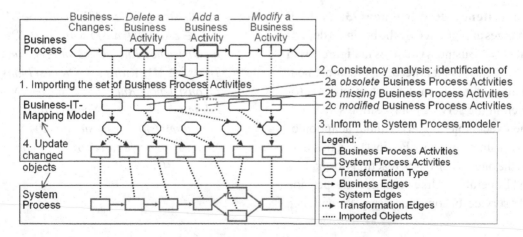

exist in which business process activities are modeled sequentially in the business process and should be ordered in parallel in the system process (e.g. to reduce the execution time). Likewise, a split of a business process activity does not always result in system process activities that follow each other directly. This can not be described by a flow-control fragment in the BIMM.

Therefore, we pursue a fundamentally different way then the one described in Enhancements 1 and 2: The last existing (and extensively documented) version of the system process is remains in place (i.e. it is not discarded). Required changes (for example initiated by new business requirements) are propagated subsequently into this system process. In our opinion, this approach results not only in a better quality of system processes (now created manually), but also in less maintenance effort of the various models: The BIMM has to store only the dependencies between business process activities and system process activities. Therefore, it is not necessary to maintain complex control flow fragments or to define rules how to apply them.

PROOF-OF-CONCEPT IMPLEMENTATION

In the following section, we describe how to realize a BIMM by using the Business Process Modeling Notation (short: BPMN). To this end, we use the application example from the Background section. We discuss the difficulties that occur during modeling. In addition, we demonstrate how our approach can be implemented with today's process modeling and process execution tools. We first use the IBM WebSphere Business Modeler 6.2 (WBM) (IBM, 2008a) tool. This tool focuses more on the specification and execution of service compositions (compared with tools for the

pure business process modeling like ARIS). In addition, it enforces the compliance with certain guidelines. For comparison, we present also an implementation in ARIS which uses BPMN notation for realizing the BIMM.

IBM WebSphere Business Modeler

A BIMM[2] can be created by IBM WebSphere Business Modeler (cf. Figure 15). The BPMN swimlane representation separates the objects (activities) from the business process and the system process, and also the transformation nodes between them. An object type categorization enables additionally marking by colors. In addition, the names of the transformation nodes are chosen in a way that the type of transformation is easily recognizable. The uniqueness of these nodes is achieved by sequential numbering. For a more detailed description, special names can be chosen for the basic transformations (e.g. "Insert: Service for changing the state in the Product Data Management System").

The creation of the BIMM with the WBM tool is more difficult because some functionality is missing. For instance, there is no comfortable possibility for copying business process activities into the BIMM and subsequently making a reference to the same Object Instance in the business process (cf. ARIS Assignments).

Further difficulties arise because of the technical focus of WBM: Since the process models have semantics for execution, it is necessary to define input and output data (known as ports) for all activities, as well as the data flow. Thus, we also have to define a data flow for the edges of the transformation nodes although it does not really exist. If we do not define all input and output data of objects in our BIMM, we get some error messages. The associated data flow objects can be chosen arbitrary. In these objects can be hidden by a special view (modeling mode) in WBM. If we use the modeling mode "basic", error mes-

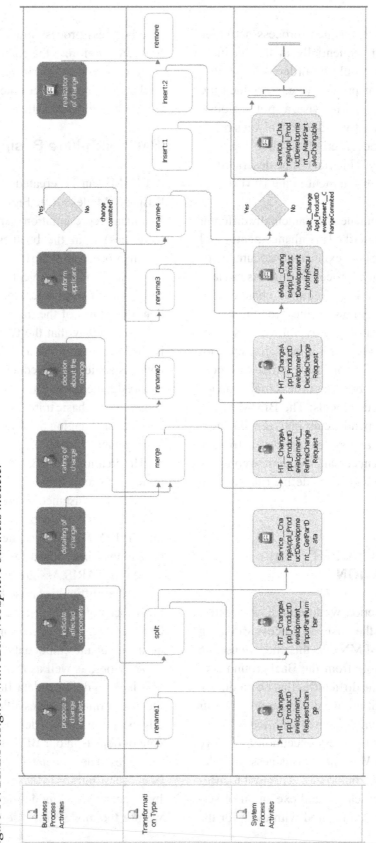

Figure 15. BIMM designed with IBM WebSphere business modeler

sages and warnings for undefined data objects are hidden. One should be aware, however, that these errors exist, even if they are not relevant because no deployment of the BIMM is planned.

ARIS Business Architect

As shown in Figure 16 it is also possible to design a BIMM by using the ARIS Business Architect 7.1. Again the model is realized in BPMN notation. The BIMM includes business process activities of a corresponding business process (cf. Figure 20) defined as an extended Event Driven Process Chain (short: eEPC) and system process activities of a corresponding system process (cf. Figure 21). The different model layers are structured by using BPMN swimlanes.

The clarity of the presentation results from using derivations of existing object types. These so-called Sub-Types can have their own styles of visualization (their own symbols). This functionality is also used to define special symbols to visualize transformation nodes in the BIMM (like in Figure 12). In addition, a special configuration of the ARIS Business Architect allows us to visualize specific attributes for each object. This allows for displaying an unambiguous name for structural nodes (e.g. for branching). It is not possible to define a special transformation edge between business process activities and transformation nodes (or between transformation nodes and system process activities) in the BIMM (cf. Figure 16). To this end, we use the edge type "is predecessor of".

Referencing business process and system process activities in the BIMM is easy to realize in ARIS: The ARIS object approach demands that each object (e.g. an activity) modeled in a diagram has exactly one corresponding object stored in the ARIS database. This allows for the copying of activities from business processes and system processes and the subsequent storing of these activities in the BIMM as so-called "assignment copies". Changes applied to objects (e.g. activities

in the business process or in the system process) affect all assignment copies, because they reference the same ARIS database object. This keeps the names of activities and other attributes up to date in the BIMM if changes occur in business processes or in system processes.

Another advantage of using ARIS is that edges between objects do not describe the data flow explicitly. Thus, the problem of WBM transformation edges will not occur because transformation edges need not be connected to specific output parameters of a business process activity in the BIMM. Similarly, it is not defined whether activities (from the BIMM) have additional output parameters or attributes, because these are exclusively specified in the corresponding business process or system process. The modeling of a BIMM with ARIS is easier than using WBM, since ARIS is less formal and has no execution semantics. The reason for this is that the tool is not intended to be used to specify the IT-view of an information system, but to design business processes.

However, this is also a disadvantage for the usage of ARIS, because the ARIS Business Architect is not a tool for users of IT departments and not commonly used for the creation of system processes. It is not expected that an IT architect will implement his (UML-) classes or data objects in ARIS in order to develop the IT specification.

Conclusion

We have examined two different modeling tools. Both tools have shown that a BIMM can be realized as a BPMN diagram in principle. The result was clear and buildable with little effort: The creation of a single transformation node with the corresponding edges and the usage of existing business process activities and system process activities is possible in a few seconds up to minutes. Therefore, both tools are suitable for the creation of a BIMM.

Although BPMN diagrams can be used for designing BIMMs, they actually describe only a

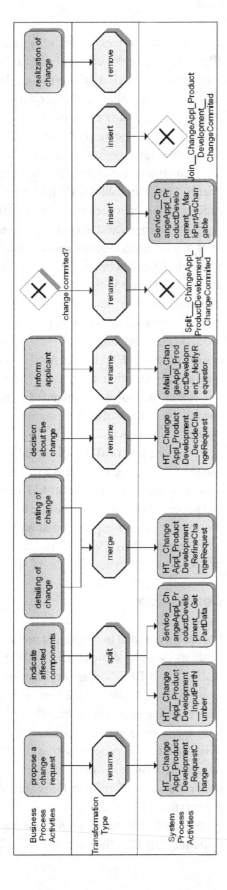

Figure 16. Business-IT-mapping model desiged by using ARIS Business Architect 7.1 (BPMN-Notation)

temporary solution. BPMN diagrams should be used only until process modeling tools implement their own type of BIMM.

RELATED WORK AND DISCUSSION

In the literature, we can find a number of approaches addressing issues related to modeled business processes and their transformation into executable models. First, we consider approaches which realize transformations between different meta-models. Subsequently, we discuss approaches such as MDA (Model-Driven Architecture) and MDSD (Model-Driven Software Development), and also the modeling methods of various manufacturers.

- **Model layer transformation:** Existing literature discusses two fundamentally different types of (meta-) model transformations: first, the direct transformation of business processes (e.g. eEPC or BPMN) into executable models (e.g. BPEL or BPMN), and second, the transformation including an additional model layer (e.g. eEPC or BPMN).

In the first case, the business process is usually limited by restrictions (e.g. non-cyclic models). Ziemann, & Mendling (2007) use the XML-based exchange format EPML (Mendling, & Nüttgens (2006)) for eEPC models to transform these into BPEL. Because of limitations in the eEPC model a direct transformation into a BPEL model can be realized. This approach has to be re-applied if changes are made at the business process layer, e.g. inserting a new business process activity. Thus, changes that have already been implemented in the BPEL model will be lost. Nevertheless, this approach provides a basic mechanism for transforming acyclic eEPC models into BPEL models.

- **There are other similar approaches:** van der Aalst, & Lassen (2005) describe how a workflow net can be transformed into a BPEL model and Gardner (2003) discusses automatic mapping of UML models into BPEL models. Basic transformations of BPMN to BPEL are described in the BPMN standard (OMG, 2009), White (2005), and Ouyang et al. (2006). The latter approach details the transformation of a non-restricted BPMN model into a BPEL model. Additionally, this approach describes an algorithm that transforms BPMN models into BPEL models automatically. First, the algorithm scans the BPMN model for certain patterns. Subsequently, it replaces them by custom-defined components that allow a direct mapping into BPEL.

In the second class of approaches, an intermediate model between the business process layer (e.g eEPC) and the executable model layer (e.g. BPEL) is introduced: Thomas, Leyking, & Dreifus (2008) describe the transformation of an eEPC model into a BPEL model and uses an additional BPMN model as intermediate layer. The idea is, analogous to our approach, to improve Business-IT alignment. However, it is not a goal to make the relationship between activities of the different layers transparent. The starting point for the transformation is the flow logic of the business process (eEPC). Previously defined mapping constructs transform the business process activities into an intermediate model (BPMN). This BPMN model is subsequently enriched by technical details (particularly for the process execution) and is transformed into a BPEL model.

Other approaches, such as Weidlich, Weske, and Mendling (2009) compare various models for similarities. If changes are made on a model, they can be assigned to similar models. Approaches concerning requirements engineering deal with the bidirectional propagation of changes on requirements and related UML models (Rupp, 2007).

- **Model driven approaches:** Several related works are based on standardized approaches such as MDA and MDSD.

Allweyer (2007) describes an approach that is independent form the modeling notation, which transforms (coarse granular) business processes into executable processes. To realize such a transformation, different patterns will be defined in the business model (eEPC). These patterns specify the technical detailing of objects (e.g. business objects from the business process) and describe how these objects may be transferred into the executable model (BPMN). Subsequently, transformation rules implement such transformations.

Bauler et al. (2008) describes how to define business patterns and technical patterns and how to apply them on various business processes. Thereto, business patterns are applied on coarse granular BPMN models. The resulting model is called "extended BPMN model". Based on this model an automatically transformation generates an executable model (so-called pseudo-BPEL). It is transferred in a further step into an executable model (BPEL) by using additional technical patterns.

The OrVia project (Stein et al, 2008) uses a similar approach: it describes a method for an automatic and tool-assisted transformation of eEPC models into executable BPEL models. Predefined patterns are used here as well. eEPC models will be transformed into BPEL models by the usage of such patterns.

Model driven approaches generate their executable models by using patterns. However, such approaches for the generation of executable models are not always realizable. This also applies to our scenario where *free* modeling of the system process is required: Therefore, for business processes (mostly described coarsely granular and vaguely), a structural adaptation at the system process layer is necessary. To realize such an adaption using automatically applicable patterns would be too complex and costly, because extensive transformations between objects from the business process (e.g. activities) and objects from the system process have to be defined. Additionally, transformations like inserting new activities in the system process are hard to realize, since there exist no corresponding activity in the business process to which a pattern can be applied. In our scenarios, business processes are different, so that a reuse of predefined patterns in various business processes is not realistic. In addition, the "technical problem" with pattern definition that was mentioned at Enhancement 2 occurs with these approaches. Therefore, for each business process, it must be decided individually how a corresponding technical representation can be realized in the system process.

In addition to these model-driven approaches, there are service-oriented approaches which support a model-driven development of information systems (De Castro, Marcos, & Wieringa, 2009). Furthermore, there are approaches describing how to transform models into another notation. Ouyang et al (2009) present a technique that allows transforming BPMN models into readable (block-structured) BPEL models. Such a transformation is defined unidirectional. As a result, inconsistencies occur if changes are made in the BPEL model.

Methods of software manufacturers: Software manufacturers usually recommend a different approach. Similar to our proposal, they introduce an additional model layer between the business model layer and the executable model layer.

The modeling methodology M3 of the company MID is based on a MDA approach. This methodology is subdivided into three variants (Pera, & Rintelmann, 2005). When compared to our approach some similarities are interesting to note for the variant "M3 for SOA". This method provides extensions for Innovator (MID, 2008) for each model type in the form of UML "stereo-

type". The modeling takes place at three levels. The first level describes the business model, in which business processes are defined freely and without modeling restrictions. Subsequently, use cases are derived from the business process description. The latter describe the requirements for the information system to be developed. Based on these use cases and additional information from the business processes, a platform-independent "analysis model" is generated. This second layer is comparable to our system model layer. It describes, for example, classes and data models, and also process descriptions that are required to implement the business processes. At the third model level a platform-specific model is described which specifies the target platform and language. This platform-specific model is supplemented by technical information.

Other manufacturers like IBM (Arsanjani et al, 2008; Arsanjani, 2004), IDS Scheer (Klückmann, 2007), Enterprise SOA (Woods, Mattern, 2006), Model-Driven Integration of Process driven SOA Models (Zdun, Dustdar, 2007; Tran, Zudan, & Dustdar, 2008) or Quasar Enterprise (Engels, & Voss, 2008) describe similar methods in order to transfer business processes into an IT implementation. They also use different model layers to realize the mapping between business processes and their IT implementation. However, none of these methods document the dependencies between business process activities of various levels in a traceable and understandable way.

Conclusion

In our project ENPROSO, we use these approaches as a basis in order to realize fundamental transformations between different modeling languages. At some approaches, the necessity of an intermediate model (system model) is identified and partially implemented. A BIMM that ensures traceability between a business process and a system process has not been discussed in any previously existing approach.

CONCLUSION

Business processes (created by business departments) must be adapted structurally before they can be implemented within a workflow management system. This chapter describes an approach which allows for a quick and transparent transfer of business requirements into information systems (cf. Figure 16). To achieve this, we introduced a new model layer (system model) between the business model and executable model. This model is in the responsibility of the IT department and serves as specification for the IT implementation. An additional Business-IT-Mapping Model (that is part of the system model) enables the transparent documentation of the transformations that were applied to the business processes in order to define the system process and the executable process (service composition schema). This traceability is used to create or adapt an IT implementation more quickly. It also ensures the consistency between the model layers. The approach for the realization

Figure 17. ENPROSO three-level modeling method

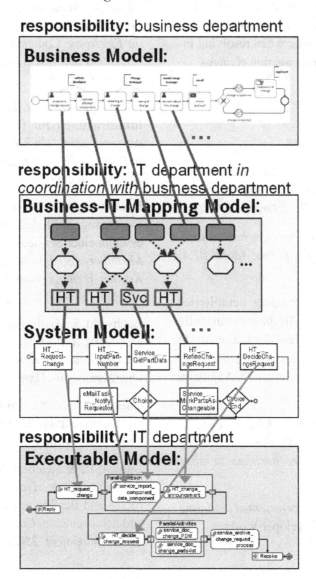

of a Business-IT-Mapping Model is described in detail and realized prototypically.

We have shown how flexibility can be increased in the development of service- and process-oriented information systems. Our approach ENPROSO (Figure 17) enables the realization of business requirements by an IT implementation with a higher quality and more quickly by:

- ensuring bidirectional traceability between business activities and system activities
- enabling localization of changes in the corresponding model
- enabling automatic identification of inconsistencies between different models
- supporting the modeler when resolving inconsistencies and propagating changes

REFERENCES

Agrawal, A. (2007a). *WS-BPEL extension for people specification. Technical Report, Active Endpoints, Adobe, BEA, IBM, Oracle*. SAP AG.

Agrawal, A. (2007b). *Web services human task. Technical Report, Active Endpoints, Adobe, BEA, IBM, Oracle*. SAP AG.

Allweyer, T. (2007). Erzeugung detaillierter und ausführbarer Geschäftsprozessmodelle durch Modell-zu-Modell-Transformationen. *In 6. Workshop Geschäftsprozessmanagement mit Ereignisgesteuerten Prozessketten,* St. Augustin, Germany (pp. 23-38).

Amnajmongkol, J., Angani, Y., Che, Y., Fox, T., Lim, A., & Keen, M. (2008). *Business activity monitoring with Websphere business monitor V6.1*. IBM Redbooks.

Arsanjani, A. (2004). *Service-oriented modeling and architecture*. IBM Developer Works.

Arsanjani, A., Ghosh, S., Allam, A., Abdollah, T., Ganapathy, S., & Holley, K. (2008). SOMA - A method for developing service-oriented solutions. *IBM Systems Journal, 47*.

Barry, D. K. (2003). *Web services and service-oriented architectures*. Morgan Kaufmann.

Bauler, P., et al. (2008). Usage of model driven engineering in the context of business process management. In *Proc. 4th GI Workshop XML Integration and Transformation for Business Process Management,* (pp. 1963-1974).

Bobrik, R., Bauer, T., & Reichert, M. (2006). Proviado – Personalized and configurable visualizations of business processes. In *Proc. 7th Int'l Conf. on Electronic Commerce and Web Technologies (EC-WEB'06), LNCS 4082,* (pp. 61-71). Krakow, Poland: Springer.

Buchwald, S., Bauer, T., & Pryss, R. (2009). IT-Infrastrukturen für flexible, service-orientierte Anwendungen - ein Rahmenwerk zur Bewertung. In *Proc. 13. GI-Fachtagung Datenbanksysteme in Business, Technologie und Web,* (pp. 524–543).

Buchwald, S., Bauer, T., & Reichert, M. (2010). Durchgängige Modellierung von Geschäftsprozessen in einer Service-orientierten Architektur. In *Modellierung'10, March 2010, Klagenfurt, Austria. Koellen-Verlag, Lecture Notes in Informatics (LNI) 161,* (pp. 203-211).

Buchwald, S., Tiedeken, J., Bauer, T., & Reichert, M. (2010). *Anforderungen an ein Metamodell für SOA-Repositories, Zentral-europäischer Workshop über Services und ihre Komposition*.

Chen, H.-M. (2008). Towards service engineering, service orientation and business-IT alignment. In *Proc. 41st Hawaii Int. Conf. on System Sciences*.

Dadam, P., & Reichert, M. (2009). The ADEPT Project: A decade of research and development for robust and flexible process support - Challenges and achievements. *Computer Science - Research and Development, 23*(2), 81-97. ISSN 1865-2034

De Castro, V., Marcos, E., & Wieringa, R. (2009). Towards a service-oriented MDA-based approach to the alignment of business processes with IT systems: From the business model to a Web Service composition model. *International Journal of Cooperative Information Systems, 18*(2), 25–260. doi:10.1142/S0218843009002038

Erl, T. (2005). *Service-oriented architecture: Concepts, technology, and design*. Prentice Hall.

Erl, T. (2007). *Service-oriented architecture: Principles of service design*. Prentice Hall.

Erl, T., Karmarkar, A., Walmsley, P., Haas, H., Yalcinalp, U., Liu, C. K., et al. Pasley, J. (2009). *Web service contract design and versioning for SOA*. Prentice Hall. Engels, G., & Voss, M. (2008). Quasar enterprise. *Informatik Spektrum, 31*, 548–555.

Gardner, T. (2003). UML modelling of automated business processes with a mapping to BPEL4WS. In *Proc. of the First European, Workshop on Object Orientation and Web Services at ECOOP.*

IBM. (2005). *WebSphere MQ Workflow Workflow: Getting started with Buildtime*, ver. 3.6. Product documentation, Document Number SH12-6286-10.

IBM. (2008a). *WebSphere business modeler*, ver. 6.2. White Paper.

IBM. (2008b). *WebSphere process server*, ver. 6.2. White Paper.

Josuttis, N. M. (2007). *SOA in practice - The art of distributed system design*. O'Reilly.

Klückmann, J. (2007). *10 steps to business-driven SOA*. IDS Scheer AG.

Mendling, J., & Nüttgens, M. (2006). EPC markup language (EPML): An XML-based interchange format for event-driven process chains (EPC). *Inf. Syst. E-Business Management, 4*, 245–263.

MID. (2008). *Innovator object – Objektorientiertes Software Engineering mit der UML*. White Paper.

Mutschler, B., Reichert, M., & Bumiller, J. (2008). *Unleashing the effectiveness of process-oriented information systems: Problem analysis, critical success factors and implications. IEEE Transactions on Systems, 38.* IEEE Computer Society Press.

OASIS. (2007). *Web services business process execution language, ver. 2.0*. OASIS Standard.

OMG. (2004). *UML 2.0 superstructure specification*. OMG.

OMG. (2009). *Business process model and notation (BPMN) specification 2.0, V0.9.14, revised submission draft*. OMG.

Ouyang, C., Dumas, M., Van der Aalst, W. M. P., Hofstede, A. H. M., & Mendling, J. (2009). From Business process model to process-oriented software systems. *ACM Transactions on Software Engineering and Methodology, 19*(1). doi:10.1145/1555392.1555395

Ouyang, C., Van der Aalst, W. M. P., Dumas, M., & Hofstede, A. H. M. (2006). *Translating BPMN to BPEL*. BPM Center Report, BPM-06-02.

Pera, O., & Rintelmann, B. (2005). *Von betrieblichen Geschäftsprozessen zu einer SOA, 18*. Deutsche ORACLE-Anwenderkonferenz.

Reichert, M., & Dadam, P. (2009). Enabling adaptive process-aware Information Systems with ADEPT2. In Cardoso, J., & van der Alst, W. (Eds.), *Handbook of research on business process modeling* (pp. 173–203). New York, NY: Information Science Reference. doi:10.4018/978-1-60566-288-6.ch008

Rinderle-Ma, S., & Reichert, M. (2009). Comprehensive life cycle support for access rules in Information Systems: The CEOSIS Project. *Enterprise Information Systems, 3*(3), 219–251. doi:10.1080/17517570903045609

Rupp, C. (2007). *Requirements-Engineering und Management*. Hanser.

Scheer, A. W., Thomas, O., & Adam, O. (2005). Process modeling using event-driven process chains. In Dumas, M., & van der Alst, W. (Eds.), *Process-aware Information Systems: Bridging people and software through process technology* (pp. 119–145). doi:10.1002/0471741442.ch6

Stein, S. (2009). *Modeling method extension for service-oriented business process management*. Dissertation, Christian-Albrechts-Universität zu Kiel.

Stein, S., Kühne, S., Drawehn, J., Feja, S., & Rotzoll, W. (2008). Evaluation of OrViA framework for model-driven SOA implementations: An industrial case study. In M. Dumas, M. Reichert, & M.-C. Shan (Eds.), *Business Process Management: 6th International Conference, BPM 2008, LNCS 5240* (pp. 310–325). Milan, Italy: Springer.

Thomas, O., Leyking, K., & Dreifus, F. (2008). Using process models for the design of service-oriented architectures: Methodology and E-commerce case study. In *Proceedings of the 41st Annual Hawaii International Conference on System Sciences* (p.109). Washington, DC: IEEE Computer Society.

Tran, H., Zdun, U., & Dustdar, S. (2008). *View-based integration of process-driven SOA models at various abstraction levels*. In R.-D. Kutsche & N. Milanovic (Eds.), *Proceedings of First International Workshop on Model-Based Software and Data Integration* MBSDI, Berlin, CCIS, vol. 8, (pp. 55-66). Springer.

Van der Aalst, W. M. P., & Lassen, K. B. (2005). *Translating WORKflOW NETS to BPEL4WS. BPM-05-16*. Eindhoven, Netherlands: BPM Center.

Weber, B., Reichert, M., & Rinderle-Ma, S. (2008). Change patterns and change support features - Enhancing flexibility in process-aware Information Systems. [Elsevier Science.]. *Data & Knowledge Engineering*, *66*(3), 438–466. doi:10.1016/j.datak.2008.05.001

Weber, B., Reichert, M., Wild, W., & Rinderle-Ma, S. (2009). Providing integrated life cycle support in process-aware Information Systems. [IJCIS]. *Int'l Journal of Cooperative Information Systems*, *18*(1), 115–165. doi:10.1142/S0218843009001999

Weber, B., Sadiq, S., & Reichert, M. (2009). Beyond rigidity - Dynamic process lifecycle support: A survey on dynamic changes in process-aware Information Systems. *Computer Science - Research and Development, 23*(2), 47-65. Springer. ISSN 1865-2034

Weidlich, M., Weske, M., & Mendling, J. (2009). *Change propagation in process models using behavioral profiles*, IEEE International Conference on Services Computing.

Werth, D., Leyking, K., Dreifus, F., Ziemann, J., & Martin, A. (2006). *Managing SOA through business services - A business-oriented approach to service-oriented architectures*. ICSOC Workshop, Springer.

Weske, M. (2007). *Business process management - Concepts, languages, architectures*. Springer.

White, S. (2005). *Using BPMN to model a BPEL process*. BPTrends.

Woods, D., & Mattern, T. (2006*). Enterprise SOA: Designing IT for business innovation*. O'Reily Media.

Yvanov, K. (2006). *ARIS value engineering for SOA*. IDS Scheer AG.

Zdun, U., & Dustdar, S. (2007). Model-driven integration of process-driven SOA-models. *International Journal of Business Process Integration and Management*, 2(2), 109–119. doi:10.1504/IJBPIM.2007.015135

Ziemann, J., & Mendling, J. (2007). EPC-based modeling of BPEL processes: A pragmatic transformation approach. In *MITIP 2005*. Italy Architectures. Springer.

KEY TERMS AND DEFINITIONS

Business Process: Serves a particular business goal (e.g., to handle customer orders, to deliver goods or to manage product changes) and it constitutes a recurring sequence of business functions whose execution has to meet certain rules. Furthermore, a business process model documents business requirements in respect to the process- and service-oriented information system to be designed. These business requirements are often elicited by interviewing end users as well as process owners. The graphical representation and documentation of business processes is usually supported by respective business process modeling (BPM) tools.

Business-IT Alignment: Targets at closing the gap between business processes and their IT implementations (e.g., service composition specifications). This goal can be achieved, for example, by improving the interactions between business and IT departments during the service development process as well as during service maintenance. The latter becomes possible with the Business-IT-Mapping Model described in this handbook. Amongst others, this mapping model explicitly maintains the relationships between business process models and their implementation in a process- and service-oriented information system.

Business-IT-Mapping Model (BIMM): Defines a connection between a business process model and a service composition specification. Currently, this link is neither supported by business process modeling nor by CASE tools. In particular, BIMM allows to store and maintain the complex dependencies between business process models and service composition specifications in a traceable way.

Service Composition Schema: Represents the technical and platform-specific specification of a business process. For the implementation of process- and service-oriented information systems, additional information which goes beyond the one from the respective business process model are required; e.g., technical specifications of data objects and data types, implemented services, user interfaces, business rules, and access control policies. The service composition schema has to meet a number of constraints in order to be executable by a service orchestration engine; e.g., specification of transition conditions, assurance of soundness (e.g., proper completion, no deadlocks) or completeness of the specified data flow (e.g., no missing input data upon invocation of a single activity and service respectively.

ENDNOTES

[1]   A detailed description of all BPMN 2.0 modeling components can be found on http://bpmb.de/poster.

[2]   The corresponding Business Process Diagram (cf. Figure 18) and the system process Diagram (cf. Figure 19) can be found in the appendix.

APPENDIX

A prototypical implementation of the BIMM was realized with the IBM WebSphere Business Modeler and ARIS. In the following we show the corresponding business processes and system processes. These directly realize the scenario introduced in the Background section (see Figure 1). Figure 18 and Figure 19 show the BPMN implementation of the business process and the system process in IBM WebSphere Business Modeler (WBM).

Figure 18. Business process designed in IBM WebSphere business modeler

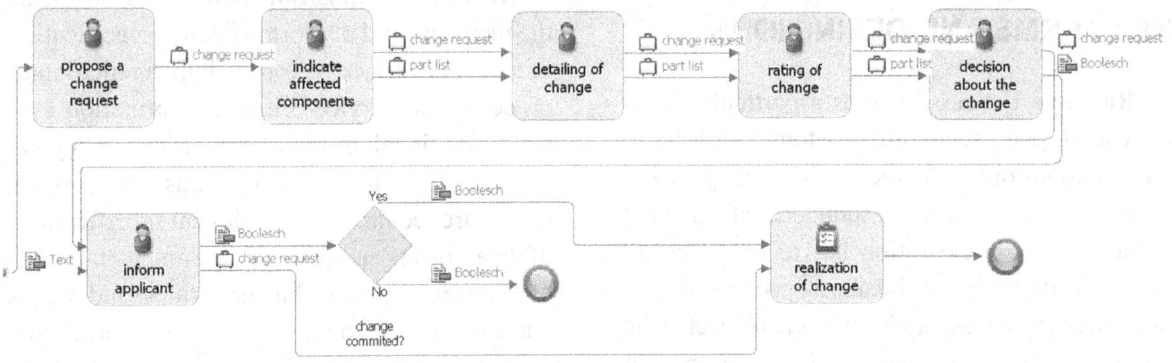

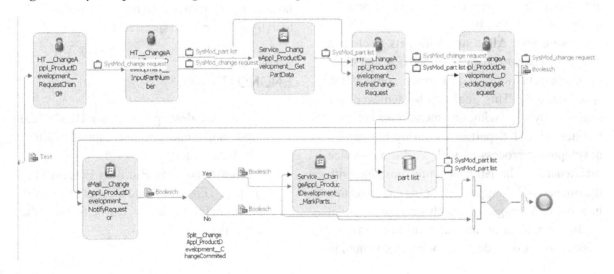

Figure 19. System process designed in IBM WebSphere business modeler

Figure 20 shows the eEPC implementation of the business process in ARIS Business Architect. The corresponding BPMN implementation of the system process is shown in Figure 21.

Figure 20. Business process modeled in ARIS

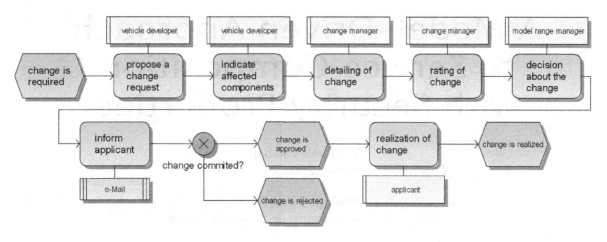

Figure 21. System process modeled in ARIS

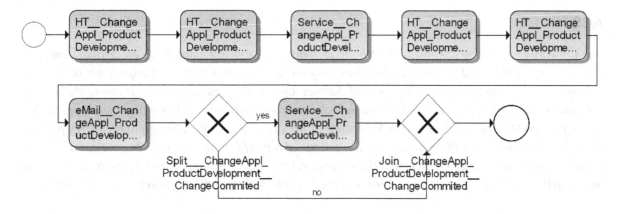

Chapter 8
A Model–Driven Approach to Service Composition with Security Properties

Stéphanie Chollet
Laboratoire d'Informatique de Grenoble, France

Philippe Lalanda
Laboratoire d'Informatique de Grenoble, France

ABSTRACT

The software engineering community is striving to handle a significant number of new critical demands. Productivity, quality, and runtime flexibility are only few of them. To satisfy such requirements, new development paradigms are regularly proposed. Service-Oriented Computing (SOC) is one of them. SOC is based on the notion of services, which are well-defined composition units, to support rapid application development. This chapter presents a brief state of the art of services. Although SOC brings properties of major interest, it suffers from usual limitations of reused-based approach. In particular, service composition is much more complicated than often pretended. In this chapter, we propose to present a model-driven approach to service composition dealing with non-functional aspects, including security.

INTRODUCTION

The need for advanced development technologies and tools providing appropriate support in the software industry is greater than ever. We believe that this is essentially due to the diversity of software developments undergone nowadays

and to an ever increasing pressure. Software systems pervade every aspects of our life and, subsequently, place very different and demanding requirements on the development projects. In some domains, unprecedented pressure is put on cost and time-to-market. Time-to-market in the mobile phone industry for instance has dropped down to six months. In other domains, the main difficulty resides in new, stringent non functional

DOI: 10.4018/978-1-61350-159-7.ch008

requirements. For instance, pervasive applications are characterized by complex requirements in terms of dynamism, context awareness and autonomy. New development paradigms have been proposed to face these demanding conditions. For instance, approaches like component-based software engineering, aspect-oriented programming or service-oriented computing have been recently defined to facilitate the development of modular, dynamic applications.

It however turns out that the community is striving to use efficiently these new technologies and to deliver the expected level of software quality. We believe that an effective approach to improve productivity and quality is to hide technical complexity through the use of generative programming techniques. The purpose of generative programming is to enable the production of software through the automatic generation of applications from specifications written in a Domain-Specific Language (DSL). A DSL offers, through appropriate notations and abstractions, expressive power focused on, and usually restricted to, a particular problem domain. It allows developers to manipulate familiar domain concepts at the different phases of software production. Although, tools based on DSL are naturally expected by the industry, very few of them are actually delivered. One of the main blocking factors is the cost of producing such tools that must incorporate many software engineering practices in order to cover the whole software lifecycle. Also, in order to be really useful, a tool has to be dedicated to the domain it deals with. Unfortunately, developing a tool in a narrow domain is generally not cost effective and very few companies can afford such an investment. Most companies then rely on generic tools that are getting unfitted to modern software.

This chapter presents a model-based approach for the composition of secured services. The purpose of this approach is to generate part of the code related to security, which is complex and error-prone, from domain-specific models. It is based on the separation of concerns principle in

the sense that different models, and associated meta-models, are used to specify different aspects of the service composition.

It is structured as it follows. First, we define the Service-Oriented Computing (SOC), the service composition and the service technologies used in different domains such as application integration, pervasive environment... The second section deals with the security in SOC, particularly the security between the service consumer and the service provider. We detail the security problems, solutions and technologies adapted to the service domain. The third section presents a model-driven approach to facilitate the composition of heterogeneous and secured services. The last section presents the results of experiments applied to an implementation of the model-driven approach.

SERVICES

Service Definition

Service-Oriented Computing (SOC) is a reuse-based approach for the development of modern software applications. The key concept of this approach is the notion of service. Several definitions have actually been proposed for software services. Let us review the major ones.

First, Papazoglou (2003) proposed the following definition:

"Services are self-describing, platform agnostic computational elements."

A service is then a software composition unit defined through an explicit description. A service can be discovered, selected and used by a consumer based upon this description. Service consumers are usually unaware of the service implementation technology or of the underlying runtime platform. Similarly, a service does not know the runtime contexts in which it is used. This double independence is a major property of the service-oriented approach, as it facilitates loose-coupling at the application level. This definition is however limited in the sense that it presumes that a service is executed on a remote platform and cannot be imported on a local platform.

The OASIS consortium, which is responsible for the standardization of Internet applications, defined services as it follows:

"A service is a mechanism to enable access to one or more capabilities, where the access is provided by using a prescribed interface and is exercised consistent with constraints and policies as specified by the service composition. A service is accessed by means of a service interface where the interface comprises the specifics of how to access the underlying capabilities. There are no constraints on what constitutes the underlying capability or how access is implemented by the service provider. A service is opaque in that its implementation is typically hidden from the service consumer except for (1) the information and behavior models exposed through the service interface and (2) the information required by service consumers to determine whether a given service is appropriate for their needs." (OASIS, 2006)

According to the OASIS, a service provides a set of functionalities that are specified in a service description. The description comprises an interface exposing the available function in a programmatic way, and a set of constraints and access policies characterizing the offered functionalities. The service implementation is not visible to service consumers. Only the information that can help determine whether the service corresponds to the consumer requirements is available. However, it is notably difficult to distinguish between necessary and unnecessary information regarding service selection.

Arsanjani provided his own vision of software services. He focused on the interactions needed to get the service functionalities:

"A service is a software resource (discoverable) with an externalized service description. This service description is available for searching, binding, and invocation by a service consumer. Services should ideally be governed by declarative policies and thus support a dynamically reconfigurable architectural style." (Arsanjani, 2004)

This definition focuses on the importance of the service description. Indeed, the whole process starts with a potential consumer search for a service meeting its needs and requirements. The search is based on the description of the needs and on the services description. Once a service is found the consumer connects to the service and invokes it. These actions may be performed before or during the execution of a service-oriented application.

In the rest of this chapter, and in accordance with the previous definitions, we see a service in the following way:

"A software entity that provides a set of functionalities described in a service description. The service description contains information on the service's functional part, but also on its non-functional aspects. Based on such specification, a service consumer can search for services that meet its requirements, select a compliant service and invoke it."

Service-Oriented Computing

The goal of Service-Oriented Computing (SOC) is to enable the creation of applications from specific entities, *i.e.* services, while ensuring the loose-coupling of these assembled entities. This is not a technology, but rather an architectural style (Shaw, 1996) relying on an interaction pattern among different actors, as illustrated by Figure 1.

Three actors can be identified in the interaction pattern:

Figure 1. Actors and interactions in SOC

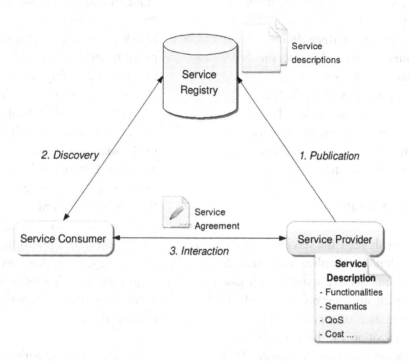

- The service provider offers a service, described in a service specification.
- The service consumer uses services offered by service providers.
- The service registry stores all the service descriptions published by service providers. Additionally, the service registry enables consumers to search and select the services they require. There are many ways to implement such a registry that can be global or local for instance.

Three communication primitives can be defined for the aforementioned actors:

- **Service publication:** a service provider registers its services in the service registry.
- **Service discovery:** a service consumer searches the service registry for a service meeting its criteria.

- **Service binding and invocation:** once a consumer has selected a service provider, it can set a binding and use the provider's service.

The main advantage of a Service-Oriented Architecture (SOA) is that only the service descriptions are shared between the different actors. This allows for interconnected services to remain loosely-coupled. Depending on the adopted approach, service descriptions can have different forms and levels of detail. In all cases, the main purpose of a service description is to specify the service functionalities. The loose-coupling characteristic of SOA brings about an additional advantage: the heterogeneity of service implementations and runtime platforms, as well as the service location are hidden from service consumers. Another beneficial effect of the SOA loose-coupling characteristic is the substitutability property. Precisely, one service can be transparently replaced by another service, as long as both services implement the interface defined in the provider-consumer contract. Finally, the SOA facilitates the communication between service consumers and service providers that belong to different administrative authorities. This is an important characteristic of the service-oriented approach, even if in most cases the entire service-oriented application belongs to a single enterprise.

Service Composition

As we have previously seen, the service-oriented approach allows building applications through service composition. Service composition can be viewed as a mechanism for building applications via the integration of services. The result of a service composition can be considered as a new service, called a composite service. This type of composition is referred to as recursive or hierarchical composition. A service application can be built from a set of available services in a service registry.

However, in order to obtain a well-structured service composition from a set of services, a certain number of steps must be followed. These steps start from the composition specification and continue until a concrete and executable implementation is obtained:

- **Functional architecture definition:** this phase identifies the functionalities expected from the resulting application, or service composition. Some approaches that provide support for this phase are currently available.
- **Service identification:** this phase determines the services required for the composition, depending on the composition's expected functionalities.
- **Selection of services and of their implementation:** this phase selects services and implementations that meet the necessary

requirements, for all services identified in the previous step.

- **Service mediation:** this phase deals with possible service integration incompatibilities. Despite having selected the most suitable services in the previous phase, it is generally impossible to directly assemble them without modification. Some sort of mediation is often required (*e.g.* semantic mediation), in order for the integrated services to behave as expected.
- **Service deployment and invocation:** this phase is concerned with deploying services on the execution platforms, once the service composition has been successfully completed. It is then possible to invoke the services in order to obtain their concrete composition.

Despite this decomposition into tasks, the construction of applications by means of service composition remains a difficult and potentially long process. Each task can be divided into further subtasks, which developers must sometimes perform manually. Ideal situations where developers only have to deal with "good" services are rare (*i.e.* compatible services providing the expected functionalities). Most of the time, developers have to solve incompatibility issues by introducing mediation layers that adapt services to each other. For example, developers must solve incompatibilities between the integrated services' input and output data type.

We believe that the complexity of building applications through service composition comes from two main aspects: (i) the complexity of implementing the desired application functionalities, requiring domain-specific expertise; (ii) the complexity of implementing the service-oriented architecture itself.

Service composition is specified according to some service coordination logic. Namely, it is defined according to the service composition control, which may be intrinsic or extrinsic. These two control possibilities define the following composition styles: process-based composition (or behavioral composition) and structural composition. The two styles are presented in the following sections.

Process-Based Composition

In this composition style, a process specifies the services coordination logic. A process is represented by an oriented graph of activities, and by a control flow dictating the activities execution order. Each activity represents a functionality which is implemented by a concrete service.

In practice, process-based composition is described by a specific language and interpreted by an execution engine. The engine handles all service communications and potential errors.

We distinguish two process-based composition forms:

- **Service orchestration** describes a service's interactions and internal steps between interactions (Peltz, 2003) (*e.g.* data transformations and internal module invocations). This is a centralized view of services.
- **Service choreography** describes collaboration among a set of services that aim to achieve a given objective. Collaborating services achieve their shared goal via orderly message exchanges (Austin, 2003). In this case, there is a global view of services and their interactions.

These two points of view of the process-based composition are only currently employed for Web services. WS-BPEL (*Web Service Business Process Execution Language*) (OASIS, 2007) is an example of Web services orchestration language. WS-CDL (*Web Service Choreography Description Language*) (W3C, 2004) is a Web services choreography description language.

Process-based composition allows a clear separation between application control and provided functionalities. Therefore, developers use this composition type for building applications from software parts whose internal operations are unknown. Such software parts are seen as "black boxes". In this manner, identified functionalities can be reused across various compositions and the control logic remains simple to express. However, only few interactions can be specified between the assembled activities, since composition languages do not allow the expression of complex algorithms. Moreover, the types of interactions between the assembled activities cannot be detailed. Process-based composition offers a control approach that is useful but that remains limited to certain domains.

Structural Composition

In contrast to process-based composition, structural composition control is expressed inside the services. Only service developers are aware of the services control logic. The only externally available information is the services' provided and required functionalities.

In structural composition, services are clearly identified with their interactions. In order to ensure valid compositions, syntactic and semantic dependencies of services must be resolved at service assembly time. Therefore, in order to define a composition's operation, developers also deliver the composition coordination logic. The coordination logic can be implemented for example via a Java class. At present, the SCA (Service Component Architecture) (OSOA, 2007) specification and the approach presented in (Lalanda, 2007) are some of the few proposed structural composition specifications.

In contrast to process-based composition, structural composition does not allow for the easy reuse of composition services, since the composition control is internal to services. However, structural composition is more efficient than process-based composition, since service communication is direct rather than passing through an intermediary. In addition, as the service contents are implemented by the developer, the interaction algorithms between services can be more complex than those of process-based composition that are based on a restricted language.

Service Technologies

Web Services

Web Services are the most popular and well-known technology for implementing Service-Oriented Architectures, both in the industry and the academia. In this section, we present the main Web Services principles. The main purpose of Web Services was to render applications available via the Internet or within an Intranet. Web Services comply with the service-oriented approach principles previously presented, meaning they are described, published and discovered. A service provider describes service functional and non-functional characteristics in a WSDL file and then registers the service description in an UDDI service registry. A client, or consumer, searches the UDDI registry for services that meet their requirements.

From the consumer point of view, a Web Service is a black box that provides no technical details on its implementation. The only available information includes the Web Service functionalities, certain properties, its location and the invocation instructions. Consumers use the SOAP protocol to communicate with Web Services.

The Web Service architecture hides the Web Services implementation complexity from the user. Hence, a Web service may use other services (*i.e.* Web services, or of other types) in order to provide its functionalities. The Web Service's users remain completely unaware of such aspects. Certain coordination is required among the different service calls.

However, these technologies do not take into account some important non-functional properties,

even if they can be specified with WS-* specifications. But, they are so many of them today that it's difficult to be an expert on them.

Assembling Web Services relies on service orchestration. There is no structural composition for Web services. WS-BPEL (OASIS, 2007), which is the acronym for *Web Services Business Process Execution Language*, is an OASIS consortium specification. The latest version of the WS-BPEL specification is 2.0, since March 2007. This specification is one of the best known specifications for Web Services orchestration. It replaces previous specifications, such as Microsoft's XLANG (http://www.ebpml.org/xlang.htm) and IBM's WSFL (*Web Services Flow Language*), (http://xml.coverpages.org/wsfl.html).

Web Services step forwards in terms of service composition due to WS-BPEL specification. This composition is based on service orchestration, hence presenting the advantages of workflow-based composition, as well as the disadvantage of the centralized execution engine. However, Web services do not support the mechanisms necessary for providing dynamic service-oriented architectures.

Services and Devices

Home automation environments have commonly been based on a large part of SOA characteristics, such as weak coupling, heterogeneous devices and dynamism. The popularity of communicating objects, such as cell phones and PDA, have pushed the creation of communication technologies like Bluetooth (http://www.bluetooth.com/), UPnP and DPWS. These are high level protocols hiding the complexity of used technologies while permitting not only wireless communication between heterogeneous devices, but also device discovery. UPnP and DPWS are two specifications based on the dynamic service-oriented architecture principles, and are commonly used in home and office networks.

UPnP (UPnP Forum, 2008) is the acronym for *Universal Plug and Play*. It is a specification defined from an industrial initiative and is currently run by the UPnP Forum. The goal of this specification is to simplify connections between heterogeneous communicating devices and the construction of home networks. UPnP was inspired and eventually derived from the *Plug and Play* technology, which allows dynamically connecting peripherals to a computer.

The UPnP specification proposes a group of protocols, themselves based on standard Internet protocols. These protocols allow implementing a dynamic service-oriented architecture specialized for home automation. The goal of UPnP is to discover new devices connected to a network. This is why devices and their services are described in an UPnP specific format and is based on XML. When a device joins the network, it announces itself to all the other devices present on the network. A device can submit a request on the network in order to obtain information regarding other connected devices. In the case of a dynamic service-oriented architecture, it is also possible for a device to be stopped. In this case, the device is capable of sending a message to notify other devices of its departure.

Finally, UPnP offers a specification for discovering and communicating with devices and their services in home and office networks. UPnP has become a popular standard thanks to the evolution of technologies in home automation and the need for applications to react according to the devices detected.

It is clear that UPnP is centered on devices more than applications that can be created using these devices. This is an obstacle for integrating devices into applications. Also, UPnP lacks important functionality, such as security, which is not considered at all, even when it is essential in the home automation context to be capable of restricting devices and/or services using, for example, an authentication procedure.

DPWS (Jammes, 2005), (Zeeb, 2007) is the acronym for *Device Profile for Web Services*. It is a specification (Microsoft, 2006) proposed and maintained by Microsoft. Windows Vista, the latest operating system from Microsoft, natively integrates this specification. This simplifies integrating devices into a home or office network. DPWS is thus presented by Microsoft as a replacement for UPnP, although it is part of a monopolistic strategy.

The DPWS specification is based on the Web Services technology. It starts from the premise that Web Services are a technology rich in standards and in features and has consistently met many varying requirements However, to be adaptable to all web services, Microsoft proposes a core set of features based on the web service specifications:

- **secure sending and receiving** of messages for Web Services using the WS-Security (OASIS, 2004) specification,
- **dynamic discovery** of Web Services using the WS-Discovery(Microsoft, 2005) specification,
- **description** of a Web Services using the WS-MetadataExchange (W3C, 2008) specification,
- **subscription and reception** of events by a web service using the WS-Eventing (W3C, 2005) specification.

The DPWS architecture follows the service oriented architecture principles. More particularly, DPWS is based on the principles of web services. After obtaining an IP address (with WS-Addressing (W3C, 2004)), a device must discover all other network devices and reports its own existence and the services it offers. In general, these communications are conducted in a *multicast* mode. The device features are given in an extended WSDL description file. Then, a device's service may be used. Communication between devices is done using SOAP and can be asynchronous.

Finally, the DPWS specification is strongly inspired by that of UPnP. It is indeed intended to be the new version of UPnP. The features offered are similar to those of UPnP, with the difference that they are provided in a cleaner and more precise manner, largely thanks to the Web Services specifications. Another advantage of this specification is the addition of security features. However, despite improvements and efforts by Microsoft, DPWS is implemented in very few devices and is limited to local networks. The adoption of this standard will certainly take some time.

SECURITY AND SERVICES

Attacks and Threats in SOA

Information Disclosure

Service consumer and service provider use the network to communicate. The communications can be intercepted by malicious people or machines for criminal purposes. Figure 2 is an illustration of this attack.

The aim of this attack is to collect information from service consumer and from service provider. All the communications (request and response) are sniffed. The main problem is the in-formation disclosure. Then, information can be divulged to anyone. To address this problem, exchanged information must be confidential on the network. Only the service consumer and the service provider must understand the information. The solution to keep confidential information is to cipher the content of messages.

Identity Usurpation

Identity usurpation is a more sophisticated attack than information disclosure. A malicious person or machine deceives the service provider about his/its "real" identity. The malicious machine with the identity of a "real" service consumer exchanges messages with the service provider. The content of the response can contain confidential information. Figure 3 synthesizes how this attack works.

The malicious machine steals the identity of a "real" service consumer. The messages are exchanged without the service provider is aware of the trick. This attack can be made after the sniffing of the network and/or with the theft of the client information on the client machine.

To avoid this kind of attack, the service provider must be sure of the client identity. A system of authentication must be required to differentiate the "real" client from the malicious client. Moreover, the authentication information is exchanged and

Figure 2. Information disclosure

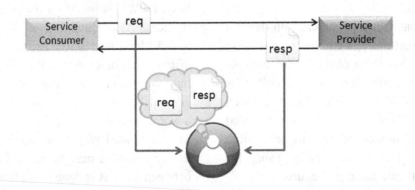

Figure 3. Identity usurpation

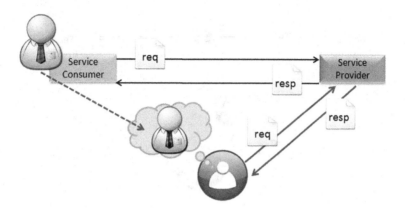

must be confidential between the consumer and the provider to avoid the theft of the authentication information.

Misappropriation of Information

The misappropriation of information is an attack different from information disclosure and identity usurpation. Consumer messages are hijacked by a malicious person or machine. Then, messages are modified for criminal purpose.

The principle of this attack is to alter the content of the messages in order to damage the service provider. A malicious person or machine intercepts a message from a "real" service consumer to a service provider. He/It modifies the initial content with an insertion of malicious code. Then, the malicious message is sent to the service provider. The service provider processes the message as a normal request from the service consumer. The malicious code can be, for example, a virus that damages the service provider. Figure 4 illustrates the scenario of this attack.

An immediate consequence of this attack is that the content of the message is lost. The damage of the provider server is a second consequence. The service provider is not able to accurately work, *i.e.* to reply to all clients requests.

To address this problem, the integrity of exchanged information must be ensured. The messages must not be modified, altered or destroyed to the service provider. A standard solution is to cipher the content of the message and to add a checksum.

Denial of Service

The denial of service is an attack that overloads the service provider. Its aim is that the service provider is not available and unable to treat all the requests. The objective is only to damage the performance and the reputation of the service provider. The service provider can then loose the consumer trust.

The principle of this attack is to overload the service provider with numerous malicious messages. For example, the service provider can have an infinite loop in the message in order to parse the request. Or, the malicious machine can send a great number of messages. The service provider has not the sufficient resources. It spends all one's time responding to the malicious client instead of to react to the "real" client. Many solutions (Yunus, 2005) exist to overload a service provider. Figure 5 is an illustration of the overloaded service attack.

Figure 4. Virus

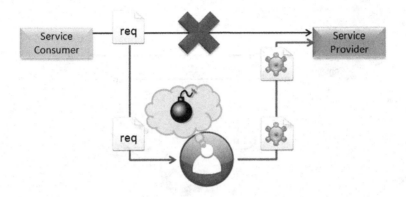

To conclude, the solutions to overload a service are simple difficult to detect. The malicious messages are like the "real" messages. The consequences are the service disruption and the system damage. To avoid this type of attack, the service provider must have a supervision system in order to detect runtime fault.

Security: Objective, Definition, and Concepts

Principle and Definition

Security can be defined as a set of measures taken as a precaution against theft or espionage or sabotage. In computer science, security makes use of many technical, organizational, juridical and human means. These means are used to ensure the security of a complete system. At each step of the system life cycle, security increments exist.

At the specification level, analysts must study all the risks. An evaluation of these risks enables to know their probability or frequency. Analysts examine also the cost of each risk. Only the knowledge of the risks and their impacts allows defining an adequate protection policy for the system.

According to the results of the analysis step, security policies are defined at design time. Among all the risks, the analysts choose the ones to be treated by the system. Security policies enable to define the required techniques to be applied.

Figure 5. Denial of service

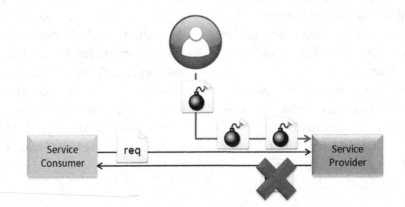

The goal of the development phase is to make specific tools for the secured system. Developers integrate security techniques in reply to the risks specified in the previous step.

Concepts

The main concepts of security are the following:

- **Authentication** guarantees the identity of a person and the origin of information. Authentication is often coupled with a mechanism of authorization to control system access.
- **Data integrity** guarantees that some data has not been changed, destroyed, or lost in an unauthorized or accidental manner.
- **Data confidentiality** guarantees that some information is not made available or disclosed to any unauthorized parties.
- **Traceability** corresponds to the log and the audit of the events.
- **Non-repudiation** guarantees that the system is operating at a specified time.

Microsoft (Microsoft) defines the transfer security concept that encompasses three major security functions: data integrity, data confidentiality and authentication. Transfer security is applied in distributed environments such as the service domain. The content of the messages exchanged between the different stakeholders of the SOA are one of the most vulnerable components.

Technical Solutions

The purpose of this section is to present the available technical solutions. These are techniques associated to the security concepts previously detailed. They ensure a set of properties.

Authentication allows proving identity. Technical solutions to implement authentication are the use of a username with a password or a certificate. These two mechanisms consist in inserting an identity proof in a message. The sender adds in the message his identity and the receiver verifies the validity of the identity with an access control system. The receiver must have previously defined a set of access policies to check access control.

Data protection implies two security properties: data integrity and data confidentiality. A signature ensures that the data have not been altered or destroyed. In order to keep confidential information, the solution is the cipher.

The logs of events are the solution to apply the traceability properties. The difficulty is to know which event is interesting to log in order to detect an intrusion in the system.

The availability and the non-repudiation require more complex solutions and more adapted to the system. They are linked with the system.

Security Technologies Adapted to Services

For many service technologies, the messages exchanged between the service consumer and the service provider are expressed with an XML-based language. It exist two recommendations proposed by W3C to ensure the data integrity and confidentiality of XML information. XML Digital Signature (W3C, 2008) is used to sign an XML document. XML Encryption (W3C, 2002) is used to encrypt and to decrypt XML document. With XML, it is possible to express with different asserts the same content. For example, <node a="1"/> is equivalent to <node a = "1"></node>. In the security point of view, these two expressions are not equivalent, while their signatures are different. To avoid this problem, it exists recommendations (Canonical XML (W3C, 2001) and/or Exclusive XML Canonicalization (W3C, 2002)) to normalize the XML document. The main advantage of XML Digital Signature and XML Encryption is that signature and encryption can be applied to a specified part of an XML document.

- *XKMS* (*XML Key Management Specification*) (W3C, 2005) is a W3C protocol. It facilitates the development of secure inter-application communication using public key infrastructure. It is composed of two standards: X-KRSS (*XML Key Registration Service Specification*) and X-KISS (*XML Key Information Service Specification*). X-KRSS is used to register, to reissue, to revoke and to recover keys. X-KISS allows to locate and to validate public keys.

- *XACML* (*eXtensible Access Control Markup Language*) (OASIS, 2005) is an OASIS specification. It is a declarative access control policy language implemented in XML. It contains a processing model describing how to interpret the policies. *XrML* (*eXtensible rights Markup Language*) (ContentGuard) is a language based on XML to describe rights, fees and conditions.

- *Single Sign On* (SSO) is a method of access control of multiple, related, but independent software systems. A user logs in once and gains access to all systems without prompted to log in again at each of them. For example, Google Account gives you an access to Gmail, Blogger, Google Groups, Google Wave,…

- *SAML* (*Security Assertion Markup Language*) (OASIS, 2005) is an OASIS protocol based on XML. It is a language for exchanging authentication and authorization data between different security domains.

- *WS-Security* (OASIS, 2004) is an OASIS recommendation proposed in 2004. This recommendation is an extension of the SOAP protocol. It proposes to add security information into the message exchanged between the client and the provider of Web Service. It is based on the XML Encryption and XML Digital Signature to ensure the data confidentiality and data integrity.

The WS-Security recommendation ensure the transfer security properties (authentication, data integrity and data confidentiality). It is based on security technologies such as username/password, X.509 certificate, SAML token… to ensure the authentication. It explains how to add security technologies into the header and the body of SOAP messages. This recommendation has been adapted by the DPWS technology.

There are security technologies that implement the WS-Security recommendation. Apache WSS4J (Apache, 2006) (*WS-Security for Java*) is a Java library used with Apache Axis 1.4 (Apache, 2006). Apache Rampart (Apache, 2009) is the last version of this library for Apache Axis 2.0. These implementations propose to intercept the SOAP messages at sending and at receipt in order to add the security parameters.

A MODEL-DRIVEN APPROACH TO SECURED SERVICE COMPOSITION

In the previous sections, we have presented the notions of software services and security. We also insisted on the difficulty to develop an application made of secured services. This is due to various reasons. First, there are today many technologies for describing, publishing and composing services. Depending on the target application domain, different protocols and mechanisms are used to implement a SOA. For instance, Web Services (www.w3c.org) are dominant to integrate IT applications. UPnP (www.upnp.org) or DPWS (*Devices Profile for Web Services*) are preferred in small area networks. OSGi (www.osgi.org) is often used in centralized, embedded equipments. These technologies require deep expertise. Cross-technology applications require almost unavailable skills. In addition, as of today's state-of-the-art, service composition cannot be based only upon service specifications. Syntactic compatibility does not ensure semantic compatibility. In practice, service composition is based on unexpressed assumptions and rules allowing reaching the expected results. A composition of services has also to reach a set of pre-defined non functional qualities like security which requires the production of complex, often non flexible code. In the general case, such code cannot be automatically generated at composition time.

We believe that without effective solutions for easy and correct service composition, SOC orientation will be limited to narrow, very specific domains of applications. In this paper, we present a generative model-based approach to handle the composition of secured services

Background on Model-Driven Engineering

Model-Driven Engineering has been defined by R. France and B. Rumpe as it follows:

"The term Model-Driven Engineering (MDE) is typically used to describe software development approaches in which abstract models of software systems are created and systematically transformed to concrete implementation." (France, 2007)

The goal of model-driven engineering approach is to reduce the gap between the problem domain and software implementations. This approach proposes a set of technologies allowing refining successively models. These models are an abstract representation of the system at different steps. The refinements are transformations from the abstract problem to the software implementation. The advantage of the model-driven engineering is that the complexity of the implementation is hidden. Moreover, the communication between the different stakeholders is improved during the software lifecycle. R. France and B. Rumpe (France, 2007) have a more ambitious view of model-driven engineering: models are used for software design but also during the software

runtime. The models used at runtime are named models@runtime.In this case, they can be used to supervise the system at runtime.

The model concept is the main element of model-driven engineering. There is no real consensus to define a model and different definitions have been proposed:

"A model is a simplification of a system built with an intended goal in mind" (Bézivin, 2001).

"A model is an abstraction of some aspect of a system. The system described by a model may or may not exist at the time the model is created. Models are created to serve particular purposes, for example, to present a human understandable description of some aspect of a system or to present information in a form that can be mechanically analyzed." (France, 2007)

A model simplifies a real system. It facilitates the understanding or the analysis of reality. A system can be described by one or several models. Each model represents a particular point of view at a particular level. As a model represents a particular point of view, it is then partial. Note that a model can be made whereas the system does not exist. To simplify their use, models are often represented with graphs (Kuhne, 2006). A node represents a concept; the links represent the relations between the concepts. Cardinalities specify the number of instances taking part in a relation. The class diagram of UML (OMG, 2009) is an example of a model represented by a graph.

There are many methods to categorize models (Ludewig, 2003), (Fowler, 1999). For example, models can be classified according to their role. This classification, proposed in the 2000's, separates productive models and contemplative models. Contemplative models are only used to improve the communication between the different stakeholders. Productive models enable to implement a system after multiple transformations.

A model must be expressed with a formal language in order to be used by machines. The formal language must be clear, precise and non-ambiguous. Then, the formal language must be specified; it becomes a subject to model. This idea introduces the notion of meta-model. A meta-model can be defined as follows:

"A meta-model is a model that defines the language for expressing a model." (OMG, 2002)

A meta-model can be also expressed by a graph. In the particular case of UML, a meta-model is also represented by a class diagram. Meta-models define a grammar and a vocabulary. If the model is correctly built, then the model can be automatically transformed. They are various levels of conformity. In the rest of this paper, the conformity term is used to the instantiation conformity. If a meta-model contains elements (relations/links, classes/objects) that can be instantiated, then a model made by instantiation of the elements is conformed to the meta-model.

Previously, we have explained that a system can be described by many models. Each model describes a particular point of view. If we need a productive model, it is required to compose all the models to have a global view of the system. The model composition can be defined as follows:

"Model composition is an operation that combines two or more models into a single one." (Del Fabro, 2006)

"Model composition in its simplest form refers to the mechanism of combining two models into a new one." (Herrmann, 2007)

The model composition can be also applied to meta-model because a meta-model is a model. The meta-model composition is the result of the meta-models union with additional links between the concepts of meta-models.

A Model-Driven Approach

The principle of our approach is to express service composition at a high level of abstraction and then to generate the composition code and glue code (non-functional code: security…). This approach can be divided into two parts, as illustrated by the Figure 6:

- First, the design step allows to express the service composition with models of functional and non-functional properties;
- Second, the runtime step allows generating the appropriate code to execute service composition according to the available services.

This approach is applied to the process-based service composition. The service composition is a service orchestration with security constraints. To remind, a service orchestration is executed by an orchestration engine which manages the order of the service calls. The difference with the other orchestration technologies, we are interested in the orchestration of heterogeneous and secured services in a dynamic environment. The services can be Web Services, UPnP services, DPWS services… And the services can appear and disappear in the runtime context. This approach proposes mechanisms to hide the technological complexity of services and security. It adds a model@ runtime to manage the dynamic environment. This model-driven approach has been also applied to structural composition in static (Lalanda, 2007) and dynamic environment (Yu, 2008).

In the following sections, we detail each part of the approach and we discuss the advantages and the disadvantages to adopt a model-driven approach to service composition problem.

Design

The design step allows to hide the technical details of services implementations, the complexity of

Figure 6. Model-driven approach

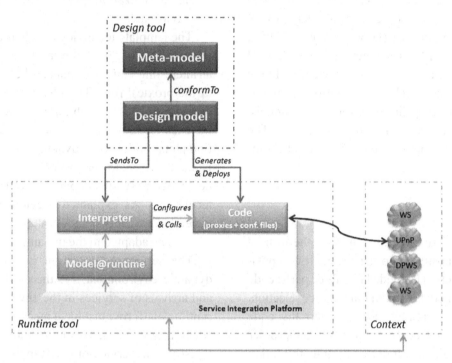

service composition mechanisms and the context dynamism. Service composition is defined by a model. To ensure the validity and the conformance of the model, a meta-model of service composition is required. At the model level, the domain concepts are used and not the domain objects. The main domain concept is "abstract service". An abstract service is a global description of concrete services implemented in the multiple service technologies. An abstract service is:

- An functional interface that specifies the functionalities provided by the service;
- A set of non-functional properties that can be runtime or static features (Badr, 2008).

If we consider the process-based service composition, the abstract orchestration must also be defined. The concrete orchestration corresponds to the call of concrete services. An abstract orches-

tration is represented by an oriented graph, *i.e.* nodes are abstract services, and edges are dataflow between services. The service composition model provides the reusability properties. The service composition is implementation independent.

To simplify the service composition, separation of concerns paradigm can be applied. Functional and non-functional properties can be separated. The functional properties are defined in a model of the orchestration of abstract and heterogeneous services. Each non-functional property is defined in a non-functional model. And the non-functional models are linked to the functional model. The functional model plays the central role. To ensure the coherence and the validity of the models, meta-models are used. Each meta-model defines the concepts of the domain which can be used at model level. Figure 7 is an illustration of the separation of concerns at meta-model and model level.

With the separation of concerns, each model can be replaced by another. The modularity of the approach is improved (Grønmo, 2004), (Ortiz, 2009). Additionally, each meta-model is defined by a domain expert; each model is defined by a domain engineer. The composition of meta-models is made by links between meta-models. These links are defined by both of experts. The communication between the different stakeholders is also improved.

Runtime

The goal of the runtime is to transform the abstract service composition into an executable composition. This section is divided into three parts: code generation, model@runtime and service selection.

The transformation consists into the code generation. The code corresponds to the proxies to call the available services. This transformation must take into consideration the heterogeneity of the service technologies and the dynamism of the environment. The solution is to generate the proxies' files into two steps with templates files. The first step consists in the generation of generic proxies' files for each abstract service defined in the model. The second step consists

in the specialization of these files according to the environment.

The template technology such as JET (http://www.eclipse.org/modeling/m2t/?project=jet) is an interesting solution to manage the heterogeneity of the proxies' files. The idea is to code the required templates for each supported technologies, i.e. each technology expressed in the orchestration meta-model. The advantage of this solution is that it is easy to support new technology. The developer must add template files adapted to this technology. As explained previously, the files generated are generic; they contain parameters in order to be adapted to the dynamic environment.

The service composition is executed in a dynamic environment, *i.e.* there are departures and arrivals of services in the environment. The runtime platform must have mechanisms to self-adapt at these events. A solution is to use the service registry of the service-oriented approach. The service registry must keep a view of the environment with the available services. In the model-driven engineering domain, this service registry is named a model@runtime. The model@runtime contains the functional and non-functional properties of services defined according to the service point of view. The separation of concerns paradigm can be applied to this model, *i.e.* it can be decomposed

Figure 7. Separation of concerns

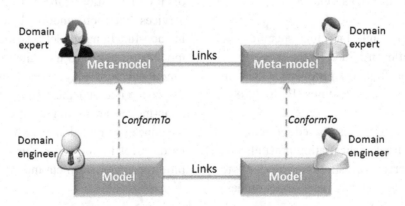

into functional and non-functional part. It brings the modularity and the reusability properties.

The generated code contains parameters such as the concrete address (IP address) of the service. These parameters are completed with the selection of an appropriate service in the service registry. The service selection requires that (1) the service must be available, (2) it must ensure the functionalities defined in the specifications, (3) it must respect the non-functional constraints defined in the specifications. Many approaches (Mabrouk, 2009), (Chollet, 2010) have been proposed to solve the selection problem, particularly in the service domain. The algorithm of service selection returns concrete information for the selected service. This information is used to parameter the proxies files. In a dynamic environment, it should be interesting to apply the selection algorithm just before the service call.

LESSONS LEARNED

Using a model-driven approach brings clear benefits to service composition such as productivity and quality improvements. Regarding quality, we can mention the following findings:

- **Design models are easier and faster to produce.** Domain expert defines service composition only with domain-specific concepts which are much more accessible for them.
- **Design effort is focused on applications**, not on platform details. The abstraction level of the service composition efficiently hides the complexity of the underlying technologies. An abstract service can be a Web Service, a DPWS or an UPnP device. But, the designer has not to deal with the specificities of these technologies.

Figure 8. User learning

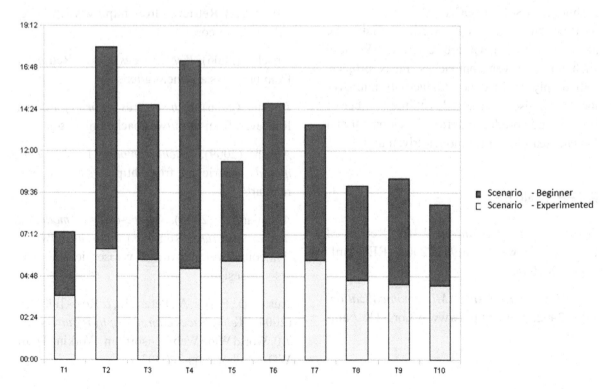

- **Labor-intensive and error-prone development tasks are automated.** Non-functional code, usually named glue code, is a repetitive and error-prone task. The model-driven approach eliminates a large part of this development task.
- **Reuse of designs and tests between platforms is enabled.** In fact, abstract workflow can be easily reused. The concrete services can be changed as the domain workflow remains unchanged.

The model-driven approach has been validated with Secure FOCAS tool (Chollet, 2009). One of the experiments was the measure of the user learning with a tool able to generate the functional and security code from a model of service orchestration. To compare a developer needs approximately 48 hours to develop the security code for an orchestration with ten services. With Secure FOCAS, the same task is made in 15 minutes for beginners and 5 minutes for experimented developers (Figure 8). Additionally, the security is entirely generated from the orchestration at a high level in Secure FOCAS tool.

Regarding productivity, we have first to be aware that skills in SOC are very scarce. Without such model-driven approaches, many projects will simply not be done. Productivity improvements can also be assessed with the number of lines of code produced during development and the user learning of the model-driven tool.

REFERENCES

W3C. (2001). *Canonical XML*. Retrieved from http://www.w3.org/TR/2001 /REC-xml-c14n-20010315

W3C. (2002). *Exclusive XML canonicalization*. July, 2002, from http://www.w3.org/TR /xml-exc-c14n/

W3C. (2002). *XML encryption syntax and processing*. Retrieved from http://www.w3.org/TR/xmlenc-core/

W3C. (2004). Web services addressing (WS-Addressing). Retrieved from http://www.w3.org/Submission/ ws-addressing/

W3C. (2004). *Web services choreography description language*, version 1.0. Retrieved from http://www.w3.org/TR/2004/ WD-ws-cdl-10-20041217/

W3C. (2005). *Web services eventing* (WS-Eventing). Retrieved from http://www.w3.org/Submission /WS-Eventing/

W3C. (2005). *XML key management specification* (XKMS 2.0). Retrieved from http://www.w3.org/TR/2005/ REC-xkms2-20050628/.

W3C. (2008). Web services metadata exchange (WS-MetadataExchange). Retrieved from http://www.w3.org/Submission/2008 /SUBM-WS-MetadataExchange-20080813/

W3C. (2008). *XML signature syntax and processing* (2nd ed.). Retrieved from http://www.w3.org/TR/ xmldsig-core/

Apache. (2006). *Web services – Axis*. Retrieved from http://ws.apache.org/axis/.

Apache. (2006). *Web services security for Java*. Retrieved from http://ws.apache.org/wss4j/.

Apache. (2009). *Apache Rampart - Axis2 security module*. Retrieved from http://ws.apache.org/rampart/

Arsanjani, A. (2004). *Service-oriented modeling and architecture*. Retrieved from http://www.ibm.com/developerworks/ webservices/library/ws-soa-design1/

Austin, D., Barbir, A., Peters, E., & Ross-Talbot, S (2004). *Web services choreography requirements 1.0*. World Wide Web Consortium, Working Draft WD-ws-chor-reqs-20040311.

Badr, Y., Abraham, A., Biennier, F., & Grosan, C. (2008). Enhancing Web Service selection by user preferences of non-functional features. In *Proceedings of the 2008 4th International Conference on Next Generation Web Services Practices* (pp. 60-65). IEEE Computer Society.

Bézivin, J., & Gerbé, O. (2001). Towards a precise definition of the OMG/MDA framework. In *ASE '01: Proceedings of the 16th IEEE International Conference on Automated Software Engineering* (p. 273). IEEE Computer Society.

Chollet, S., & Lalanda, P. (2009). An extensible abstract service orchestration framework. In *Proceedings of ICWS'09: 2009 IEEE International Conference on Web Services (IEEE ICWS 09), Applications & Industry Track* (pp. 831-838). IEEE Computer Society.

Chollet, S., Lestideau, V., Lalanda, P., Colomb, P., & Moreno, D. (2010). Heterogeneous service selection based on formal concept analysis. In *IEEE Proceedings of Congress on Services (SERVICES 2010) - IEEE 2010 International Workshop on Net-Centric Service Enterprises: Theory and Application (NCSE 2010)*.

ContentGuard. (n.d.). *XrML: The digital rights language for trusted content and services*. Retrieved from http://www.xrml.org/

Del Fabro, M. D., Bézivin, J., & Valduriez, P. (2006). *Weaving models with the Eclipse AMW plugin*. In Eclipse Modeling Symposium, Eclipse Summit Europe 2006. Esslingen, Germany.

Fowler, M., & Scott, K. (1999). *UML distilled: A brief guide to the standard object modeling language* (2nd ed.). Addison-Wesley Professional.

France, R., & Rumpe, B. (2007). Model-driven development of complex software: A research roadmap. In *FOSE '07: 2007 Future of Software Engineering* (pp. 37-54). IEEE Computer Society.

Grønmo, R., Skogan, D., Solheim, I., & Oldevik, J. (2004). Model-driven Web services development. In *IEEE International Conference on e-Technology, e-Commerce, and e-Services* (pp. 42-45). Los Alamitos, CA, USA. IEEE Computer Society.

Herrmann, C., Holger Krahn, H., Rumpe, B., Schindler, M., & Völkel, S. (2007). An algebraic view on the semantics of model composition. In *Model Driven Architecture- Foundations and Applications* [Berlin, Germany: Springer.]. *Lecture Notes in Computer Science, 4530*, 99–113. doi:10.1007/978-3-540-72901-3_8

Jammes, F., Mensch, A., & Smit, H. (2005). Service-oriented device communications using the devices profile for Web Services. In *MPAC'05: Proceedings of the 3rd International Workshop on Middleware for pervasive And Ad-hoc cOmputing* (pp. 1-8). ACM.

Kuhne, T. (2006). Matters of (meta-) modeling. [SoSyM]. *Software and Systems Modeling, 5*(4), 369–385. doi:10.1007/s10270-006-0017-9

Lalanda, P., & Marin, C. (2007). A domain-configurable development environment for service-oriented applications. *IEEE Software, 24*(6), 31–38. doi:10.1109/MS.2007.154

Ludewig, J. (2003). Models in software engineering - An introduction. *Software and Systems Modeling, 2*(1), 5–14. doi:10.1007/s10270-003-0020-3

Mabrouk, N. B., Beauche, S., Kuznetsova, E., Georgantas, N., & Issarny, V. (2009). QoS-aware service composition in dynamic service oriented environments. In *Middleware '09: Proceedings of the 10th ACM/IFIP/USENIX International Conference on Middleware* (pp. 1-20). Springer-Verlag.

Microsoft Corporation. (2005). *Web services dynamic discovery* (WS-Discovery). Retrieved from http://schemas.xmlsoap.org/ws /2005/04/discovery/

Microsoft Corporation. (2006). *Devices profile for Web services*. Retrieved from http://specs.xml-soap.org/ws/2006/02/devprof/devicesprofile.pdf

Microsoft Corporation. (n.d.). *Security overview*. http://msdn.microsoft.com/en-uk/library/ms735093.aspx.

OASIS. (2004). *Web services security: SOAP message security 1.0*. Retrieved from http://docs.oasis-open.org/wss/2004/01/oasis-200401-wss-soap-message-security-1.0.pdf

OASIS. (2005). *eXtensible access control markup language* (XACML) version 2.0. Retrieved from http://docs.oasis-open.org/xacml/2.0/access_control-xacml-2.0-core-spec-os.pdf.

OASIS. (2005). *Assertions and protocols for the OASIS security assertion markup language* (SAML) V2.0. Retrieved from http://docs.oasis-open.org/security/saml/v2.0/saml-core-2.0-os.pdf

OASIS. (2006). *Reference model for service oriented architecture*. Retrieved from http://docs.oasis-open.org/soa-rm/v1.0/soa-rm.pdf

OASIS. (2007). *Web services business process execution language*, version 2.0. Retrieved from http://docs.oasis-open.org/wsbpel/2.0/OS/wsbpel-v2.0-OS.html

OMG. (2002). *Meta-object facility (MOF) specification*, version 1.4. Retrieved from http://www.omg.org/cgi-bin/doc?formal/2002-04-03

OMG. (2009). *Unified modeling language* (UML). Retrieved from http://www.omg.org/technology/documents/modeling_spec_catalog.htm#UML

Ortiz, G., & García de Prado, A. (2009). Adapting Web Services for multiple devices: A model-driven, aspect-oriented approach. In *Proceedings International SERVICES Conference* (pp. 754-761). Washington, DC: IEEE Computer Society.

OSOA. (2007). SCA: Service component architectre. Retrieved from http://www.osoa.org/display/Main/Service+Component+Architecture+Specification

Papazoglou, M. P. (2003). Service-oriented computing: Concepts, characteristics and directions. In *WISE'03: Proceedings of the Fourth International Conference on Web Information Systems Engineering* (pp. 3-12). Washington, DC: IEEE Computer Society.

Peltz, C. (2003). Web services orchestration and choreography. *Computer, 36*(10), 46–52. doi:10.1109/MC.2003.1236471

Shaw, M., & Garlan, D. (1996). *Software architecture: Perspectives on an emerging discipline*. Upper Saddle River, NJ: Prentice Hall.

UPnP Forum. (2008). *UPnPTM device architecture* 1.1. Retrieved from http://www.upnp.org/specs/arch/UPnP-arch-DeviceArchitecture-v1.1.pdf

Yu, J., Lalanda, P., & Chollet, S. (2008). Development tool for service-oriented applications in smart homes. In *Proceeding IEEE International Conference on Services Computing (SCC'08)*, (pp. 239-246). IEEE Computer Society.

Yunus, M., & Mallal, R. (2005). An empirical study of security threats and countermeasures in Web services-based services oriented architectures. In *Web Information Systems Engineering – WISE 2005* [Springer.]. *Lecture Notes in Computer Science, 3806*, 653–659. doi:10.1007/11581062_72

Zeeb, E., Bobek, A., Bohn, H., & Golatowski, F. (2007). Service-oriented architectures for embedded systems using devices profile for Web Services. In *AINAW '07: Proceedings of the 21st International Conference on Advanced Information Networking and Applications Workshops* (pp. 956-963). IEEE Computer Society.

Chapter 9
Adaptive and Dynamic Service Compositions in the OSGi Service Platform

Lionel Touseau
Université de Grenoble, France

Kiev Gama
Université de Grenoble, France

Didier Donsez
Université de Grenoble, France

Walter Rudametkin
Université de Grenoble, France

ABSTRACT

Service-oriented architectures provide a good level of decoupling between the elements that compose an application. Service compositions may take into account that services that take part in the composition can appear and disappear. This is typically not the case when using Web Services. In dynamic environments this uncertain service availability is a recurrent scenario. Applications should be ready to handle that and dynamically adapt their behavior based on the application's context and the available services. Although typically presented using Web Services, there are also SOAs that use other technologies. In this chapter we provide an overview on some dynamic service oriented platforms, giving special focus on the OSGi Service Platform. Also, we present what principles and mechanisms help to handle dynamicity, and we provide information on the dynamic service-based component models targeting the OSGi platform. These models allow the realization of applications that are adaptive upon dynamic scenarios where service availability is uncertain.

DOI: 10.4018/978-1-61350-159-7.ch009

INTRODUCTION

Software systems are required to become more and more dynamic, flexible and adaptive. There are different factors at runtime that lead to these properties. For example, changing business requirements or application context changes require an application to be easily reconfigurable without stopping its execution. In such highly dynamic scenarios, applications should be able to adapt their behavior autonomously, and be ready to handle failures and unavailability, as well as the apparition, of component services, performing the necessary configurations at runtime (Di Nitto, 2008).

Dynamic adaptation is required in various application domains relying on service-oriented computing (SOC) principles (Papazoglou, 2003). In a business context, it is crucial to adapt to market changes, and to take advantage of available service providers to successfully achieve business goals through service composition.

In another emerging context such as ubiquitous computing, also referred to ambient intelligence, systems and applications must adapt to a continuously evolving environment, since they must cope with the characteristics of devices composing those systems. Among these characteristics, mobility is a primary cause of dynamic availability. Data storage and processing units have become smaller and smaller, while radio communication protocols have multiplied (e.g., BlueTooth, 6LoWPAN, WiFi, WiMax, Radio-Frequency IDentification, Near-Field Communication, 3G,...) and battery life of mobile devices has been considerably extended. All of these factors have resulted in a dissemination of computing resources enabling pervasive and mobile computing, where resources are not static and the services they provide are dynamically available (Weiser, 1993).

SOC has also started being used to provide a flexible and extensible infrastructure for modular applications such as "a la carte" Java EE applica-

tion servers (e.g., Glassfish or Jonas servers) or plug-in-based applications like the well-known Eclipse IDE. Such systems are likely to evolve at runtime (e.g., the addition, update or removal of new plug-ins and technical services), and thus require the underlying service platform to provide dynamic adaptation capabilities.

Although Service Oriented Architectures are well known through the usage of Web Services, other types of technology take advantage of SOAs and the loose coupling inherent to these architectures to leverage application infrastructure in different scenarios. In this chapter we present some of these technologies, and show how they enable dynamic adaptation, allowing applications to react to changes in the set of services provided in an application's context.

First, this chapter explains the differences between static service-oriented architectures and dynamic service-oriented architectures, and then it presents the requirements needed for a service platform to enable dynamic adaptation. Next, several dynamic service platforms are described, including the OSGi specification. The second part of this chapter explains the software engineering challenges faced when developing dynamic adaptable service-based applications, and the benefits of service-oriented component models in handling dynamism. It then describes several component models, most of which target the OSGi service platform, which is the main topic of this chapter.

BACKGROUND

Before diving into the depths of dynamic adaptation of service-based applications, here is a background summing up required notions such as the principles of service-oriented computing, the notion of service-based application, and what differs between static and dynamic service composition.

Service-Orientation Principles and Service-Based Applications

The Service-oriented approach, which has been popularized by the standardization of Web Services, consists of the use and reuse of a functional entity: the service. A service is described by a contract that is independent from its implementations (Beugnard, 1999). A service provider publishes a service implementation that can be discovered and used by service consumers (Erl, 2007). The pivot between these entities is the service specification. This approach enables a loose coupling between service providers and consumers, and therefore late-binding.

Late-binding, which is a first step towards dynamic applications, allows a service consumer to bind to a specific service implementation at runtime, not at design time. Only the service specification is chosen at design time. For instance, a media application uses a media renderer to play a video. Yet, the media renderer used to play a video clip is chosen at runtime, not at the time the application was written.

The last entity composing a SOA is the service registry, or service broker. Service publication and discovery rely on a service registry, which can be centralized or distributed, unique or duplicated, or even virtual (i.e., each service consumer must keep its own service registry up to date) like in the UPnP service platform. It can also be passive or provide brokering features, that is, matching service consumers to service providers.

Figure 1 describes the three basic interaction phases of a service-oriented architecture (SOA):

- **Service publication:** a service provider publishes the service specification it implements and a way to use its service;
- **Service discovery and selection:** once service providers are discovered, a service consumer can select the ones it wants to interact with;
- **Service binding:** a service consumer must bind to a service provider before using the service.

A service-based application is basically an application that relies on services to operate. Such an application may consume several different services to achieve its goals, and even expose its functionalities through the publication of one or more services.

Sometimes, service applications are also referred to as the set of components (service consumers and service providers) composing the whole application.

Figure 1. Service interaction patterns in a service oriented architecture

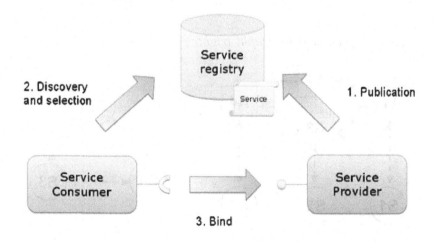

In both cases, services are composed to enable the execution of the application.

Static and Dynamic Service Composition

Individual services may be composed for realizing coarse grained tasks, such as a *travel* (using fine grained services such as *flight reservation, car rental* and *hotel booking*) or the processing of a purchase in an e-commerce system (in this case fine grained services are credit card payment, purchase orders to partners or suppliers, shipping and handling).

Static composition is made at design-time when the architecture and the design of the system are being planned, which may work fine as long as the service components and environment do not change very often (Dustdar, 2005). A vision of static and dynamic service compositions in the Web Services world is provided in (Bucchiarone, 2006). Two approaches, mostly used for business processes, are seen for static service composition: orchestration and choreography. An orchestration consists of a series of activities that require services. The composition logic is at the level of the orchestrator, which is a central coordinator, responsible for invoking and combining the services that are part of the composition. In choreography of services, composition logic is embedded in the service. There is no central coordinator but rather

a set of complex tasks by means of conversations that are undertaken by each participant.

On top of the basic functionality of an SOA we can find approaches for the coordination of services, supporting the composition of services (Figure 2). The choreography and orchestration are two forms of statically defined behavioural composition according to (Peltz, 2003), corresponding to business processes that are normally composed. Regarding the behavioural composition, Web services offer two specifications: WS-BPEL (Business Process Execution Language, formerly BPEL4WS) (Jordan, 2007) for orchestration and WS-CDL for choreography (Qiu et al, 2007).

Dynamic composition is often related to the usage of semantic Web Services, using an ontology-based layer to achieve semantic matches for Web services (Dustdar, 2005). However, others see it as service compositions that have adaptive characteristics. According to (Casati, 2001), service compositions need to work in an adaptive fashion avoiding human intervention if they need to adjust themselves to environmental condition changes. Dynamic service discovery is one of the enablers for such adaptive behaviour. Such needs are similar to those of dynamic compositions in component-based adaptive applications, where it is possible to add, remove, or reconfigure components within an application during its execution. In order to enable dynamic recomposition, a component-based framework needs late binding (McKinley, 2004).

Figure 2. Orchestration (left) and Choreography (right)

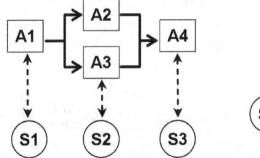 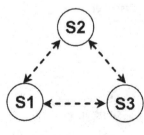

DYNAMIC SERVICE PLATFORMS

Why

As explained in the introduction of this chapter, dynamic adaptation has become a key requirement for applications, and therefore for service-based applications. Late-binding provides a first level of dynamism. But solely late-binding is not sufficient to build efficient adaptive applications.

Dynamic SOC should not be confused with late-binding. Late-binding is a mechanism inherent to SOC provided by loose coupling which allows service implementations to be chosen at runtime. Actually, at selection time, the service consumer only knows the service specification, not the implementation details which depend on the service implementation instances published by service providers. The binding between the consumer and the service instance occurs at the latest possible moment, that is, when the consumer actually needs the service for the first time. However, once a service consumer is bound to a service provider, the binding generally does not evolve anymore, and consequently the application cannot adapt to future changes.

In dynamic SOC, services can be registered and unregistered at anytime, and service consumers can be notified of these changes. A service provider can therefore be dynamically substituted by another if the provider disappears or if another provider offers better contract conditions (Bottaro, 2007).

Requirements to Enable Dynamic Adaptation and Composition in Service-oriented Architectures

To be adaptive, that is, able to react to changes in service availability, the underlying SOA needs to offer additional features, in addition to basic SOC primitives (i.e., service publication, discovery and binding).

The first step is about service provisioning. A service provider should be able not only to pub-

lish its service, but also to withdraw it when it is not available anymore, and replace it to support versioning. The second requirement to enable dynamic service composition is a passive service discovery mechanism: service consumers should be notified of service publications, updates or withdrawals, in order to react to these changes.

The weak coupling brought by the service approach brings flexibility to service-oriented architectures, which do not need to be bound to a specific service implementation since they basically rely on the service contract. However, a service consumer, in principle, has no control over the life cycle of a service provider to whom it is bound and therefore has no guarantees of the provider's availability.

In addition, we can affirm that a service consumer can not know if the service provider being used will be available at the time it will actually be invoked.

Therefore, typical service-oriented architectures as presented in the previous chapters cannot build dynamic service-oriented applications where such service unavailability may be frequent, due to whatever reason.

In order to use a SOA as the basis for building dynamic applications, the basic functions of publication, discovery, selection and binding are not enough. Nevertheless it is possible to extend such basic patterns of interaction to make a SOA dynamic. In this desired context, the dynamic arrival and departure of service providers must be taken into account by service consumers. Therefore, in addition to the basic SOA functions, one would need also the following primitives:

- The withdrawal of services (i.e., a service is no longer available)
- The update of a service version (i.e., replacing a service implementation by another version or modifying its properties)
- The notification of services arrival (publication), update, and departure (withdrawal).

Rather than having to constantly query the service registry in order to verify if a service provider is still available, it is more appropriate that the registry keeps the service consumers informed if the services in which they are interested in are available or not. These two modes would respectively correspond to pull and push approaches for accessing information (in this case the presence of the service provider in the registry).

In a classic SOA, a service consumer is expected to actively query (pull approach) a passive service registry which is basically limited to keeping information about services, which are published by providers, as well as answering to queries made by service consumers looking for service providers.

By adding a feature allowing the service provider to withdraw (i.e., unregister) itself from the service registry and update the provided service, as well as a mechanism for notifying both publication and withdrawal of services, the registry takes a more active role and thus inverses the service discovery mechanism which becomes passive on the consumer side. The notification mode could be general or specific. In a general mode service consumers are notified of any service publication and it is up to the service consumer to do the filtering in order to select which service(s) it would bind to. In a specific mode there could be some sort of pre-selection where the service consumer subscribes to the service registry indicating which service contracts (and possibly additional filters) it is interested in consuming. The main difference between these two approaches is that the former generates more communication than the latter. The overhead may be insignificant in a centralized platform but may hinder performance in distributed scenarios.

This notification mechanism, shown in the Figure 3, allows consumers to respond to changes in the availability of providers and paves the way for adaptive (or reconfigurable) applications, which can evolve at runtime through dynamic service bindings.

Overview of Several Dynamic Service Platforms

Most service platforms supporting dynamic SOC primarily target systems where service availability evolves continuously, unlike web services published by reliable enterprise servers which are rather highly available. For example, UPnP and DPWS explicitly target ad-hoc and local networks of communicating devices. Likewise, Jini was designed to build service-based applications across Java Virtual Machines distributed over a Local Area Network (LAN), and OSGi initially targeted home gateways.

Jini

Jini is a Java-based service platform specified by Sun in 1999 (Waldo, 1999), and now it has become part of the Apache River project. The Jini specification targets dynamic local area networks. It relies on service-orientation principles to bring flexibility into distributed applications where devices and machines (i.e., network nodes) can be discovered dynamically. The Jini platform thus allows developers to design dynamic distributed applications without dealing with the underlying network layer.

From a technical point of view, Jini relies on the Java RMI (*Remote Method Invocation*) communication protocol, and service specifications are syntactically expressed by Java interfaces. Java method calls are processed by proxies (stub and skeletons) since Jini manages serialization and code loading.

When a service provider publishes its service, it sends a Java object that implements the service interface to a *Lookup Service* (i.e., Jini service registry). The provider can also optionally publish attributes (service properties) along with the service interface. Attributes are objects subtyping the Entry class that can be used during the selection process. Service providers must also associate a *lease* (duration) to the published service. This leas-

Figure 3. Dynamic SOA mechanisms

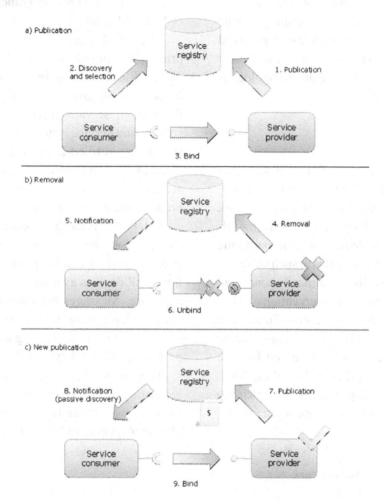

ing mechanism is specific to Jini and absent from other service platforms. Once the lease expires, the service offer is removed from the service registry. Service providers may renew a lease before its expiration or cancel it to unregister its offer. A service provider can also update the attributes attached to its published services. Services can be grouped together inside *federations* managed by the service registry.

To discover services, consumers send unicast or multicast discovery requests to service registries. Yet, Jini lookup services do not offer flexible mechanisms to filter and select service providers. A service consumer request consists of a required service specification (a Java interface) plus an optional set of required attributes. Matching providers are selected on the sole basis of syntactically matching interfaces and identical values of attributes. Jini also enables passive discovery, and therefore dynamic adaptation. A service consumer can subscribe to the lookup service and give a particular service type to be notified of providers' arrivals and departures. A lease is also granted for this subscription. A consumer should renew its lease to continue being notified, or cancel it to stop notifications.

In conclusion, lease and passive service discovery mechanisms make Jini a dynamic service platform that enables the design of dynamic distributed Java and service-based applications.

However, Jini does not specify any facilities for service composition and architecture dynamic adaptation. These tasks are left to developers, and the resulting complexity may explain the rather low adoption rate of Jini while this technology is an early service platform.

UPnP

Universal Plug and Play (UPnP) is a set of specifications defined by the UPnP Forum (UPnP, 2010). UPnP aims at providing a transparent network infrastructure for SOHO (Small Office Home Office), that is, small scale networks similar to the one depicted on Figure 4. Nodes of such networks are devices that should be dynamically connected or disconnected without the intervention of a human operator (zero administration). To achieve this goal, UPnP devices are self-configurable and self-descriptive. UPnP is based on Internet standards such as IP, TCP, UDP, HTTP and XML and is consequently independent from implementation programming language, operating system,

or communication modes (Ethernet IEEE 802.3 or WiFi IEEE 802.11).

UPnP nodes are either *devices* (e.g., light, printer, TV) or *control points* (e.g., PDA, media player). Since control points use services delivered by devices, the latter are service consumers, and the former, service providers. UPnP does not specify any service registry entity. Service consumers are notified by devices when their state changes. Each consumer has to keep its own local service registry up to date according to the events broadcasted on the network.

In UPnP, service discovery is based on SSDP (Simple Service Discovery Protocol (Goland et al, 1999)). A control point first has to look for UPnP devices available on the network, not a service. Messages are sent over HTTP/UDP non-standardized protocols in unicast (HTTPU) or multicast (HTTPMU). Figure 5 describes the protocol stack used by UPnP.

Then, self-descriptive devices indicate to the requesting control point the service they provide via a service description expressed in an XML grammar specific to UPnP. This description pro-

Figure 4. Domestic UPnP network

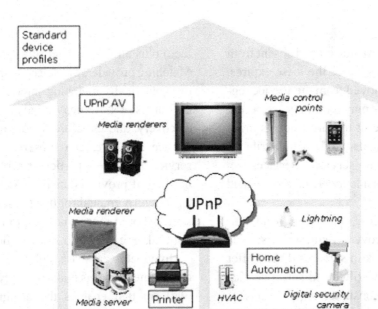

Figure 5. UPnP and DPWS protocol stacks

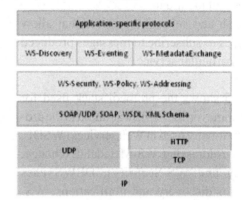

vides the device URL (IP address and port) and a link to more detailed description which specifies the syntactical service interface (state variables, available actions and their parameters). In addition, this description can optionally provide icons for graphical control points, or other information related to the device manufacturer and vendor. Once a service has been discovered, it can be invoked like a web service, using SOAP RPC.

In addition to passive discovery enabled by SSDP notifications, UPnP proposes a notification mechanism to monitor the state of devices. This mechanism is based on GENA (General Event Notification Architecture) (Cohen et al, 1999). When a state variable is modified, the device sends a notification containing the device identifier, the state variable and its updated value. Notifications and state variables are the only way to interact asynchronously with UPnP devices.

UPnP Forum also specifies domain-specific standard device profiles. Some profiles are shown in rectangles in Figure 4 above. For instance, the UPnP AV profile provides descriptions for media renderers and media servers, while the Home Automation profile deals with lightning, HVAC systems (heating, ventilating, and air conditioning) or security video.

The UPnP Forum and UPnP community are still active. Recent products are equipped with UPnP technology (e.g., Microsoft Xbox 360, Sony Playstation 3). Yet, the use of heterogeneous protocols complicates UPnP integration with other technologies. Moreover, service consumers must first discover devices, and then ask for services.

DPWS

The DPWS (Devices Profile for Web Services) specification targets the same networks as UPnP, following the same approach. It is considered as the successor of the latter, except that DPWS is based on a set of standard technologies from Web services, which gives it a greater potential for integration. DPWS is built on a subset of the Web services specification that allows devices to use this industry standard mechanism to communicate with other equipment, computers, and Web services.

The DPWS specification defines two types of services: hosting services and hosted services. A hosting service is linked to a device and plays an important role in the discovery phase, while a hosted service depends on the device that hosts it. In addition to these services, DPWS integrates a set of services:

- Discovery services that can send multicast messages to find other equipment,

- Metadata exchange services that provide dynamic access to a device's hosted services and meta-data
- Publish and subscribe services that allow devices to subscribe to messages produced by a particular service.

Figure 5 shows the protocol stack used for DPWS (Jammes et al, 2005). In addition to the protocols traditionally used in Web services (WSDL, SOAP, WS-Addressing, WS-MetadataExchange, WS-Policy and WS-Security), DPWS uses protocols for discovery and notifications. WS-Discovery is a multicast protocol for plug-and-play and ad-hoc discovery of devices connected to a network, allowing to search for and to locate devices as well as exposing services provided by such devices. The WS-Eventing protocol defines how to manage publish and subscribe events, which allow UPnP devices to be informed of changes in services from other devices.

However, DPWS suffers the same problem as UPnP: consumers of services must keep their own service registry. A practical example is WSD (Web Services for Devices) (Microsoft, 2010), which is Microsoft's implementation of the DPWS specification included in the Windows Vista operating system, allowing devices such as printers or scanners to interact with Windows over an IP network. Windows Vista provides a searchable services directory which can be queried by applications in order to compensate the lack of a centralized DPWS service registry in the network. Moreover, the discovery protocols do not allow the direct discovery of services. It is the device that is discovered in the first place. It can be done either actively by sending messages on the network, by WS-Discovery, or passively listening to the device announcements joining the network.

Finally, although DPWS specifies how it is possible to interact with devices, the client-side specification is vague, which could eventually pose compatibility problems between clients and devices (Zeeb et al, 2007).

The OSGi Service Platform

The OSGi platform specifies a framework that allows the dynamic deployment of Java components and services. The most popular implementations of the OSGi specification are Eclipse Equinox (Eclipse, 2010), Apache Felix (Apache, 2010) and Knopflerfish (Knopflerfish, 2010). OSGi applications can take advantage of Java's dynamic class loading features to update software components without the need to stop the application. One of the peculiarities of the OSGi platform is the fact that unlike other service platforms, it is centralized, that is to say, not distributed. The services running in it are co-located within a single Java Virtual Machine (JVM).

The OSGi specification was established by the OSGi Alliance, a consortium of major industry players such as IBM, Nokia, Motorola and Oracle (OSGi, 2010). The OSGi specification originally targeted applications and technical services for home gateways. The spectrum of targets has subsequently extended. First vehicular embedded systems began using OSGi, and more recently mobile devices (Sprint, 2008) and other small devices whose ressources are limited. On the other side of the spectrum, large modular applications have also begun using OSGi, such as Java Enterprise Edition application servers like Glassfish (Glassfish, 2010) and OW2 JOnAS (JOnAS, 2010) (modularized as an OSGi application in (Desertot, 2006) before going into production servers) or plugin-based architectures such as the Eclipse Platform (Gruber et al, 2005). The OSGi technology is now considered the *de-facto* standard for modular and dynamic Java applications.

The OSGi framework is composed of four layers depicted in Figure 6. Thus, the deployment units which are called *bundles* can:

- be executed on an OSGi platform,
- benefit from a modular approach and communicate with other bundles,

Figure 6. OSGi framework architecture

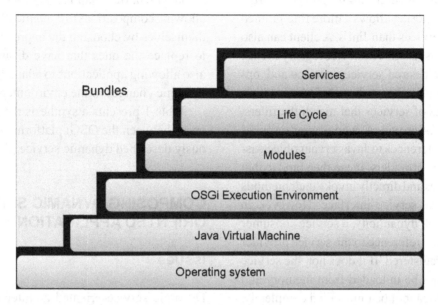

- have their life-cycle managed by the OSGi container,
- consume and provide services thanks to the service layer.

A bundle is a compressed Java archive (jar) which can contain code, resources and native libraries. The jar file manifest contains OSGi specific attributes describing the bundle, providing metadata and the bundle dependencies (e.g. a list of imported and exported class packages). Bundles can interact with each other through the OSGi platform by providing and requiring services and packages (Java types). A bundle needs to have its type dependencies resolved before it can be started. In fact, there are two levels of dependencies: package dependencies (types), and service dependencies (objects). The former are dynamically resolved and necessary for bundle activation, while the latter are also dynamically resolved but not necessary for bundle activation (i.e., services can be discovered during bundle execution). A bundle can be dynamically managed at runtime: it can be installed, uninstalled, started, stopped, updated, that is to say without having to interrupt the platform execution.

In addition to this view related to deployment, the platform offers infrastructure for services as it implements SOA mechanisms providing a dynamic service-oriented architecture. Each bundle can indeed consume and provide services dynamically since OSGi allows the insertion and removal of bundles at runtime, and thus the dynamic arrival and departure services. The OSGi platform defines a service registry, where service instances can be registered and unregistered during application execution. An OSGi service consists of a Java interface and a set of properties (all <key, value>) which can provide information on the service provider or the service provided. A provider may publish in the registry the services it provides, but may also withdraw a provided service and change the properties associated with an existing service publication. The service provider registers with the service registry an object instance which implements the service (by implementing the service interface).

The registry provides both active and passive discovery of services. A consumer can query the registry to retrieve a list of providers of a given service interface. This list can be narrowed down by a LDAP (Lightweight Directory Access Protocol) filter parameter describing the properties of the service. This filtering allows a more fine-grained selection of services than Jini's. A client can also use a listener to subscribe to service registry events, specifying the desired service interface and, optionally an LDAP filter, to be notified of arrivals and departures of services that match the filters. From this list of providers, a consumer retrieves one or more references to Java servant objects issued by service providers. It can then bind to that object instances and directly invoke their methods specified in the service interface. However, in order to manage dynamicity, a service consumer must release the reference to the service provider when it is unregistered. If it does not, the service provider cannot be unloaded from memory and the old bundle cannot be uninstalled completely, leading to dangling objects and stale references which are unknown to most OSGi application developers (Gama, 2008).

Optionally, an OSGi bundle can provide an Activator class, specified in the manifest, that is instantiated and called when the bundle is started. At that moment of startup the activator code can spawn threads and register services in the OSGi service registry. There are also many users who use OSGi just as a deployment platform for applications, ignoring the service oriented approach and the features that allow establishing highly dynamic service-oriented architectures.

The OSGi dynamic composition mechanisms rely on a service-oriented composition approach. OSGi uses service-oriented principles for providing loose coupling between components. Since OSGi does not define a compositional model, any composition of services is the responsibility of the developer as well as the dynamicity influencing this composition, in a similar way to Jini. However, to cope with this complexity, in addition to following good programming practices, there are component models targeting the OSGi platform, which are described later in this chapter. One of the goals is to relieve the developer from the composition of services and from the error-prone

management of dynamism and at the same time allowing compositions to dynamically recompose themselves by choosing the appropriate services to replace the ones that have disappeared, and also allowing applications to adapt themselves to dynamic changes in the environment.

Table 1 presents a synthesis the main differences between the OSGi platform and the previously described dynamic service platforms.

COMPOSING DYNAMIC SERVICE-ORIENTED APPLICATIONS

Issues

Dynamic service-oriented architectures require careful management of service dynamism. The code managing the dynamic binding and unbinding between service consumers and service providers can be found mixed with their business code, therefore increasing the complexity of applications that can react to the dynamic availability of services. Indeed, managing service bindings between service consumers and providers in a composition results in additional non-functional code. Moreover, due to the complexity of binding management, the code tends to be more error-prone. In order to alleviate programmers from such error prone tasks, dynamic service-oriented composition mechanisms are put into action.

Service-Oriented Components

The application of component-based software engineering (CBSE) (Szyperski, 1998) to service-oriented computing allows separating the code managing service bindings from the application code. Thus, developers can focus on functional concerns. Services are published and withdrawn by the component-container of provider components while they are discovered by the container of consumer components. The component-container

Table 1. Main characteristics of dynamic service platforms

	Jini	UPnP	DPWS	OSGi
Programming language	Java	Not specified	Not specified	Java
Service specification	Java interface and attributes	Specific XML-based description	WSDL and extensions	Java interface and service properties
Service registry	Distributed federation; Exposes a *lookup service*	Virtual: consumers have to keep their own local registry up to date	Virtual (cf. UPnP)	Unique and centralized
Publication and removal	Using the *lookup service* and a *lease* mechanism	Multicast announcements (GENA and SSDP events)	Multicast announcements (WS-Eventing)	Register and unregister services through the *bundle context*
Passive discovery	RemoteEvent	SSDP	WS-Eventing	ServiceEvent notifications
Selection	On exact attributes matching	No selection mechanism (depends on the service descriptor)	No selection mechanism	Using LDAP filter on service properties
Binding	Java/RMI	HTTP/SOAP	HTTP/SOAP	Local Java reference

also handles service bindings between consumers and providers using binding policies.

Service-oriented component models combine a SOC approach with component models: the services are provided and consumed by software components that rely on services and trading mechanisms for composition. Service-oriented architectures (SOA) essentially specify the mechanisms for publication, discovery and binding of services. Binding is often performed through the perspective of consumers. Especially in web services the emphasis is placed on the service interface, not the way to provide it. Generally nothing is said about how to provide a service. In addition, the way of designing a service provider is often left to the initiative of the developer.

The component approach applied to SOA is a relatively new initiative. We can cite as pioneer research projects such as ServiceBinder (Cervantes, 2002) in the context of the OSGi platform, and more recently the technology agnostic Service Component Architecture (SCA) (Beisiegel et al, 2007). This approach consists of externalizing specific code related to the platform services, but orthogonal to the business logic that is part of the service. That is to say that publication, discovery

and selection of services can be made by the component container. It can be done either programmatically or declaratively. In the former way the component uses control interfaces provided by the container to bind to a service provider or publish a service. In the latter form, the container interprets metadata in external files or annotations associated with the component code and resolves service dependencies by looking for adequate service providers.

The container can also take over the management of dynamism in SOAs that are described as dynamic, that is to say, the architectures that provide consumers with mechanisms to keep them informed of arrivals and departures of services. The interesting part of the approach lies in the fact that the container can automatically publish or unregister a service (from a registry) based on the life cycle of the component that provides it. When the component is disabled or stopped, the service is removed from the directory. When it is activated or started, the service is published.

Similarly, if a component service consumer delegates the management of service dependencies to the container of a service-oriented component model, the bindings (when a provider exposes its service) and unbindings (when a provider un-registers) will be done automatically. In order to achieve self-adaptivity in components membrane, service bindings are managed by policies. Policies range from static to highly dynamic ones.

When a consumer uses a static binding policy, once it binds to a provider (at runtime through a late-binding mechanism), the binding cannot be reconfigured, and if the service provider is no longer available, the consumer application is stopped. On the contrary, a dynamic binding policy will enable component self-reconfiguration and dynamic adaptation. As soon as a provider of a required service registers or unregisters its service, the bindings of the service consumer application will be reconfigured. This way, service substitution can be performed by the container: a leaving service provider can be replaced by a provider of the same service, or a service provider with a better quality of service can substitute one with lower capabilities (Bottaro, 2006).

Nevertheless, other approaches exist to counter the flaws of a dynamic policy. Service availability cannot be guaranteed and service-based applications have to cope with service disruptions. Typically, the update of a service provider component results in short service disruptions that are not harmful to the application's overall availability. However, following a dynamic binding policy the consumer component will unbind and rebind to the same provider in reaction to an update of the latter. Temporal (e.g., timeouts in SpringDM (Colyer et al 2007) or iPOJO (Temporal, 2010) or SLA-based (Touseau 2008) binding policies provide tolerance to service disruptions and offer a trade-off between the static and dynamic approaches.

Study of Service-Oriented Component Models

In this section we present the main OSGi service-oriented component models like Service Binder, Declarative Services, DependencyManager,

iPOJO and Spring Dynamic Modules, and lastly, although not OSGi-specific, we give an overview of SCA (Service Component Architecture) which is a technology agnostic service-oriented component model.

Service Binder

Service Binder is a component model aiming to facilitate service publication and discovery as well as the bindings of such services in the OSGi platform (Cervantes, 2004). The configuration of the component is expressed in a metadata file embedded in the OSGi bundle. It includes the component class, the provided services, configuration properties, information about the required services and the callback methods to be invoked when a requested service is registered or unregistered. By exploiting this configuration, the Service Binder container handles the publication and the withdrawal of services in the OSGi service registry, but it serves primarily to track the arrival and departure of services.

The selection of services does not differ from the OSGi model; it is based on the service specification (interface) and a set of properties. Thus it is possible to declare a filter in the configuration of the component so it binds only to those providers that match the filter. Then, through the declaration of bind and unbind callback methods implemented by a service consumer component, references to the service objects are injected in the component during execution via these methods. This allows the component to dynamically adapt to changing context and to the dynamic availability of services.

Declarative Services

Declarative Services, which is part of the OSGi specification v.4, is based on the concepts proposed in the Service Binder component model. The specification uses the same objectives and uses the same primitives (bind / unbind) as well as the declarative description of the component through a metadata file.

The life cycle of the component is managed by the container. The component has to implement a control interface including activation and deactivation methods which are respectively called when all required services are available and when a service becomes unavailable and is withdrawn. Thus the life cycle of the component is subject to the dynamic availability of services it requires.

Therefore, if a component that implements a service specification (i.e. a Java interface) says it provides that service, the container of the DS component automatically publishes that service upon component activation and also removes it from the registry upon its deactivation. The context object passed to the components in the activation and deactivation methods can use features that facilitate service lookup and can also provide access to the properties described in the component metadata.

Declarative Services, just like Service Binder, focuses on managing the publication and withdrawal of services in OSGi's service registry as well as the dynamic creation and destruction of service bindings, and the life cycle of components. The DS container can be configured by a declarative description in a metadata file following an XML-based grammar, or by annotations in the component code. The usage of these component models simplifies the task of application developers when using OSGi services, alleviating them from the burden of providing code, often error prone, for ensuring programmatic monitoring of service discovery, binding and publication. Therefore, they can concentrate on the business code of applications.

Dependency Manager

Apache Felix Dependency Manager (Offermans, 2010) is another component model targeting the OSGi platform. DM's specific goal is the construction of service dependencies program-matically instead of using a declarative approach as described in Declarative Services and Service Binder. Yet the principle remains the same and the connections of a service consumer to providers are created and destroyed dynamically based on the component configuration and the dynamic availability of service providers. This offers the same adaptability of service-oriented components built by the declarative models for OSGi described in the previous section.

Using a programming interface provides greater flexibility since new bindings can be created dynamically, while in the case of declarative metadata the configuration description of a component does not evolve after the deployment phase (with the exception of external tools like SOSOC (Donsez, 2009), but it requires externally redefining the metadata anyways). On the other hand, although the code for service dependencies and binding management facilitates the use of basic mechanisms of OSGi, it gets mixed up with business code. Therefore it constitutes a potential source of error in comparison to approaches that do the externalization of service binding through configuration metadata. In addition, a declarative approach allows quickly understanding the application's architecture and dependencies without needing to inspect the source code for that purpose.

iPOJO

iPOJO (Escoffier, 2007) is a subproject of Apache Felix, incorporating the principles of Service Binder and Declarative Services by going further. This component model focuses not only on a more fine grained management of service dependencies, but it also aims to provide hierarchical composition mechanisms, and the possibility to orthogonally deal with other extra-functional concerns in an extensible way. It tries to provide as much transparency as possible for the developer that ideally only manipulates business objects called POJOs (Plain Old Java Object) (Richardson, 2006). The iPOJO infrastructure is responsible for injecting the specified extra-functional properties, leaving the developer to concentrate only on the business code.

iPOJO uses the concept of service dependency. When an iPOJO component requires a service (any ordinary OSGi service, either wrapped by iPOJO or not), then we say it has a dependency on that service. The dependency can be resolved or not. While it is not resolved the service consumer is not valid, that is to say, while the consumer is not bound to a provider meeting the conditions expressed by the dependency. Just like in the Service Binder and Declarative Services approaches, the component remains disabled in that case. Similarly, when all service dependencies are resolved, the component is valid and activated. However we will see below that this is not always true and that the life cycle of an iPOJO component may be affected by other events.

Service dependencies are injected into a POJO by iPOJO's injection mechanism which relies on Java bytecode manipulation (either at build time or deploy time) and inversion of control. Thus the component developer has only to declare the used services as fields of his business object (the POJO) and use them normally, since the injection of those fields will be managed by iPOJO. The iPOJO container is responsible for injecting at runtime the references to the required services.

It can either inject them directly in the fields or pass them as parameters to callback methods in the same way Service Binder and Declarative Services work.

Besides its corresponding POJO, an iPOJO component is formed by its configuration and its modular container. The configuration expressed in the form of metadata which can be either in an XML file or embedded in the POJO code as annotations. The membrane is composed of modular software components called *handlers*. Figure 7 describes an interaction between two components via the handler mechanism.

Each handler manages a non-functional aspect. The configuration of an iPOJO component actually describes the configuration of each handler that composes the component membrane. There are different handlers provided by the iPOJO runtime, but two are dedicated to the dynamic management of services: a handler for service delivery, and another one for dependency management. The former concerns the publication and the withdrawal of the provided service (an iPOJO component) and its properties in the OSGi registry. The latter allows the passive discovery, selection and binding of services. Being much richer than Declarative Services, iPOJO offers various configuration options for a finer grained configuration of bindings. For instance, a consumer

Figure 7. Structure of iPOJO components and interactions between a service consumer and a service provider

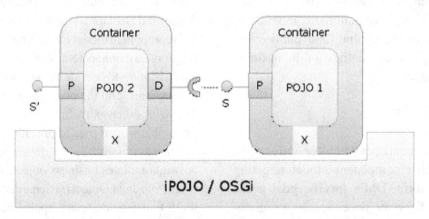

component can provide a default implementation that will be used when there are no service providers available.

Two other handlers present in the iPOJO core runtime allow the configuration of a component's instance by the definition of properties, and to drive the component life cycle, respectively.

The life cycle of an iPOJO component is conditioned by the state of its handlers. While all handlers used by the component are not valid, the component is disabled. It is activated only when its handlers are valid. For example if the service dependencies of a component that provides a service are no longer satisfied, the dependency manager becomes invalid and the components become disabled, resulting in the automatic withdrawal of the service represented by that iPOJO component from service registry.

In addition to the core handlers, the iPOJO container can be extended by custom external handlers. An example is the JMX (Java Management eXtension) handler which dynamically creates MBeans exposing the methods and attributes specified in the component configuration. Another example is the external handler TemporalHandler that extends the management of connections allowing developers to specify a timeout for service bindings. This is intended to provide a certain level of tolerance for disruptions.

The extensibility gained with that modular container approach allows iPOJO to potentially inject any extra-functional property via this handler mechanism.

To better illustrate the handler mechanism, in Figure 7 the POJO 1 component publishes a service S through the handler P (ProvidedService handler). The POJO 2 component is both a service consumer and service provider. By using the service S which it binds to through the handler D (Dependency handler), it is able to provide and publish a service S'. The handler X is an external handler used by both components.

Finally, the iPOJO component model offers composition mechanisms inherited from compo-

nent-based software engineering. The so-called horizontal (or functional) composition based on service delivery and services dependencies: a component can be built from other services in order to provide another service. The vertical (or structural) composition corresponds to the creation of hierarchical composites whose internal structure is built from other components, which may also be composite. These internal components are not visible or usable by other iPOJO components other than the composite containing them, unless the composite exports the services from those components. Figure 8 shows the two schemes supported by iPOJO composition.

Spring Dynamic Modules

Spring Dynamic Modules (Colyer et al 2007) is another service component model on top of OSGi. The Spring framework (Spring, 2010) targets lightweight application servers and has been ported to OSGi to take advantage of its modularity, deployment capabilities and scalability. As one of the consequences, Spring Dynamic Modules has added the concepts of service to its framework so that Spring components, called Spring beans, can provide and use OSGi services. The main idea of Spring Dynamic Modules is to create groups of components called application contexts within OSGi bundles. In an application context, the components communicate using the mechanisms provided by Spring. But between two groups (thus two bundles as there is one context per bundle) communication is done through OSGi services.

An application context descriptor describes both the configuration of a group of components and the services bindings with other applications. The bindings are expressed as dependencies to a required service interface. Like other models for OSGi components, each dependency can specify the following attributes: the filter, the required service provider, the optionality, the cardinality, the ranking of suppliers and the maximum waiting time. The waiting time is used when components

Figure 8. iPOJO supports two types of composition: functional (top) and structural (bottom)

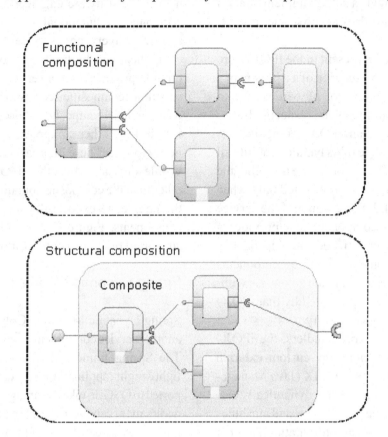

attempt to access a service that is not available. If the service is still not accessible after the time specified, an exception is thrown.

Spring Dynamic Modules uses inversion of control based on dependency injection. As in Service Binder, service dependencies are injected via reflection methods. Like other service-oriented component models presented previously, Spring Dynamic Modules conditions the life cycle of services according to the state of service dependencies. When the service dependencies of a bean are not met, the services provided by the bean are not published.

From the composition perspective, Spring Dynamic Modules provides a mechanism for structural composition, as iPOJO, since the application contexts are composites comprising several beans. However, unlike iPOJO, communication within a group of components does not follow the paradigm of the service approach and are specific to Spring.

Spring Dynamic Modules nevertheless has the advantage of offering a single development model (based also on the principles of POJO) and an effective infrastructure to create dynamic service-based applications. However, the proposed composition model is limited, it does not replace a service provider within a composition, and an application context is not dynamically reconfigurable, which is usually the typical scenario of OSGi-based applications.

Others

There are other approaches that are not part of mainstream OSGi component models but utilize interesting concepts. Extended ServiceBinder (Bottaro, 2006), offers the possibility to import and export local and remote OSGi services as well as non-OSGi services (Jini, UPnP), thus allowing the usage of distributed services over ServiceBinder. With ambient intelligence in mind, extended ServiceBinder enriches the description of component-level service properties. From the perspective of the service provider, this extension provides an alternative for describing static properties of services. The properties can indeed be retrieved dynamically through a method called by the container before the publication of the service and its properties. And from the service consumer's perspective, Extended ServiceBinder allows to specify a service providers sorting method (or utility function) in order to not limit the selection of service criteria defined statically in the description of the component. Typically, if a user moves their context may change. Therefore, preferences concerning the location of the service evolve accordingly, and the dynamic needs can no longer be statically expressed in a declarative way.

Also, we find other approach for enhancing the static description of components in SOSOC (for Service Oriented Oriented Components and Script) (Donsez, 2009). SOSOC consists of a component model developed with scripting languages, which allows reconfiguring the implementation of SCR components (for Service Component Runtime which is the implementation of the Apache Felix Declarative Services). The idea behind SOSOC is to use the dynamic nature of scripting languages to provide flexibility to the static and declarative component models so they can be adapted and reconfigured at runtime, changing the behavior of executing service instances without losing their internal state.

The Peaberry project (Peaberry, 2010) is an extension for Google-Guice (Guice, 2010) that supports dynamic service dependency injection using an annotation-based mechanism. Google-Guice is an injection mechanism trying to simplify business code by using annotations and the factory design pattern. Peaberry fits perfectly in with OSGi, but also provides an extensible plug-

in based mechanism that allows supporting other service registries, and therefore other platforms. The Peaberry component model comes in the form of an OSGi bundle that can be deployed on any OSGi platform compatible with the R4 specification, such as Apache Felix or Eclipse / Equinox.

Service Component Architecture

Service Component Architecture (SCA) (Beisiegel et al 2007) is a set of specifications established by the OSOA consortium bringing together several major industrial groups (IBM, BEA, Oracle, SAP, SUN, Siemens). Since 2007 the specifications are being standardized by the OASIS organization. These specifications describe a structural model for building applications using a SOA. The purpose of SCA is to simplify the writing of application regardless of the technologies used for implementation (e.g. Java, BPEL, EJB, C). The best known implementations of SCA are IBM WebSphere, BEA Aqualogic, and the open-source implementation Apache Tuscany (Tuscany, 2010).

The SCA specification targets the construction of component-based service-oriented architectures. Among other things, the specification provides:

- An implementation model describing the structure of a component.
- An assembly model specifying how compositions and applications are built.

An SCA component, whether primitive or composite (see Figure 9), has a container which consists of three parts:

- Services, which are the features it offers to other components. Although SCA is technology agnostic, service specifications are expressed in the language of the service platform being used. Most often these are WSDL descriptors or Java interfaces.

Figure 9. SCA assembly model

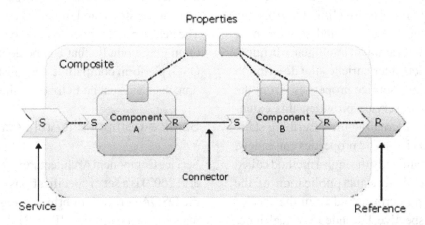

- References, which express the services required by the component to ensure its operation. These required services may be either provided by SCA components or by third party systems (exposing Web Services or communicating via JMS, for example). This is expressed through bindings (e.g., SOAP / HTTP, JMS, JCA, IIOP). The references are a sort of service dependency. Thus, a component must describe for each reference the required interface, cardinality, optionality and can declaratively define the policies on extra-functional properties (security, transaction, etc) to be ensured, as well as a unique identifier.
- Properties that correspond to the configuration of the component. These properties are configured when the component is constructed, that is, when instantiating the SCA component.

The assembly model proposed by SCA is a structural composition model. SCA defines a compositional language called SCDL (for Service Component Definition Language) to describe applications. Thus, in SCA, an application is actually an assembly of component types communicating via services. A component type can have multiple implementations, but all must follow the pattern defined in the component type. The implementations are chosen when deploying the application. Inside of a composite, the components are connected using connectors called fixed wires. Once the binding is performed, these connectors cannot change during the execution of the application: the composition is established based on unique identifier references.

Moreover, the composition model described in SCA is hierarchical. That is to say that a composite made from components of rank N is a component of rank N +1, and behaves according to SCA's implementation model: it can provide services, depend on references and be configured with properties.

Finally, SCA defines the notion of domain. Each domain corresponds to an implementation of the SCA specification. Thus it is not always possible for SCA applications of two different domains (built on top of two different infrastructures) to interoperate. This is due to the fact that SCA is not tied to a specific technology and each implementation of SCA supports a set of technologies, not necessarily being compatible with one another.

The technological independence of SCA allows many platforms to take advantage of its strengths, especially the easy integration with the services approach. This is for example the case of Apache Tuscany (Tuscany, 2010) and the Newton Component Model (Newton, 2010), both of which use OSGi for offering scalability, modularity and deployment easiness by using OSGi bundles with SCA. Thus, they benefit from the hierarchical composition model from SCA and the remote access to OSGi services. This also applies to OW2 FraSCAti (Seinturier et al, 2009) which provides support for implementing SCA components made in accordance with the principles of the Fractal component model (Bruneton et al, 2004). FraSCAti thus allows Fractal to enter the world of SOA, and the other way around, by enabling SCA to benefit from Fractal to create reconfigurable components.

However, even if SCA has the advantage of offering a technologically independent component model that supports the addition of hierarchical structural composition, some key points are left to the initiative of its implementations. For example, SCA does not define nor reuse a service description language. In addition, policies associated with the management of connectors between components are not specified and depend on each implementation. Finally, SCA shares a weakness with Web services in terms of dynamism. As the links between components explicitly reference other components via their unique identifiers, service providers are selected during the deployment phase, which prevents their substitution so execution does not support the dynamic availability of services.

CONCLUSION

Although dynamic adaptation has become a major requirement for applications, the setup of such dynamic applications is not an easy task. First, the underlying service platform must provide features required to build reactive applications.

Yet, even with such platforms, dynamically composing adaptive applications remains challenging since developers have to deal with the

code dedicated to the adaptation logic in addition to the application business code. A recent approach aims at easing this task by applying the principles of component-based software engineering to service-oriented architectures. This approach based on service-oriented component models is a good starting point for easily building applications able to autonomously adapt to context changes. Applications can indeed be seen as service compositions while context changes may result in the evolution of the availability of services or their properties.

This chapter has presented a state-of-the-art on dynamic service platforms, that is to say, the service platforms that enable the design of adaptive and reconfigurable applications following a service-oriented architecture, and a survey on existing service-oriented component models.

Regarding dynamic and autonomous reconfiguration, some issues are still open. Adapting the architecture is not always the best decision. Sometimes a reconfiguration may be inefficient or counterproductive. For instance, a leaving service might just undergo an update and reappear immediately. Moreover this decision cannot always be based on the sole information of service availability. Even if it was not tackled in this chapter, changes in the quality of service may also be a triggering factor for reconfigurations.

Service-oriented component models have paved the way towards self-adaptive service-based applications. However existing models still need improvements since they require a more complex adaptation and composition logic than what other fields of software engineering, such as autonomic computing or semantics, currently provide.

REFERENCES

Apache. (2010). *Felix iPOJO temporal dependency documentation*. Retrieved from http://felix.apache.org/site/temporal-service-dependency.html

Apache. (2010). *Felix*. Retrieved from http://felix.apache.org

Apache. (2010). *Tuscany*. Retrieved from http://tuscany.apache.org

Beisiegel, M., et al. (2007). *SCA service component architecture: Assembly model specification*, Open Service Oriented Architecture, 2007. Retrieved from http://www.osoa.org/display/Main/Service+Component+Architecture+Home

Bottaro, A., & Gérodolle, A. (2006). *Extended service binder: Dynamic service availability management in ambient intelligence*. In 1st Workshop on Future Research Challenges for Software and Services, Vienna, Austria.

Bottaro, A., & Hall, R. S. (2007). Dynamic contextual service ranking. In *Proceedings of 6th International Symposium on Software Composition* (SC 2007), Braga, Portugal, March 2007.

Bruneton, E., Coupaye, T., Leclercq, M., Quema, V., & Stefani, J.-B. (2004). An open component model and its support in Java. *7th International Symposium on Component-Based Software Engineering (CBSE), LNCS 3054*, (pp. 7-22). May 2004.

Bucchiarone, A., & Gnesi, S. (2006). A survey on services composition languages and models. *In International Workshop on Web Services Modeling and Testing* (pp. 37-49).

Casati, F., & Shan, M. C. (2001). Dynamic and adaptive composition of e-services. *Information Systems, 26*(3), 143–163. doi:10.1016/S0306-4379(01)00014-X

Cervantes, H., & Hall, R. S. (2002). Beanome: A component model for the OSGi framework. In *Proceedings of the International Workshop on Software Infrastructures for Component-Based Applications on Consumer Devices*, Lausanne, Switzerland, September 2002

Cervantes, H., & Hall, R. S. (2004). *Autonomous adaptation to dynamic availability using a service-oriented component model*. International Conference on Software Engineering (ICSE), Edinburgh, Scotland, May 2004.

Cohen, J., et al. (1999). *General event notification architecture base*. Retrieved from http://www.upnp.org/download/draftcohen-gena-client-01.txt

Colyer, A., et al. (2007). *Spring dynamic modules for OSGi 1.0.1*. Retrieved from http://static.spring-framework.org/osgi/docs/1.0.1/reference/html/

Desertot, M., Donsez, D., & Lalanda, P. (2006). *A dynamic service-oriented implementation for Java EE Servers*. In *Proceedings of the 3th IEEE International Conference on Service Computing* (SCC'06), Chicago, USA, 18-22 September 2006. IEEE Computer Society. ISBN: 0-7695-2670-5

Di Nitto, E., Ghezzi, C., Metzger, A., Papazoglou, M., & Pohl, K. (2008). A journey to highly dynamic, self-adaptive service-based applications. *Automated Software Engineering, 15*, 313–341. doi:10.1007/s10515-008-0032-x

Disruptions, in proceedings of IEEE International Conference on Services Computing (SCC'08), July 8-11, 2008. IEEE Computer Society, Washington, DC, pp. 415-422.

Donsez, D., Gama, K., & Rudametkin, W. (2009). Developing adaptable components using dynamic languages. In *Proceedings of 35th EUROMICRO Conference on Software Engineering and Advanced Applications* (SEEA). Patras, Greece, 27 August 2009.

Dustdar, S., & Schreiner, W. (2005). A survey on web services composition. *International Journal of Web and Grid Services, 1*(1), 1–30. doi:10.1504/IJWGS.2005.007545

Eclipse. (2010). *Equinox*. Retrieved from http://www.eclipse.org/equinox

Erl, T. (2007). *SOA principles of service design.* Upper Saddle River, NJ: Prentice Hall Press.

Escoffier, C., Hall, R. S., & Lalanda, P. (2007). iPOJO: An extensible service-oriented component framework. In *Proceedings of the IEEE International Conference on Services Computing* (ICSOC'07) (pp. 474-481). Washington, DC: IEEE Computer Society.

Gama, K., & Donsez, D. (2008). A practical approach for finding stale references in a dynamic service platform. In *Proceedings of 11th International Symposium on Component Based Software Engineering* (CBSE-2008), Karlsruhe, Germany, 14 October 2008.

Glassfish. (2010). Retrieved from https://glassfish.dev.java.net

Goland, Y., et al. (1999). *Simple service discovery protocol v1.0.* IETF, 1999.

Google. (2010). *Guice.* Retrieved from http://code.google.com/p/google-guice/

Gruber, O. (2005). The Eclipse 3.0 platform: Adopting OSGi technology. *IBM Systems Journal, 44*(2), 289–299. doi:10.1147/sj.442.0289

Jammes, F., Mensch, A., & Smit, H. (2005). Service-oriented device communications using the devices profile for web services. In *Proceedings of the 3rd International Workshop on Middleware for Pervasive and Ad-hoc Computing* (MPAC '05)

JOnAS. (2010). *Java open application server.* Retrieved from http://jonas.ow2.org

Knopflerfish. (2010). *Knopflerfish.* Retrieved from http://www.knopflerfish.org

McKinley, P. K., Sadjadi, S. M., Kasten, E. P., & Cheng, B. H. (2004). Composing adaptive software. *Computer, 37*(7), 56–64. doi:10.1109/MC.2004.48

Microsoft. (2010). *WSDAPI client application and device host development.* Retrieved from http://msdn.microsoft.com/en-us/library/bb821828.aspx

Newton. (2010). *Component model.* Retrieved from http://newton.codecauldron.org/site/concept/ComponentModel.html

Offermans, M. (2010). *Apache Felix dependency manager.* Retrieved from http://felix.apache.org/site/apache-felix-dependency-manager.html

OSGi Alliance. (2010). *OSGi service platform core specification.* Retrieved from http://www.osgi.org/

Papazoglou, M. P. (2003). Service-oriented computing: Concepts, characteristics and directions. In *Proceedings of the Fourth international Conference on Web information Systems Engineering.* WISE. IEEE Computer Society, Washington, DC

Peaberry Project. (2010). *Peaberry Project.* Retrieved from http://code.google.com/p/peaberry/

Peltz, C. (2003). Web services orchestration and choreography. *Computer, 36*(10), 46–52. doi:10.1109/MC.2003.1236471

Qiu, Z., Zhao, X., Cai, C., & Yang, H. (2007). Towards the theoretical foundation of choreography. In *Proceedings of the 16th International Conference on World Wide Web* (WWW'07), Banff, Alberta, Canada, May 08-12, 2007, (pp. 973-982). New York, NY: ACM.

Richardson, C. (2006). *POJOs in action: Developing enterprise applications with lightweight frameworks.* Manning Publications Co.

Seinturier, L., Merle, P., Fournier, D., Dolet, N., Schiavoni, V., & Stefani, J.-B. (2009). Reconfigurable SCA applications with the FraSCAti platform. In *Proceedings of the 2009 IEEE International Conference on Services Computing (SCC'09), Symposium on Compiler Construction,* September 21-25, 2009. IEEE Computer Society, Washington, DC, (pp. 268-275).

Spring Source. (2010). *Spring framework*. Retrieved from http://www.springframework.org

Szyperski, C. (1998). *Component software – Beyond object-oriented programming*. Addison-Wesley and ACM Press.

Touseau, L., Rudametkin, W., & Donsez, D. (2008) *Towards a SLA-based Approach to Handle Service*

Universal Plug and Play Forum. (2010). *Home page*. Retrieved from http://www.upnp.org

Waldo, J. (1999). The Jini architecture for network-centric computing. *Communications of the ACM, 42*(7), 76–82. doi:10.1145/306549.306582

Weiser, M. (1993). Ubiquitous computing. *IEEE Computer, 26*(10), 71–72.

Zeeb, E., et al. (2007). *Lessons learned from implementing the devices profile for Web services*. In *Proceedings of the IEEE-IES Digital EcoSystems and Technologies Conference,* (pp. 229-232).

KEY TERMS AND DEFINITIONS

Component: A component is a central concept in CBSE. A software component can be defined as a unit of composition. A component is designed as a black box, *i.e.* its internal structure is not available to the public. Such design allows components to be easily substituted in a software system.

Component-Based Software Engineering (CBSE): CBSE is a sub-discipline of software engineering based on the concept of separation of concerns where software systems are built as a composition of reusable components.

Enterprise JavaBeans (EJB): EJB is a component architecture written in the Java programming language for modular construction of enterprise applications.

Java Enterprise Edition (Java EE): Java EE is a platform for server development in the Java programming language. It is broadly based on modular components such as EJB running on an application server. Those components provide functionalities to deploy fault-tolerant, distributed, multi-tier Java software.

Near-Field Communication (NFC): NFC is a set of standards for short-range wireless radio-frequency based communications. These standards have been defined by NFC Forum. NFC technology can be embedded in electronic devices such as mobile phones or PDA.

OSGi: OSGi is both a component-based platform and a service platform for the Java programming language. OSGi aims to facilitate the modularization of Java applications as well as the interoperability of such applications and services over various devices.

Radio Frequency Identification (RFID): RFID is a wireless technology that allows for non contact reading. RFID is often used as an alternative to bar coding.

Service-Oriented Computing (SOC): SOC promotes the use of well-defined composition units – services – to support the rapid development of applications. The central objective of this approach is to reduce dependencies among composition units, where a unit is typically some remote functionality accessed by clients.

Section 6
Service Verification and Validation

Chapter 10
Service Composition Verification and Validation

Manuel Palomo-Duarte
University of Cadiz, Spain

ABSTRACT

Web services are changing software development thanks to their loosely coupled nature and simple adoption. They can be easily composed to create new more powerful services, allowing for large programming systems. Verification and validation techniques try to find defects in a program to minimize losses that its malfunction could cause. Although many different approaches have been developed for "traditional" program testing, none of them have proven definitive. The problem is even more challenging for new paradigms like web services and web service compositions, because of their dynamic nature and uncommon web service-specific instructions. This chapter surveys the different approaches to web service and web service composition verification and validation, paying special attention to automation. When no tools are available for a given technique, academic efforts are discussed, and challenges are presented.

INTRODUCTION

According to the Software Engineering Body of Knowledge - SWEBOK (Abran & Moore, 2004), *"verification and validation addresses software product quality directly and uses testing techniques which can locate defects so that they can be addressed"*. Software *Verification*

and Validation (V&V) has been a key problem in Computer Science since the so-called *Software Crisis*, causing monetary and human losses (Leveson, 1995). Many efforts have been made since then to develop computer programs that meet system requirements, but up to date, no solution has proven definitive (Myers, Badgett, Thomas, & Sandler, 2004). This way, a "good" quality can only be achieved by carefully combining different techniques.

DOI: 10.4018/978-1-61350-159-7.ch010

Service Oriented Architectures (SOA), and Web Services (WS) are changing software development. They greatly ease system interoperability, and new WS can be built on them using service composition technologies. But they also include some peculiarities uncommon in other paradigms (like WS-specific instructions), so V&V techniques have to be adapted accordingly (Bozkurt, Harman, & Hassoun, 2010). This chapter surveys the different approaches to web service and web service composition V&V, paying special attention to the tools available to automate them.

The rest of the chapter is divided into five sections. The first one provides some background information to make the text self-contained. The second section, *Service Verification and Validation*, deals with V&V techniques for external WS, given that we don't have access to their code (i.e. *black-box testing*). The following one explains additional techniques to test the internal logic of a composition of different WS, that is *white-box testing*. Along these two sections we comment tools[1] to automate the different software testing techniques, or proposals showing how to implement them. In the fourth and fifth sections, we compile future research directions, and draw some conclusions about the state of the art of service and service composition V&V. Finally, we include the references, some additional readings and a glossary of key terms and definitions.

BACKGROUND

Service Composition

WS usually publish their available operations using WSDL files. WSDL is the XML-based language standardized by W3C® (WSDL Technical Committee, 2007) to describe WS. WSDL description files include all the information needed for the interaction between service invoker and provider: the URI where the WS waits for requests, the different kinds of messages accepted, etc. WSDL specifications use XML Schema data types to describe the messages exchanged.

Thanks to their platform and language independence, WS can be not only invoked in traditional programs, but they can also be easily composed to create new higher-level ones that suit costumer needs (Newcomer & Lomow, 2004). This is sometimes called *programming in the large*. There are two ways of composing services: choreography and orchestration (Papazoglou, 2006). When orchestrating there is a director process that implements all the logic of the composition, whereas in choreography that logic is distributed over the different partner services.

Orchestration is simpler, as it can use independent services, and is easier to monitor. This has led to a much wider industrial support: the WS-BPEL (Web Services Business Process Execution Language) orchestration language OASIS® standardization committee was formed by specialists from the leading IT companies: Oracle®, Microsoft®, IBM®, HP®, etc. (WS-BPEL Technical Committee, 2007). Additionally, BPMN (Business Process Modeling Notation) has backed WS-BPEL supporting automatic translation from BPMN graphical models to it (Business Process Management Initiative, 2010). In contrast, the W3C language for choreography, WS-CDL, remains as a Candidate Recommendation since 2005 (Web Services Choreography Working Group, 2005).

WS-BPEL is a language for static web service orchestration. It includes the usual instructions in imperative languages for data manipulation, assignments, loops, and other WS-specific ones for web service invocation, timeout event processing, compensation for faulty WS, etc. WS-BPEL compositions are deployed in a WS-BPEL engine, usually contained in an application server, that creates a new process when an invocation to a service is received.

There are other languages that allow dynamic discovery and composition of semantic WS (WS including semantic information in their description), namely OWL-S and WSMO. Nevertheless, they are poorly supported by industry: there are few semantic WS available that can hardly be automatically discovered and composed. OWL-S was standardized by W3C in 2004, but some problems reduced its adoption (Balzer, Liebig & Wagner, 2004). OWL-S version 2 was released recently (OWL Working Group, 2009). It makes the language easier to use, but it is still soon to see if it will help to popularize it. As for WSMO, the ESSI WSMO Working Group is leading different efforts to spread its use (ESSI WSMO Working Group, 2010) with limited success for the moment.

Software Verification and Validation: The Testing Process

The Curriculum Guidelines for Undergraduate Degree Programs in Software Engineering - a Volume of the Computing Curricula Series, (The Joint Task Force on Computing Curricula, 2004) states that *"software verification and validation uses both static and dynamic techniques of system checking to ensure that the resulting program satisfies its specification and that the program as implemented meets the expectations of the stakeholders"*. Static testing techniques do not execute code to test a program, but dynamic ones do, being complementary (Bertolino & Marchetti, 2004). Next sections briefly introduce what we consider the most interesting techniques to test WS and web service compositions. For an in-depth survey see (Myers, Badgett, Thomas, & Sandler, 2004).

The testing process is a part of the development process, so it must be adapted to the development methodology and project constraints (costs, deadlines, human resources, etc.). All the techniques we will comment need the source code to operate, so they must be applied after the program has been, at least, partially implemented. Literature has shown that there are different testing strategies to lead the testing process, stating which techniques to use, who is responsible of every part of the

testing process, how to act when a bug is found, when to stop testing, etc. (Bertolino, 2007). These implementation details of the testing strategy must follow the guidelines of the software development methodology used in the project

Finally, we would like to remark the role of open-source in V&V. The main contribution of open-source software to a V&V department is not cost reduction, but freedom. In the long term, open-source software can help avoid technology dependance (something specially critical with recent companies' bankruptcy or acquisitions), and take advantage of massive usage and contributions from the community (Tapscott & Williams, 2006), as well as an increase in the in-house know-how and adaptability (Raymond, 2001). This has lead to many public institutions to create policies supporting open-source software as a priority in IT technology (Ghosh, 2006). So we recommend that any V&V department should, at least, consider open-source as a positive feature when analyzing different tools and systems to adopt. For this reason, in the text we point open-source tools when available.

Software Verification and Validation Static Techniques

On the side of static techniques, there are different ones based on human interaction (code reviews, inspections and walkthroughs), which can hardly be automated. Here, we will focus on tools to automate the process of checking certain properties of the code through models. Using formal models like Petri nets, Finite state machines or Pi-calculus, we can usually find deadlocks, unreachable sections or uninitialized variables, among other pitfalls in a program. The use of techniques based on formal approaches produces limited but almost (Hall, 1990) totally reliable results (as long as the reasoning process followed is sound), so their results can be complemented with dynamic techniques.

Software Verification and Validation Dynamic Techniques

Dynamic testing techniques execute code to check a system. So, all of them need input data to operate. The technique that aims to generate them is called *test data generation*. Test data generation creates the input needed to execute or invoke a program. If it is augmented with expected results, then it is called a *test case*. A set of test cases is called a *test suite*. Test case generation can also intentionally generate wrong input data to check that the system detects it and behaves as it supposed to do: providing a suitable error message and returning to a consistent state. This is called *robustness testing*.

Test suites are usually produced to meet a certain *adequacy criteria*. For example, a test case that executes all instructions of a program provides *instruction coverage* or *statement coverage*. It is one of the weakest structural coverage criteria. Other stronger ones are *branch coverage* (that makes every conditional expression evaluate to both true and false), *path coverage* (that makes every possible path to be executed), or *loop coverage* (that executes every loop zero, one and more than one time). Obviously, the stronger the criterion is, the better testing it provides. But also, the hardest it is to obtain, the longer it will take to execute and check. Test suite evaluation and improvement is a classical topic in testing (Myers, Badgett, Thomas, & Sandler, 2004).

Mutation testing is a testing technique, now used for more than thirty years (Woodward, 1993) to measure the quality of a test suite. To use it, a set of mutation operators needs to be defined for the target language. Operators are applied to a program to produce mutants: copies with a single change modeling a common mistake from a programmer (Jia & Harman, 2010). A typical mutation is changing an operator in a mathematical expression, for example tweaking (x=y+1) to (x=y-1). These mutated versions of the program are later run under a test suite. The output of each mutant is compared with that of the original program for the same test suite. Any difference in their outputs indicates that the test suite can detect the bug the mutant includes, so it can be considered a "good" suite.

Using the data previously obtained the system can be executed to perform, for example, *functional testing*. It checks the right behavior of a piece of software. If that software is tested apart from the rest of the system it is called *unit testing*, but if it is included in the whole system it is called *system testing*. One of the most challenging open problems in functional testing is the *oracle problem*. An oracle is a system that given a program input it tells the output that it must provide. Oracle definition and development is a classical problem in software testing, and many different approaches exist (Davis & Weyuker, 1981). Human oracles are not desirable, as they makes massive testing very expensive, and (as any other human action) are error-prone, specially with large workloads that cause fatigue.

Other robust solution for oracle problem is *reference testing*, that applies when a previous version of the program exists and can be used as an oracle. But this is only usually available when migrating or upgrading a program, for example when reimplementing a desktop program to make it available as a web service. In a similar way, *regression testing* (that tests a modified program), updates a test suite from the previous version of the program to ease testing a new version of it. Experience has shown (Myers, Badgett, Thomas, & Sandler, 2004) that a change in a program quite often adds new bugs to it, especially in large systems. So a suitable selection of valid test cases (that test features that hold between both versions) and replacement of invalid ones with new ones that test recently added features usually produces good results.

Some more specific techniques can be applied to certain cases. One of them is *metamorphic testing*, that can create new test cases based on a previous test suite, and additionally solves the oracle problem for testing (Zhou, Huang, Tse, Yang, Huang, & Chen, 2004). It is based on a certain relation hold between the specific program input and output, so that it can automatically generate new test data based on a previous test data set and calculate a new relation that must hold for the new test output. Its main drawback is that its applicability is limited to problems where relations between inputs and outputs are well-known (mainly, mathematical ones).

Dynamic invariant generation is a technique that has been successfully used to help test and improve programs (Ernst, Perkins, Guo, McCamant, Pacheco, Tschantz, & Xiao, 2007). It basically checks for assertions in a set of program traces. As those properties are not mathematically derived, but based on a set of test cases, they are called *likely invariants* or *dynamic invariants*. This technique can be used to detect bugs in the code, mitigating the oracle problem or checking for deficiencies in a test suite.

Opposite from functional testing, there is *nonfunctional testing*. It tests other different features of the system: usability, maintainability, portability, etc. Some of them can be hardly applied to web service testing. So we will only consider in *workload testing* (also known as *stress testing*), that checks that the system is able to serve a certain amount of parallel requests.

SERVICE VERIFICATION AND VALIDATION

Introduction

One of the main advantages of WS is that they can be invoked through the network independently from the hardware platform, the operating system and the programming language in the client and server sides. This way, systems can be built upon distributed services easily. But it implies a challenge for testing in many ways. To start with, independently from SOA-specific features, when the tester does not have access to the source code of the system, testing techniques are limited to black-box dynamic approaches (that is, techniques based on service execution).

Additionally, other WS-specific issues arise. For example, when a program invokes a service formerly used, can we be sure it is the same piece of software than before? We only know its WSDL definition and URL, but the service provider could have changed the implementation of the service during that time, producing messaging or functional problems. Even more, in general we cannot assume that we can make as many invocations as desired to the service under test. For example, web service invocations can be costly (like a stock market service), can block resources (like a flight reservation service), or can take too long (like a complex computation), etc. This limitation can be overcome if the server provides a "testing version" of their services. But even this is not always available, and if available, does not usually behave exactly like the actual service.

In this section we assume that we have a service we would like to use, no matter how it was discovered. After confirming its interoperability with our system, for example, through the different Basic Profiles approved by the WS-I (Web Services Interoperability Organization, 2010), backed by most products in the SOA world, we have to test it systematically before using it in production. In this section we will see the different approaches to do it: test data generation, unit testing and regression testing.

Test Data Generation

When generating test data for an external web service, all we know about it is its public interface described in a WSDL document (except for semantic WS, but as of today, they are not widely supported). The simplest approach is random test data generation. It can be automatically created from the WSDL documents, for example using WSDL-Test (Sneed & Huang, 2007) or the commercial tool Parasoft® SOAtest (Parasoft, 2010). They both can optionally check properties on web service output messages (these properties have to be provided by a human). The advantage of this method is that it is a completely automated technique. As for fault-based test case generation, it is implemented in the WebSob framework (Martin, Basu, & Xie, 2007), checking for inconsistencies in WSDL description files.

Other complementary approach is suggested by (Bai, Dong, Tsai, & Chen, 2005). It generates test data according to dependencies between operations of the same stateful service. For example, a purchase of a certain item on a shopping service probably depends on a previous stock income service invocation. This way, side effects from the invocation of a web service can be tested. The open-source tool soapUI (Eviware, 2010), allows for defining test cases that depend on the previous execution of others. The tool is backed by Eviware®, a private company that offers support and commercial versions improving its capabilities.

We have seen several black-box testing test data generation techniques, but they are all very limited, as they can only rely on the interface of the service to be tested. This way, little confidence on its validity can be assured. For example, if we generate a test suite comprising 1000 test cases, can we be sure it covers all execution paths? Inspecting the source code, we could, perhaps, check that all of those test cases execute the same path many times, while a certain path that contains a bug remains untested. Using internal information (as we will see in the next section), we could define a much better and concise test suite that executes all paths.

Unit Testing

Web service unit testing can test both functional and non-functional properties. It aims to be sure that the web service works properly, so it can be integrated into the system. Most of the techniques and tools outlined in the previous subsection produce input data, but can only automatically check general properties on web service output. To overcome these limitations and reduce human error (as assertions are usually manually inserted by a human), a method to overcome the oracle problem is needed.

In web service black-box unit testing all approaches have to take advantage of certain additional information about the service to automatically create test cases solving the oracle problem. For example, contracts supplied by the service provider (Heckel & Lohmann, 2004), test sheets (Atkinson, Brenner, Falcone, & Juhasz, 2008) or extensions of the WSDL definitions of the WS to ease their black-box testing (Tsai, Paul, Wang, Fan, & Wang, 2002).

Robustness testing considers web service behavior when a wrong input is received. The WebSob framework (Martin, Basu, & Xie, 2007) automatically generates valid and invalid input data for a web service, and checks its output for input/output message pairs that can show an inconsistency in web service functionality. Additionally, it allows to compare previous test results to implement regression testing.

Another aspect unit tests deals with is workload testing. In SOA, it is usually considered a Quality of Service (*QoS*) feature. It is specially interesting for systems with time restrictions, as service consumers often contract a certain Service Level Agreement that must be met by the services. It is addressed by the previously commented tools ParaSoft SOAtest and soapUI. In a similar way, test cases can be used as a contract between service provider and service consumer (Bruno, Canfora, Di Penta, Esposito, & Mazza, 2005). This way, they can be also used to measure functional and QoS behavior of new versions of a web service. This is part of the SeCSE project, that will be commented in detail in the next subsection on regression testing. A quality management system for QoS contracts is proposed by (Yeom, Tsai, Bai, & Min, 2009). It supports creation and deployment of contracts, registration of WS and monitoring to detect and notify contract violations.

Regression Testing

Regression testing is a technique that aims to detect bugs after upgrading a program (for example fixing bugs, adding new features, reimplementing part of the system, etc.). This problem is limited in "traditional" software, because when a program is executed, it invokes libraries that are installed in the system. And even if a new version of a library is published, the program keeps invoking the same version of the library, and the system behaves the same until the moment when the developer decides to upgrade it. But this problem becomes critical in SOA, as services are external and can change in any moment, so service users (both customers and integrators) must be specially aware of the problems that it could cause.

Concerning regression testing of WS, one of the most interesting approaches, apart from the Web-Sob framework, is the SeCSE project (Melideo, 2006). It provides free and open-source tools for service-centric systems. It considers two aspects: functional testing (including regression testing), and QoS in terms of time. It stores the information sent and received to the web service to implement regression testing, minimizing resources needed for testing. It also proposes adding test cases to the description of the service as a contract, so they can be used for regression testing (Bruno, Canfora, Di Penta, Esposito, & Mazza, 2005).

We would like to remark that, in any case, the tester has to take into account that web service regression testing has to be sometimes flexible. For example, the answers of some WS could depend on the time of the invocation, weather conditions or other information that can change over successive invocations with the same inputs. In those cases, a different behavior does not necessary mean a malfunction in the system.

Concluding Remarks

Techniques discussed in this section apply to WS in general. They provide a black-box dynamic approach, and can be applied to test a service whether we have access to its code or not (Bozkurt, Harman, & Hassoun, 2010). Given that we don't have access to its source code, main approaches test if a web service works as expected generating input data (test data generation) to invoke it, so we can check its output on that data (unit testing) or other non-functional features, and verify that internal changes in it do not affect its external behavior (regression testing). Nevertheless, there are some issues not properly addressed yet, like how to make sure that the WS we have tested remain the same when actually executing them or how to reduce the cost of testing.

Next section will discuss complementary approaches for services built upon services (service compositions), applicable when we have access to its source code. They provide deeper testing of WS, using internal information from them.

SERVICE COMPOSITION VERIFICATION AND VALIDATION

Introduction

When composing services, having tested the different partner services is not enough to assure the quality of the new compound service: the internal composition logic has to be systematically tested as well. Service composition internal logic can be simple, for example a wrapper for a legacy system, or an adapter that adds or modifies certain information to the answer of a service and sends it to the client. But it can also be very complex: modeling business activities or critical services using loops, data manipulation, fault handling, etc. (Papazoglou, 2006). This way, an undetected bug in the code can cause huge monetary losses, especially if the composition (that is a service itself) is invoked not only by costumers but also by other programs or services.

In the next six subsections, we assume that we have an executable WS-BPEL service composition ready to be deployed and invoked that has to be tested. We review classical software testing techniques, and see if there are tools supporting them for service compositions or at least some proposal showing how to adapt them. After reviewing different approaches for WS-BPEL, a section is dedicated to semantic orchestration languages and the last one compiles efforts on service choreography.

Static Techniques for WS-BPEL Verification and Validation

If we look at static techniques (Morimoto, 2008) we can see different proposals using Petri nets, abstract state machines and model checking, among others. All are based on a certain formalization of the WS-BPEL specification. This is necessary because the standard is written in natural (English) language, inherently non-rigorous (Hallwyl, Henglein, & Hildebrandt, 2010) and does not include an unambiguous specification. Depending on the formalism used, different operations can be applied to the modeled compositions to check certain properties (Van Breugel & Koshkina, 2006).

Model checking techniques basically translate a program into a formal language in which they can automatically check certain properties using a tool supporting it (Clarke, Grumberg, & Peled, 1999). There is a model-checking approach that translates a WS-BPEL composition into a formal model defined by state transition system, that is later processed using the SAL (Symbolic Analysis Laboratory) tool. Both translations are automatic via the VIATRA open-source framework (Kovacs, Gonczy, & Varro, 2008). Properties checked are expressed in LTL (Linear Temporal Logic), which can describe properties usual in classical languages (like "the program has to terminate on every execution", "every variable read has been writ-

ten before", etc.) and some other specific of web service composition: safety (certain undesirable states are impossible to reach) and reachability (certain desirable states are possible to reach).

Petri nets implement a state-based parallel flow in a graph that eases checking for different properties (Peterson, 1977). They suit the WS-BPEL definition of a composition (Lohmann, Massuthe, Stahl, & Weinberg, 2006), which has led to many works modeling WS-BPEL compositions using them. One of the most interesting defines an automatic complete translation from any standard WS-BPEL 2.0 composition to an extended Petri net, optimizing the resulting net to minimize its size (Lohmann, 2008). That translation is conducted by BPEL2oWFN, an open-source tool that can produce different output files. Using it, the following properties can be checked in a WS-BPEL execution flow: controllability, generation of the operating guideline, check for deadlocks and any temporal logic formula. For other approaches based on Petri nets refer to (Lohmann, Verbeek, Ouyang, & Stahl, 2009).

There is also a multi-agent Abstract State Machine (ASM) effort (Fahland & Reisig, 2005). It models each WS-BPEL activity into an independent agent. This way, the whole WS-BPEL composition can be modeled defining the interactions between them. The approach focuses on the negative workflow (that is, compensation caused by faults). Nevertheless, no further work appears to have been done in this field: obtaining more results from the model remains as a line of future work.

Pi-calculus is a formal process algebra to check for properties in concurrent systems, like a WS-BPEL composition (Lucchi & Mazzara, 2007). A WS-BPEL 2.0 translation to Pi-calculus is also proposed to verify behavioral compatibility and consistency between several interacting WS-BPEL processes (Weidlich, Decker, & Weske, 2007). Although the aim of the paper falls out of our scope, we recommend reading it. It includes a very interesting discussion justifying that a complete translation from WS-BPEL to a model is not necessary to verify certain properties, and that discarding some uninteresting features can lead to a much smaller and easier to handle model.

This section has reviewed different formal approaches to verify certain properties in WS-BPEL compositions. For a survey including these and other approaches refer to (Morimoto, 2008). As commented before, static techniques provide totally reliable results, but limited for a deep V&V of WS-BPEL compositions. In next sections we will see complementary dynamic approaches.

Test Case Generation for WS-BPEL Compositions

As seen before, test data generation for external WS is limited to the information available in the WSDL document. This way, it can usually only generate test data (not complete test cases), and its quality can be hardly measured. Opposite from it, when access to the WS-BPEL composition source code is available, the different techniques can offer much better results, providing a certain coverage criterion of program or data flow.

There are several efforts using the open-source system SPIN (Holzmann, 1997). SPIN receives in its input a Promela program and a set of LTL formulas to be checked. Using SPIN, there is a proposal of a non-automatic method to generate the smallest test suite that provides transition coverage criterion (García-Fanjul, Tuya, & de la Riva, 2006). A similar approach (Bentakouk, Poizat, & Zaïdi, 2009) based on Symbolic Transition Systems generates a test suite providing path length criterion (all execution paths including "n" or less instructions).

In contrast, we can find a system that implements automatic JUnit-compatible test suite generation providing state coverage and transition coverage for WS-BPEL control flow testing, and all-du-path coverage for WS-BPEL data flow testing (Zheng, Zhou, & Krause, 2007). These features are implemented in an open-source Eclipse®

Wizard. Unfortunately, the project seems abandoned. It was supported by the EU FP6 funded project Digital Business Ecosystem (Nachira, Dini, Nicolai, Le Louarn, & Rivera Leon, 2007) till 2007. Then it was renewed, but the project has taken a different aim (Peardrop Consortium, 2010). In this case, before deciding adopting this tool we strongly recommend checking if in-house or externally-contracted support can be obtained on the system.

WSOTF is an open-source tool that can create, execute and debug test cases using a TEFSM (Timed Extended Finite State Machines) model, which allows for timing constraints (Cao, Felix, & Castanet, 2010). WSOTF can be considered an improvement over the "off-line" TGSE framework. Unfortunately, it requires as input the WS-BPEL specification files translated to the format of WSOTF and its home site is poorly documented in French language (Pfe-Otasw development team, 2010).

As the number of test cases that can be created from a program can be very high (and so the time and effort needed to test them), a new paradigm is emerging: search-based software test data generation (Harman, 2008), that uses search techniques to evaluate test cases for a certain test objective. There only proposal of applying it to WS-BPEL (Blanco, García-Fanjul, Tuya, 2009) uses scatter search, a metaheuristic technique based on an evolutionary method, to search the optimal solution to a problem. Not implemented yet, it remains an open field.

WS-BPEL Unit Testing

As a contrast to "usual" software unit testing, WS-BPEL unit-testing environments have to include a service mockup mechanism, to avoid that a fault in an invoked web service can produce a malfunction in a right service composition. But that replacement must be flexible enough to simulate all aspects of web service behavior that can affect the internal composition.

Reviewing testing capabilities, most leading industrial development environments just include basic techniques. For example, Oracle BPEL Process Manager is probably the most popular and powerful orchestration system. Concerning composition testing, it includes an environment to run test cases invoking mockup services (Oracle, 2007). It supports automatic massive invocations and can check assertions on the outputs and produce a simple instruction coverage report. And the situation is similar in most other tools, being Parasoft SOAtest the most complete, including several testing tools in a solution (Parasoft, 2010).

On the academic side there are different proposals for unit testing (Zakaria, Atan, Ghani, & Sani, 2009). One of the most interesting is the open-source BPELUnit system (Fachgebiet Software Engineering, 2010). BPELUnit is a full-featured open-source system that eases unit testing, allowing automatic invocation of massive tests from the command line, an Eclipse plug-in, or a Apache® Ant script. It allows for WS replacement and test cases can include assertions to be checked on the received messages.

BPELUnit is currently maintained by Daniel Lübke (Lübke, 2007). For certain time the project was not further developed, remaining in version 1.0 after some contributions in June 2007. But in April 2009, version 1.1.0 was released and, since then, activity has risen again and a new website has been set up (BPELUnit development team, 2010). It is community-oriented and includes tutorials, a mailing list and a source code repository to support its continuous distributed development. Recent improvements in the system include automatic test case generation based on templates (from Excel® or OpenOffice® spreadsheets among others), test coverage calculation for an executed test-suite (for the moment, instruction coverage, but in near future other criteria are planned to be supported), and more realistic mockups. These new mockups allow the test suite to include a set of behaviors that are fired depending on the input message received on every execution.

Given all these features, we can consider BPELUnit a very good tool. It is mature, engine-independent (it supports several proprietary and open-source BPEL engines), and its development seems to be supported by an active community.

WS-BPEL Mutation Testing

The only WS-BPEL mutation system available nowadays is GAmera (Estero-Botaro, Palomo-Lozano, & Medina-Bulo, 2010). It is composed of two sub-systems that can be used independently: a WS-BPEL mutation system, and an automatic WS-BPEL test case generator based in the mutation system and a genetic algorithm. Only the first subsystem is fully implemented and operative. It has recently been updated to version 1.0.5, reducing a number of redundant mutants the previous version produced.

GAmera mutation operators include not only usual mistakes made when programming in classical languages, but it also WS-BPEL-specific bugs. They take into account the fact that compositions are usually programmed using a graphical IDE, so some common mistakes in other languages are not considered. Some of the mutation operators implemented are selecting a different partner for an invocation, changing the fault thrown by a throw activity or tweaking the timeout for certain actions. GAmera is an open-source system, and can be downloaded from its home site (SPI&FM Group, 2010a).

WS-BPEL Dynamic Likely Invariant Generation

Takuan (Palomo-Duarte, García-Domínguez, & Medina-Bulo, 2008) is an open-source system that dynamically generates invariants reflecting the internal logic of a WS-BPEL composition. It receives a WS-BPEL composition and a test suite in BPELUnit format. It automatically executes the composition under the test cases provided and checks for likely invariants in their traces.

Internally Takuan uses three open-source systems: BPELUnit, ActiveBPEL® 4.1 (a WS-BPEL 2.0 compliant engine) and Daikon. Takuan includes several WS-BPEL-specific optimizations to discard a number of redundant invariants and can be used from the command line or using a graphical interface (Palomo-Duarte, García-Domínguez, Medina-Bulo, Alvarez-Ayllón, & Santacruz, 2010).

Takuan can be used to find bugs and improve a test suite, typical uses of a dynamic invariant generator (Ernst, Perkins, Guo, McCamant, Pacheco, Tschantz, & Xiao, 2007). But, it can also monitor a composition if we use as input a set of traces limited to those collected in several invocations of it. This way, the invariants obtained using Takuan will not reflect the general behavior of the composition, but the specific under those executions in the real world invoking actual services.

Regression Testing in WS-BPEL

WS-BPEL regression testing is addressed by two proposals. The first one proposes checking for the differences between the old and the new versions of the composition and creating specific test cases to test the changed activities (Liu, Li, Zhu, & Tan, 2010). The second proposal defines several WS-BPEL-specific techniques to prioritize test cases according to the coverage of test data (Mei, Zhang, Chan, & Tse, 2009). Nevertheless, none of them offers any tool for automated support, so it remains as a future challenge.

Semantic Orchestration Verification and Validation

As commented in the *Background* section, semantic composition has limited industrial support for the moment. Most testing efforts are academic approaches concerning model checking and test case generation (Bozkurt, Harman, & Hassoun, 2010). For example, the BLAST model checker has been extended to handle the concurrency in OWL-S.

This, way, test cases can be generated automatically according to different criteria (Huang, Tsai, Paul, & Chen, 2005). And for WSMO, test cases that meet a certain specification can be generated using a formal B abstract state machine (Shaban, Dobbie, & Sun, 2009).

Service Choreography Verification and Validation

Due to its limited adoption there are very few works about service choreographies verification and validation. In this section we comment three interesting ones.

There is a proposal that defines several data flow testing criteria specific for WS-CDL choreography (Mei, Chan, & Tse, 2009). It uses extended Labeled Transition Systems (LTSs) to model interaction between the different WS in a choreography, and XPath Rewriting Graphs (XRGs) patterns to model how data in WSDL documents is queried using XPath according to the specification of the choreography.

A model-based testing technique is developed for Message Choreography Modeling (MCM), a proprietary choreography language developed by SAP® Research (Stefanescu, Wieczorek, & Kirshin, 2009). The proposal is interesting, as it provides automated translation from MCM to executable UML models that are tested using UML-specific testing tools. Nevertheless, we strongly recommend taking a close look at the dependencies and maturity of non-standardized and research-level tools before considering adopting it.

The authors of BPEL2oWFN have adapted it so it can be applied to test BPEL4Chor compositions (Lohmann, Kopp, Leymann, & Reisig, 2007). BPEL4Chor is a choreography language written on top of WS-BPEL. The tool is used to detect deadlocks in a choreography, but it can be applied to test more general properties as previously commented in the *Static techniques for WS-BPEL verification and validation* section.

Concluding Remarks

After reviewing the different efforts in service composition V&V we can conclude that there is a long way ahead to provide good support for testing techniques in WS-BPEL. Industrial tools include very limited testing support (mainly basic functional testing). Academia is taking the right steps in most directions, adapting techniques and facing trends. But in many cases results are not supported by automatic tools, remaining as a challenge its integration in mainstream development tools. In other cases, little work is available, like with metamorphic testing, where the only proposal found implements service compositions in C++ (Chan, Cheung, & Leung, 2007), or specific research like service exception and compensation. As for semantic orchestration and choreography, it seems that its limited industrial adoption has risen little interest in academia.

FUTURE RESEARCH DIRECTIONS

Apart from the different challenges of every field reviewed, we can highlight four trends that have to be faced in general:

- First of all, web service composition V&V efforts should focus in providing full support of the WS-BPEL 2.0 standard. It is here to stay, as it is backed by the main IT companies. And it seems to be the basis for the future technologies: BPMN, BPEL4People, semantic extensions, dynamic service composition execution, BPELScript, etc. From a research perspective, results obtained for BPEL4WS 1.1 are as valid as those obtained for WS-BPEL 2.0. But from an industrial point of view, the later are preferred.
- Secondly, tools should try to ease their use providing (when possible) two modes of operation: fully-automated and interactive.

On the one hand, the automatic operation support will allow to use the technology from other tools, easing massive usage and interoperability to build more powerful systems. The automated mode can be implemented as a library, so it can be compiled on widely used programming languages, a rich shell supporting different options, or even as a web service to receive remote invocations. On the other hand, the interactive mode must be as easy as possible to install, and intuitive for a human to operate. It can be built as a stand-alone tool (in that case we recommend multi-platform languages like Java®, Python, C++, etc.) or a plug-in for a widely used integrated development environment, like Eclipse or Netbeans. On both operation modes fully automatic translation from WS-BPEL, WSDL or any other file to models must be implemented to meet industry requirements. A good example for this is the BPELUnit system.

- Efforts (specially academic ones) should try take advantage of the community. A simple web site, offering information about the system (for example screenshots or screencasts that allow visitors to *see before you try*) and providing support on it, can help spread the use of the system. Additionally, there are other tools to complement it: wikis, forums, slide-sharing systems, webinars, introductory tutorials, etc. We also recommend considering the advantages of an open-source based model, shifting incomes from licenses to long term maintenance contracts by a larger community. This way, the step to industrial adoption can be eased.
- SOA development environments should integrate testing tools to provide fully-automated support for SOA development methodologies. Most methodologies include a testing phase, but they tend to leave parts of

Table 1. MC: model checking, P: proposal, I: implemented as an automatic tool, O: open-source

Technology	Testing	Author reference	State
Web Services	Test data generation	(Sneed & Huang, 2007)	I
		(Parasoft, 2010)	I
		(Martin, Basu, & Xie, 2007)	I
		(Bai, Dong, Tsai, & Chen, 2005)	I
		(Eviware, 2010)	I
	Unit testing	(Heckel & Lohmann, 2004)	P
		(Atkinson, Brenner, Falcone, & Juhasz, 2008)	P
		(Tsai, Paul, Wang, Fan, & Wang, 2002)	P
		(Martin, Basu, & Xie, 2007)	I
		(Parasoft, 2010)	I
		(Eviware, 2010)	I
		(Bruno, Canfora, Di Penta, Esposito, & Mazza, 2005)	P
		(Yeom, Tsai, Bai, & Min, 2009)	P
	Regression testing	(Martin, Basu, & Xie, 2007)	I
		(Melideo, 2006)	I,O
		(Bruno, Canfora, Di Penta, Esposito, & Mazza, 2005)	P
WS-BPEL compositions	MC, SAL	(Kovacs, Gonczy, & Varro, 2008)	I,O
	MC, Petri nets	(Lohmann, 2008)	P
	MC, Abstract State Machine	(Fahland & Reisig, 2005)	P
	MC, Pi-calculus	(Lucchi & Mazzara, 2007)	P
	MC, Pi-calculus	(Weidlich, Decker, & Weske, 2007)	P
	Test case generation	(García-Fanjul, Tuya, & de la Riva, 2006)	P
		(Bentakouk, Poizat, & Zaïdi, 2009)	I
		(Zheng, Zhou, & Krause, 2007)	I,O
		(Cao, Felix, & Castanet, 2010)	I
		(Blanco, García-Fanjul, Tuya, 2009)	P
	Unit testing	(Oracle, 2007)	I
		(Parasoft, 2010)	I
		(Fachgebiet Software Engineering, 2010)	I,O
	Mutation	(Estero-Botaro, Palomo-Lozano, & Medina-Bulo, 2010)	I,O
	Invariants	(Palomo-Duarte, García-Domínguez, & Medina-Bulo, 2008)	I,O
	Regression testing	(Liu, Li, Zhu, & Tan, 2010)	P
		(Mei, Zhang, Chan, & Tse, 2009)	P
OWL-S	MC, BLAST	(Huang, Tsai, Paul, & Chen, 2005)	I
WSMO	MC, B abstract state machine	(Shaban, Dobbie, & Sun, 2009)	P
WS-CDL	MC, XPath Rewriting Graphs	(Mei, Chan, & Tse, 2009)	P
MCM	Model-based testing	(Stefanescu, Wieczorek, & Kirshin, 2009)	P
BPEL4Chor	MC, Petri nets	(Lohmann, Kopp, Leymann, & Reisig, 2007)	P

it as manual activities (García-Domínguez, A., Medina-Bulo, I., & Marcos-Bárcena, M., 2010). It also applies for development techniques that could be adapted to SOA, like test driven development.

Apart from research and development trends, we would like to emphasize the lack of examples to test a tool or a technique. Most WS have a cost of use, that makes them not eligible when evaluating a testing technique. Additionally, most compositions implement business models of corporations (sometimes including decision-making management), so companies do not usually publish them (or not completely). But good testbeds are needed for assuring the quality of the testing techniques, and only a few limited efforts exist. Regarding WS there are sites compiling a list of freely available WS (XMethods, 2010), (WebserviceX.NET, 2010). As for WS-BPEL compositions, there is a collection of compositions from different papers (SPI&FM Group, 2010b), and a couple of sites including sample compositions used for unit testing of two WS-BPEL engines: WSO2® SOA Platform (WSO2 Oxygen Tank, 2010) and Apache ODE (Apache ODE development team, 2010).

CONCLUSION

This chapter has reviewed the different solutions for web service and web service composition testing. On the side of web service testing, industry offers mature and useful tools for different testing techniques. But on the side of service compositions we have to rely on academic proposals, as IT companies have done yet little work in this field beyond functional testing. Table 1 summarizes approaches and tools.

We consider this quite a logical situation: WS have been adopted for many years, and companies have been improving their systems to cover the testing phase. But service composition is just a recent technique: the WS-BPEL standard for service composition was approved in 2007 (although the proposal was on work since 2006). In semantic WS and WS choreography, no standard seems to have substantial industrial support (both in composition tools and choreography-usable or semantic WS availability).

Nevertheless, academia seems to be paving the way for future tools. There are both static and dynamic approaches to service composition white-box testing in many ways: unit testing, mutation testing, dynamic invariant generation and test case generation among others. But there a few challenges ahead: both academic and industrial efforts should try to make usable and easy-to-adopt tools that implement full support of the WS-BPEL 2.0 standard, and integrate them in leading development methodologies.

REFERENCES

Abran, A., & Moore, J. W. (2004). Software quality. In Bourque, P., & Dupuis, R. (Eds.), *Software engineering body of knowledge (SWEBOK) guide*. IEEE Computer Society.

Apache ODE Development Team. (2010). *Apache ODE WS-BPEL engine unit test compositions*. Retrieved May 10, 2010, from http://svn.apache.org/viewvc/ode/trunk/bpel-test/src/test/resources/bpel/2.0

Atkinson, C., Brenner, D., Falcone, G., & Juhasz, M. (2008). Specifying high-assurance services. *Computer*, *41*(8), 64–71. doi:10.1109/MC.2008.308

Bai, X., Dong, W., Tsai, W., & Chen, Y. (2005). WSDL-based automatic test case generation for Web Services testing. In *Proceedings of the 2005 IEEE International Workshop on Service-Oriented System Engineering* (pp. 215-220). IEEE Computer Society.

Balzer, S., Liebig, T., & Wagner, M. (2004). Pitfalls of OWL-S: A practical Semantic Web use case. In M. Aiello, M. Aoyama, F. Curbera, & M. P. Papazoglou (Eds.), *Proceedings of the Second International Conference on Service Oriented Computing* (pp. 289-298). Association for Computing Machinery.

Bentakouk, L., Poizat, P., & Zaïdi, F. (2009). A formal framework for service orchestration testing based on symbolic transition systems. *Proceedings of the 21ˢᵗ Testing of Software and Communication Systems Conference*, (pp. 16-32).

Bertolino, A. (2007). Software testing research: Achievements, challenges, dreams. In [IEEE Computer Society]. *Proceedings of the Future of Software Engineering at ICSE, 2007*, 85–103.

Bertolino, A., & Marchetti, E. (2004). *A brief essay on software testing*. Submitted to Software Engineering, IEEE Computer Society, Technical report, 2004.

Blanco, R., García-Fanjul, J., & Tuya, J. (2009). A first approach to test case generation for BPEL compositions of Web Services using scatter search. In *Proceedings of the IEEE International Conference on Software Testing, Verification, and Validation Workshops* (pp. 131-140). IEEE Computer Society.

Bozkurt, M., Harman, M., & Hassoun, Y. (2010). *Testing Web services: A survey* (No. TR-10-01). Department of Computer Science, King's College London.

BPELUnit. (2010). *Development team*. Retrieved May 10, 2010, from http://github.com/bpelunit/bpelunit

Bruno, M., Canfora, G., Di Penta, M., Esposito, G., & Mazza, V. (2005). Using test cases as contract to ensure service compliance across releases. In Benatallah, B., Casati, F., & Traverso P. (Eds.), *Proceedings of the Third International Conference Service-Oriented Computing - ICSOC 2005, Lecture Notes in Computer Science: Vol. 3826* (pp. 87-100). Springer-Verlag®.

Business Process Management Initiative. (2010). *BPMN FAQ*. Retrieved May 10, 2010, from http://www.bpmn.org/Documents/FAQ.htm

Cao, T. D., Felix, P., & Castanet, R. (2010). WSOTF: An automatic testing tool for Web Services composition. In *Fifth International Conference on Internet and Web Applications and Services 2010* (pp. 7-12).

Chan, W. K., Cheung, S. C., & Leung, K. R. (2007). A metamorphic testing approach for online testing of service-oriented software applications. *International Journal of Web Services Research, 4*(2), 61–81. doi:10.4018/jwsr.2007040103

Clarke, E. M., Grumberg, O., & Peled, D. A. (1999). *Model checking*. The MIT Press.

Davis, M. D., & Weyuker, E. J. (1981). Pseudo-oracles for non-testable programs. In Levy, B. (Ed.) *Proceedings of the ACM '81 Conference* (pp. 254-257). Association for Computing Machinery.

Ernst, M. D., Perkins, J. H., Guo, P. J., McCamant, S., Pacheco, C., Tschantz, M. S., & Xiao, C. (2007). The Daikon system for dynamic detection of likely invariants. *Science of Computer Programming, 69*(1-3), 35–45. doi:10.1016/j.scico.2007.01.015

ESSI WSMO Working Group. (2010). *WSMO home site*. Retrieved May 10, 2010, from http://www.wsmo.org

Estero-Botaro, A., Palomo-Lozano, F., & Medina-Bulo, I. (2010). Quantitative evaluation of mutation operators for WS-BPEL compositions. In [IEEE Computer Society.]. *Proceedings of the International Conference on Software Testing, Verification, and Validation Workshops, 2010*, 142–150. doi:10.1109/ICSTW.2010.36

Eviware. (2010). *SoapUI*. Retrieved May 10, 2010, from http://www.soapui.org

Fachgebiet Software Engineering. (2010). *BPELUnit home site*. Retrieved May 10, 2010, from http://www.se.uni-hannover.de/forschung/soa/bpelunit

Fahland, D., & Reisig, W. (2005). ASM-based semantics for BPEL: The negative control flow. In D. Beauquier, E. Börger, & A. Slissenko (Ed.), *Proceedings of the 12th International Workshop on Abstract State Machines 2005* (pp. 131-151).

García-Domínguez, A., Medina-Bulo, I., & Marcos-Bárcena, M. (2010). Inference of performance constraints in Web Service composition models. In V. De Castro, J. M. Vara, E. Marcos, M. Papazoglou, & W. Van den Heuvel (Eds.), *CEUR Workshop Proceedings of the 2nd International Workshop on Model-Driven Service Engineering* (pp. 55-66).

García-Fanjul, J., Tuya, J., & de la Riva, C. (2006). Generating test cases specifications for BPEL compositions of Web Services using SPIN. In *Proceedings of the International Workshop on Web Services: Modeling and Testing - WS-MaTe 2006* (pp. 83-94).

Ghosh, R. A. (2006). *The impact of free/libre/open-source software on innovation and competitiveness of the European Union*. Brussels, Belgium: European Commission. Retrieved May 10, 2010, from http://www.flossimpact.eu

Hall, A. (1990). Seven myths of formal methods. *IEEE Software, 7*(5), 11–19. doi:10.1109/52.57887

Hallwyl, T., Henglein, F., & Hildebrandt, T. (2010). A standard-driven implementation of WS-BPEL 2.0. In S. Y. Shin, S. Ossowski, M. Schumacher, M. J. Palakal, & C. Hung (Eds.), *SAC '10: Proceedings of the 2010 ACM Symposium on Applied Computing* (pp. 2472-2476).

Harman, M. (2008). Search based software engineering. *Computers & Operations Research, 35*(10), 3049–3051. doi:10.1016/j.cor.2007.01.008

Heckel, R., & Lohmann, M. (2004). Towards contract-based testing of Web Services. *Electronic Notes in Theoretical Computer Science, 116*, 145–156. doi:10.1016/j.entcs.2004.02.073

Holzmann, G. J. (1997). The model checker SPIN. *IEEE Transactions on Software Engineering, 23*(5), 279–295. doi:10.1109/32.588521

Huang, H., Tsai, W., Paul, R., & Chen, Y. (2005). Automated model checking and testing for composite Web Services. In *IEEE International Symposium on Object-Oriented Real-Time Distributed Computing* (pp. 300-307). IEEE Computer Society.

Jia, Y., & Harman, M. (2010). An analysis and survey of the development of mutation testing. *IEEE Transactions on Software Engineering, 99*.

Kovacs, M., Gonczy, L., & Varro, D. (2008). Formal analysis of BPEL workflows with compensation by model checking. *International Journal of Computer Systems and Engineering, 23*.

Leveson, N. G. (1995). *Safeware: System safety and computers*. Addison-Wesley Professional.

Liu, H., Li, Z., Zhu, J., & Tan, H. (2010). Business process regression testing. In Krämer, B. J., Lin, K.-J., & Narasimhan, P. (Eds.), *Service-Oriented Computing - ICSOC 2007, Lecture Notes in Computer Science* (*Vol. 4749*, pp. 157–168). Springer-Verlag. doi:10.1007/978-3-540-74974-5_13

Lohmann, N. (2008). A feature-complete petri net semantics for WS-BPEL 2.0. In M. Dumas, & R. Heckel (Ed.), *4th International Workshop on Web Services and Formal Methods - WS-FM 2007, Lecture Notes in Computer Science: Vol. 4937* (pp. 77-91). Springer-Verlag.

Lohmann, N., Kopp, O., Leymann, F., & Reisig, W. (2007). Analyzing BPEL4Chor: Verification and participant synthesis. In M. Dumas, & R. Heckel (Eds.) *4th International Workshop on Web Services and Formal Methods - WS-FM 2007, Lecture Notes in Computer Science: Vol. 4937* (pp. 46-60). Springer-Verlag.

Lohmann, N., Massuthe, P., Stahl, C., & Weinberg, D. (2006). Analyzing interacting BPEL processes. In S. Dustdar, J. L. Fiadeiro & A. P. Sheth (Ed.), *Proceedings of the 4th International Conference on Business Process Management - BPM2006, Lecture Notes in Computer Science: Vol. 4102* (pp. 17-32). Springer-Verlag.

Lohmann, N., Verbeek, E., Ouyang, C., & Stahl, C. (2009). Comparing and evaluating Petri net semantics for BPEL. *International Journal of Business Process Integration and Management, 4*(1), 60–73. doi:10.1504/IJBPIM.2009.026986

Lübke, D. (2007). Unit testing BPEL compositions. In Baresi, L., & Di Nitto, E. (Eds.), *Test and analysis of Web services* (pp. 149–171). Springer-Verlag. doi:10.1007/978-3-540-72912-9_6

Lucchi, R., & Mazzara, M. (2007). A pi-calculus based semantics for WS-BPEL. *Journal of Logic and Algebraic Programming, 70*(1), 118, 96.

Martin, E., Basu, S., & Xie, T. (2007). Automated testing and response analysis of Web Services. In *IEEE International Conference on Web Services* (pp. 647-654). Los Alamitos, CA: IEEE Computer Society.

Mei, L., Chan, W. K., & Tse, T. H. (2009). Data flow testing of service choreography. In H. van Vliet, & V. Issarny (Eds.), *Proceedings of the 7th Joint Meeting of the European Software Engineering Conference and the ACM SIGSOFT Symposium on The Foundations of Software Engineering on European Software Engineering Conference and Foundations of Software Engineering Symposium* (pp. 151-160). Association for Computing Machinery.

Mei, L., Zhang, Z., Chan, W. K., & Tse, T. H. (2009). Test case prioritization for regression testing of service-oriented business applications. In J. Quemada, G. León, Y. S. Maarek & W. Nejdl (Eds.), *Proceedings of the 18th International Conference on World Wide Web* (pp. 901-910). Madrid, Spain: Association for Computing Machinery.

Melideo, M. (2006). *SeCSE project home site.* Retrieved May 10, 2010, from http://www.secse-project.eu

Morimoto, S. (2008). A survey of formal verification for business process modeling. In M. Bubak, G. D. Albada, J. Dongarra, & P. M. Sloot (Eds.), *Proceedings of the 8th international conference on Computational Science, Part II, Lecture Notes in Computer Science: Vol. 5102* (pp. 514-522). Springer-Verlag.

Myers, G. J., Badgett, T., Thomas, T. M., & Sandler, C. (2004). *The art of software testing.* John Wiley and Sons.

Nachira, F., Dini, P., Nicolai, A., Le Louarn, M., & Rivera Leon, L. (Eds.). (2007). *Digital business ecosystems book.* Luxembourg: European Commission.

Newcomer, E., & Lomow, G. (2004). *Understanding SOA with Web Services (independent technology guides).* Addison-Wesley Professional.

Oracle. (2007). *Testing BPEL processes.* Oracle Application Server 10g Documentation. Oracle

OWL Working Group. (2009). *OWL 2 Web ontology language.* Retrieved May 10, 2010, from http://www.w3.org/TR/owl2-overview

Palomo-Duarte, M., García-Domínguez, A., & Medina-Bulo, I. (2008). Takuan: A dynamic invariant generation system for WS-BPEL compositions. In C. Pahl, S. Clarke, & R. Eshuis (Eds.), *European Conference on Web Services* (pp. 63-72). Los Alamitos, CA: IEEE Computer Society.

Palomo-Duarte, M., García-Domínguez, A., Medina-Bulo, I., Alvarez-Ayllón, A., & Santacruz, J. (2010). Takuan: A tool for WS-BPEL composition testing using dynamic invariant generation. In B. Benatallah, (Ed.), *10th International Conference on Web Engineering - ICWE 2010, Lecture Notes In Computer Science: Vol. 6189* (pp. 532-535). Springer-Verlag.

Papazoglou, M. P. (2006). Web services technologies and standards. *ACM Computing Surveys.*

Parasoft. (2010). *Parasoft SOAtest.* Retrieved May 10, 2010, from http://www.parasoft.com/jsp/solutions/soa_solution.jsp?itemId=319#bpel

Peardrop Consortium. (2010). *Peardrop Project home site.* Retrieved May 10, 2010, from http://www.peardrop.eu/about/Pages/index.aspx

Peterson, J. L. (1977). Petri Nets. [Association for Computing Machinery.]. *Computing Surveys, 9*(3), 223–252. doi:10.1145/356698.356702

Pfe-Otasw Development Team. (2010). *Pfe-Otasw home site.* Retrieved May 10, 2010, from http://code.google.com/p/pfe-otasw

Raymond, E. S. (2001). *The cathedral & the bazaar: Musings on Linux and open-source by an accidental revolutionary.* Sebastopol, CA: O'Reilly Media.

Shaban, M., Dobbie, G., & Sun, J. (2009), A framework for testing Semantic Web Services using model checking. In D. Dranidis, & I. Stamatopoulou (Eds.), *Fourth South-East European Workshop on Formal Methods* (pp. 17-24).

Sneed, H. M., & Huang, S. (2007). The design and use of WSDL-test: A tool for testing Web Services: Special issue articles. *Journal of Software Maintenance and Evolution, 19*(5), 297–314. doi:10.1002/smr.354

SPI&FM Group. (2010a). *GAmera home site.* Retrieved May 19, 2010, from https://neptuno.uca.es/redmine/projects/gamera

SPI&FM Group. (2010b). *WS-BPEL composition repository.* Retrieved May 10, 2010, from https://neptuno.uca.es/redmine/projects/wsbpel-comp-repo/wiki

Stefanescu, A., Wieczorek, S., & Kirshin, A. (2009). MBT4Chor: A model-based testing approach for service choreographies. In R. F. Paige, A. Hartman, & A. Rensink (Eds.) *Proceedings of the 5th European Conference on Model Driven Architecture - Foundations and Application, Lecture Notes in Computer Science: Vol. 5562* (pp. 313-324). Springer-Verlag.

Tapscott, D., & Williams, A. D. (2006). *Wikinomics: How mass collaboration changes everything.* Portfolio Hardcover.

The Joint Task Force on Computing Curricula. (2004). *Computing curricula - Software engineering 2004.* IEEE Computer Society and Association for Computing Machinery.

Tsai, W. T., Paul, R., Wang, Y., Fan, C., & Wang, D. (2002). Extending WSDL to facilitate Web Services testing. In *IEEE International Symposium on High-Assurance Systems Engineering – HASE 2002* (pp. 171-172). Los Alamitos, CA: IEEE Computer Society.

Van Breugel, F., & Koshkina, M. (2006). *Models and verification of BPEL*. Unpublished draft.

Web Services Choreography Working Group. (2005). *Web Services choreography description language version 1.0*. Retrieved May 10, 2010, from http://www.w3.org/TR/ws-cdl-10

Web Services Interoperability Organization. (2010). *WS-I Organization's Home Site*. Retrieved May 10, 2010, from http://www.ws-i.org

Webservice, X. net. (2010). *List of available Web Services*. Retrieved May 10, 2010, from http://www.webservicex.net

Weidlich, M., Decker, G., & Weske, M. (2007). Efficient analysis of BPEL 2.0 processes using Pi-Calculus. In J. Li, M. Guo, Q. Jin, Y. Zhang, L.-J. Zhang, H. Jin, M. Mambo, J. Tanaka, & H. Hayashi (Eds.), *Proceedings of the IEEE Asia-Pacific Services Computing Conference APSCC'07*, (pp. 266-274). Tsukuba Science City, Japan: IEEE Computer Society.

Woodward, M. R. (1993). Mutation testing - Its origin and evolution. *Information and Software Technology*, 35(3), 163–169. doi:10.1016/0950-5849(93)90053-6

WS-BPEL Technical Committee. (2007). *Web services business process execution language version 2.0*. Retrieved May 10, 2010, from http://docs.oasis-open.org/wsbpel/2.0/wsbpel-v2.0.html

WSO2 Oxygen Tank. (2010). *WSO2 business process server WS-BPEL samples*. Retrieved May 10, 2010, from https://wso2.org/repos/wso2/branches/bps/1.1.0/product/modules/samples/src/main/resources/bpel/2.0

WSDL Technical Committee. (2007). *Web services description language version 2.0*. Retrieved May 10, 2010, from http://www.w3.org/TR/wsdl20

Xmethods. (2010). *List of free Web Services*. Retrieved May 10, 2010, from http://www.xmethods.net

Yeom, G., Tsai, W., Bai, X., & Min, D. (2009). Design of a contract-based Web Services QoS management system. In *International Conference on Distributed Computing Systems Workshops*, (pp. 306-311). Los Alamitos, CA: IEEE Computer Society.

Zakaria, Z., Atan, R., Ghani, A. A. A., & Sani, N. F. M. (2009). Unit testing approaches for BPEL: A systematic review. In S. Sulaiman, & N. M. M. Noor (Eds.), *Asia-Pacific Software Engineering Conference* (pp. 316-322). Los Alamitos, CA: IEEE Computer Society.

Zheng, Y., Zhou, J., & Krause, P. (2007). An automatic test case generation framework for Web Services. *Journal of Software*, 2(3), 64–77. doi:10.4304/jsw.2.3.64-77

Zhou, Z., Huang, D., Tse, T., Yang, Z., Huang, H., & Chen, T. (2004). Metamorphic testing and its applications. In *Proceedings of the 8th International Symposium on Future Software Technology - ISFST 2004*, (pp. 316-322).

ADDITIONAL READING

Baresi, L., Ehrig, K., & Heckel, R. (2006). Verification of Model Transformations: A Case Study with BPEL. *Trustworthy Global Computing*, 183-199. Springer-Verlag.

Beek, M., Bucchiarone, A., & Gnesi, S. (2006). *A Survey on Service Composition Approaches: From Industrial Standards to Formal Methods*. Technical Report 2006-TR-15.

Bucchiarone, A., Melgratti, H., & Severoni, F. (2007). Testing Service Composition. In *Proceedings of the 8th Argentine Symposium on Software Engineering - ASSE 2007*.

Endo, A. T., & da Silva Simao, A. (2010). *Formal Testing Approaches for Service-Oriented Architectures and Web Services: a Systematic Review*. Instituto de Ciências Matemáticas e de Computação Technical Report 348.

Fogel, K. (2005). *Producing open-source Software: How to Run a Successful Free Software Project*. O'Reilly Media.

Foster, H., & Mayer, P. (2008). Leveraging Integrated Tools for Model-Based Analysis of Service Compositions. In Mellouk, A., Bi, J., Ortiz, G., Chiu, D. K. W., Popescu M. (Ed.) *International Conference on Internet and Web Applications and Services* (pp. 72-77). Los Alamitos, California, USA: IEEE Computer Society.

García-Fanjul, J., Palacios-Gutiérrez, M., Tuya-González, J., & de la Riva-Alvarez, C. (2009). Methods for Testing Web Service Compositions. *UPGRADE. European Journal for the Informatics Professional*, 5(X), 62–66.

Glossary Working Party - International Software Testing Qualification Board. (2004). *Glossary of terms used in Software Testing. Version 1.0*. Retrieved May 10, 2010, from http://www.istqb.org/downloads/glossary-1.0.pdf

Papazoglou, M. (2007). *Web Services: Principles and Technology*. Prentice Hall.

Weyuker, E. (1982). On Testing Non-Testable Programs. *The Computer Journal, 25*(4), 470, 465.

Xie, T. 2010. *Software Testing Research Survey Bibliography*. Retrieved May 10, 2010, from http://people.engr.ncsu.edu/txie/testingresearch-survey.htm

KEY TERMS AND DEFINITIONS

Dynamic Testing Techniques: Techniques that aim to find bugs in a program executing it.

Software Validation: Process to check if resulting product meets user requirements, so it is valid for use.

Software Verification: Process to verify if the resulting product meets initial requirements.

Static Testing Techniques: Techniques that aim to find bugs in a program analyzing its source code.

Test Case: Input values that can be used to execute a piece of software and results it has to provide when executed on them.

Test Data: Input values that can be used to execute a piece of software.

Test Suite: Set of test cases, usually grouped because they, as a group, hold some property.

Testing: Software engineering technique that aims to find bugs in a system.

ENDNOTE

[1] Brand names, product names or trademark belong to their respective owners.

Section 7
Service Management

Chapter 11
Towards a High-Availability-Driven Service Composition Framework

Jonathan Lee
National Central University, Taiwan

Shang-Pin Ma
National Taiwan Ocean University, Taiwan

Shin-Jie Lee
National Central University, Taiwan

Chia-Ling Wu
National Central University, Taiwan

Chiung-Hon Leon Lee
Nanhua University, Taiwan

ABSTRACT

Service-Oriented Computing (SOC), a main trend in software engineering, promotes the construction of applications based on the notion of services. SOC has recently attracted a great deal of attention from researchers, and has been comprehensively adopted by industry. However, service composition enabling the aggregation of existing services into composite services still imposes a great challenge to service-oriented technology. Web service composition requires component Web services to be available in request, to behave correctly in operation, and to be replaceable flexibly in failure. Although availability of Web services plays a crucial role in building robust SOC-based applications, it has been largely neglected, especially for service composition. In this chapter, we propose a service composition framework that integrates a set of composition-based service discovery mechanisms, a user-oriented service delivery approach, as well as a service management mechanism for composite services.

DOI: 10.4018/978-1-61350-159-7.ch011

INTRODUCTION

Service-Oriented Computing (SOC) has become a main trend in software engineering that exploits both Web services and Service-Oriented Architecture (SOA) as fundamental elements for developing on-demand applications. Web services are self-described, self-contained, platform-independent computational elements that can be published, discovered, and composed using standard protocols to build applications across various platforms and organizations. Recently, research in both industry and academia has alleviated issues in service-oriented technologies, including semantic service discovery, automatic service composition, and QoWS aware service management. Notably the composition of multiple Web services into a composite service has been widely accepted as more beneficial to users than an atomic service. In further service compositions to service clients, resulting composite services can be used as atomic services. However, Web service composition requires component Web services to be available and to behave correctly. In fact, if any component Web service fails, the entire service flow must be aborted. This shows the importance of including mechanisms of maintaining service availability in Web service compositions. Although Web service availability is a critical issue for building robust SOA-based applications, it has been largely neglected, especially for service composition. Current specifications like WS-ReliableMessaging and WS-Transaction do not focus on the availability of Web services (Abraham, 2005). WS-Reliability guarantees that a message is delivered to a recipient even if the recipient is down temporarily. Similarly WS-Transaction guarantees that a client does not stay in an invalid state when any Web service in the transaction is not operational. Accordingly, we still need a systematical methodology to enhance or maintain service availability, especially for composite services. To achieve the goal, we have identified three key issues:

- **How to handle the openness issue of Web services?** The implementation of the service-oriented architecture can be classified as two categories, one for the intranet and the other for the Internet. For the SOA implementations within the intranet, the organization-level management administers all component services, therefore, existing methods of system availability assurance, such as load balance, failover mechanism, or even manual control by the system management personnel, can attain the required service availability. However, the SOA implementations over the Internet imply that all services reside in an open environment and component services in a composition may belong to multiple different service providers from different organizations. Thus, maintaining the service availability through central control and management is arduous, increasing the difficulty of achieving a high service availability of composite services.

- **How to handle the dynamic issue (Cervantes, 2005) of Web services?** As mentioned above, most Web services reside in an open environment. The large number of services together with their communication links and information sources may appear and disappear dynamically in the Internet. Moreover, Web services may suffer from long response times or temporary non-availability. Such outages for mission critical systems are unacceptable and can even cause fatal damages. Handling the dynamic issue, that is, detecting the permanently or temporarily failed services and finding required services that can be re-bound and react appropriately in a composition, is significant to providing dependable SOA-based applications.

- **How to decide service recovery strategies?** When a composite service detects any failure from its component service, several possible remedies may be applied to, including some intuitive solutions such as restarting failed service directly and re-invoking component services after waiting for a period of time, or a far more complicated design of substituting a functionally equivalent service for the failed one. Swapping services relies on a combination of various search strategies, including searching for services of better quality, services that many users use, or client-specified services. A mechanism is in need to assist the service manager in choosing the most appropriate recovery strategy to satisfy managers' expectations or users' demands.

To address the above research issues, we propose a high-availability-driven service composition framework to attain and guarantee high-availability of composite Web services, including the following features:

- To incorporate considerable service-orientation characteristics (Erl, 2005) including service binding, service discovery, service composition, service contracting, service delivery, service monitoring, and service recovery.
- To construct a service lifecycle model to show phases and activities of the service composition process.
- To provide a technical and management framework for applying methods, tools, and relevant stakeholders to maintain high service availability.

This book chapter is organized as follows: In the next section, we introduce the infrastructure of SOA, including the fundamental elements such as SOAP, WSDL, and WS-BPEL, as well as the collaboration model of SOA. In Section 3, we present important background work related to Web service availability. In section 4, we exam-

ine and compare the extant solutions, which are devised for attaining or guaranteeing Web service availability. In Section 5, we describe in detail our proposed approach to enhance Web-service availability, called Availability-Enhanced Service Composition Lifecycle. Finally, we summarize the benefits of our approach in the conclusion session.

INFRASTRUCTURE OF SERVICE-ORIENTED ARCHITECTURE

A Web service is an interface describing a collection of operations that are network accessible through a standard XML messaging (Er1, 2004). As the interface hides implementation details, the service architecture allows the services to be used irrespective of the hardware and software platform on which they are implemented. Based on the service architecture, the Service-Oriented Architecture is responsible for the dynamic behaviors among multiple services and entities. SOA involves three main actors (See Figure 1): the Service Provider, the Service Registry, and the Service Requester, and three main operations defining the interactions between the components: publish, find, and bind. The collaborations include: (1) the service provider publishes services by sending the service description to the service registry; (2) the service requester finds the required services from the service registry, and finally (3) the requester binds services in the client application.

In addition, numerous specifications and standards exist to support the Web service and Service-Oriented Architecture:

- **XML:** The base technology XML is the building block of Web services, and almost all related specifications are regulated based on XML.
- **SOAP:** The Simple Object Access Protocol (SOAP) is used for XML messaging and making remote procedure calls between applications. SOAP is basically an HTTP

Figure 1. Service-oriented architecture

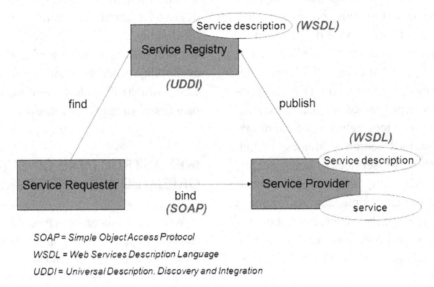

post with an XML envelope as the payload. It defines a standard mechanism of sending messages using SOAP headers and encoded operations.

- **WSDL:** The Web Services Description Language (WSDL) is an XML language for describing Web services as a set of network endpoints that can operate messages. It allows service descriptions in a standard format.
- **UDDI:** The UDDI (Universal Description, Discovery and Integration) layer facilitates the publishing and discovery of Web services.

For the common implementation of SOA, all message exchanges follow SOAP standard, service descriptions are developed according to WSDL standard, and the service registry architecture and its data models are establish based on UDDI standard.

Except the above-mentioned specifications, several XML-based languages for Web service composition have also emerged, for example, WSFL, WS-BPEL, and WSCI. WS-BPEL (Web Services Business Process Execution Language,

also known as BPEL) is notable for combining the best of other standards of Web service composition, allowing for a mixture of block-structured and graph-structured process models. A BPEL specification describes how different services should be invoked in terms of ordering and parallelism and how the service data can be created, used, updated, and merged into a process. Consequently, BPEL has been adopted industrial-wide as the *de facto* service composition standard. A composite service is often treated as a fully automated service flow that orchestrates activities of multiple software components exposed as Web services. Many studies and advanced research on service composition are based on the BPEL standard.

WEB SERVICE AVAILABILITY

To explore the key features of service availability management, important concepts and definitions related service availability are fully discussed below.

The Definitions of Service Availability

Service availability has a variety of definitions. Menascé and Almeida (2001) defined availability as the probability that a system is up, and unavailability as the probability that a system is down. Paspallis *et al.* (2006) mentioned service availability as the percentage that a Web service is available and functioning within its operational requirements. Al-Masri *et al.* (2008) proposed that service availability is the percentage of successful service invocations in all service invocations. In summary, two major categories divide the definitions of service availability: the first is based on available service time, and the second is based on successful service calls and is relatively easy to implement. Besides, to achieve High-Availability (also called HA), a service needs to maximize its uptime and minimize its downtime based on the above definitions.

The Definitions of Failure, Error, and Fault

When devising a method for attaining high availability, the definitions of three confusable terms—failure, error, and fault (Jayasinghe, 2005)—must be clarified:

- **Failure:** A failure occurs when the delivered service deviates from its specification.
- **Error:** An error is a part of the system state and can be an indication that a failure is occurring or has occurred.
- **Fault:** A fault is defined as an abnormal condition or defect (Chan, 2007) which may be the cause of an error.

The ultimate goal of fault handling is to remove errors before a failure occurs, and to prevent faults from activating again. At least, we should take recovery actions when the any failure occurs, and

record the revealing errors and faults of each failure as the foundation of performance improvement.

Classifications of Faults

Faults can be divided into three major groups: physical, development, and interaction faults (Chan, 2007):

- **Physical Faults:** physical faults cause failures in the network medium, or failures on the server side. Two common cases of physical faults are when a service is down or the network connection to the service is down.
- **Development Faults:** human developers or development tools may introduce development faults. Interface mismatch, workflow inconsistency, and non-deterministic actions are well-known development faults. Interface mismatch faults may occur due to service interface changes or updates, and then a workflow inconsistency problem may emerge causing the interface change. A fault due to non-deterministic actions is a case where a service has more than one possible outcome. By following development guidelines or utilizing appropriate supporting tools, this kind of fault can be avoided.
- **Interaction Faults:** an interaction faults occurs when the given composite service fails at runtime, which can be sub-divided into:
  - **Content Fault:** occurs when the content of the service delivered deviates from the expected composite service. Content faults include incorrect service, misunderstood behavior, response error, and QoWS.
  - **Timing Fault:** timing failures are concerned with the time of arrival or the timing of the service delivery that result in the system deviating from

its originally specified functional requirement. Timing faults include incorrect order, time out, and misbehaving workflow faults. If the execution order in a composite service is fixed, timing faults do not occur.

Active and Passive Replication

Replication refers to the use of redundant resources (also called "replica" or "failover" components), including software or hardware components, to improve availability, reliability, fault-tolerance, and performance. The replication can be treated as the *de facto* solution to the availability concern of applications (Maarmar, 2009). There are two well-known techniques for fault tolerance in a distributed system: "active replication" and "passive replication" (Jayasinghe, 2005).

- **Active Replication:** Active replication means creating redundant application servers, namely replicas. When the system receives a request from a client, the request is forwarded to all replicas. Each replica processes the request and generates results independently, conveying the results to the "voter" component. The voter decides the final result based on the predefined strategy, such as maximum occurrence of the same result, and returns the final result to the client.
- **Passive Replication:** Passive replication is also called primary backup replication. In this method, only one server acts as the primary one to do the assigned job. If the primary server fails, the backup server takes over.

Classifications of Service Availability

Many extant techniques focus on enhancing or guaranteeing the availability of the system that provides web services. These solutions primarily fall into the three categories (Abraham, 2005):

- **Infrastructure Availability:** the goal of this kind of work is to maintain the high-availability of the underlying infrastructure that supplies the web service. Replication can be applied between servers, networks, and disk arrays.
- **Middleware Availability:** the aim of this kind of work is to ensure that the middleware stack is highly available. Replication is utilized among distributed systems that host multiple versions of the database, web application server, and messaging bus if one of the underlying components fails.
- **Application Availability:** this kind of work focuses on the availability of the applications that provide the web service built on top of the infrastructure and middleware. If any application node fails, another node takes over based on the replication mechanism.

Therefore, we observe that factors such as network connectivity, server failures, and middleware breakdowns negatively affect availability. For enhancing availability of Web services, infrastructure, middleware, and application availability may be examined and applied first. In fact, in current availability research, these concerns have been considered and these extant solutions are relatively mature whereas the availability guarantee for Web services remains a new research field. Meanwhile, the current literature on service availability mostly explores issues and solutions for the availability of the back-end server or merely for the atomic Web service, not for composite services. Therefore, the ultimate goal of this study is to propose an appropriate framework that enhances and maintains the high-availability of composite Web services. Replication or failover widely achieves high availability and fault tolerance. We adopt the replication mechanism as the main notion to enhance Web service availability and mitigate damage caused by physical and interaction faults. Moreover, our proposed framework employs passive replication since active replication needs a high cost to perform a large numbers of duplicate service invocations.

LITERATURE REVIEW OF SERVICE AVAILABILITY ATTAINING

This section reviews several representative efforts of Web service availability, attaining, and guarantee, and summarizes common features of these approaches as well as their shortcomings.

Self-Serv

Self-Serv (Benatallah, 2003) is a middleware infrastructure for the composition of web services. Self-Serv enables the declarative composition, the multi-attribute dynamic selection of component services, and peer-to-peer orchestrations. It is an important research work in the field of service composition. Self-Serv proposes the concept of a service container that facilitates the composition of a potentially large and changing set of services. A container is a service that aggregates several other substitutable services—those that provide the same set of operations either directly or through an intermediary mapping. Since the component services can be substituted dynamically for design time and runtime, the availability of the whole composite service can be assured.

Birman's Extensions to Web Service Model

Birman *et al.* (2004) proposed extensions to the web services model that supported monitoring the health of the system, self-diagnosis of faults, self-repair of applications and event reporting. This solution emphasizes scalability issues especially for a system, including large numbers of light-weight components, such as web service clients and small web service servers; it also builds on existing technologies, such as WS-Transactions and WS-Reliability. In general, this approach ensures a "server-level" availability that can offer fault-tolerance mechanisms that client systems can remain unmodified or linked to a new library at run time.

Vilas' Virtualization Framework

Vilas *et al.* (2004) proposed virtualization, in which new virtual web services (VWS) are created instead of actual ones, and real web services are internally managed in a cluster in the back of the virtual service. The clients communicate with the virtual web services as if they were utilizing the real one. The cluster decides which component services are bound per each client request. In summary, this solution realizes three specified requirements: detecting faulty servers, providing maintenance mechanisms for the cluster, and providing mechanisms for adding and removing servers in the cluster. In general, by maintaining "server-level" availability, this approach achieves web service availability.

Abraham's Web Service Model Enhancement

Abraham *et al.* (2005) introduced a web service model enhancement that fuses the failover mechanism at the transport level. This work devises two main components, including an enterprise level gateway that operates at the enterprise level and plays a monitoring role, as well as a central hub that manages invocation from several requesters and determines the best response. The enterprise level gateway passes a request to the appropriate service or if the desired service is not healthy, redirects it to another service. The central hub sends the request messages to multiple services, analyzes responses, and sends the most appropriate response back to the requester based on the specified criteria. The enterprise level gateway seems like passive replication whereas the central hub is more like active replication.

Ye's Middleware Architecture

Ye and Shen (2005) presented a middleware architecture that maintains a consistency of service replica states, accepts synchronous and asynchronous calls from client applications to web services, and returns results back to clients. Two main entities comprise the replicas in this work: a web service site and proxy web service site. A web service site is a conventional web service provider that hosts the code and data needed for implementing web service functionality. A proxy web service site is a middleware between clients and the web service site, ensuring consistency and recovery in cases where the web service site fails.

IBM FAWS System

IPM proposed FAWS (Fault tolerance for web services) (Jayasinghe, 2005) to provide a fault tolerance system for SOAP-based web services. It uses passive replication to supply fault tolerance for the web service technology. FAWS features two techniques, namely "client-transparent fault tolerance" and "non-transparent fault tolerance". In the case of non-transparent fault tolerance, the client sends the request to one of the list of service providers, and fault handling is achieved by invoking the next service provider on the client side. In the case of client-transparent fault tolerance, the client sends the request and waits for the response; faults are handled on the server side. FAWS provides a high-level components architecture that is consisted of four major components, which are FT-Front, FTY-Admin, FT-Detector, and FT-Monitor, to achieve client-transparent fault tolerance. Using the proposed architecture, the client is unaware of any server failure and need not resend the request when the web service fails. This approach is a good demonstration of

how the replication mechanism guarantees the high-availability of Web services.

Smart-Stubs and Smart-Skeletons

Paspallis *et al.* (2006) presented an approach to enable high availability and dynamic upgradability. The authors proposed three main requirements: (1) detect when service responsiveness becomes unsatisfactory (2) manage the availability infrastructure, (3) support dynamic upgrades. Based on the requirements, they devised a mechanism called smart-stubs and smart skeletons, which are proxies generated dynamically by HA-aware WSDL compilers. Smart-stubs and smart skeletons allow for automatic rerouting of SOAP messages to ensure availability in the event of faults, and block and adapt SOAP messages to enable dynamic software upgrades.

WS-Replication

To develop highly available web service in mission-critical systems, Sales *et al.* (2006) proposed a framework, namely WS-Replication. WS-Replication adopts an active replication strategy, using SOAP-based multicast to communicate with all web service replicas. WS-Replication satisfies availability requirements of mission-critical applications since current specifications such as WS-Reliability mainly focus on the message level only.

Dahlem's Mediation Model

Dahlem *et al.* (2007) presented a mediation model for improving the availability of composed services. The proposed mediation model is based on a multi-layered architecture with three layers: the service layer, composition layer and mediation layer. The model masks failures in a service composition by transparently selecting and executing an alternative composition while using the same logic at runtime. This approach threatens the composite service flow as a black box and can swap the whole flow directly when the failure occurs.

FTWS (Fault-Tolerant Web Services)

Laranjeiro and Vieira (2007) addressed web services availability from a fault-tolerance perspective. This approach proposed a mechanism named FTWS (Fault-Tolerant Web Services) to allow programmers to specify alternative web services that are grouped by functionality for each operation in a service composition. FTWS deals with the tasks of redundant web service invocation and response voting. FTWS is headed by an adapter that assesses the status of each member web service in a group using QoWS metrics, namely response time, response correctness, response availability, and a composed metric; it either simultaneously or sequentially invokes the alternative web services prior.

Maamar's Community Approach

To sustain the high availability of web services engaged in composition scenarios, Maamar *et al.* (2009) proposed a community-based approach. In this approach, a set of protocols is specified, including community management, web service attraction and retention, and web services identification for composition. By following these protocols, a community can be established and dismantled, allowing web services to enter and depart at their convenience. A master web service leads a community and is responsible for attracting web services to its community using awards, convincing web services to stay longer, and identifying the web services to partake in composite web services. In this approach, availability is achieved based on substituting traditional replica web services with communities of similar web services.

Hu's Analysis and Design Approach

Hu *et al.* (2009) presented an approach of analyzing and designing composite services based on both the system and client perspectives. From the system's view, the availability of a composite web service is calculated by its composite pattern, including Sequence, AND-join, AND-split, Or-join, Or-split, Do-iteration, and While-iteration. From the client's view, the three types of availability, i.e. non-redundant service, part-redundant service, and all redundant service, are analyzed. The all-redundant system that provides backup services for all service nodes yields much better availability.

Schneider's Orchestration Service

Schneider *et al.* (2009) proposed a mechanism of controlling the interaction within service compositions by means of a pluggable component, i.e. Orchestration Service. The Orchestration Service acts as a proxy for all partner services, as well as centrally coordinates the service composition flow through the interception and relay of messages exchanged among these partner services. This approach does not concern the behavior of the involved services, but focuses on their interactions in service composition. In this way, the Orchestration Service engages in obligations monitoring and interactions logging, ensuring the correct enforcement of stipulated policies without extensive modifications to existing service compositions.

May's Redundancy Strategies

To resolving high-availability issues of Web services, May *et al.* (2009) proposed two service redundancy strategies for SOA-based systems, including serial redundancy and parallel redundancy. Serial redundancy is an active strategy, letting the service consumer maintain an ordered list of service replicas via a request to one service replica at a time until the response is received or fails in each invocation due to time constraints. In contrast, parallel redundancy lets the service consumer send simultaneous requests to all the replicas until the first response is returned or no response is received within the limited time duration. In addition, a testing framework for evaluating performance and sustaining Web-service availability is accordingly proposed.

Sheng's On-Demand Service Replication Approach

Sheng *et al.* (2009) developed an on-demand service replication approach to achieve robust Web services provisioning based on dynamic and proactive deployment of replicas. To reduce the unavailability of Web services, this work adopted a well-known service replication mechanism to devise a replication decision model that mainly determines the number of the replicas, as well as when and where these replicas should be created and deployed. This approach is based on the separation of service provisioning and service computing to enable the decoupling of service providers and their service host providers selected to proactively deploy the appropriate replicas for a desired availability level. Additionally, a proposed mechanism for host matchmaking and selection advances the success of the on-demand service replication model.

Summary for Literature Review

By examining and comparing these research results, we summarize some observations:

1. The application replication mechanism motivates most approaches. Some methods utilize active or passive replication mechanisms directly whereas others propose augmented replication methods such as service proxy, clustering, virtualization, and service community.

2. Most methods can be applied to atomic Web services only, not composite Web services. A systematic method for attaining and maintaining composite services in different lifecycle stages requires development.

3. Most do not analyze the effect of service discovery as well as how and when to select failover/replica services. However, service discovery is an important activity in realizing the replication mechanism of Web services.

AVAILABILITY-ENHANCED SERVICE COMPOSITION LIFECYCLE

To construct a framework that guarantees high-availability of composite services, critical characteristics related to service composition and service availability, such as service composition, service binding, service change, and service contracting, should be investigated and analyzed first; based on the analysis results, an availability-enhanced service composition lifecycle is devised.

Service Composition: Starting from the Service Composition Lifecycle

As mentioned, service composition technology has gained a lot of attention and offers add-on values when delivering Web services to clients. According to existing literature (Yang, 2004; Esfandiari, 2005; Lee, 2008), a service composition lifecycle should include the following (See Figure 2).

1. **Service design:** this phase develops a composite service scheme that describes the service execution flow and service data manipulation. The *de facto* language of composite service scheme is WS-BPEL.

2. **Service deployment:** this phase deploys composite services in the service composition execution engine by uploading the composite service schema and performing configurations. An executable composite service is generated by the execution engine,

Figure 2. Service composition lifecycle

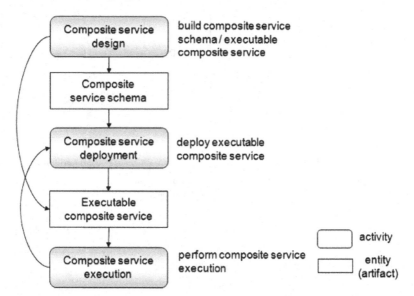

which listens to service requests from the client.

3. **Service execution:** this phase is responsible for performing tasks involved in the composite service. The service execution engine that hosts the composite services controls the execution flow, maintains the service data, and delivers service results to the client

In other words, a composite service provider should design the abstract composite service first, then deploy the service on the execution engine. Afterwards, the service requester can invoke the composite service by sending requests to the execution engine that processes the service request according to the composite service scheme.

Service Binding

The core concept of SOA shall be loops of "publish→search→binding" activities. In practice, the service proxy is often a bridge linking service requesters and remote Web services. Service proxy (or called service stub) is developed manually in accordance with the service description document (namely WSDL file), or

even generated automatically through a variety of services tools (such as WSDL2JAVA or various IDE environments) directly. The service proxy has the same interface with the remote Web service, and can be used as a local object for clients. Besides, the service proxy knows how to encode and decode messages which are sent to and received from the remote Web service. The client can invoke the proxy without worrying about the implementation details of how to communicate with the remote services.

Because WSDL separates interface and implementation, Web services realize "low coupling" characteristic, which means that a service proxy links to any concrete Web service as long as the service provides functionalities in conformance with the specified service interface (See Figure 3). In other words, service proxy decides the Internet address (so-called endpoint) of any service node dynamically to achieve "dynamic binding" or "dynamic swapping". This concept is similar to the "plug and play (PNP)" concept for hardware. New service components can be linked to existing application systems without restarting the server.

For service composition, a composite service is a service flow initially consisting of abstract

Figure 3. Service binding

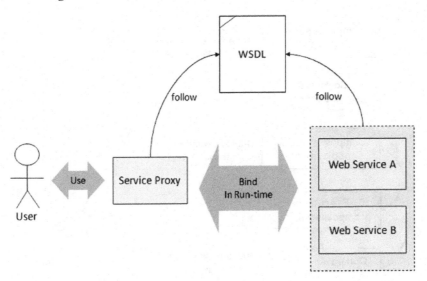

component services (or called service nodes). Concrete component services corresponding to an abstract service are functionally equivalent and serve as replacements with one another (also via WSDL conformance). Concrete services are bound statically or dynamically into the abstract composite service to construct an executable composite service. Thus, selecting and binding appropriate concrete component services in a composition is a very critical issue for building a composite service of good quality.

Service Change

As mentioned above, the dynamic feature of Web services is an important factor that impacts service quality. To address it, we need a detailed analysis of this factor. First of all, the service execution engine, which is responsible for controlling and managing composite services, is always the central service bus in the IT infrastructure. Thus, the execution engine is most likely given better hardware resources than individual SOAP server, and applied more mature fault tolerance mechanisms at the operating system level or web server level to achieve higher stability and availability.

Therefore, we focus on the changes to component services, defining the change as, "The functionality or quality of the component service does not work well as prescribed in the service contract." We classify the service changes as follows:

- **Change reversibility:** change in component services may be (1) permanent (failure) or (2) temporal (failure). Different models shall be devised for various changes.
- **The sources of service changes:** we classify the service changes by the source causing the changes (which are faults mostly). Two situations are identified: (1) user change: a change emerges due to requests from users. An available service for a user may be unavailable and unacceptable for another user due to different user requirements; (2) service change: a change occurs because of a service missing or service malfunctioning.
- **The impact of service changes:** the impact of changes also affects the remedy actions. Categories in this manner include:

○ **Unavailability:** the component service cannot be linked to or cannot be invoked.

○ **Mal-function:** the component service cannot deliver the desired functionality.

○ **Low-Quality:** the quality of the component service is lower than the service agreement level.

Service Composition, Binding, and Service Change

On the basis of the fore-mentioned analysis, we summarize the relationships among composition, change, and binding (See Figure 4):

- Abstract service composition embodies the service process to generate an executable composite service through service binding.
- Changes of any component services often cause a failure of service binding (namely invalid service binding).
- Changes of any component services also damage functions or QoWS (Quality of

Web services) of the composite service due to invalid service binding.

- The composite service should detect changes of its component services, understand the causes of the changes, and perform follow-ups of the service recovery actions.
- According to the user intentions and the system context, the composite services can change (substitute) the service-binding configuration, which should swap their component services.
- Swapping service bindings, which is usually an effective service recovery method, can reduce or mitigate the damages caused by service changes.

Service Contracting: Using Extended Contract Net Protocol (ECNP)

After introducing the above concepts, we bring up the service-contracting notion. The Contract Net Protocol (CNP) (Smith, 1980) is a specification of problem-solving communication and control for nodes in a distributed problem solver. Its significance lies in that it is the first work to use a negotiation process involving a mutual selection

Figure 4. Relationships among composition, change and binding

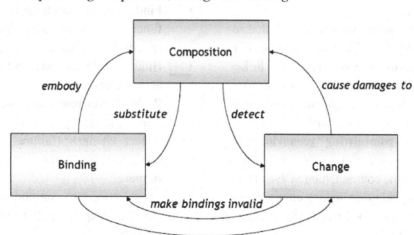

by both managers and contractors. In contract net, the agents are totally cooperative, and the selection of a contractor is based on suitability, adjacency, processing capability, and current agent load. The main steps in contract net protocol are (1) request for bids: A manager requests all bidders to submit bids; (2) submission of bids: The bidder prepares a bid and submits it to the manager for evaluation; (3) awarding of contracts: The manager evaluates the bid, which could (or not) be awarded as a contract to the bidder; (4) acceptance of contracts: If the contract is awarded, the bidder is requested to accept (or decline) the execution of the contract; and (5) submission of results: The bidder submits the results of executing the contract.

The Extended Contract Net Protocol (ECNP) (Lee, 2008) method extends CNP for both static and dynamic service composition to identify the components of the service (component service), to bind these components services, and execute the composite service. There are four scenarios in ECNP:

1. **"Making contracts" scenario:** In this scenario of ECNP, Service Composition Engine (SCE) makes contracts with component services by mediation of Service Matchmaking Engine (SME) ensuring the support for use of those component services hosted on Service Provision Engine (SPE) in the future.

2. **"Awarding tasks" scenario:** SCE that receives a request (by the service requester) awards tasks to component services. The key step in this scenario is that SCE requests SME for appropriate services again in a semantic manner before awarding tasks.

3. **"Normal de-committing" scenario:** If the provider of some component service wishes to repudiate the contract, then SCE can take the actions, including making contracts and awarding tasks, as described in the previous scenario of ECNP.

4. **"Abnormal de-committing" scenario:** A component service may de-commit the contracts without un-advertising itself. If SCE obtains error messages when awarding tasks, then it recognizes that contract de-committing event occurs. Afterwards, SCE can also take the actions prescribed in Scenarios 1 and 2.

Enhanced Service Composition Lifecycle

Composition-related activities, including composite service design, deployment and execution, are insufficient on their own. Enhancements to the service composition lifecycle are based on the fore-mentioned analysis results for the highly available service composition. To realize the concept of a passive replication method, we adjust the original form of replication due to the lack of providers of duplicate resources (so-called replicas). Meanwhile, some important issues such as code management and state synchronization between software copies are no longer required. Hence, we propose applying service discovery mechanisms to prepare replica services, selecting failover services and achieving service hot-swapping on-the-fly. We identified several requirements that should be addressed in our solution framework:

- Find concrete component services with functionalities in accordance with the specified interface at development phase.
- Bind suitable concrete component services at development time.
- Re-bind concrete component services at runtime to satisfy the user's expectations.
- Detect changes (failures or unexpected conditions) when the composite service is running.
- Swap concrete component services at runtime if applying the dynamic binding strategy.

- Deliver composite services to end-users by infusing user interactions and user interfaces into the composite service flow.
- Recover the service from the damages caused by changes according to predefined recovery strategies.

According to the above requirements, the original service composition lifecycle (See Figure 5) should be tailored to fit the requirements via adding notions of service binding and hot-swapping along three dimensions:

1. to propose a suite of service discovery activities, including interface-based matching, QoWS-based matching, semantic matching, and run-time matching, facilitating the selection of services by a set of composition-based service discovery mechanisms;
2. to provide a couple of service management activities, including service monitoring and dynamic service recovery, ensuring achievement of service recovery;

3. to devise the service delivery activities, namely service user interfaces design and rendering, infusing user interactions into composite services to improve composite service usability.

Responsibility Augments for Service Composition Activities

Obviously, the original service composition lifecycle cannot address issues of service availability, thus, the first step of lifecycle enhancements is to augment responsibilities for each activity:

- **Service Design:** to ease further service binding and re-binding, the service design activity can be adjusted as follows: the designer should first pick up abstract component services and then establish an abstract composite service flow. Next, multiple interface-compliant concrete services should be located or prepared for each service node (i.e. abstract component

Figure 5. Enhanced service composition lifecycle

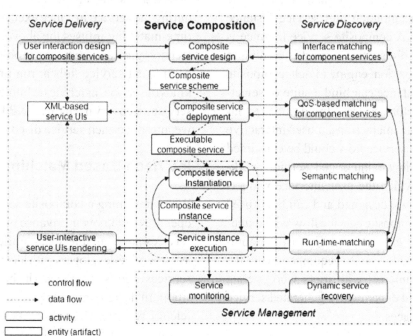

service); these services can be candidates for binding.

- **Service Deployment:** in this phase, we must identify the default binding service for each node as well as decide which concrete services can be qualified as binding services. Whether a component service is "qualified" or not usually depends on two criteria: interface conformity and Quality of Web Service (QoWS). Moreover, according to the regulations of ECNP, the composite service should make contract with the qualified component services to ensure the availability.

- **Service Execution:** in the original service composition lifecycle, the service execution activity is responsible for performing tasks of a composite service, and does not consider the parallel usage of different users. However, a composite service supposedly can serve for multiple users simultaneously. Every user should be able to decide his/her preferred service bindings in the composite service. Accordingly, we divide the original service execution activity into two sub-activities, namely composite service instantiation and service instance execution. A composite service instance is generated if a service request is coming to the composition engine. Each composite service instance can bind a suite of selected contractor services. In addition, to facilitate user interactions, a user-interactive composite service flow could be consumed directly via an integrated service workspace in which the user interface widgets are abstractly designed and can be infused into the composite service flow with extensions (Lee *et al.* 2009). That is, the composite service can be equipped with the ability to interact with users who operate the rich and dynamically-generated service user interfaces.

Extensions: Service Discovery Activities

To achieve better service availability, or even better service usability, we should strengthen the activities related to service discovery via a variety of service matchmaking mechanisms. We should indentify the required service matching methods based on the augmented service composition activities and the ECNP protocol. In the composite service design phase, service interface-based matching mechanism (hereinafter referred to as interface matching) is necessary to find abstract component services as well as concrete component services that can be bound into the service node in the composition; in the composite service deployment phase (the contracting phase in ECNP), QoWS-based matching mechanism (hereinafter referred to as QoWS matching) determines which quality level of the service establishes the service as the contractor service in the composition; In the composite service instantiation phase (the task awarding phase in ECNP), semantics-based matching mechanism (hereinafter referred to as semantic matching) meets the client's requirements, and determines the actual service bindings; during the service instance execution phase, runtime-matching infuses the above three matching technologies and resolves problems when any component service fails at run time. These four kinds of service matching technologies satisfy the service discovery needs in ECNP. In next sections, we introduce each service discovery technology.

Interface-Based Matching

When designing a composite service, the developer may not know in advance which component services are available and qualified, thus it must assist service developers with locating appropriate services used as components in the service composition. In design time, a keyword search function fetches Web services (abstract or concrete) first. An interface-based search facility sifts through appropriate services with inputs and outputs that fit the developer's intentions. From the replication perspective, we prepare component services that are possible as replicas through Interface-based matching.

QoWS Matching

For selecting or choosing services in a composition, Quality of Web Service (QoWS) is always treated as an important concern. QoWS can be represented as attributes like response time, cost, availability, and responsibility (Menascé, 2004), and a user can specify QoWS constraints or preferences that affect the results of service discovery. A lot of solutions have been proposed to realize QoWS-aware service selection and composition (Aggarwal, 2004; Canfora, 2008; Zeng, 2003). In the proposed framework, QoWS matching identifies candidate contractor services. Only qualified concrete component services are selected according to the quality requirements of the composite service and then these services are attached to a service node in the composition. SLA (service-level agreement) may be applied to regulate that the component service provide appropriate quality as specified in the contract. From the replication view, through QoWS matching we identify replica services that can takeover in the event of failure. Each service node in the composite service is attached with a community or a cluster containing a group of replica services with the same or similar functionalities.

Semantic Matching

In the semantics community, performing service discovery from the semantic viewpoint is a main research track. Extant efforts are largely focused on modeling Web services as ontology to facilitate semantic matching. For example, Paolucci *et al.* (2002) augmented WSDL and UDDI based on DAML-S, an otology language, to perform semantic matching. Sycara *et al.* (2004& 2009)

also proposed a semantic language, namely OWL-S, to allow semantic annotations and semantic discovery for SOA. In our proposed framework, semantic matching determines binding component services from the contractor services. Either domain-independent or domain-dependent ontology should be prepared and utilized to assure the linking component services that satisfy client requirements. Semantic matching mainly addresses the client's view to enhance availability, i.e. semantic matching offers specific "available" services to the specific service requester.

Moreover, this framework applies Possibilistic-Petri-Nets-Based (PPN-Based) (Lee, 2004; Lee, 2005) Service Matchmaker to fulfill partial requirements of these types of service discovery. A standard service matchmaking is merely based on keyword search whereas the PPN-based matchmaker addresses partial matching. PPN-based matchmaker performs not only interface matching for component services, but also conditional matching with semantics to locate services based on domain-dependent or domain-independent properties such as service type, service fee, and service level.

Extensions: Service Delivery

Service-oriented architecture is an ideal application integration mechanism. However, at the service presentation layer, its core principles of loose coupling and reusability are not applied. A service user interface is necessary for users to consume services. From the user's perspective, an interaction with a highly available composite service is the import part of user experience. The user experience is a major evaluation factor for composite service. A service delivery platform applies to both services and consumers, and interacts among them, bringing users an optimal experience. It typically integrates a series of techniques involved in the service life-cycle, especially the service composition technique, working together with the service orchestration system to deliver business functions, perform interactions among composite services and consumers, and eventually offer feedback to user experience derived from the interactions, which further improves the availability and usability of composite services. The service delivery category captures two major activities, including the user interaction design and the user-interactive service delivery. In the following sub-sections, we describe the activities in detail.

User Interaction Design

A composite service interacts with clients, typically Web browsers, through a series of service requests and responses carrying the delivered service data together with its user interfaces; therefore, the presentation layer effect actually serves as a key element in the design and development of composite services. In traditional service consumption, we must carefully study a composite service to interact with it, understanding its usage story, and implement some special-purpose codes. In particular, the user interface is manually developed in the early stages of service lifecycle. In other words, an ad-doc implementation is mainly handles service delivery. In recent years, much research has addressed this issue, attempting to deal with it in flexible and extensible ways (Lee, 2009; Tsai, 2008; Song, 2008; Vermeulen, 2007; Spillner, 2007; Khushraj, 2005; Kassoff, 2003). In these works, no matter how the problems are resolved, the XML-based approach to modeling service user interface is comprehensively adopted due to the flexibility, portability, and extensibility of XML. Via XML-based modeling, the service request and response messages can also be visualized without tedious coding.

User interaction is a desirable feature of service delivery, which can be abstractly declared in XML-based composite service scheme, such as BPEL, and combined with associated service user interfaces in design phase; it also successfully delivers composite service functions (Lee, 2009).

Two key elements support our solution to provide composite services with user interactions: (1) the rendering of the XML-based service user interfaces; and (2) an interaction mechanism between a long-running service flow and its participants. Both elements are based on the definition of extension activity in BPEL specifications. User interaction improves interplay between service composition and service delivery, and successful user interaction design may yield service usability.

User-Interactive Service Delivery

The major tasks of user-interactive service delivery are to handle user interactions during composite services, to render the service user interfaces against the interactions, and to feedback user experience for evaluation. By working with the service composition system in the service execution stage, the service delivery platform initially performs dynamic transformation from XML-based service user interfaces to consumer-readable or multimodal GUIs, such as HTML for Web consumer or embedded GUI for mobile device; then, it handles the inner workings of user interactions in composite services, by which clients consume and interact with composite services through a serious of service requests and service responses without any ad-hoc implementation. As mentioned above, the service management activities show how an existing composite service can be made more robust and qualified by monitoring desired services, evaluating recovery mechanisms, and replacing them upon failure. The feedback mechanism in user interactions can also facilitate the interplay between user interaction design and usability evaluation. Therefore, involving the service delivery platform into our enhanced service composite framework fuses user interactions with service compositions. It not only enhances communication between service composition and service delivery, but also aiding usability and availability.

Extensions: Service Management Activities

Although service discovery and service delivery activities achieve most requirements for a highly available service system, it lacks a number of important features, including: (1) how to determine whether a component services is no longer available? (2) If a composite service does not work as usual, what kind of remedy or recovery methods should be used? Obviously, these two issues cannot be covered in discovery-related and delivery-related activities. Therefore, "service management" activities should be considered to complement service discovery and delivery activities and become integrated into the service composition framework for strengthening the composition lifecycle and enhancing the quality of composite services.

Two major tasks in service management category are service monitoring and dynamic service recovery. Service monitoring technology measures and collects service quality data and determines the service status. Dynamic service recovery can dynamically decide the service remedy method based on the "fault location" in the service flow based on requirements or constraints offered by the user when any component services fail or unexpected conditions occur. Through applying these service management-related technologies, we realize regulations in ECNP more completely and systematically improve composite services availability.

Semantic Monitoring

Service monitoring gathers information and decides if the service result is unsatisfactory or the performance deviates from the specified QoWS attributes significantly. A human manager should define QoWS attributes and constraints as well as set event trigger conditions. Service monitoring functions should involve auditing events or data generated by component services and composite services, recoding the execution logs for each instance of service flow, and generating statistics reports. Meanwhile, service monitoring should also analyze the health of a Web service by recording the "heartbeats" of the service, or probe performance data by periodic service invoking. According to the monitoring report, corresponding events are triggered and inform the Dynamic Service Recovery component to take over the remainder of composite service execution and restore normal service operation. Besides, the service quality data serving as a basis of QoWS matching is stored in the quality database.

Dynamic Service Recovery

The main goal of the dynamic service recovery component is to avoid SOAP faults or transport-level failures such as connection timeout exceptions or socket closed exceptions when the user consumes the composite service. Therefore, when Service Monitor sends out any notification of failure, we need to dynamically decide the service remedy method to "heal" the failed service in run time and return acceptable service results to the user. Except for the traditional recovery strategies such as restarting failed service directly or re-invoking component services after waiting for a period of time, we may also swap component services. To apply recovery strategies efficiently, we should identify the execution rules for all strategies and specify the execution priority based on requirements or constraints offered by the user. Meanwhile, before taking recovery actions, "fault location" in the service flow is indentified. For example, when any fault appears or any failure occurs, the system solves the problem by following these procedures:

1. After waiting 10 seconds, the system re-invokes the failed component service.
2. If the failure cannot be eliminated, the system decides whether to ignore this component

service and continue the service execution according to its importance.

3. If the component service cannot be passed by, the system selects a failover service (according to its semantic satisfaction or QoWS criteria) from the contractor services list, re-binds the service, and continues the service execution.

4. If there currently is no candidate service, the system re-discovers functionally equivalent component services, selects and signs an appropriate failover service (according to its semantic satisfaction or QoWS), re-binds the service, and continues the service execution.

CONCLUSION

Web service availability plays a pivotal role in establishing a dependable SOA-based composite application. In this chapter, we examine the present efforts in Web service availability, investigate availability issues in Web service composition, present a software framework for composite Web service analysis, and improve service availability. Through the proposed approach, a suite of service discovery, service management, and service delivery facilities resolve and recover openness and dynamic issues. Consequently, the availability of composite services can be attained and maintained, and end users can consume highly available composite services in the service working space.

The benefits of this work are fourfold: (1) to obtain better service availability by selecting and attaching multiple candidate services for future binding, (2) to bind appropriate services to form an executable composite service per each client's request at run time, (3) to infuse user interactions and user interfaces into service composition for delivering composite service to end users, and (4) to avert service failures by performing service recovery strategies when receiving trigger event sent by the service monitor.

REFERENCES

Abraham, S., Thomas, M., & Thomas, J. (2005). *Enhancing Web services availability*. Paper presented at the IEEE International Conference on e-Business Engineering, Beijing, China.

Aggarwal, R., Kunal, V., Miller, J., & Milnor, W. (2004). Constraint Driven Web Service Composition in METEOR-S. Paper presented at the SCC 2004: 2004 IEEE International Conference on Services Computing.

Al-Masri, E., & Mahmoud, Q. H. (2008). Toward quality-driven Web Service discovery. *IT Professional, 10*(3), 24–28. doi:10.1109/MITP.2008.59

Andrews, T., Curbera, F., Dholakia, H., Goland, Y., Klein, J., Leymann, F., & Thatte, S. (2003). *Business process execution language for web services (BPEL4WS) 1.1: Technical report*. BEA Systems and International Business Machines Corporation and Microsoft Corporation and SAP AG and Siebel Systems.

Benatallah, B., Sheng, Q. Z., & Dumas, M. (2003). The Self-Serv environment for Web services composition. *IEEE Internet Computing, 7*(1), 40–48. doi:10.1109/MIC.2003.1167338

Birman, K., van Renesse, R., & Vogels, W. (2004, 23-28 May 2004). *Adding high availability and autonomic behavior to Web services*. Paper presented at the 26th International Conference on Software Engineering, 2004. ICSE 2004.

Box, D., Ehnebuske, D., Kakivaya, G., Layman, A., Mendelsohn, N., Nielsen, H., & Winer, D. (2000). *Simple object access protocol* (SOAP) 1.1: May.

Canfora, G., Di Penta, M., Esposito, R., & Villani, M. (2008). A framework for QoS-aware binding and re-binding of composite web services. *Journal of Systems and Software, 81*(10), 1754–1769. doi:10.1016/j.jss.2007.12.792

Cervantes, H., & Hall, R. S. (2005). *Service oriented concepts and technologies in service-oriented software system engineering: Challenges and practices*. Hershey, PA: Idea Group Publishing.

Chan, K. S. M., Bishop, J., Steyn, J., Baresi, L., & Guinea, S. (2007). A fault taxonomy for Web Service composition. *Proceedings of the 3rd International Workshop on Engineering Service Oriented Applications* (WESOA'07), Springer, LNCS.

Christensen, E., Curbera, F., Meredith, G., & Weerawarana, S. (2001). *Web services description language* (WSDL) 1.1.

Clement, L., Hately, A., von Riegen, C., & Rogers, T. (2004). *UDDI version 3.0. 2*. UDDI Spec Technical Committee Draft, 10.

Dahlem, D., Nickel, L., Sacha, J., Biskupski, B., Dowling, J., & Meier, R. (2007, 21-23 February). *Towards improving the availability of service compositions*. Paper presented at the Digital EcoSystems and Technologies Conference, 2007. DEST '07. Inaugural IEEE-IES.

Erl, T. (2004). *Service-oriented architecture: A field guide to integrating XML and web services*. Upper Saddle River, NJ: Prentice Hall PTR.

Erl, T. (2005). *Service-oriented architecture: Concepts, technology, and design*. Upper Saddle River, NJ: Prentice Hall PTR.

Esfandiari, B., & Tosic, V. (2005, 11-15 July). *Towards a Web service composition management framework*. Paper presented at the 2005 IEEE International Conference on Web Services, 2005. ICWS 2005.

Iwasa, K., Durand, J., Rutt, T., Peel, M., Kunisetty, S., & Bunting, D. (2004). *WS-Reliability 1.1. Organization for the Advancement of Structured Information Standards*. OASIS.

Jayasinghe, D. (2005). *FAWS for SOAP-based Web services*.

Jordan, D., Evdemon, J., Alves, A., Arkin, A., Askary, S., Barreto, C., & Goland, Y. (2007). *Web services business process execution language version 2.0*. OASIS Standard, 11.

Kassoff, M., Kato, D., & Mohsin, W. (2003). Creating GUIs for Web services. *IEEE Internet Computing, 7*(5), 66–73. doi:10.1109/MIC.2003.1232520

Khushraj, D., & Lassila, O. (2005). Ontological approach to generating personalized user interfaces for web services. *The Semantic Web VISWC, 2005*, 916–927.

Klusch, M., Fries, B., & Sycara, K. (2009). OWLS-MX: A hybrid Semantic Web service matchmaker for OWL-S services. *Web Semantics: Science. Services and Agents on the World Wide Web, 7*(2), 121–133. doi:10.1016/j.websem.2008.10.001

Kreger, H. (2001). Web services conceptual architecture (WSCA 1.0). *IBM Software Group Journal, 5*, 6–7.

Laranjeiro, N., & Vieira, M. (2007). Towards fault tolerance in web service compositions. *Proceedings of the 2007 Workshop on Engineering Fault Tolerant Systems*.

Lee, J., Lin, Y. Y., Ma, S. P., & Lee, S. J. (2009). BPEL extensions to user-interactive service delivery. *Journal of Information Science and Engineering, 25*(5), 1427–1445.

Lee, J., Liu, K., Wang, Y., & Chiang, W. (2004). Possibilistic Petri nets as a basis for agent service description language. *Fuzzy Sets and Systems, 144*(1), 105–126. doi:10.1016/j.fss.2003.10.016

Lee, J., Liu, K. F. R., & Weiling, C. (2003). Modeling uncertainty reasoning with possibilistic Petri nets. *IEEE Transactions on Systems, Man, and Cybernetics. Part B, Cybernetics, 33*(2), 214–224. doi:10.1109/TSMCB.2003.810446

Lee, J., Ma, S. P., Lin, Y. Y., Lee, S. J., & Wang, Y. C. (2008). Dynamic service composition: A discovery-based approach. *International Journal of Software Engineering and Knowledge Engineering, 18*(2), 199–222. doi:10.1142/S0218194008003635

Lee, J., Wang, Y. C., Wu, C.-L., Lee, S.-J., Ma, S.-P., & Deng, W. Y. (2005). A possibilistic Petri-Nets-based service matchmaker for multi-agent system. *International Journal of Fuzzy Systems, 7*(4), 199–213.

Maamar, Z., Sheng, Q., Tata, S., Benslimane, D., & Sellami, M. (2009). Towards an approach to sustain web services high-availability using communities of web services. *International Journal of Web Information Systems, 5*(1), 32–55. doi:10.1108/17440080910947303

Martin, D., Burstein, M., Hobbs, J., Lassila, O., McDermott, D., McIlraith, S., & Payne, T. (2004). *OWL-S: Semantic markup for web services*. W3C Member Submission.

May, N. R., Schmidt, H. W., & Thomas, I. E. (2009, 27-29 Aug. 2009). *Service redundancy strategies in service-oriented architectures*. Paper presented at the 35th Euromicro Conference on Software Engineering and Advanced Applications, 2009. SEAA '09.

McGuinness, D., & Van Harmelen, F. (2004). *OWL web ontology language overview*. W3C recommendation, 10, 2004-2003.

Menasce, D., & Almeida, V. (2001). *Capacity planning for Web Services: Metrics, models, and methods*. Upper Saddle River, NJ: Prentice Hall.

Menasce, D. A. (2004). Composing Web Services: A QoS view. *IEEE Internet Computing, 8*(6), 88–90. doi:10.1109/MIC.2004.57

OASIS Web Services Business Process Execution Language (WS-BPEL) TC. (2007). *Web services business process execution language,* version 2.0 OASIS Standard.

OASIS Web Services Transaction (WS-TX) TC. (2009). *Web Services atomic transaction* (WS-AtomicTransaction) Version 1.2.

OASIS Web Services Transaction (WS-TX) TC. (2009). *Web Services business activity* (WS-BusinessActivity) Version 1.2.

Paolucci, M., Kawamura, T., Payne, T., & Sycara, K. (2002). *Semantic matching of web services capabilities*. First International Semantic Web Conference.

Paolucci, M., & Sycara, K. (2003). Autonomous Semantic Web services. *IEEE Internet Computing, 7*(5), 34–41. doi:10.1109/MIC.2003.1232516

Paspallis, N., & Papadopoulos, G. (2007). An architecture for highly available and dynamically upgradeable Web Services. In Knapp, G., & Zupancic, J. (Eds.), *Advances in Information Systems development: New methods and practice for the networked society* (p. 147).

Salas, J., Perez-Sorrosal, F., Patino-Martinez, M., & Jimenez-Peris, R. (2006). *WS-replication: A framework for highly available web services.*

Schneider, C., Stumpf, F., & Eckert, C. (2009, 16-19 March). *Enhancing control of service compositions in service-oriented architectures*. Paper presented at the International Conference on Availability, Reliability and Security, 2009. ARES '09.

Sheng, Q., Maamar, Z., Yu, J., & Ngu, A. (2009). Robust web services provisioning through on-demand replication. *Information Systems: Modeling, Development, and Integration. Lecture Notes in Business Informatics, 20,* 4–16. doi:10.1007/978-3-642-01112-2_3

Smith, R. G. (1980). The contract net protocol: High-level communication and control in a distributed problem solver. *IEEE Transactions on Computers, 29*(12), 1104–1113. doi:10.1109/TC.1980.1675516

Song, K., & Lee, K.-H. (2008). Generating multimodal user interfaces for Web Services. *Interacting with Computers, 20*(4-5), 480–490. doi:10.1016/j.intcom.2008.07.001

Spillner, J., Braun, I., & Schill, A. (2007, June 2007). *Flexible human service interfaces*. Paper presented at the 9th International Conference on Enterprise Information Systems (ICEIS).

Stojanovi, Z., & Dahanayake, A. (2004). *Service-oriented software system engineering: Challenges and practices*. Hershey, PA: IGI Global. doi:10.4018/978-1-59140-426-2

Sycara, K., Paolucci, M., Ankolekar, A., & Srinivasan, N. (2003). Automated discovery, interaction and composition of Semantic Web Services. *Journal of Web Semantics, 1*(1), 27–49. doi:10.1016/j.websem.2003.07.002

Sycara, K. P. (2004). Dynamic discovery, invocation and composition of semantic web services. *Proceedings of the Third Helenic Conference on AI.*

Tao, H., Song, G., Minyi, G., Feilong, T., & Mianxiong, D. (2009, 17-19 December). *Analysis of the availability of composite Web Services*. Paper presented at the Fourth International Conference on Frontier of Computer Science and Technology, 2009. FCST '09.

Tsai, W.-T., Huang, Q., Elston, J., & Chen, Y. (2008, 22-24 Oct. 2008). *Service-oriented user interface modeling and composition*. Paper presented at the IEEE International Conference on e-Business Engineering, ICEBE '08.

Vermeulen, J., Vandriessche, Y., Clerckx, T., Luyten, K., & Coninx, K. (2008, March 2007). *Service-interaction descriptions: Augmenting services with user interface models*. Paper presented at the Engineering Interactive Systems.

Vilas, J., Arias, J., & Vilas, A. (2004). High availability with clusters of web services. *Advanced Web Technologies and Applications, Proceedings of the 6ᵗʰ Asia Pacific Web Conference*, (pp. 644-653).

Yang, J., & Papazoglou, M. (2004). Service components for managing the life-cycle of service compositions. *Information Systems, 29*(2), 97–125. doi:10.1016/S0306-4379(03)00051-6

Ye, X., & Shen, Y. (2005, 11-15 July). *A middleware for replicated Web services*. Paper presented at the IEEE International Conference on Web Services, 2005. ICWS 2005.

Zeng, L., Benatallah, B., Dumas, M., Kalagnanam, J., & Sheng, Q. (2003, May). *Quality driven Web Services composition*. Paper presented at the 12th International Conference on World Wide Web (WWW 2003).

Section 8
SOA Applications

Chapter 12
SOA Designed Health Care System for Taiwan Government

Jun-Bin Shi
Industrial Technology Research Institute, Taiwan

Shu-Fen Yang
Industrial Technology Research Institute, Taiwan

Tsung-Jen Huang
Industrial Technology Research Institute, Taiwan

ABSTRACT

SOA (Service-Oriented Architecture) is gaining popularity in becoming the mainstream in corporate integrated applications in recent years. However, at the early stage of proposal for SOA, due to the lack of a completion in relevant standards and infrastructure, corporations still need to evaluate the effect and risks involved in investment for SOA. For this reason, the introduction for SOA among corporations becomes relatively conservative. In contrast to the conservation projected by corporations at the initial stage, the government agents took position in promoting SOA and developing e-Government, who were the forerunners first committed in the integration of SOA applications.

BACKGROUND

Among these agencies, The Research, Development and Evaluation Commission (RDEC) of the Executive Yuan, has long schemed a service platform for e-Government (2011), using Web Services and XML as standards development and key technologies. Meanwhile, the RDEC also visited multiple countries and assimilated the experiences on implementing digitization from other advanced nations. The RDEC also built a governmental service platform with an overall planning in consideration of progressive steps for different stages. In the preliminary stage, the RDEC built a government portal, followed by promoting authorization, authentication, and electronic payment in the second stage to public services. In the third stage, the RDEC conducted counseling on existing systems of specific agencies by transforming these systems into application systems of medium environment with access to Web Services, thereby integrating

DOI: 10.4018/978-1-61350-159-7.ch012

specific services. Finally in the fourth stage, the RDEC implemented interdepartmental innovative services. The objective of the third stage aims to complete framework design for e-Government service platform based mainly in view of IT technical architecture, taking into consideration of functional and non-functional in the design principles to accomplish an infrastructure that support e-Government Portal and cross authority service integration, in addition to complete construction of service platform using SOA service design integrated with various modules.

INTRODUCTION

The Information and Communications Research Laboratories (ICL) also committed in service-oriented architecture related promotion and research at the initial stage of SOA development, which mainly takes responsibility in service platform related to the Department of Health from the e-Government service platform, with emphasis on the establishment of SOA service system regarding medical information and health care. Additionally, due to the security issue for SOA is regarded as the critical module in whether if the service platform is able to be successfully introduced, it is therefore used as evaluation reference for corporations in the introduction of SOA. Consequently, the institution also emphasize on studies related to SOA security issues. The paper is divided into three major sections, introducing the promotion and research on SOA related applications from the ICL.

Service System for Medical Information

Electronic Personal Health Record (PHR) refers to electronically storing personal health related medical information records that generally provide purposes similar to Electronic Medical Record (EMR). Recently due to rise in health care, the significance of personal health record gradually expands to the self-physiological measurement records of the public, hospital and laboratory records, health examination records, and insurance documents. The advantages of electronization not only reduces the inconvenience of management in physical papers but also the largest benefit lies creating the possibility in sharing health records, which can be used to integrate a person's current and past heath records into more comprehensive information through connection of computer or internet. Electronic personal health records can also offer other advanced applications such as demographic information and needs for other medical research purposes.

The development of common standards becomes one important step to improve the use efficiency of data under medical environment and to strengthen integration of analysis and application. The information exchange of Health Level 7 (HL7) refers to the specific proposal of electronic data format and operational process (Health Level 7 International, 2011) with emphasis on the medical records, clinical, examination, insurance, patient referral, care, and hospital transfer between medical information systems. Although the use of uniform data standards may technical barriers issues of integrated personal health records, the privacy of medical information and how to properly save and use information, are issues which require prudential judgment in implementation; moreover, the actual integration or convergence of scattered data is likely to result in issues on how to maintain and update follow-up data. Therefore, the program proposes an interface design similar to "passport" for data linking and integration. Simply put, the index data of basic information and access to medical institutions published in the passport are used as reference to units participating in health care system, to transfer, exchange and integration data through such intermediary information design.

The program probes into two aspects: (1) Information exchange standards for applications, develop unified exchange interface, and obtain complete personal health record. (2) Apply web services technology, construct operation environment for integration. Web services technology is a new method for system integration which has been widely used in distributed application integration architecture; due to the features to simplify of this technology in system development, which consequently and directly affect the implementation of traditional procedures and lifecycles. The program looks into the perspective of Service Oriented Architecture (SOA) and discusses how systems achieve integration in regards to mutual control in addition to the impact of such architecture on constructing health care applications.

Health Care System

The demographic information of Taiwan promulgated by Ministry of Interior, the rate of aging in Taiwan ranked second in the world, while the long-term care population exceeded over 400,000 people. The health care issues for senior citizens reveal the importance and urgency. Therefore the government actively engages planning and establishment of integrated IT technology with the industry for senior citizen care. Administrative policies related to the Ministry of Economic Affairs and Department of Health aim at building an electronic service industry for warm and caring service that gradually establish models of social innovation from senior citizen care, family care, community care and society care. Such policies also take initiatives in caring for senior citizens from the mind, body and soul by linking the content and technology of various services from SOA-based, open technology platform and proposing specific and feasible applications and integrated services derived.

On the other hand, changes in global health care industry have contributed to the shift in health care services from traditional bedside services in the hospital to mostly home care and life services of discharged patients; whereas the focus also shifts from emergency treatment to health care system

development based on the concept of preventive health care. For these reasons, prevention, treatment and care or even items in extension to life support, have all become indispensable links in health care system. Therefore, the applications on preventive health care, medical treatment and care related services also become more widespread. Using Service-Oriented Architectures (abbreviated as SOA) based open information platform to link the content and technology of various services and to propose specific and feasible applications and integrated services derived, have become one of the important policies in expectation for solving health care demand in the future.

The program adopts service oriented architecture based concept and its design model to organize functions included in system applications into services of interoperability and standardization in the future, while these services can also be combined rapidly and used repeatedly to meet integration requirement. The information service platform constructed by the program link with the system network from customer premise equipment, service provider, content provider, medical institutions, and distributors. The method of implementation applies new web services and service oriented architecture to mutually combine peer-to-peer collaborative business models with a series of service process from the above-mentioned four networks. Additionally, the repeated use of standard interface for integrating internal applications of operating business with external system and services from customers and suppliers may easily and rapidly expand heterogeneous and diversified services.

Web Services Security Gateway Systems

Both integrations of governmental and commercialized applications are involved with security and management issues in the data transmission process. Therefore issues on web service security and management are also discussed following the rise in web services. Moreover, failure to resolve service security and management will only make a halt on new technology at the stage of assessment for use due to lack of trust. As a result, medical information and health care platform particularly emphasize on web service security and management related issues.

The implementation of connecting medical information and health care platform systems with the network from customers, suppliers and distributors depends on the use of new web services and SOA to complete the peer-to-peer collaborative business models. Furthermore, security and management requirement for web services will appear following the expansion in scale, which also show inclination towards centralized management. To meet requirement for Web Services Control and Management, the Web Services Security Gateway (WSSG) developed by ICL of Industrial Technology Research Institute (ITRI) is applied in medical information an health care platform.

The above is a brief introduction to the three programs committed to Service-Oriented Architecture by Information and Communications Research Laboratories. We have accumulated relevant development experiences for Service Oriented Architecture in addition to encountering and solving some issues found in SOA in the process of implementing these programs. The experiences obtained by ICL in the process of implementing Service Oriented Architecture programs are divided into the following chapters and topics: 3. Web Services and Service Oriented Architecture, introducing relevant web services and Service Oriented Architecture technology in the implementation of medical information and health care platform with WSSG. 4. Applications on medical information and health care system, introducing concept in information management required for health care and medical information system to propose web services and Service Oriented Architecture. 5. Web Service Design, this chapter covers brief introduction on the Web Service process architecture between medical

information and health service system and the discussion on constructing medical information and health care service system through service oriented development process. 6. Web Service security and management. This chapter introduces management and security related security and standards that are required by web services. 7. Web Services Security Gateway, this chapter describes the Web Service Security Gateway architecture developed by ICL and its position in Service Oriented Architecture in the health care and medical information service oriented architecture.

WEB SERVICES AND SERVICE ORIENTED ARCHITECTURE

Web Services

System integration is an important means for heterogeneous environment in resource and information sharing. The definitions of integration between heterogeneous platforms require protocols, operation method and even development language that are recognized by both sides, while the level of mutual control is used as indicator for integration assessment. Middleware is an important means for recent applications in system integration. For example, the Component Object Model (COM) and Common Object Request Object Architecture (CORBA) from OMG organization are two most common distributed computing architecture approaches in commercial applications. Nonetheless, the above-mentioned middleware contain a complex and abstruse specification framework, resulting in difficulty of use by developers.

Web service technology uses XML messaging to replace middleware in system integration. Due to the nature of XML as Text-based document, and the format of Text is based on ASCII code, therefore under the premise of the majority of machines accepting SCICC codes at current state, messaging interoperability is inevitably higher than middleware [8] and the application systems completes communication through messaging. Web service technology can be traced by to the XML-RPC proposed by Microsoft and UserLand in1998. The initial intention was to solve system integration issues caused by limitations in operating systems; the technology was subsequently proposed to World Wide Web Consortium (W3C) for continuous development and standardization. After undergoing continuous revision, the standards were officially announced in 2003 while the various supporting development tools were also gradually completed. For example, the main application development languages such as Java and.Net (Medjahed et al., 2003), application server software such as IBM WebSphere and BEA WebLogic, and public service agency such as Microsoft and IBM, show the flourishing development of application system development based on Web Service technology. As commented earlier, web service technology has become one of the important architecture in application integration.

Web service technology contains two advantages: (1) Straightforward. Web service is document oriented application system integration. It uses packaging, transmission and interpretation for messages to complete the interoperability to be overcome by heterogeneous environment. It

has a lower level in development in comparison with traditional middleware. (2) Based on existing technology. The core of web services is based on exiting XML technology while the protocols also adopts application specifications Open Systems Interconnection (OSI) standards released by OSI organization, therefore the development method is not limited to any programming language or application software (Medjahed et al.).

Service-Oriented System Design

Service-Oriented Architecture divides network users into service requester, service provider, and service broker. The message passing environment commonly structured is shown in Figure 1. All communication approaches between each role (such as query, release and implementation) are completed in Simple Object Access Protocol (SOAP) message (XML messaging) (W3C, 2011) Service Oriented Architecture frequently applies the three specifications in the interpretation of interactions and operation reference between the roles. The description is summarized as the follows:

Figure 1. Members and corresponding standards of service-oriented architecture

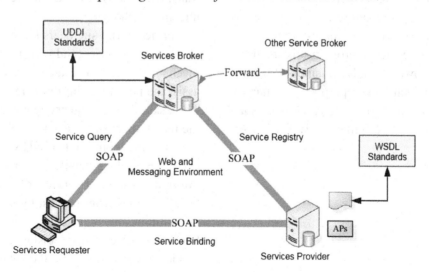

- **Simple Object Access Protocol (SOAP):** This standard is based on the foregoing XML messaging format, in other ones a XML Schema, whereas users make a document on messages according to this format, which plays a media that works around the entire Service Oriented Architecture. Although this specification is used in communication, it does not define its proprietary protocol layer. The current SOAP adopts HTTP as main transmission protocols however not limited to the use of other protocols in OSI application layer (such as FTP, and SMTP).
- **Web Services Description Language (WSDL):** The standard is a XML Schema which is used record relevant information to services, such as agreement, association and implementation details. The standard is referred by service providers in describing its service content. It is also a "document" in terms of real output. For service requesters, obtaining WSDL document for services is equivalent to acquiring execution right to the service.
- **Universal Description, Discovery, and Integration Protocol (UDDI):** This standard is developed by UDDI organization, mainly to provide standards for establishing service broker center in addition to involving in operational reference for broker center from service providers or requesters. The broker center referred in this standard is also known as UDDI Business Registry (UBR), which serves purposes similar to web searching engine, nonetheless the targets of search are limited to web services (W3C).

APPLICATION FOR MEDICAL INFORMATION AND HEALTH CARE SYSTEMS

Medical Information System

The program proposes an "integration service portal" design that emphasizes on the information management concept required by health e-Healthcare Record information system. The problem faced by health care information system is a typical distributed environmental integration. Due to the difficulty of obtaining consistency in the operation platforms, system development, and application approaches for various institutions and organizations, therefore internet service and service-oriented architecture are fundamental technology used in system development. The integrated service portal outlined in this program will collaboratively construct message exchanging environment with various institutions in distributed environments including medical institutions, various care responsibility units, public, to health and governmental agencies. In response to the possibly different developing environment used by various participating institutions, the study requires the operations must be structured under the Service Oriented Architecture and that each institution application system is required to transfer SOP message to complete cross-platform message exchange.

Service portal site bears the responsibility of "broker" web service, and a service registry center mechanism must be established in response to assist the portal site in implementing such task. The tasks of UDDI registry center aims to support the registration and query for web services. The registration is commonly used by service providers for recording detailed information on unit information and web services of providers; query usually comes from request by service requesters without any requirement for identification. Service providers must register their distribution service beforehand while the subsequent information update and deletion will go through this registry center. Web service portal sites use tools to establish their own proprietary service registry center, with major methods for selection including: (1) Install service registry center on a Microsoft platform using the built-in functions of server operating system. For example, Microsoft Server 2003 supports the above-mentioned function; (2) Using the API and database of establishment registration center or other open software such as UDDI4J on Java-based AP server platform. Basically, the establishment of service registry center also contains standard methods and tools; however the difficulty lies on the management, implementation and maintenance on data of registry.

The concept of "health e-Healthcare Record" aims to assist the collection and recording of public data summarized on health e-Healthcare Record using the processing capacity of information technology. The public or care responsibility unit may obtain a simple list of health records through a convenient web environment. Should the public encounter the need to inspect more detailed information, they may access to the data

system of original care responsibility unit through the link provided by the center. Figure 2 refers to the process design of "health e-Healthcare Record" for changes in relevant data. The figure on the left column is the process for care responsibility unit (including hospital, institutions, and community). In the event of the public encountering changes in care related data, the care responsibility unit system is responsible to update information to health service platform. The data transfer between health service platform and various care responsibility unit systems will be carried out through web services. The right and security issues required may be referred to relevant WS-Security standards for design. The figure on the right is the process of how the public obtain records of care summary. The middle section of the figure refers to the schematic diagram for passport application process.

Health Care Service System

The existing health care service systems emphasized on the particular services for users and sold to them. But the particular services are not

Figure 2. Schematic diagram for the application, change and query of health e-healthcare record

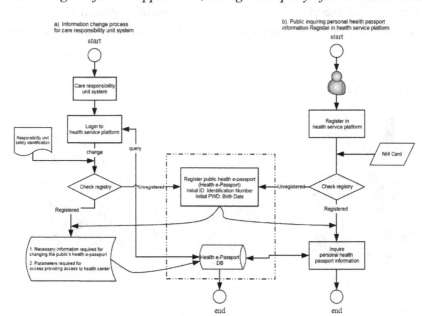

integrated with each other and the user needs to do integration for the services and information by himself. The user feels inconvenient and not satisfied because of facing the separate services and information without any interfaces for inter-communication.

This project provides the service oriented architecture first on analyzing the home care service and then indicates the requirements based the results. An integrated interface and protocol are constructed with the SOA technique to support the extensions in the future.

To meet the need for senior citizen health care stated in this program, various service providers are integrated to provide users with SECOM and Chia-Yi Christian Hospital (current service provider) according to different requirement. The Figure 3 shows the working system in Chia-Yi Chritian Hospital for Volunteer Management System, the positioning system of emergency aid and the Vital Signs Monitoring System are the working systems in the Taiwan SECOM. Due to different users require different services under different stages and scenarios, how to provide a single-service interface and integrating service information and service centers will allow service providers to provide services required by users at anytime, anywhere, which therefore meets the requirement for self-service through information

platform to integrate existing service technology of each provider. In addition, the program will also continue to integrate other service providers in the future, in order to transform and store message on technological architecture and information exchange protocols. Thereby a common platform interface is requited for formulation.

The program implements SOA technology to construct a complete platform using the two service providers during the planning stage as core to integrating information system of various information suppliers. The requirement assessed by consumers and care centers to provide appropriate services and implementation of information. Meanwhile, SOA collaborative platform provide plug-n-play information integration interface to assist service providers integrate their services at anytime according to customer requirement for selection.

WEB SERVICES OPERATION DESIGN

Service-Oriented Development Process and Methods

The medical system based on service oriented architecture adopts a service oriented architecture

Figure 3. SOA collaborative platform

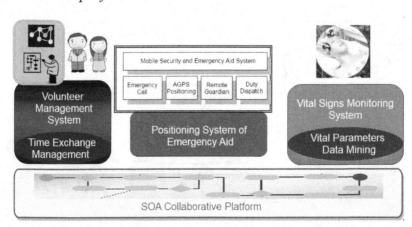

is basically indifferent from the one adopted by IT. The ultimate goal aims to include functions of various medical information and health care service system, and to organize the functions into standard services of mutual control and communication. These services can be accessed through standardized interface. Each service refers to a partial function which clearly corresponds to a certain step in operation process. The services are re-structured or repackaged through the system function modules of application program isolated from existing cooperation partners, which are then exposed using standard web service interface.

Medical information and health care service system can build a directory service based on these basic services components, accessing and repeating use of operation functions in different systems, or construct service infrastructure by rapidly combining into another service according to system requirement. These services can further meet operation requirement according to system requirement for combination and repeated use.

Before undergoing the design for web service interface, we must first establish a Business Scenario because we could find the actual requirement for enterprises in the real world through this Scenario, followed by developing a SOA solution based on Service-Oriented Architecture Approach

to solve this problem and to meet corporate requirement (Figure 4).

Figure 5 refers to a Business Scenario of "Query for Physiological Signal Measuring Date." In this example, "Measuring Management" will store the physiological signal data measured for each member to the database and this data will record the basic information of undergoing measuring instrument and the standard values of various physiological signals. When the Call Center receives request for "Query for Physiological Signal Measuring Data" from the members, they can connect to the Portal and input user account to query and authenticate membership. Upon validation of authentication, the physiological signal measuring data will be given and provided with health consultation and suggestion according to the standard values of each physiological signal.

We have established a Business Scenario of "Query for Physiological Signal Measuring Date" in the above-mentioned example, which briefly explains the actual operation process. Next, Service-Oriented Architecture Approach is implemented to develop a SOA solution.

A Top-down approach (Arsanjani, 2004) is applied to develop a SOA solution and to find out all services. Currently there are three types of identify candidate services, including top-down

Figure 4. SOA infrastructure

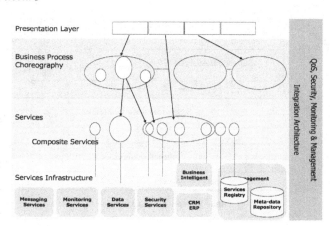

Figure 5. Business scenario of "query for physiological signal measuring date"

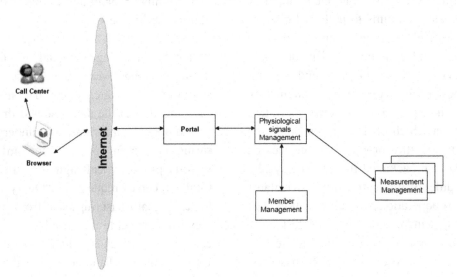

domain decomposition, bottom-up analysis of existing system and center-aligned business objectives modeling, respectively. We choose the top-down approach mainly due to the medical information and health care service system is innovative system development that lacks existing system for analysis.

SOA Approach includes five steps, which are Domain Decomposition, Goal Service Model Creation, Subsystem Analysis, Services Specification, and Structure Services, as shown in Figure 6.

The entire SOA Approach analysis and Development process starts from a Business Problem and we must first understand what kind of problem the enterprise needs to solve and the kind of Business Services that the enterprise could provide for such problem.

Figure 6. Five main steps of the SOA approach

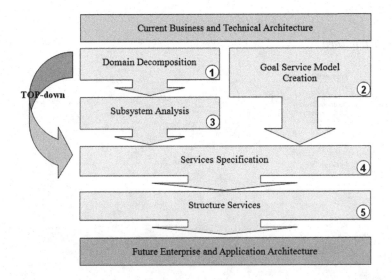

With this level of understanding, the SOA Approach is used through Top-down approach to find out all possible Business functions, processes, and sub-processes to solve this problem, followed by presenting the above-mentioned functions and process during use care and goal-service model, in order to converge Business Problem and find out Business Services. Finally the implementation of technical details for these services and the SOP of entire information process transfer are defined.

We discover web services related to medical information and health care service system through Service Oriented Architecture and development process in the follows:

Medical Information System

Medical information system uses Service Oriented Architecture to establish and integrate operating environment following SOP messaging with basis on the public's health e-Healthcare Record as operating core. A collaborative operational web service for response should be developed between the medical information system and each collaborative care responsibility unit, by playing mutual roles between service requesters or service providers. The interactive relationship is shown in Figure 7 with detailed design described below:

Medical information system: Including health e-Healthcare Record data base, care change service, information query service, and use log.

- **Health Care Database:** Responsible for data change of public access to each care unit. The database accepts update on "e-Healthcare Record change service" through web services at each care responsibility unit system, which also serves as the index center for detailed care records.
- **Passport Change Service:** Accepting calls for use of web services (or application system) from each care responsibility unit system to transfer SOAP request to health care system for updating change in database. Each collaborative institution must register service description and WSDL document.
- **Information Query Service:** Transferring SOAP request to specific care responsibility unit system and access detailed care records according to the parameter criteria. The record data for each care unit is feedback through data convergence. The service replies data via another window after dismantling and restructuring.

Care Responsibility Unit System: Service in coordination with the "health e-Healthcare Record" from the medical information system with development including change/registry service, record/access service and use log.

Figure 7. Medical Information System and care responsibility unit system based Web Service operation

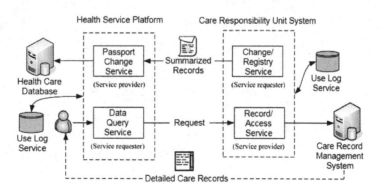

- **Change/Registry Service:** The care responsibility unit system updates care data to the database of health care system through SOAP approach and implemented by the "passport change service" of care system.
- **Record/Access Service:** The care responsibility unit shall provide a permanent web service to accept query request from medical information system or other authorized care responsibility unit system. Such service will render query result via HTML format.

Health Care Service System

Due to the broad coverage of multiple service provider systems, the information platform for development by health care service system adopts SOA platform (Figure 8) to achieve information integration and plug-n-play. Multiple service providers can collaborate in operation through SOAP messaging with at least five major core modules of web service operations planned:

Registry service, directory service, authorization and authentication service, service integration, and information interchange as shown in Figure 8, SOA Platform, are described in the following services provided by each module:

- **Registry Service:** The registry service mechanism of SOA platform aims at the basic items of implementation required for complex collaborative implementation environment when providing services. Due to the large number and distributed information exchange involved in platform operations (including user information, supplier information, and operation services), the registry service formulates a set of encoding rules of object identifiers for operating platform, as shown in Figure 9. According to the encoding rules of ASN.1. The only object identifier (OID) for providing these data objects of exchange is used as identification and management of the identity, thereby converging features such as registry and management of the

Figure 8. SOA Platform

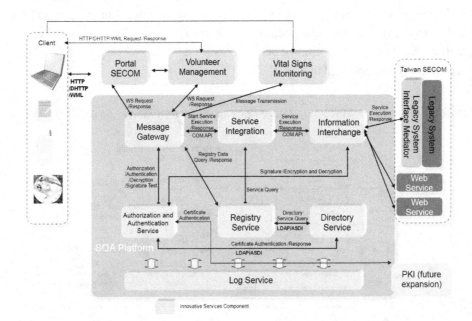

platform on user information, supplier information, and service content.

- **Directory Service:** The Platform Directory Service (PDS) of SOA platform is established in compliance with relevant X.500 international standards and supports directory server of LDAP v3 Directory Access Protocol(RFC 2251 □RFC 2252 □ RFC 2253) This platform is an important fundamental platform of the program and used as a unified storage location for common information to be accessed by core suppliers, users, public, and operation service of the internal units of medical institutions and external care institutions. The data will be ensure for consistency, sharing and easy maintenance, which concurrently provides the API planned and developed by the team as registry module, authorization/authentication service module, and interface for communication with Government Directory Service (GDS) and Local Directory Service (LDS) in data exchange modules (As shown in Figure 10).

- **Authorization and Authentication Service:** The function of safety certification aims to identify the service requester according to the credentials (account/password, electronic credentials) provided by service requesters in order to generate a "Token 1" that responds to service requester as the single signed-in credentials for common operating platform application system. The relevant description for the interface is shown in Figure 11. The authorization service refers to the permissions given for specific service requirement inquired by the requester when the platform follows "Token 1" from service requester and service request object identify (service request OID), which shall return a "Token 2" as reference for communication and identification with the platform. The external system shall Trust such "Token 2" and provide the service required.

- **Service Integration:** Application design requirement that closely integrates service integration with registry service to meet operating service. The application shall closely integrates other modules of the platform during implementation, correctly process service request proposed by users, and provide service managers and system managers with effective tracking and monitoring to this module.

- **Information Interchange:** Information Interchange Infrastructure is the legacy system interface for the developed system and existing system. It provides the calling form the developed systems to the registered service of the existing system or receiving the incoming message for the developed system to process. As the Figure 12 shows, the Information Interchange Infrastructure does the information interchange by the Web Services and provides two functions: A. Transform the service agreement to information process, B. Process the encapsulation and decapsulation of the request message and the request-for-response message.

WEB SERVICE SECURITY AND MANAGEMENT

When web services become increasingly widespread I IT applications, the issues on relevant security, management and service quality also become increasingly important. For any application program involving security issues, the safety to save information access is the most fundamental requirement. Nonetheless the practical service based on construction of SOA principles is more likely to expose weakness of existing safety practices due to the loose coupling characteristics of

Figure 9. SOA registry service

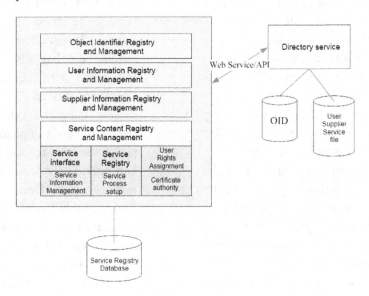

inter-organizational operations, hence the information security become even more important on a SOA platform environment. The relationship between enterprise, cooperative partners, customers and employees on a SOA platform environment usually changes. Therefore the SOA management used to establish and stop dynamic association also becomes increasingly important. Moreover, the management of service combination between corporate enterprises is even more complex. On

Figure 10. SOA directory service

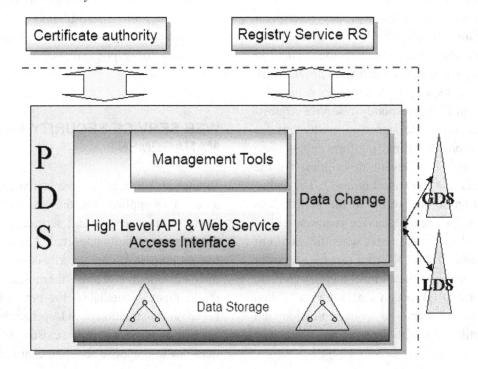

Figure 11. Authorization and authentication service

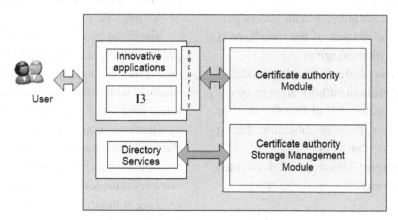

Figure 12. Information interchange

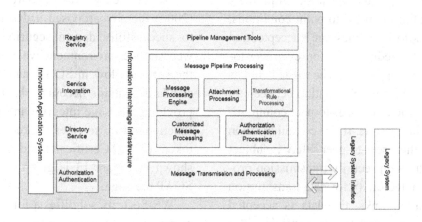

the other hand, message exchange must also change following the difference in environment, Business Model, and cooperative suppliers on the medical information and health care platform. In addition to safety and association management, how to maintain the system feasibility to 7x24 after establishing web services and deployment to SOA platform, and to provide tracking and statistical report for web service use in auditing operations, are both basic requirements for service quality on a SOA platform.

The ICL of ITRI has developed the Web Services Security Gateway solution in response to these issues on web service management. The ITRI mainly took Service Level Agreement (RDEC, 1992) formulated in the outsourcing project of

governmental agency information business as reference to web service quality. The Web Services Security Gateway is used to provide availability, efficiency, security, and audit of control system for web service.

One question must be clarified before discussing web service related security. Why does the existing SSL (n.d.) or IPSec (n.d.). fail to meet the requirement for web service security? First of all, web service security must be able to meet the following requirement.

- **Confidentiality:** The data must be able to guarantee the non-availability and non-openness to individuals, entity or programs without proper authorization.

- **Authorization:** Including access permission given in accordance with access permission and guarantee of the transferee is authorized with messaging.
- **Data integrity:** Referring to data modified or damaged without authorization or by users without authorization thereby ensures messaging free from modification during the transmission process.
- **Proof of Origin:** Messages received must be able to be identified with the sender.

Security transmission protocols such as SSL and IPSec can provide message integrity and confidentiality during the transmission process, however only limited point to point conditions. Nonetheless due to SOAP message is accepted and processed by intermediary, therefore even peer-to-peer communication links can be trusted, and as long as there is not trust association between all intermediaries, then safe peer-to-peer communication will be impossible. If one communication link is unsafe, then peer-to-peer safety is subject to damage. Although security transmission protocol can guarantee safety for data transmission in communication links, the data is accepted and decoded after completing transmission. The safety transmission protocols cannot guarantee the data free from access without authorization and changes. Due to the characteristics of web service storing message and resend thereon, the protection for SOAP message become necessary. In view of this, general security transmission protocols are insufficient for the safety protection SOAP messages.

Since the promulgation of SOAP standards (W3C, 2007), security mechanisms such as the encryption, authorization and authentication have received widespread attention from people. These three points are also issues which corporation applications should emphasized on, nonetheless, the SOAP standards are not comprehensive with regards to security in formulation. Simplicity is one important design objective for SOAP, utilizing existing standards and agreement to realize corresponding functions possibly. Therefore SOAP standard has its flaw in coherent security.

Web service security standards (WS-Security) (2006) thereby proposed a description in how to successfully design security functions for web service environment which emphasize on the security flow in SOAP standards. The first standard contains necessary basic elements by providing message integrity and confidentiality function to web services. Moreover, the security tokens (X.509 Certificates and Kerberos tickets) shown in Figure 13 is given to association to SOAP message.

WS-Security solidifies a foundation for web security architecture in development. Following the pass of time, other standards, in addition to basic security architecture, are gradually introduced to solve relevant issues on security strategies, trust, privacy and authorization. Figure 14 refers the web service security architecture diagram.

Figure 13. Web Service security tokens

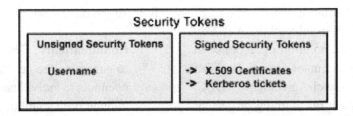

Figure 14. Web Service security architecture

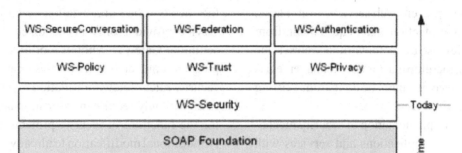

With regards security standards to web services, WS-Security agreements include how to guarantee integrity and confidentiality standards for Web service message. WSS agreement includes detailed message on Security Assertion Markup Language (SAML), Kerberos and certificate format (such as X. 509), which also describes on how to sign and encrypt SOAP message. In addition, the agreement describes on how to add security token into message, including binary security token such as X. 509 certificates and Kerberos ticket. The security features are placed into a message of SOAP message through WS-Security, thereby such agreement guarantees security for peer to peer.

WS-Policy (Web Services Policy Framework) permits Web Services to contain a set of standards that must satisfy (or use) the rules. For example, the Client uses Web Services must understand the WS-Policy provided at the Service end to ensure whether if the Client follows these policies when using this service. Therefore, when the Services end request encryption or signature for all Messages with specific methods, the Client end may not process service call on message without encryption or signature. Moreover, Policy Web Services for timestamp with specific requirement may not transmit messages without timestamp. Hence, these are the objective of WS-Policy: Assign WS-Policy to be followed by Web Services Requester to undergo service call.

The security and management of web services are achieved through WS Security agreement and WS-Policy agreement. The most straightforward approach is to directly write logistics related to security and management to the applications of web services. However, such approach to embed security and management logistics in the program becomes a headache for updating, maintenance and management in the future. Therefore the Web Services Security Gateway developed by ICL is used for converged web service security and management module.

WEB SERVICES SECURITY GATEWAY

The links between medical information and health care system with customer, supplier and distributor network applies the Web Service and SOA architecture to accomplish peer to peer collaborative commercial models. Following the expansion in scale, the management and security requirement in Web Services start to emerge and show a, inclination towards converged management. For this reason, the program plans on introducing the Web Services Security Gateway developed by the ICL of ITRI, to meet requirement for Web Services Security Control and Management.

The lack of protective work on the application layer with emphasis on the characteristics of web services from current web security mechanism has driven to the development of WSSG which can be used to prevent web services from hacks. The keys to protection and requirement from characteristics also differ for various web service applications; therefore customized management is required however it cannot be done from existing network security mechanism.

The direct implementation of security mechanism on various applications and services with emphasis on these security characteristics will cause complexity in system maintenance due to distributed characteristics. The management with regards to the configuration on security policies is also difficult, which inevitably becomes a dreadful nightmare in terms of system maintenance. Therefore the combination of web firewall convergence and establishment of various protective functions on firewall for providing converged security management of various application system, can offer a more convenient and simple system maintenance for MIS with dual features in security and convenience. Moreover, these characteristics can be combined with other web security protection mechanism can help service providers with more concentration on developing services they provide. The issues on management of web security by web security experts will construct better services under a more rigorous security protection. When taking into consideration of web service applications and security management requirement for customization, the WSSG unifies the management mechanism as "separation of security control and management and development of web services in addition to reduction in system development complexity and improve system security policy changes and flexibility," with regards to the advantages of security protection system control. The separation of security control and management with system development can help service providers stay free from web attacks and concentrate on the execution of services provided, in order to simplify system development at back end. With regards to enhance system security policy changes and flexibility, in the event of opening a web service to a newly allied organization or customer, the service provider only needs to change Policy setting at Gateway without modification to any programming codes. The modification to old security rules or new formulation to new security rules will only require modification and enhancing the functions in security protection systems. No additional modification to already established (multiple) web services is required, which thereby substantially reduces the complexity and costs in system development and maintenance.

The WSSG system from the ICL of ITRI as shown in Figure 15 provides Security Control & Management requirement from Web Services. All Web Services Message through SOA platform will undergo security added-value processing through WSSG, while the implementation of Web Services Message Security is also processed by WSSG. Regardless of Web Services system provided by the internal or external services of the company, either undergoes rigorous protective measures through this WSSG system, which effectively provides security management mechanism and maintain a carefree state when providing services. The system eventually intercepts malicious attacks to web exchange documents and the damaging impact caused to the system.

The Web Services Security Gateway from ICL of ITRI provides convenient Security Policy Wizard which allows managers to set up customized security management requirement on single Web Service application. The WS-Security and SAML standard are applied to undergo identification and permission control (Authorization). The system contains the following characteristics:

- **Rapidly and effectively integrate with corporate information security infrastructure:** The system adopts integral Adapter design to rapidly integrate with the existing information security infrastructure with the corporations.

Figure 15. Web service security gateway architecture

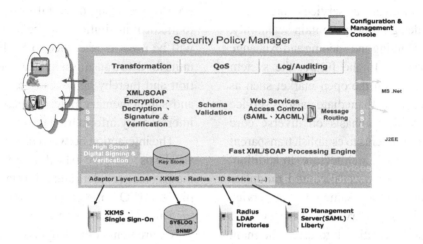

- **Support for integral Web Services Security related Standards:** The system may coordinate with traditional SSL encryption transmission, which also supports complete XML Security standards such as XML Digital Signature, WS-Security, and SAML. Providing enterprises integrated Web Services Security solutions to meet the requirement of corporations on Web Services security.

- **Independent security and management:** Separate security control and management from Web services development to reduce the complexity in system development and enhance system security policy changes and flexibility.

Supporting Specifications

1. Web Services Standards
   - XML 1.0
   - SOAP 1.1
   - WSDL 1.1 (Web Services Definition Language)
   - W3C XML Schema 1.0
   - XPath 1.0 (XML Path Language)
2. Web Services Security

- HTTPS (SSL v2/v3, TLS v1) refer to openssl
- XML Digital Signature 1.0□XML Encryption 1.0
- OASIS Web Services Security: SOAP Message Security 1.0 (WS-Security 2004)
- WS-I Basic Security Profile v1.0
- SAML

FUTURE RESEARCH DIRECTIONS

Following the increasingly growing problems in population aging, the issues on home care also become relatively urgent. The medical information and health care service system combined with SOA significantly show the following advantages:

1. Using SOA designed information platform to connect with network from future operational enterprises and customers, service providers, content providers, and distributors by implementing new Web Services and SOA architecture into mutually controlled standardized services with the functional organizations included in the systems. These services can rapidly structure and repeat usage to meet customer requirement.

2. The Marketplace is an open market operation for mediating various service contents and the SOA design concept contain Scalability, Dynamic Binding and opening and exchange characteristics. In the future, the system will be based on the open market such as the Marketplace to mediate various service contents with emphasis on diverse core service components to establish transparent service provision architecture. In addition, the system will generalize and modulate some common and same-concept service functions into core Services Components and to provide integration interface. The main objectives of the system aims to provide users with customization and simplified user environment, which concurrently supports service providers with rapid and flexible development and deployment of new-pattern services.

However, the current medical information and health care service system projects come from the SOA platform developed by business corporations, who provide services by integrating service suppliers, content supplier and distributors. It is inevitably difficult for customers to transfer to different platforms medical records can easily be transferred through health e-Healthcare Record. However due to lack of relevant information exchange standards in current health e-Healthcare Record, therefore under SOA architecture, how to construct relevant health care information change standards is an important research in the future.

Results

The ITRI successfully integrates SOA with medical information and health care from the above-mentioned program. With regards to medical information, a successful foundation based on service oriented architecture with emphasis on personal health record connecting with integration issues, an interface design concept similar to

"Passport" is introduced with indexed information for recording basic information and access to medical institutions on the passport. The data will be used as reference to health care system units for data transmission, exchange and integration and thereby achieves objectives in control and supplementary practical care through such intermediary information design.

The interaction between users and care center will be used as core in health care service system; the service providers and information integration platform (SOA platform) provide appropriate service and information implementation according to requirement commonly assessed by the users and care center. Meanwhile, the SOA platform provides plug-n-play information integration interface to allow service provides with integration of services at any time. Additionally, care upon request will be provided according to user needs.

WSSG provides a web service converged management platform which reduces complexity in system development and enhances system security policy change and flexibility through separating security control and management in addition to development in web services. Encryption, filtering, digital signature, Schema validation, WS-Security, access control, XPath, and detailed logging methods are also applied to reduce threat from web service transactions and enhance security. XML firewall containing simple operation, service layer management and strengthening access control, allow medical information and health care service systems to concentrate on service development, which also provides greater flexibility in future service management.

REFERENCES

W3C. (2007). SOAP version 1.2. Retrieved from http://www.w3.org/TR/soap12-part1/

Arsanjani, A. (2004). *Service-oriented modeling and architecture*. Retrieved from http://www.ibm.com/developerworks/library/ws-soa-design1/

Health Level Seven International (HL7). (2011). *Website*. Retrieved from http://www.hl7.org

IPsec. (n.d.). Retrieved from http://en.wikipedia.org/wiki/IPsec

Medjahed, B., Benatallah, B., Bouguettaya, A., Ngu, A. H., & Elmagarmid, A. K. (2003). Business to business interactions: Issues and enabling technologies. *The VLDB Journal, 12*(1), 59–85. doi:10.1007/s00778-003-0087-z

OASIS. (2006). OASIS Web services security (WSS) TC. Retrieved from http://www.oasis-open.org/committees/wss/

RDEC. (1992). *Operation manual of service level agreement for governmental agency information business outsourcing projects*. Retrieved from http://www.rdec.gov.tw/public/Data/852014512671.pdf

RDEC. (2011). E-government service platform (GSP). Retrieved from http://www.rdec.gov.tw/lp.asp?ctNode=12144&CtUnit=1735&BaseDSD=7&mp=100

Transport Layer Security. (n.d.). Retrieved from http://en.wikipedia.org/wiki/Secure_Sockets_Layer

World Wide Web Consortium. (W3C). (2011). *Website*. Retrieved from http://www.w3c.org

APPENDIX: SYSTEM ANALYSIS OF E-HEALTHCARE RECORD SERVICE

Use Case Modeling

Figure 16. Use case diagram of e-healthcare record service

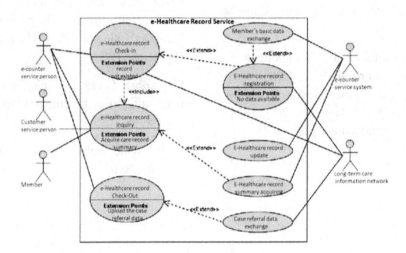

A.1 e-Healthcare Record Check-in

1. Brief Description of Use Case:After accepting a case, the e-counter service person should process the e-Healthcare record check-in entry through the remote care information platform's portal website or e-counter system. After checking in, you have right to inquire and update members' e-Healthcare records. If any member has no e-Healthcare record, the system will trigger the e-Healthcare record registration procedure to complete the registration, and then complete the e-Healthcare record check-in procedure.
2. Participant Character/Role:E-counter service persons and the long-term care information network
3. Pre-Conditions
    (1) The SSO (Single Sign-On) mechanism should be integrated at the remote care information platform and the e-counter system.
    (2) E-counter service persons should acquire members' NHI IC cards in case of accepting cases.
4. Post-Conditions
    (1) Store the e-Healthcare record check-in information in member's e-Healthcare record index.
    (2) Acquire the e-Healthcare record index, and complete the interconnection of the long-term care information network for accessing member's discharge planning information.
5. Basic Flows:
    (1) After the e-counter service person completes the case accepting procedure, the e-Healthcare record check-in should be processed through the e-counter system or service portal; at this time, the e-counter service person will be asked to insert NHI IC card for confirmation and authorization.

(2)   After any e-counter service person inserts member's NHI IC card and confirmation, the e-Healthcare record check-in components should process the NHI IC information confirmation and the authorization verification.

(3)   The e-counter service person should process the check-in procedure in accordance with the ID no. and name etc. derived from the NHI ID card, and wherein the e-Healthcare record registration procedure should be processed if any one has no care membership (see Alternative Flows 3.1).

(4)   After checking in, the e-Healthcare record check-in components should store data in member's e-Healthcare record in accordance with the acquired member and e-counter information.

(5)   After completing the check-in procedure, the e-Healthcare record check-in components provide members' e-Healthcare records, including member's basic data and e-Healthcare record index (refer to the Use Case of inquiring the e-Healthcare records).

(6)   The e-Healthcare record check-in components acquire the discharge planning information for any e-counter service person's reference through the interconnection of the long-term care information network.

(7)   The e-Healthcare record check-in operation should be thus completed.

6.   Alternative Flows

   (3.1)   e-Healthcare Record Registration Flow:

   a.   In accordance with the member's ID no., the e-Healthcare record registration components may acquire member's related basic data (member's ID no., name, gender and birth date, etc. included in NHI IC card) though the discharge planning or the case assessment information accessed through the integrated long-term care information network.

   b.   In case of the long-term care information network not containing this member, the e-Healthcare record registration components will ask the e-counter service person to enter basic personal data or export them from the e-counter system through the service portal for registering member's e-Healthcare records.

   c.   After establishing member's e-Healthcare records, the e-Healthcare record registration components will create username and password for service portal, and thus members can access care service information and resource through the network service portal.

   d.   The e-Healthcare record registration components issue message to inform member to enter username and password.

   e.   The e-Healthcare record registration operation should be thus completed.

7.   Exceptional Flows:

   (2.1)   In case of the failure of the NHI IC card verification, terminate the Use Case.

   (4.1)   In case of the failure of updating e-Healthcare record index information, the update failure message will appear, and you will be asked to process check-in operation again and terminate the Use Case.

   (7.1)   In case of the failure of the interconnection of the long-term care information network, the connection failure message will appear, and you will be asked to inquire information again and don't terminate the Use Case.

A.2 e-Healthcare Record Check-Out

1. Brief Description of Use Case: After the e-counter service person closes the case or completes the case referral procedure, the e-Healthcare record check-out procedure should be processed. After completing the check-out procedure, the system should store related historical information in member's health care record index, and if necessary, the case referral data should be uploaded to the long-term care information network.
2. Participant Character/Role: E-counter service persons.
3. Pre-Conditions:
   (1) The SSO (Single Sign-On) and the information security mechanisms should be integrated at the remote care information platform and the e-counter system.
4. Post-Conditions:
   (1) Store the e-Healthcare check-out information in member's e-Healthcare record index.
5. Basic Flows:
   (1) After any e-counter service person completes the case closing procedure, the health care check-out function should be checked through the user interface provided by e-counter system or service portal, and the e-counter service person will be asked to enter member's PID.
   (2) The e-Healthcare record check-out components should first check the desired member who is a member being checked in at this counter.
   (3) The e-counter service persons should make sure whether to process the check-out procedure, in order to avoid fault operation.
   (4) During the check-out process, the e-counter service persons will be prompted to upload the case referral data to the long-term care information network (refer to the Use Case diagram relevant to the case referral data exchange).
   (5) After completing the check-out procedure, the e-Healthcare record check-out components should store related historical information in member's health care record index, and appears the completion message.
   (6) The e-Healthcare record check-out operation should be completed.
6. Alternative Flows:
   None.
7. Exceptional Flows:
   (2.1)   In case of the failure of member's PID verification or any one who is not a legal member after inquiry, terminate the Use Case.
   (3.1)   if the member is not the one who is checked in at the counter, the system should provide "not permitted" message, and terminate the Use Case.
   (6.1)   In case of the failure of updating e-Healthcare record index information, the update failure message should appear, and you will be asked to process check-out operation, and terminate the Use Case.

A.3 e-Healthcare Record Updating

1. Brief Description of Use Case: After the e-counter (the e-Healthcare record check-in procedure completed) is authorized, member's e-Healthcare record index information may be continuously

updated through the e-counter system, and the integrity and the continuity of member's e-Healthcare record may also be maintained.

2. Participant Character/Role: An e-counter system.
3. Pre-Conditions:
   (1) The SSO and the information security mechanisms should be integrated at the information platform and the e-counter system.
4. Post-Conditions:
   (1) Member's e-Healthcare record index information should be successfully updated at the e-counter system.
5. Basic Flows:
   (1) The e-Healthcare record should be updated by the e-Healthcare system through the information platform for e-Healthcare record index information mapping.
   (2) The e-Healthcare record update components should confirm the desired members who are checked in at this counter.
   (3) The e-Healthcare record update components should complete the e-Healthcare record index information update, and the completion message should appear.
   (4) The e-Healthcare record update operation should be completed.
6. Alternative Flows:
   None
87. Exceptional Flows:
   (2.1)   if this member is not the one who checked in at the e-counter, the system should provide "Update not permitted" message, and terminate the Use Case.
   (3.1)   In case of the failure of updating the health care record index information, the update failure message should appear, and the update operation should be processed again, and terminate the Use Case.

A.4 e-Healthcare Record Inquiring

1. Brief Description of Use Case: Members, e-counter service persons, and customer service persons may inquire member'se-Healthcare records through the service portal or the e-counter system.
2. Participant Character/Role: E-counter service persons / Customer service persons/Members
3. Pre-Conditions:
   (1) The SSO and the information security mechanisms should be integrated at the information platform and the e-counter system.
4. Post-Conditions:
   (1) Member's e-Healthcare records should be successfully inquired.
5. Basic Flows:
   (1) Members, e-counter service persons or customer service persons inquire the e-Healthcare records.
   (2) The e-Healthcare record inquiry components ask you to enter member's PID.
   (3) The e-Healthcare record inquiry operation will investigate the e-Healthcare records. When clicking the e-Healthcare record index to acquire the e-Healthcare record summary, the e-Healthcare record summary investigation procedure (refer to the Use Case relevant to the e-Healthcare record summary investigation) should be processed.

(4)   The e-Healthcare record inquiry operation should be completed.

6.   Alternative Flows:
None
7.   Exceptional Flows:
(2.1)   In case of the failure of the PID verification, terminate the Use Case.
(3.1)   In case of the failure of the e-Healthcare record inquiry, the failure message should appear, and request for inquiry operation again and continue the Use Case.

A.5 e-Healthcare Record Summary Investigation

1.   Brief Description of Use Case: Members, e-counter service persons or customer service persons may real-time investigation on the e-Healthcare record summary stored in the e-Healthcare system through the connection of the care service record index information.
2.   Participant Character/Role: An e-counter system.
3.   Pre-Conditions:
(1)   The SSO and the information security mechanisms should be integrated at the information platform and the e-counter system.
4.   Post-Conditions:
(1)   Member's e-Healthcare record summary should be successfully looked up and displayed.
5.   Basic Flows:
(1)   Members, e-counter service persons or customer service persons may process the e-card record summary investigation in accordance with the e-Healthcare record index.
(2)   The e-Healthcare record summary investigation components should be connected to the e-counter system, and acquire the e-Healthcare record summary needed.
(3)   The e-Healthcare record inquiry operation should be completed.
6.   Alternative Flows:
None
7.   Exceptional Flows:
(2.1)   In case of the failure of the investigation or the network connection, the failure message should appear, and request for investigation operation again, and continue the Use Case.

A.6 Member's Basic Data Exchange

1.   Brief Description of Use Case: In case of accepting a case, the e-counter system may acquire member's basic data from the remote care information platform, and thus the unnecessarily repeated basic data entry may be reduced. On the other hand, at the time of registering member's e-Healthcare records or updating member's basic data, the e-counter system may map member's basic data to the remote care information platform in order to ensure the integrity and the consistency of member's data.
2.   Participant Character/Role: An e-counter system.
3.   Pre-Conditions:
(1)   The SSO and the information security mechanisms should be integrated at the information platform and the e-counter system.

4.   Post-Conditions:
     (1)   Member's basic information should be successfully exchanged.
5.   Basic Flows:
     (1)   E-counter system and member's basic data exchange components should be interconnected, and member's basic data exchange procedure should be also processed.
     (2)   Member's basic exchange operation should be completed.
6.   Alternative Flows:
     None
7.   Exceptional Flows:
     (1.1)   In case of the failure of information exchange, the failure message should appear, and request for data exchange operation again, and terminate the Use Case.

A.7 Case Referral Data Exchange

1.   Brief Description of Use Case: An e-counter system may map case referral data to the long-term care information network at the time of the e-Healthcare record check-out.
2.   Participant Character/Role: An e-counter system.
3.   Pre-Conditions:
     (1)   The SSO and the information security mechanisms should be integrated at the information platform and the e-counter system.
4.   Post-Conditions:
     (1)   The case referral data should be successfully uploaded to the long-term care information network.
5.   Basic Flows:
     (1)   The e-counter system and the case referral data exchange components should be interconnected, and the case referral data exchange procedure should be also processed.
     (2)   The case referral data exchange operation should be completed.
6.   Alternative Flows:
     None
7.   Exceptional Flows:
     (1.1)   In case of the failure of information exchange, the failure message should appear, and request for data exchange operation again, and terminate the Use Case.

Chapter 13
Case Study on SOA Implementation Framework and Applications

Tzu-Chun Weng
Institute of Information Industry (III), Taiwan

Yu-Ting Lin
Institute of Information Industry (III), Taiwan

Jay Stu
Institute of Information Industry (III), Taiwan

ABSTRACT

As industry shows increasingly meager profits, increasing value-added products is imperative to enhance profits. Across all industries, executives are demanding more and more value and specific character-istics from their strategic business processes. The CEOs of enterprises engage in integrating their IT organizations to measurably improve the flow of data and information driving key business decisions. The Enterprise Service Bus (ESB) provides a set of infrastructure capabilities, implemented by middle-ware technology, that enable the integration of services in the Service Oriented Architecture (SOA). The ESB concept already has a number of uses that solve some very common and challenging integra-tion problems. Innovative Digitech-Enabled Applications & Services Institute (IDEAS) of Institute for Information Industry (III) executed many projects, which support technology transfer to and assist some industries, subsidized by Economic department of Taiwan. Three relatively industrial applications with EBS are discussed.

DOI: 10.4018/978-1-61350-159-7.ch013

INTRODUCTION

Integration of applications within a business and between different businesses is becoming more and more important in this rapid changing world. The needs for real time and update information that is accessible to every business require developers find solutions for integrating diverse, heterogeneous applications, developed in different architectures and programming languages and on different platforms. Business have to do this quickly and cost effectively, but still preserve the architecture and deliver robust solutions that are maintainable over time. But integration is a difficult task. With different dimension data from distinct resources, integration technology applied SOA concept address backend service control process. When the service system is triggered by the front end business request, back end service components should find applicable data from different resources to meet the service need. The back end data service is often a service bus or a repository that data can converge to a united conceptual data stream. There is still a lot of heavy lifting to do integration and a need for a well defined approach (methodology) and a set of best practices.

Enterprise service bus thus would enable low cost integration and would be used by companies with limited IT resources. Enterprise service bus is from service-oriented architecture evolved, in describing one kinds of IT infrastructure application integration model, through one kinds of clearly defined class of structure, coupled with each other and form. ESB is a pre-assembled units which were completed in SOA practice of mechanisms, including the practice of SOA inside layered target functional elements needed basis. With the concept of ESB for the construction of the information development platform, operating through decentralized management mechanism, event-driven, data-driven processing mode, etc., and then have the ability to support plant content-based routing and filtering capabilities,

in addition, its also provides a very rich standard interface, but also with complex data transmission capacity. ESB is divided into four modules, Event-Service, Message-Service, Data-Service and Process-Service. We integrate them to implement the concept of ESB to complete enterprise applications.

This chapter focuses on the newly developed solutions to integrate existing applications, using modern technologies, particularly enterprise service bus architecture including four service modules: Event-Service, Message-Service, Data-Service and Process-Service. In the following sections, the objective of the chapter define critical concept for integration, what integration patterns to use, which technologies to use, and how to best integrate existing applications with modern e-business solutions by exemplifying three industrial applications. In view of theses real cases including E-learning, Smart Store, and Medical System, SOA implementation framework with more flexible ESB development guidelines completely yields systems that are more amenable to change. From higher quality to more reuse to better scalability and availability, the benefits of implementing service architecture far outweigh the cost and extra effort involved.

BACKGROUND AND LITERATURE REVIEW

The importance of web application and advanced technology has attracted increasing attention as among the concerns of various industries. Today with an emerging service experience economy, developers increasingly desire efficient/effective principals from design to development, publish, and management. Systems thus evolve into flexible service system consisted of 4I service technologies (i.e., interface technology, intelligence technology, integration technology and infrastructure technology) to realize elasticity of this changing demand world. Integration technology particularly applied service oriented architecture coordinates the front-end business logic tasks and the exact back-end IT components needed to execute the task. Hence, the enterprise service bus provides a set of infrastructure capabilities, implemented by middleware technology, that enable the integration of services.

Service System

Service System is a composition of technology designed to deliver services that satisfy the needs of customers. A general service system is an ecosystem of all action roles (people, businesses, or nations) in a designed scenario. All action roles can share valued information with each other. Service technologies help action roles to communicate with each other and reduce the processing time of service action. Service system replies customers' requests sensitively, quickly and correctly. Quinn and Paquette (1990) have stated their insight of service system: "Properly designed service technology systems allow relatively inexperienced people to perform very sophisticated tasks quickly — vaulting them over normal learning curve delays." Fast food chained restaurant is a classic example of service system. The cooking system in a fast food restaurant is operated smoothly by their employees because the system has identified the clear goal of their output: quality and fast food on their menu. Besides, the system provides entirely support of the whole service process. Receptionists check the customer's orders and forward the order information to infield personnel, they cook food by standard facilities designed by the chain restaurant to assure all the dishes have the same taste. The instance describes a typical service system in service industry. A service system may not include many employees like receptionist. For example, a vending machine can provide selling service to customers by friendly user interface, but maintenance. Technology is the key component to form a service system and people are always the gasoline to run a service system.

Mediation

In the early days, there was little attention paid to the concept of sharing application logic and data across multiple machines in business computing and therefore many issues were caused. The big question faced by an organization was how to develop computer systems to successfully automate previously manual operations such as billing, accounting, payroll, and order management. In order to solve any one of these individual problems, it was challenging enough without considering the possibility of basing all of a company's systems on a common, reusable architecture.

With the majority of operational business functions now automated, the next phase of evolution revolves around improving the ability of these systems to meet new requirements. Information technology (IT) departments are adding new user interfaces, combining multiple data sources into a single view, exploring methods for extending applications to mobile devices, and initiating efforts to replace old applications with more modern ones. These are common reasons given by CIOs for investing in new projects.

The industry also must face a paradigm shift toward service-oriented development and architectures based upon services. While service-oriented architecture (SOA) has been around for more than a decade, the concept is now becoming more main-stream because of Web services and is gathering momentum as the IT world makes the truly important shift from developing new systems to getting more out of earlier investments. Developing services and deploying them using an SOA is the best way to utilize existing IT systems to meet new challenges.

The common goal of applying technologies such as SOA, EAI, B2B, and web services is to create architecture for integration that can be pervasive across an extended enterprise and beyond. For an integration infrastructure to achieve this pervasiveness, it must have the following characteristics:

- It needs the more flexibility and ability to react to and meet the needs with changing business requirements and competitive pressures.
- It must extend beyond the boundaries of a single corporate IT data center and into automating partner relationships such as B2B and supply-chain scenarios.
- It must adapt to suit the needs of general-purpose integration projects across a variety of integration situations, large and small. Adaptability includes providing a durable architecture that is capable of withstanding evolutions in protocols, interface technology, and even process modeling trends.
- It must have simplicity of design and low barriers to entry, enabling the everyday IT professional to become a self-empowered integration architect.
- It must provide an SOA across the pervasive integration that enables integration architects to have a broad, abstract view of corporate application assets and automated business processes.
- It must link together applications that span the extended enterprise using a single unified approach and a common infrastructure.

Mediation's architecture should address these needs, and is capable of being adopted for any general-purpose integration project. It is also capable of scaling pervasively across enterprise applications, regardless of physical location and technology platform. Any application can plug into mediation network using a number of connectivity options, and immediately participate in data sharing with other applications that are exposed across the bus as shared services. After all, data with value called as content is the most important thing in a service system.

A mediation must provides a highly distributed approach to integration, with unique capabilities that allow individual departments or business units to build out their integration projects in incremental, digestible chunks. Using the mediation, departments and business units can continue to maintain their own local control and autonomy in individual integration projects, while still being able to connect each integration project into a larger, more global integration network or grid.

4I: Interface, Integration, Intelligence, and Infrastructure

Technology plays an important role to develop a complete service system. Service technology framework contains four key items: interface technology, intelligence technology, integration technology and infrastructure technology. From the front-end device machine, meddle content analysis, back-end service to virtual service center, these four innovative system total solutions provides different layers technical problems. The 4I framework can provide a reference to locate technology resources in a service design.

Interface technology manages the communication between user and machine / machine and machine. The communication protocols have to be determined with interface technology. It should have the capability to receive the signal sent by human/machine and interpret it to understandable message in service system. The trend of interface technology is to be more natural than traditional input devices such like keyboards and mouse. The natural interface technology is to let users use their instincts to communicate with computer like gestures or touch screen.

Intelligence technology refers to the data analysis mission. It collects all the helpful data from different resources that related to service system. After collecting data, intelligence technology transforms this data into information and even into knowledge. The output information/ knowledge can help service system provide appropriate action to its user or other components in the system. Intelligence technology usually uses statistics, artificial intelligence, text mining and data modeling skills to accomplish analysis task.

Integration technology applies backend service control process. The data integration is the main purpose of integration technology. The distributed database is generally seen in nowadays information system. When the service system is triggered by the front end request, back end service should find the applicable data from different resources to meet the service need. The back end data service is often a service bus or a repository that data can converge to a united conceptual data stream. Moreover, linking different dimension data is another key ability in integration technology. For example, a geospatial service bus is a back end service to support mobile search. This geospatial service contains at least three data types: geospatial database, temporal database and ontology database. To generate the correct feedback to the user's search intent, the service bus hast to link all the three data types and forward the result to front end.

Infrastructure technology is the foundation of 4I framework. One of the main tasks of infrastructure technology is to manage all the hardware facility resource like computing power, data storage capacity and network infrastructure. Information technology service system can't be operated without hardware infrastructure. The essential software is another key component in infrastructure technology. It can deal with data processing and process sharing in a service system. For example, an operating system helps people manipulate computers to perform service task. E-mail is another classic instance of essential software to let people exchange their messages in digital format.

Figure 1 4I service technology and examples in III shows the examples of four technologies in III IDEAS service design house. The 4I framework can apply to any system to check the technology completeness.

Service Oriented Architecture (SOA)

Just like object a generation ago, service is now the killer buzzword. However, SOA is often a misunderstood topic in IT today. Before elaborating the concept, we need to define web services first in order to construct the whole knowledge. Services may mean different things to different people. From Gartner point of view, web services are loosely coupled software components that interact with one another *dynamically* via *standard Internet* technologies. In addition, W3C regards web services as software application identified by

Figure 1. 4I service technology and examples in III

Technology	Example
Interface technology	❑ Machine-Machine: interface between heterogeneous machines, web service, electronic data interchange ❑Human-Machine: speech recognition, haptic technology
Intelligence technology	❑Semantic analysis ❑Artificial intelligence, decision support technology ❑(Data/Text/Web) mining
Integration technology	❑Geospatial Service Bus (GSB) ❑Content Repository ❑RFID-enabled Application Platform (REAP) ❑Enterprise Service Bus (ESB) ❑Service Cloud (with IBM Watson Research Center)
Infrastructure technology	❑Common service like category service ❑Monitoring, auto detection ❑Computing resource management ❑Utility Cloud infrastructure (with IBM Cloud Computing)

a URI, whose interfaces and binding are capable of being defined, described, and discovered by XML artifacts and supports direct interactions with other software applications using XML-based messages via *Internet-based protocols*. As for Microsoft and IBM, a piece of business logic accessible via the *Internet* using *open standards*, and *self-contained reusable* software modules that are *independent* of applications and the computing platform are defined as web services respectively. As a result, SOA definition is still evolving now:

- A set of components which can be invoked, and whose interface description can be published and discovered (W3C).

- Service-oriented architecture is a client/server design approach in which an application consists of software services and software service consumers (also known as clients or service requesters). SOA differs from the more general client/server model in its definitive emphasis on loose coupling between software components, and in its use of separately standing interfaces (Gartner).

- Service-Oriented Architecture is a business-driven IT architecture approach that supports integrating your business as linked, repeatable business tasks, or services. SOA helps today's business innovate by ensuring that IT systems can adapt quickly, easily and economically to support rapidly changing business needs. SOA helps customers increase the flexibility of their business processes, strengthen their underlying IT infrastructure and reuse their existing IT investments by creating connections among disparate applications and information sources. (IBM)

In short, services with well-defined *interfaces* allow a *one to one mapping* between business tasks and the exact IT components needed to execute the task. The fundamental SOA spirit is taking individual functions or systems into services. In other words, SOA is an application framework using common service interface to communicate each other in order to integrate and to reuse services. (Tibco, 2004) This architecture is targeted at solving the problem which traditional distributed applications lack of uniform communicating protocols. Owing to web services with standard techniques such as HTTP, XML, SOAP, and WSDL, the integration realizes on multi-platforms and multi-languages. SOA enables IT organizations to better align them with the business by more quickly and cost-effectively delivering and modifying applications and services that address new and changing business requirements.

Enterprise Service Bus (ESB)

As previously mentioned, in recent years an architectural approach which the SOA provides brings the flexibility and agility required by today's global business environment. (Freund, & Niblett, 2008) addressed that an Enterprise Service Bus (ESB) acts a conductor as a vital ingredient of SOA which facilitates the interaction of business services by mediating the message exchange.

An ESB is an architectural pattern to integrate and manage services, not a software product. An ESB offers a software infrastructure that simplifies the integration and flexible reuse of business components within a SOA and provides a dependable and scalable infrastructure that connects disparate applications and information technology resources, orchestrates their interactions, mediates their incompatibilities, and makes them broadly available as services for additional uses. The basic functions of an ESB include message transformation, service call, application integration, service quality, security service and system management (David, 2004).

The book in (David, 2004) indicated that an ESB provides the implementation backbone for an SOA. That is, it provides a loosely coupled, event-driven SOA with a highly distributed universe of named routing destinations across a multiprotocol message bus. Applications (and integration components) in the ESB are abstractly decoupled from each other, and connect together through the bus as logical endpoints that are exposed as event-driven services.

(Hermann, etc., 2005) described that an ESB is an architectural platform. Many applications are created by composing software components in the ESB together in such a way that complete business processes are reflected. The software components are packaged as high-level "services", which are platform-neutral.

(Schmidt, etc., 2005) noted that an ESB provides the infrastructure for releasing service-oriented architecture and the runtime environment for deploying your services which do not interact with each other, rather the ESB acts as a mediator. The ESB is providing technological solutions to intercept messages between Web Services and to translate or route them to help the integration of business applications. The general architecture of

an ESB with components connected to it is shown in Figure 2 General ESB architecture (Colombe, etc., 2005). Components can take on the role of service producers (often called 'services') or service consumers. Services can be special components, such as orchestration engines, adapters to data resources or adapters to external systems which need message transformation or transport protocol conversion.

(Leusse, etc., 2007) show a basic ESB infrastructure in which services can communicate through an abstracted interface provided by the bus. Once a message is received by the bus end point, series of actions can take place. The type of actions taking place is influenced by both the content of the messages received and the way the bus has been configured to handle them.

(Goel, 2007) pointed out that the ESB is an infrastructure to facilitate SOA. The given API can be used to develop services and makes services interact with each other reliably. Technically ESB is a messaging backbone which does protocol

Figure 2. General ESB architecture (Colombe, etc., 2005)

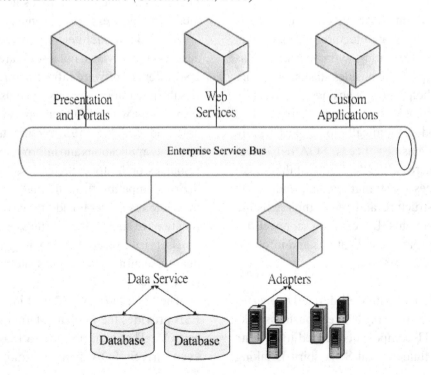

conversion, message format transformation, routing, accepting and delivering messages from various services and application which are linked to the ESB. The ESB enables a more efficient value-added integration of numerous different application components by positioning them behind a service-oriented facade and applying web services technology to interoperate.

(Papazoglou, etc., 2007) illustrated the capability of ESB that can connect diverse applications and technologies. A primary use case of the ESB is act as the intermediary layer between a portal server and the back-end data sources. A portal is an aggregation point of various resources that user will need and these resources represent as services. Retail portal, divisional portal, corporate employee portal, and business partner portal are examples of portals.

We describe the ESB as providing a set of infrastructure capabilities, implemented by middleware technology, that enable the integration of services in the SOA. The ESB to this conception is from service-oriented architecture evolved, in describing one kinds of IT infrastructure application integration model, through one kinds of clearly defined class of structure, coupled with each other and form. The ESB is a pre-assembled unit which was completed in SOA practice of mechanisms, including the practice of the SOA inside layered target functional elements needed basis.

Existing ESB Review: Open Enterprise Service Bus

Open ESB is an Open Source project creating a platform for Business Integration, Enterprise Application Integration (EAI), and Service-Oriented Architecture (SOA). Open ESB is a Java based open source enterprise service bus. Open ESB can be used as a platform for both Enterprise Application Integration (EAI), and Service-Oriented Architecture (SOA). A large number of components are being developed in

the Open ESB community: e.g. for accessing back-end systems and other ESBs or SOA platforms, for message transformation, etc. Unlike proprietary ESBs, Open ESB is purely based on open standards (e.g. JBI and Java EE). This prevents vendor lock-in.

Other open standards that are supported help with interoperability with other ESB/SOA products. The NetBeans based IDE makes it very easy to create integration solutions or composite applications.

- **Open Standards:** Open ESB is based on open standards. Avoid vendor lock-in - not only is Open ESB based on open standards, it also supports open standards for interoperability with other products.
- **Productivity:** Open ESB has made integration more productive by providing out-of-the box components for both simple and complex tasks. From simply picking up files or accessing a database through to Complex Event Processing, the Open ESB components in addition manage the many non-functional requirements, such as error handling, locking and concurrency. Open ESB enables you to realize such features easily and, typically through configuration, without writing code.
- **Patterns:** Open ESB provides components for inherently difficult problems. Consider a use-case that would require a lot of effort to implement, such as building asynchronous web service invocations with fault compensation handlers, correlation, and reliability in a cluster. An out of the box solution for this problem is provided through utilizing the BPEL SE, where business logic is expressed in WS-BPEL, and where otherwise complex logic is then reduced to far fewer lines of code.

Open ESB which is the realization of many years of innovation in integration is complete. Open ESB is freedom because No vendor lock-in. Open ESB's strategic policy is that Open Standards and Source facilitate the continuous assurance in your investment.

Existing ESB Review: IBM WebSphere Enterprise Service Bus

IBM WebSphere ESB provides an Enterprise Service Bus for IT environments built on open standards, SOA, messaging and Web services technologies of WebSphere Application Server. WebSphere ESB is aimed at businesses looking for Web services-based connectivity and service-oriented integration. IBM WebSphere Enterprise Service Bus helps enable fast and flexible application integration with reduced cost and bridging to next-generation interconnectivity.

- Decouple complex integration logic from each application with a central, integration solution eliminating point-to-point connectivity programming.
- Expose existing applications and data as new business services opportunities without impact to the current IT environment.
- Leverage existing ESB infrastructure for universal service delivery and extend easily to federated ESB and service federation model.
- Integrate seamlessly with existing SOA and BPM platform while optimized for WebSphere Application Sever as well as products within the IBM SOA Foundation.
- Reduce ongoing maintenance costs by decoupling connectivity and integration logic from each and every application.
- Maximize effectiveness of your SOA environment with dynamic service connectivity and control leveraging WSRR to increase business agility and growth.

Existing ESB Review: Sonic Enterprise Service Bus

Traditionally, enterprises connected systems using point-to-point links and custom code. More recently, integration brokers — proprietary software for creating connections among multiple systems — emerged as another solution. However, point-to-point connections are expensive to maintain, and integration brokers have been expensive to buy.

Sonic ESB is one of a new set of products billed as enterprise service buses (ESBs), lightweight integration brokers based on standards such as XML and SOAP designed to work in a distributed environment.

Sonic ESB advances service-oriented architecture (SOA) and enterprise integration by bringing you the power and flexibility of an open services and integration standards-based development model. With Sonic ESB, you will get dynamic multi-site operations management and deployment capabilities backed by the industry's only true 100% up-time enterprise messaging infrastructure.

Sonic ESB advances the state of the art in SOA infrastructure and enterprise integration by bringing to bear the power and flexibility of an open services and integration standards development model with unmatched dynamic multi-site operations management and deployment capabilities backed by the industry's only true, 100% up-time messaging infrastructure. And, with fully integrated end-to-end operational visibility and semantic data transformation support, re-draws the lines of competition.

Existing ESB Review: Oracle Enterprise Service Bus

An enterprise service bus moves data among multiple endpoints, both within and outside of an enterprise. It uses open standards to connect, transform, and route business documents as Extensible Markup Language (XML) messages, among disparate applications. It enables monitoring and management of business data, with minimal impact on existing applications. An enterprise service bus is the underlying infrastructure for delivering a service-oriented architecture (SOA) and event-driven architecture (EDA).

Oracle Enterprise Service Bus is the foundation for services using SOA and EDA. At its core, it is a loosely coupled application framework that provides your business with increased flexibility, reusability, and overall responsiveness in a distributed, heterogeneous, message-oriented environment using industry standards.

Oracle Enterprise Service Bus is a component of Oracle SOA Suite. Oracle SOA Suite is a standards-based suite that provides an integrated design-time environment and a common architecture for developing enterprise applications. Oracle SOA Suite enables services to be created, managed, and orchestrated into composite applications and business processes.

Existing ESB Review: WebOTX Enterprise Service Bus

Enterprise information systems have dramatically changed and progressed in several years. Management environment has largely changed by corporation merger, internal control and regulatory compliance control in order to personal information protection. New business is launched because of tough competition. New system to support decision making is constructed. Systems are improved in existing business to increase profit. As a result, various systems exist in silos of different departments that are operated and managed separately.

Such situation cause not only increased overall system maintenance cost but also diminished enterprise management efficiency. Enterprise information systems require "highly adaptable" and "highly flexible" system architecture and implementation.

Information systems are becoming more and more complex by the day. On the other hand, there is a strong demand for low-cost and quick system development. This demand can be satisfied by utilizing the existing systems as well as the Web services and Web API's that are available to the public, by minimizing newly developed part, and by the proper combination of the elements above. To achieve this, SOA and its underlying middleware are necessary. Service Oriented Architecture (SOA) is focused from such demand and Enterprise Service Bus (ESB) is the SOA integration technology that provides a unified architecture for high reusability.

WebOTX Enterprise Service Bus (ESB) virtualizes every system, resource, and application as services and controls these services, communication protocols, and message formats used for exchanging information among the services, while also managing sequences for executing multiple services. The system is shown in Figure 3.

WebOTX ESB has the following features.

- **Continuing to utilize designed resources as is:** WebOTX Enterprise Service Bus complies with Java Business Integration (JBI) 1.0, the Java system integration standard. JBI will be built into Java EE 6 or later. In other words, WebOTX Enterprise Service Bus provides the advanced technology necessary to set up systems capable of using future Java EE versions. Therefore, WebOTX ESB has benefit of standard based implementation that the functionality of WebOTX Enterprise Service Bus can be enhanced by incorporating open source software and third party software products.
- **Mediating communication among various services with superior performance:** WebOTX Enterprise Service Bus can access services by way of the eight communication protocols SOAP, HTTP, FTP, JMS, JCA, RMI, CORBA, and JDBC, as well as files, thereby it can translate from one communication protocol to the other

Figure 3. Example of system mediation using ESB (provided by WebOTX ESB)

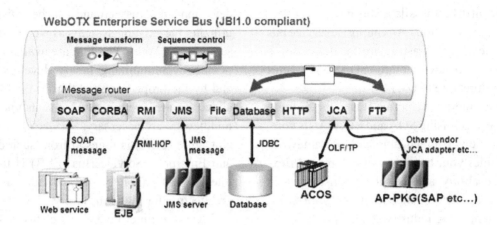

one used by services to interoperate services using different protocols.

- **Efficient mediation of existing services:** WebOTX Enterprise Service Bus can use two message transform methods namely XSLT and a built-in Java application at the same time leading to messages among services being compatible and it flexibly handles these messages in various formats. One can choose either CHDL (ContentHandler Description Language) which utilizes proprietary NEC technology, or Apache Xalan as the XSLT processor. CHDL provides three times (*) the transform performance of the conventional Xalan.

Existing ESB Review: Mule ESB

Mule ESB is the world's most widely used open source enterprise service bus, with over 1.5 million downloads and 2,500 production deployments. Mule is a light-weight and integration framework that allows developers to connect applications together quickly and easily, enabling them to exchange data. Mule ESB enables easy integration of existing systems, regardless of the different technologies that the applications use, including JMS, Web Services, JDBC, HTTP, and more.

The key advantage of an ESB is that it allows different applications to communicate with each other by acting as a transit system for carrying data between applications within your enterprise or across the Internet. Mule ESB includes powerful capabilities that include:

- **Service creation and hosting:** expose and host reusable services, using Mule ESB as a lightweight service container.
- **Service mediation:** shield services from message formats and protocols, separate business logic from messaging, and enable location-independent service calls.
- **Message routing:** route, filter, aggregate, and re-sequence messages based on content and rules.
- **Data transformation:** exchange data across varying formats and transport protocols.

MAIN FOCUS OF THE CHAPTER: INTEGRATION CHALLENGE FACED BY INDUSTRY

As the industry increasingly meager profits, to increase the value-added products is imperative

Figure 4. Mule enterprise service bus (provided by Mule ESB Community)

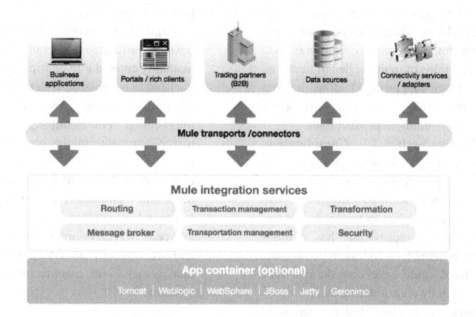

that businesses have done to enhance profits. Across all industries, executives are demanding more and more value and specific characteristics from their strategic business processes. The CEOs of enterprises engage in integrating their IT organizations to measurably improve the flow of data and information driving key business decisions. Whether a transport firm support real time information of goods status for consumers, a financial services firm is to seek a competitive advantage by guaranteeing a higher volume of faster foreign exchange trades, a retail chain is to look for accelerating the flow of store data back to brand managers at corporate headquarters, or a building materials supplier strive to optimize order and transport flow through a complex distribution chain, there are common and significant technical challenges to be overcome. Information is locked up in applications within different departments and organizations, and it is both time-consuming and costly to pry that data loose. In short, the enterprise is far from integrated.

However, integration is a difficult task to every business. Integration of applications within an enterprise and between different enterprises is becoming more and more essential in this dynamic global world. The needs for up-to-date information that is accessible from almost everywhere require developers find solutions for integrating diverse, heterogeneous applications, developed in different architectures and programming languages and on different platforms. They have to do this quickly and cost effectively, but still preserve the architecture and deliver robust solutions that are maintainable over time. Some common reasons for investing in integration solutions include (Newcomer, 2005):

- **Mergers and Acquisitions (M & A):** M & A activity typically happened in businesses. Once the distinct businesses need to consolidate similar transactions within multiple platforms, the integration becomes a vital problem to be solved. For example, different companies have their own customer databases, how to merge them with various data types could be an annoying process to deal with.

- **Internal Reorganization:** Like M&A, internal reorganizations face many of the same problems which often occur more frequently. Internal reorganizations may combine functions of multiple departments, including their supporting IT infrastructures, such as combining manufacturing operations across multiple product lines.
- **Application/System Consolidation:** Multiple IT systems often can be consolidated or replaced to save money, maximize efficiency of IT staff, and streamline business operations. For example, a telecommunications company that has multiple billing systems for wireless, wire line, and broadband could save considerable time and money by consolidating them.
- **Inconsistent/Duplicated/Fragmented Data:** Important business data may be spread across many systems and must be consolidated or "cleansed" to facilitate better decision making. For example, most businesses want to give service representatives a single view of the customer, which can only be accomplished if all of the pertinent customer information, contained in a variety of different systems, can be shared.
- **New Business Strategies:** Innovative companies frequently implement new business strategies that redefine the business environment and require IT systems to work together in novel ways. Eventually, other companies in the same industry have to adopt the same changes to stay competitive. Classic examples include just in time manufacturing and straight through processing of financial transactions.
- **Compliance with Government Regulations:** New government regulations may require redefining business processes to protect consumers and meet new information reporting requirements. For example, Sarbanes Oxley requires signifi-

cant investment in reporting, auditing, and process improvement.

- **Streamlining Business Processes:** Old business processes that required data to be manually entered into multiple systems often need to be replaced with newer systems where transactions flow without human intervention. For example, a Web commerce company might previously have received orders via the Internet, but manually entered them into the order management and manufacturing control systems. Improved integration solutions allow the company to receive orders via the Web site and automatically enter them into the order management and manufacturing control systems.

Above illustrated integration problems are often not as simple as making two disparate systems work together. Because integration can represent a multifaceted problem, many different technologies, products, and processes have been used over the years to address it. Recent experience with Web services and SOA-based solutions shows that a better answer is available. Instead of attempting to deal directly with the complexity of multiple incompatible applications on multiple computers through a single type of product such as application server, it is now possible to add a layer of abstraction that is open and standards based, and through its neutral architecture is easy to integrate with virtually any new or existing environment.

A number of factors, both business and technical, have led to the need for a new approach to integration. There are business drivers such as changes in economic conditions, regulatory compliance, and the introduction of new disruptive hardware technology such as Radio Frequency Identification (RFID) tags, all of which foreshadow significant changes in the way businesses view application integration and data sharing. These drivers seem at odds with the current state of integration within enterprises, which is not as advanced as you might think. As we will explore in this chapter, the majority of applications that ought to be integrated simply aren't, and those that are integrated suffer from overly complex integration approaches that have grown unmanageable over time, due to a lack of a cohesive integration strategy that can be applied broadly.

In past several years, there have been some significant technologies, such as Service-Oriented Architecture (SOA), web services, Enterprise Application Integration (EAI), etc. These technologies attempted to address the challenges of improving the results and increasing the value of integrated business data and processes.

Service-Oriented Architecture (SOA) has been adapted by businesses to improve their flexibility, recently with a focus on dynamic outsourcing of business processes. Enterprises need a more sophisticated, manageable infrastructure that can support high volumes of individual interactions to implement an SOA. Additionally, any such infrastructure should support more established integration styles, such as message-oriented and event-driven integration, or at least integrate with existing infrastructures. Such an infrastructure should support enterprise-level qualities of service. A cornerstone of an SOA is an ESB, which is used to loosely connect services by the means of message exchange. The ESB is emerging as the unifying concept for such infrastructure which underpins a fully integrated and flexible end-to-end service-oriented architecture and draws the best traits from these and other technology trends. In other words, enterprise service bus as a solution model would enable low cost integration and would be used by companies with limited IT resources.

SOLUTIONS AND RECOMMENDATIONS: ENTERPRISE SERVICE BUS

Major vendors first sold message queuing as the ultimate interoperability solution, then SOAP and REST, before realizing that multiple applications need to share data but had significant interface differences. Architects and vendors suggested many approaches to solving this issue, from writing wrappers using a common protocol to porting legacy systems to Java or.Net and, in the process, create a modern interface that fit in the enterprise architecture. None of these approaches is practical because they are code-intensive, expensive, and are coupled to specific systems, programming languages, and protocols.

Early attempts at solving this issue involved creating a "bus" using a common transport like MQ Series and defining a common message format (positional or XML). Systems participating in data exchanges would implement messages with specific attributes and place them in a queue. This soon becomes impractical because message formats need to be revised too often to accommodate new attributes and exponentially increases regression testing and debugging time and expense. Similar problems occur when using SOAP, REST, or almost any protocol.

The solution to this problem is elegant and obvious: let the applications communicate with one another in the protocols they already support, from EDI to SOAP, over a common transport aggregator independent of the native protocols, and adding application- or protocol-specific translation modules or message routing only where required at the endpoints. This approach allows a mainframe application written in COBOL to interoperate with a mobile device written with J2ME without either end knowing anything about the other's characteristics.

An enterprise service bus (ESB) enables a business to make use of a comprehensive, flexible and consistent approach to integration while also reducing the complexity of the applications being integrated. Due to the complex and varying nature of business needs, ESB is an evolutionary progression that unifies message oriented, event driven and service oriented approaches for integrating applications and service. Implementing an ESB facilitates greater reuse of IT assets by separating application logics and integration tasks, so you can reduce the number, size, and complexity of integration interfaces. In doing so, you can add or change services with minimal interruption to existing IT environment; reduce cost and risk involved as business changes and new opportunities arise.

In the following section, Enterprise Service Bus (ESB) including Event-Service module, Message-Service module, Data-Service module and Process-Service module are discussed to provide a total solution for above common and challenges presented in the preceding section.

The ESB connects with different services and components through the message communication, conversion and messaging of the Road Trail, and does most of the information format conversion, so to build the SOA. The ESB needs to flexibly and easily combine and re-assemble components in order to meet changing requirements anywhere, so it should connect components in a loosely coupled way. The ESB implementation for this business scenario is applied to the decomposition of the ESB runtime pattern. In Figure 5 Situation

of the Enterprise Service Bus (ESB), we depict the basic situation of the ESB.

The complexity and maintenance cost increase when we add a new application to this application landscape. We imagine that this new application must communicate with the ERP, customer relationship management (CRM), COBOL, and other application. This means that we must need to implement more than one new integration solution to be able to integrate this new application into the existing environment. In this kind of system environment with heterogeneity application, there are many reasons that enterprises should consider an integration solution like an ESB.

The true value of the ESB concept, however, is to enable the infrastructure for SOA in a way that reflects the needs of today's enterprise, to provide suitable service levels and manageability, and to operate and integrate in a heterogeneous environment. More recently the ESB concept has emerged in the context of B2B (Business to Business). The ESB incorporates the concept of mediation to facilitate the design of application based on Web-services. (Bussler, 2003)

Figure 5. Situation of the enterprise service bus (ESB)

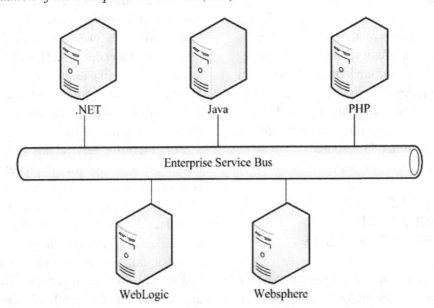

An ESB provides an architectural overview which shows how it can bring the task of integration of enterprise applications and services built on J2EE,.NET, C/C++, and other legacy environments into the reach of the IT professional every day. Through the study of real-world use cases drawn from several industries using the ESB, we clearly and coherently outline the benefits of moving toward this integration strategy. An ESB is to use the service clients and providers of these services as an intermediary between, which handles the connection between them the task, which simplifies the client and provider. The following is the definition of eight principles: (Bobby, & James, 2005)

- **Universal:** available across the entire extended enterprise environment, link layer.
- **Heterogeneous:** to provide information-oriented multi-platform, multi-protocol and multi API support level, able to integrate heterogeneous systems.
- **Interoperability:** providing open support for the agreement and support from multiple vendors for interoperability between systems.
- **Incremental integration:** to provide on-demand dynamic expansion of system capabilities.
- **Service Quality:** providing quality of service, such as security, performance, reliability, scalability, etc.
- **Replace:** to use an open API to ensure that the replacement of suppliers to achieve.
- **Event location:** to provide the event will generate business applications and submit applications to respond to these events the ability to separate.
- **Service location:** by following Service-Oriented Architecture (SOA) design methodology, so that the critical function of an abstract way for the service to provide separation of application functionality.

With the concept of the ESB for the construction of the information development platform, it operates through decentralized management mechanism, event-driven, data-driven processing mode, and etc. The platform has the ability to support plant content-based routing and filtering capabilities. In addition, it also provides a very rich standard interface, but also with complex data transmission capacity.

In Figure 6, Architecture of Enterprise Service Bus (ESB), service development platform consists of four service modules divided into four modules: Event-Service, Message-Service, Data-Service and Process-Service. This platform can be used to develop domain-specific business components and applications. The four software modules are listed below:

- **Event service module:** offers dynamic plug-on event rule and inference engine to build event monitors and process activators.
- **Message service module:** provides Web service to construct secured and reliable communication channels for inter-platform and internet. The communication channel can carry both synchronous and asynchronous messages. This module facilitates seamless application integration.
- **Process service module:** offers a workflow engine to build an automatic clinical process flow.
- **Data service module:** provides flexible, secured and distributed data exchange as well as retrieval mechanism to enable data sharing in a complex distributed infrastructure.

Event-Service

Web transaction, B2B system and instant workflow and so on, are getting complicated with the development of the e-commerce and the improvement of the transaction process. The traditional serial

Figure 6. Architecture of enterprise service bus (ESB)

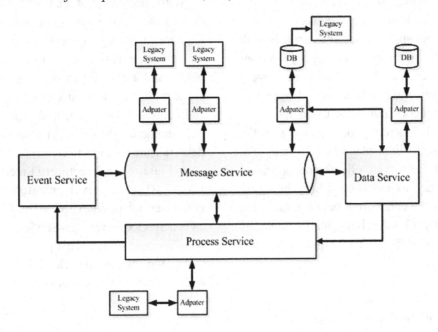

process is unable to deal with the business on the internet anymore. Therefore, the service oriented architecture and the event driven architecture are proposed.

SOA originated from the distributed application system deployed in the heterogeneous platform and network environments. In recent years, open network service standards and SOA are widely adopted; the distributed application system has migrated toward event-driven service oriented architecture. Based on the event notifications, the services are dynamically coordinated to offer more flexible and timely solutions which are complied with so called process fusion and zero latency.

Standard of open internet-service technology and SOA are all extensively applied. Distributed application system can enhance to become an event-driven SOA. Application can activate fit activities according to event notification application system in order to achieve the goal of flexible and accurate process fusion with no zero latency. Through the common event specification, a dynamic event subscribes to send, to complete a complex event monitoring and management.

Event-driven service-oriented system architecture can be viewed as a service operation system automatically and synchronously. We can enhance the performance and quality of service occupation by information technology.

One of the more important concepts in the domain of SOA is that of an Event-Driven Architecture (EDA). The EDA specifies how "services" are hooked into "business events".

Most business events—ranging from the arrival of an order or request for quote to the hiring of a new employee or the delivery of some piece of equipment—trigger several responses across an organization. At a slightly more detailed level, there are events within process steps—such as failure to invoke a service, crossing a predefined threshold, or reaching a specific target—that may interest parties external to the process itself.

The EDA allows you to publish all these events from the process that creates or encounters them to a central event-handling backbone, thereby making them available from there to all interested parties. The process or service where the event originates needn't concern itself with these external parties; otherwise, in addition to straining the execution of that particular process, you would end up with tightly intertwined systems (and hence a maintenance nightmare).

Generally speaking, event-driven business applications can be sorted into four categories:

- Simple event-driven (or message-driven) applications, where application programs explicitly send and receive messages directly to and from each other — for example, through message-oriented middleware (MOM) or Web services
- Event-driven applications that are mediated by integration brokers, which transform and route simple event messages according to logical rules
- Event-driven applications that are directed by business process management (BPM) engines that manage the end-to-end flow of a multi-step process using special, BPM-oriented types of events
- Complex-event processing (CEP) applications, where a sophisticated event manager logically evaluates multiple events to enable decoupled, parallel, or asynchronous application processing.

Message-Service

All of the interactions between clients and services within the ESB occur via the exchange of messages. Therefore, development using a message-exchange pattern is recommended, as this will encourage loose coupling. Requests and responses should be independent messages, correlated where necessary by the infrastructure or the application. Programs constructed in this way will be more tolerant of failure and give developers more flexibility to select their deployment and message delivery requirements.

Message-Service provides a reliable and safe message as well as supplies information of the subscribers to send and the development of many to many of the messages to transmit.

Message Service is one of the most mentioned services from ESB vendors and there is a very good reason for this. Most ESB are based on the Java Business Integration (JBI) specification that was developed under the Java Community Process (JCP). The JBI specification seeks to create a standard for EAI and B2B integration and attempts to do so by "adopting a SOA, which maximizes the decoupling between components, and creates well-defined interoperation semantics which are founded on standards-based messaging". JBI defines an architecture that allows the construction of integration systems from plug-in components that interoperate through mediated message exchange.

Data-Service

To keep pace with growing data demands and infrastructure complexity, organizations need a new architecture, one designed for extensibility and flexibility, which is a SOA. Informative approach to data integration and data quality is unique in that it enables shared data services for access, integration, auditing, and reporting to come together on an as-needed basis. Information can be flexibly and easily deployed, and smartly shared by data services that eliminate data silos and simplify integration efforts for organization-wide access to consistent information. With this architecture, Information Technology can extend the utility of existing systems without changing them, and substantially reduce costs and business risks of high-value Information Technology projects.

Although the theoretical promise of enterprise agility is core to the benefits of a SOA, many organizations have found that when they have implemented the SOA in their application integration layer, they have struggled with the complexities of data fragmentation. This is because traditional SOA-enabling toolsets typically provide only simple data access and lack sophisticated data services. A data service is a modular, reusable, well-defined, business-relevant service that enables the access, integration, and right-time delivery of enterprise data throughout the enterprise and across corporate firewalls. Information is unique in its ability to provide the widest spectrum of data services encompassing data access services, data discovery services, data cleansing services, data integration services, data delivery services, and metadata services.

Data-Service provides strategy-type data to copy the backup and complete information in XML format as well as a simple query at the same time to monitor changes in information content at any time aware of information, and integrate heterogeneous data. Data Service delivers continuously updated serials and publisher information that libraries and other organizations can integrate into their homegrown and open-source applications and provides metadata for all of the serials in the knowledgebase, which includes all publication types, formats, and frequencies. The new service completely replaces an existing raw data service that provided ASCII flat-file output with limited updating capability.

Process-Service

Organizations that have employed EAI middleware products to automate business processes or to integrate various legacy environments will likely already be familiar with the concept of orchestration. In these systems, a centrally controlled set of workflow logic facilitates interoperability between two or more different applications. A common implementation of orchestration is the hub-and-spoke model that allows multiple external participants to interface with a central orchestration engine.

One of the driving requirements behind the creation of these solutions is to accommodate the merging of large business processes. With orchestration, different processes can be connected without having to redevelop the solutions that originally automated the processes individually.

Orchestration bridges this gap by introducing new workflow logic.

The role of orchestration broadens in service-oriented environments. Through the use of extensions that allow for business process logic to be expressed via services, orchestration can represent and express business logic in a standardized, services-based venue. When building service-oriented solutions, this provides an extremely attractive means of housing and controlling this logic in one central physical location (the orchestration platform).

The orchestration service layer establishes a parent business process layer that can be expressed through service composition technologies, such as Business Process Execution Language (BPEL). A business process definition created using BPEL can be represented in its entirety by a Web service, introducing a new service model that can simply be called the process service.

In line with service-oriented architecture, process management solution can be added complex event, content-aware and other advanced features, and develop a compatible suite of BEPL.

Services implement the business processes of an organization by composing the functionality and tying them together with business logic within the Process Service to define the business operation. An example of a Process Service is the Reconcile Constituent Process Service used to create, locate, and update constituent data based on an incoming message.

In the ESB, services can be configured rather than coded. Process flow and service invocations can transparently span the entire distributed bus. The ESB provides a highly distributed integration environment that spans well beyond the reach of hub-and-spoke architectures, and a clear separation of business logic and integration logic such as routing and data transformation. The ESB architecture forms an interconnected grid of messaging hubs and integration services, with the intelligence and functionality of the integration network distributed throughout.

INDUSTRIAL APPLICATIONS: E-LEARNING, SMART STORE, MEDICAL SYSTEM

A lot of technologies suffer from the issue of gaining adoption by trying to find a problem to solve. The ESB concepts have evolved out of necessity via industry-leading architects working with vendors in the technology community to define and build it, so the ESB has been adopted as it has been built. The ESB is already being put to use in a variety of industries, including financial services, insurance, manufacturing, retail, telecom, energy, food distribution, and government.

- **Manufacturing:** A manufacturer of countertops and flooring use an ESB to improve supply chain predictability and reduce shortage conditions by implementing a co-managed inventory system and availability to promise (ATP) query system and another major manufacturer of lighting, televisions, and medical imaging equipment use an ESB to create a unified integration backbone to connect all its data centers across its global business units, and to create a unified view of product data and billing information to customers worldwide.
- **Telecom:** A web portal at a major phone carrier relies on an ESB to provide a real time analytics on click-through tracking, processing a lot of messages per day and an U.S. telecom carrier provider uses an ESB to provide information from internal systems to competitive carriers.
- **Energy/Utility:** An electric utility firm implemented an ESB which connects systems both internally and with government-imposed applications. Information can be provided in real time for executive reporting, billing, system management, and regulatory-mandated information sharing with its competitors.

Innovative Digitech-Enabled Applications & Services Institute (IDEAS) of Institute for Information Industry (III) executed many projects, which support technology transfer to and assist some industries, subsidized by Economic department of Taiwan. Three relatively industrial applications are discussed in the following sections.

E-Learning

The importance of web application and advanced technology has attracted increasing attention as both the concerns of digital content and publishers in education industry. E-learning, as an educational technology, has already revolutionized the way we learn since the past decades. Take this widespread publicity and the awareness of flexible design principles as an opportunity.

E-learning application is not only a general application that users learn by themselves. The trend of E-learning is to learn interactively with computer or to learn with humans by the support of technology. Innovative Digitech-Enabled Applications & Services Institute (IDEAS) of Institute for Information Industry (III) has proposed and ran a creative E-learning project called Content Web Intelligent Computing research. This research aimed to discover knowledge and valuable information from different resources and create mobile application to realize mobile-learning scenario. The content computing research includes collecting Chinese lexicon repository, constructing Chinese language relation model, semantic computing technology and language learning service software. Learning resources might be well-desined courses or even a blog content. This project wants to process and collect various types of content to deliver to learners by a service system.

E-learning application is developed via Enterprise Service Bus architecture in this project. By receiving real-time request which is noted as event-service, E-learning application performs appropriate process (e.g. video/audio streaming services) from content repository of teaching material. Thus, both instructors and students synchronously transmit teaching messages or learning history to keep learning more efficient and effective. Based on Enterprise Service Bus architecture, Institute for Information Industry (III) has developed a series mobile learning applications on different hardware devices.

(1) ChineseBlvd (Chinese Boulevard)- Chinese learning platform

Cooperate with local University to edit Chinese learning courses. III develops online learning platform that allows user to search, browse and play courses on their computers. Students can download mp3 files from the platform to listen Chinese sentences everywhere. The platform is developed based on Adobe AIR architecture. The solution provides a customized application that makes students access online courses. The application can be operated on windows, mac OS, linux and android operation system that creates cross-platform mobility. This service is currently operated in Vietnam to help people who need to learn Chinese. There is an effective learning function on this platform that students can practice their pronunciation by talking to the oral rating system. The system is capable to give a score according to user's speech sentence. The platform also provides video streaming function to connect teachers and students. Teachers can create virtual classrooms to teach multiple students in the same time but cross different geographical places. Students are also allowed to discuss with classmates or teachers by one on one video streaming function. The fusion learning model is created by composed functions of ChineseBlvd. Students may practice pronunciation first then enter the virtual classroom to learn advanced knowledge later. This model is useful to many students in Vietnam. On the students' side, the platform provides an event service of ESB by software application on various client devices. The server side host data service to provide plentiful courses.

Figure 7. ChinesBlvd fusion learning model

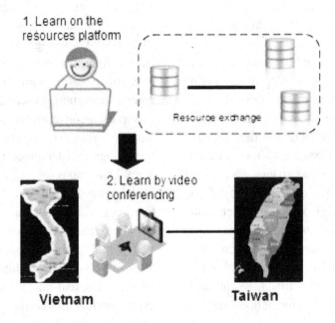

(2)   M-Taiwan mobile learning service

M-Taiwan is a national project about mobile application and internet infrastructure. III develop a portable multimedia player application with content provider and service provider. This is the first WiMAX mobile learning platform that integrated with digital content, end devices, telecom service and physical cram school. This platform can link to database to perform online streaming play or play content after downloading entire course. The product package includes net book device that can be brought conveniently and the internet connection is charged by WiMAX 4G service that create fast wireless access. The product is operated by Gjun English in Taiwan and is very successful. It's the similar model like ChineseBlvd that server side provides data service to fulfill users' needs. The special feature here is that the 4G connection plays an important role to provide message and process service.

(3)   iPhone mobile learning

Smartphone is very popular nowadays and innovative services can be designed on its advanced computing power and potable ability. The App store derived by Apple has made tremendous success. According to mobile advertising startup AdMob, there are some $200 million worth of applications sold in Apple's iPhone store every month, or about $2.4 billion a year. Learning is an application category in smart phone app store. III and LiveABC, a local content provider in Taiwan have developed an iPhone application together. Content is the king. Content is always the most important thing in learning service system. LiveABC publish the content in both physical and digital type. III design the software architecture with the content. The application is relatively tiny but useful for light learner who carried a smart phone. The content and user interface must be friendly and relaxed. The whole service architecture is built and maintained by Apple but the core application

Figure 8. Mobile learning multimedia player

is designed under overall circumstance. This case is quite smart and useful to expand e-learning content and service. Content provider discovers the user needs and proves that the right content itself can apply data service of ESB architecture.

Smart Store

The service-oriented machine is a trend in the business world, such as ATM machines, photo kiosk machines, self-service ticket machines, and vending machines. Due to the development and advancement of technology, more and more information systems are applied on these machines to supply personal and customization services. A host of technologies has emerged to provide machines new benefits in recent years by (Elliot, 2009).

Front-end revolution of machine providing services has been gradually extended to all industries and applications market (such as retail, machine tools and advertising services). In order to integrate all services of industries and reduce cooperation doorsill, how to integrate value chain across designer, manufacturer and retailer is the most key point. Among them, different cross-industry software and hardware integration of design

completed, need to take the step up through the value chain of upstream and downstream plants.

The Smart Store, later proposed by Innovative Digitech-Enabled Applications & Services Institute (IDEAS) of Institute for Information Industry (III), is such a creative and innovative conception which offers customers value-added services through information technologies. Smart Stores are similar to retail or convenience stores; however, they can be combined with features such as innovative service, more convenient avant-garde customer service, advanced electronic control, and refrigeration monitoring of your stores.

The Smart Store integrates the information and communication technologies (ICT) and innovation of related services. Smart Store is based on a technological platform that offers the support for some attractive and efficient services for customers and administrative staff. In Figure 9, the Smart Store concept is shown.

In 2006, the Institute for Information Industry (III) executed the project "An Experiment on Distribution-service Smart-Stores Project" subsidized by Economic department of Taiwan, in which they tried to conduct a smart auto-service store business.

Figure 9. The Smart Store concept. IDEAS of Institute for Information Industry (2009)

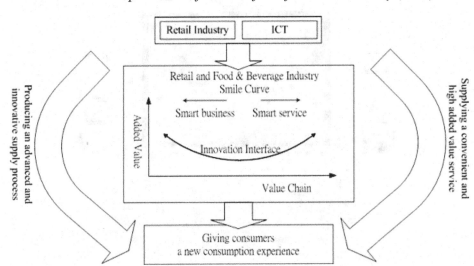

According to the analysis done by Gartner, a research institution, technologies are more feasible and have lower risk and lower cost at the moment. Some examples are described as follows:

- ALONA, established in 1980, is a professional vending machine producer. ALONA designs and manufactures a series of vending machines, leads the vending machine market and integrates kiosk contract manufacturing services and cash flow to meet customer demands in Taiwan.
- Fujitsu, established in 1935, is a leading provider of IT-based business solutions for the global marketplace. Fujitsu pursues innovation and a prosperous future to fulfill the dreams of people throughout the world and provides all-directional software and hardware, including POS, Server, system Integration, 24HR Help Desk, Maintenance Service, etc to meet the requirements of consumers.
- Acer, found in 1976, is among the world's top five branded PC vendors. It designs and produces variable products and owns technologies closer to customers including desktops and laptops, as well as PDAs, servers, storages, displays, peripherals, and e-business services for business, government, education, and home users. Acer specialized in integrating and developing trading systems for cash flows between banks and stores and combines diversified payment mechanisms to satisfy demand and improve consumer loyalty.
- In 1924, Computing-Tabulating-Recording Company (CTR), established in 1911, changed the company's name to International Business Machines Corporation (IBM). IBM focuses on emerging geographic markets and drives the new conception of self-service including POS, kiosk, Retail on Demand, e-Marketing. IBM Taiwan makes the best effort to support retail and CPG market.

- NEC, founded in 1899, is a Japanese multinational IT company which provides information technology and network solutions to business enterprises, communications services providers and governments and seeks to develop products and services that are simpler and more convenient for everyone. NEC Taiwan provides optimal service systems in combination with retail POS, ERP, and CRM solutions to help clients obtain maximum benefit.

The content of the project is to develop middle platform between the front device of service-oriented facility and the back device of integrated services. It collects and analyzes machine information by network-connection devices to offer services.

In the Figure 10, front-end facility of machine emphasizes the integration of heterogeneity and interaction of users. The front-end facility extends the conception of servicing from machine to people. The same idea can expand to retailer, machine tools and Digital Signage. The platform development addresses dynamic integration of service which can supply conception of lease. The roadmap of maintain platform emphasizes service monitor and remote assistance to complete the goals of green energy platform eventually.

Following the development of Smart Store system, many industries apply customer services combined with Smart Store apparatus to satisfy diversification of customer requirement. An Enterprise Service Bus platform of the Smart Store supports front-end services, the development of pilot applications, providing a flexible, security and stability in the Service Intelligent & Integration Platform (SIIP).

(1) Event bulletin

The Smart Stores integrate services, through the dynamic event processing, to provide remote monitoring and management, and information

Figure 10. Open platform development blueprint of service-oriented machine

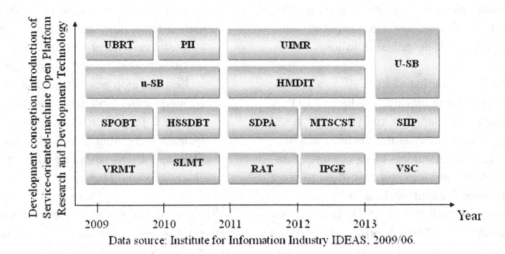

Data source: Institute for Information Industry IDEAS, 2009/06.

collection and conduct business intelligence operations to support services and content.

In Figure 11, the development of front-end hardware (machines and equipment) and interactive interface integration technologies, including interactive signage technology which provides multiple natural interface of two-way interaction with the content, composite service machine interface through a single integrated standard to sell all kinds of machine, Kiosk of the flexible cross-flow control device, machine monitor pre-diagnosis through the reception signal transmission technology, the integrative health status of the machine model which support efficient monitoring and analysis, and content across devices roaming sub-devices for mobile content transfer and use of inter-process synchronization, provide users with seamless operation experience.

(2)   Message delivery

The message service enables and increases interoperability, flexibility, and portability of applications. It enables communication between applications over distributed and heterogeneous platforms and reduces complexity because it hides the communication details and the details of platforms and protocols involved.

The message delivery is based on Internet. It provides asynchronous communication and uses message queues to store the messages temporarily. The applications can thus exchange messages without taking care of the details of other applications, architectures, and platforms involved. The messages can contain almost any type of data, asynchronous nature of communication enables the communication to continue even if the receiver is temporary not available. The basic architecture is shown in Figure 12.

(3)   Service process integration

In the Smart Store, there are many service components including transaction data service, transaction analysis, business intelligence, commodity data management, machine slot management, inventory monitoring, fault notification, E-mail message and so on.

The Service process integration provides the ability to represent business logic as a reusable component which can be easily integrated when assembling an application or solution. When an application of maintain service is implemented, fault notification and E-mail message together build a composite application. Other applications are the same.

Figure 11. The event interaction conception

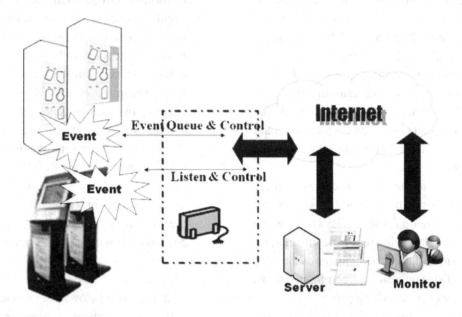

Figure 12. The basic architecture of message delivery

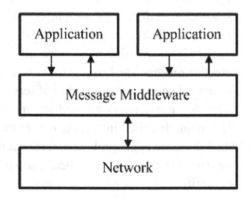

This integration application will be built to design a system which processes management application from operators worked via a web front-end. Every composite contains several components, of which interact to provide a service to operator.

With the Enterprise Service Bus, it improves Connection, Mediation and Control. The Enterprise Service Bus is the industry's first, best-in-class enterprise service bus allows organizations to better accomplish the major tasks necessary to exploit the value of service oriented architecture.

- **Connect:** Simplify the connection of new applications, web services and legacy technologies.
- **Mediate:** Reconcile incompatible protocols, data formats and interaction patterns; eliminate hard-coded service dependencies between applications; and make it easier to combine and extend existing services to meet new requirements.
- **Control:** Simplify deployment of services across a distributed environment; deploy configuration changes remotely; and provide detailed statistics to monitor performance, detect faults, and diagnose problems.

Medical System

The Enterprise Service Bus builds a service network platform to support the convergence of real-time information across the system as well as build out of the individual industry platform for the exchange of information in a timely manner. For the medical industry, the national blood bags of blood inventory build the real-time exchange platform, the traditional communication processes are turned into information systems and the various information stations such as around the blood centers, medical centers and regional hospitals, the Department of Health Disease Control Bureau and etc., will support all aspects of real-time exchange of information.

In the traditional manual processes, if there are problems found in the blood to inform the hospital needed blood for seven days time, was a big delay period; but using real-time information exchange system, there is any danger of the bags on the use of IT system, real-time communications, monitoring, or event handling process.

In order to address the above problems, we design a web-based respiratory care alarm monitoring system to assist physicians to monitor patient status. By this way, we can keep the true alarm and notify physicians automatically when alarm events occur and pass the related information to physicians. The system has four major features; reliable event generation, reliable message delivery, Anti-fraudulency, and service availability which are necessary requirements to design a trusty medical information system.

Design of this platform provides multiple mechanisms to ensure data authenticity and security as well as delivery reliability. Authenticity is considered in the data input phase. Reliability guarantees data delivery. Anti-fraudulency aims to prevent malicious modification of alarm content. Operation stability mechanism can activate the alarm process during system failure. The reliability issues are addressed from the user interface, application functionalities to hardware. The digital signature mechanism addresses the authenticity of alarm event. The data encryption ensures the privacy of the alarm data. The design features are elaborated as below:

1. **Reliable event generation:** The true alarm event is generated by processing raw data in duration and frequency constraints.

2. **Reliable message delivery:** The message delivery is based on Web service. The message is encapsulated in the http protocol using queuing like compensated re-transmission mechanism. The current method aims on finish feedback re-sending function using HTTP package storage with queuing mechanism. Inside that, it's necessary to consider the measures for re-sending and neglect mechanism of duplicate sending.

3. **Anti-fraudulency:** Digital signature is used to ensure data authenticity and integrity to filter out non-trusted sources. The process flow is shown below: We use message signature plus application program to ensure the source of message toward the notification of false alarm event. We should also neglect unbelievable source. Hence, it can save resources of computing at high extent.

4. **Service availability:** Service availability is maintained by using mesh network like detection mechanism. Ensure mechanism of system existence contains ensure of service status. We use network method and multi-multi point detection in order to ensure that when there are some problems occurred in one machine, they will be detected, solved, and notified to enter related process.

Service Web development platform consists of five service modules. This platform can be used to develop domain-specific business components and applications. The five software modules are listed below:

- **Event web service module:** offers dynamic plug-on event rule and inference engine to build event monitors and process activators.

- **Message web service module:** provides Web service to construct secured and reliable communication channels for inter-platform and internet. The communication channel can carry both synchronous and asynchronous messages. This module facilitates seamless application integration.
- **Process web service module:** offers a workflow engine to build an automatic clinical process flow.
- **Resource web service module:** offers a resource allocation and negotiation mechanism to build staff dispatch service.
- **Data web service module:** provides flexible, secured and distributed data exchange as well as retrieval mechanism to enable data sharing in a complex distributed infrastructure.

Respiratory care alarm monitoring system has been evaluated in the respiratory care ward (RCW). The plat form features are listed as below: (Lee, etc., 2006))

1. **24-hour continuous respiratory data recording and alarm monitoring:** Remote respiratory care system is deployed at the patient bedside to retrieve data and alarm. It samples the respiratory data and deliver to the remote repository in real-time. The generation of the alarm is based on probabilistic network to eliminate false alarms.

2. **Instant, prioritized alarm notification:** When alarm is generated, it will be delivered to the remote terminals. Alarms are prioritized based on their emergent levels, namely, red, yellow, and green.

3. **Intelligent multi-tier alarm notification:** The system also adopts RF-ID application. When the alarm is notified, the first tier care team will arrive within certain time limit and their presences are detected by the RF-ID readers. If the first tier staffs do no arrive in

time, system will notify second-line people, such as doctors, respiratory therapists, or other staffs on the duty schedule. Everyone is equipped with a PHS phone. Alarms will be displayed on the panel.

4. **Physicians have more time for patient care:** It takes average ten minutes to collect physiological data and submit for insurance reimbursement per bed per day. The accumulated time for thirty beds can be as high as 300 minutes which is equivalent to one physician's daily hour. With the assistance of the automatic monitoring and billing system, time can re-used for a better patient care.

CONCLUSION AND FUTURE RESEARCH DIRECTIONS

The global industry is to process all the thousands of small and large purchase and consolidation. However, common problem is that one company bought another company, in addition to personnel changes in the structure, business objectives and brand strategy to change the amendment, the existing IT systems can adapt to business after the change to the new environment. How can be new profitable business objectives? These problems will become the wave of this wave of corporate consolidation brought about by the follow-up tasks. The SOA of the proposed for the new challenges of the IT environment has brought gratifying to answer.

The ESB concept already has a number of uses that solve some very common and challenging integration problems. While this is not an exhaustive list of all the integration patterns that are in use today, it should be enough to give you an idea of how an ESB can be used in real integration scenarios.

SOA brings cost effective, reusable and low lead time solutions to an organization and the ESB would enable low cost integration and would be used by companies with limited IT resources and environments that involve a handful of systems and moderate transaction volumes.

The ESB provides a build and deployment of enterprise SOA, new thinking. The ESB is increasingly attracting attention of architects and developers to the concept of a common problem because it provides an effective solution, including service arrangements (service orchestration), data synchronization applications and business activity monitoring.

Specifically, the ESB can be described as an implicit communication infrastructure services, container, with connection-oriented the character, and then be able to under the SOA framework, responsible for the management and the cascading of the application service. The technologies can significantly alter the traditional software architecture, not only be providing a cheaper than traditional middleware solutions, but also between different application systems to eliminate the technical differences, to enable the coordination of different application server to operation, and to facilitate the integration between heterogeneous services, interoperability.

The ESB market in 2006 was two hundred million, is expected to grow in 2013 to five hundred million. The factors underpinning the growth response to rapid product life cycle of technology and fierce competition on the demand for flexible IT architecture. The ESB acts as a catalyst to achieve the main role of the architecture.

There are more and more standards to make service architecture flexible. For example, SCA (Service Component Architecture) is made by IBM and other leading company. It defines all communicate way between service and work out a SOA design principal. For integrity of a service system, the communication and integration way between hardware and software should be considered well in advance.

REFERENCES

Bobby, W., & James, S. (2005). *Simplify integration architectures with an enterprise service bus*. IBM Corporation.

Bussler, C. (2003). *B2B integration*. Springer-Verlag.

Colombe, H. GaÄel, T., & Philippe, L. (2005). Mediation and enterprise service bus: A position paper. In M. Hepp, A. Polleres, F. v. Harmelen, & M. Genesereth (Eds.), *First International Workshop on Mediation in Semantic Web Services (MEDIATE 2005) in conjunction with the 3rd International Conference on Service-Oriented Computing: Vol. 168. Perspectives on motivation* (pp. 67-80).

David, A. C. (2004). *Enterprise service bus*. O'reilly Media.

de Leusse, P., Periorellis, P., & Watson, P. (2005). *Enterprise service bus: An overview*. Technical Report Series, University of Newcastle upon Tyne, England: Publisher.

Elliot, M. (2009). Recession drives profit protection initiatives. *2009 State of the Vending Industry Report*, (pp. 28-42).

Freund, T., & Niblett, P. (2008). *ESB interoperability standards*. IBM Corporation.

Goel, A. (2007). *Enterprise integration - EAI vs. SOA vs. ESB*. Infosys Technologies White Paper.

Hermann, E., & Kessler, D. (2005). XML Signatures in an Enterprise Service Bus Environment. In Dittmann, J., Katzenbeisser, S., & Uhl, A. (Eds.), *IFIP International Federation for Information Processing. CMS 2005, LNCS 3677, Perspectives on motivation* (pp. 339–347).

IDEAS of Institute for Information Industry. (2009). *Smart Store*. Conference of 2020 Retail Technology hold by Department of Commerce Industrial Services by Ministry of Economic Affair.

Lee, G., Hsu, E., Yang, G., Tsai, A., & Weng, L. (2006) Event-driven service-oriented architecture design of respiratory care alert monitoring system. *8th International Conference on e-Health Networking, Applications and Services, HEALTHCOM 2006, Perspectives on Motivation* (pp. 101 – 107).

Newcomer, E. (2005). *The integration challenge- Developing an SOA-based integration solution using Web Services.* Retrieved May 7, 2010, from http://weblogic.sys-con.com/node/102686?page=0,0

Papazoglou, M. P., Traverso, P., Dustdar, S., & Leymann, F. (2007). Service-oriented computing: State of the art and research challenges. *IEEE Computer Society, 40*(11), 38.

Schmidt, M. T., Hutchinson, B., Lambros, P., & Phippen, R. (2005). The enterprise service bus: Making service-oriented architecture real. *IBM Systems Journal, 44*(4), 781. doi:10.1147/sj.444.0781

Sonic Software Corporation. (2005). *Sonic ESB: An architecture and lifecycle definition.* Retrieved from http://www.sonicsoftware.com/

TIBCO. (2004). Enabling real-time business through a service-oriented and event-driven architecture. Retrieved May 7, 2010, from http://www.tibco.com/software/soa/default.jsp

World Wide Web Consortium. (W3C). (2004). *Web Services glossary.* (W3C Working Group Note 11 February 2004). Retrieved May 7, 2010, from http://www.w3.org/TR/ws-gloss/

KEY TERMS AND DEFINITIONS

Business-to-Business (B2B): Describes commerce transactions between businesses, such as between a manufacturer and a wholesaler, or between a wholesaler and a retailer. B2B is also used in the context of communication and collaboration. Many businesses are now using social media to connect with their consumers (B2C); however, they are now using similar tools within the business so employees can connect with one another. When communication is taking place amongst employees, this can be referred to as "B2B" communication.

Enterprise Application Integration (EAI): Defined as the use of software and computer systems architectural principles to integrate a set of enterprise computer applications. Enterprise Application Integration is the term used to describe the integration of the computer applications of an enterprise so as to maximize their utility throughout the enterprise.

Enterprise Service Bus (ESB): An architectural pattern to integrate and manage services. ESB offers a software infrastructure that simplifies the integration and flexible reuse of business components within a SOA and provides a dependable and scalable infrastructure that connects disparate applications and information technology resources, orchestrates their interactions, mediates their incompatibilities, and makes them broadly available as services for additional uses. The basic functions of an ESB include message transformation, service call, application integration, service quality, and security service and system management.

Interface, Intelligence, Integration and Infrastructure (4I): A service technology framework proposed by Institute for Information Industry (III) in Taiwan which includes interface technology, intelligence technology, integration technology and infrastructure technology. The 4I framework provides a reference to locate technology resources in a service design. From the front-end device machine, middle content analysis, back-end service to virtual service center, these four innovative system total solutions solve the technical problems of different layers.

Paradigm Shift: The term used by Thomas Kuhn in his influential book "The Structure of Scientific Revolutions (1962)" to describe a change in basic assumptions within the ruling theory of science. It is in contrast to his idea of normal science. The term paradigm shift, as a change in a fundamental model of events, has since become widely applied to many other realms of human experience as well, even though Kuhn himself restricted the use of the term to the hard sciences.

Service Oriented Architecture (SOA): A flexible set of design principles used during the phases of systems development and integration in computing. A system based on a SOA will package functionality as a suite of interoperable services that can be used within multiple separate systems from several business domains. A service-oriented architecture is essentially a collection of services. These services communicate with each other. The communication can involve either simple data passing or it could involve two or more services coordinating some activity.

Smart Store: Integrates the information and communication technologies (ICT) and innovation of related services. Smart Store is based on a technological platform that offers the support for some attractive and efficient services for customers and administrative staff. Customers can obtain a new brand new experimental shopping environment from Smart Store which is differs from traditional one and driving customer-valued innovation through deeper insight, so innovation has become the most success factor for business survival.

Web Services: Methods of communication between two electronic devices. It is a solution logic that can be exposed over world-wide web. Web Services can convert your application into a Web-application, which can publish its function or message to the rest of the world.

Worldwide Interoperability for Microwave Access (WiMAX): A telecommunications protocol that provides fixed and mobile Internet access. WiMAX forum describes WiMAX as "a standards-based technology enabling the delivery of last mile wireless broadband access as an alternative to cable and DSL."

Chapter 14
Abstract Service for Cyber Physical Service Composition

Yajing Zhao
University of Texas at Dallas, USA

Yansheng Zhang
University of Texas at Dallas, USA

Jing Dong
University of Texas at Dallas, USA

I-Ling Yen
University of Texas at Dallas, USA

Jian Huang
University of Texas at Dallas, USA

Farokh Bastani
University of Texas at Dallas, USA

ABSTRACT

The collaboration of cyber physical systems poses many real-world challenges, such as knowledge restriction, resource contention, and communication limitation. Service oriented architecture has been proven effective in solving interoperability issues in the software engineering field. The semantic web service helps to automate service discovery and integration with semantic information. This chapter models cyber physical system functionalities as services to solve the collaboration problem using semantic web services. We extend the existing OWL-S framework to address the natures of the cyber physical systems and their functionalities, which are different from software systems and their functionalities. We also present a case study to illustrate our approach.

INTRODUCTION

A cyber physical system (CPS) has strong computational capabilities and can operate autonomously to accomplish difficult tasks. The cyber physical space is composed of a large number of cyber physical systems collaborating with each other. Given the strong capability of an individual cyber physical system, a cyber physical space may provide powerful services and functionalities. However, it is common that a CPS receives multiple tasks and chooses to accomplish only one of them. If more than one CPS chooses to accomplish the same task and temporarily ignores others tasks, multiple resources are suspended to perform one task causing other tasks to be postponed. In such situations, resources are wasted and the overall performance of the cyber physical space is impacted. To avoid such scenario, there must be an efficient mechanism that manages the

DOI: 10.4018/978-1-61350-159-7.ch014

collaboration among cyber physical systems. Such mechanism is essential in optimizing collaboration, which has a direct influence on the power of the cyber physical space, and it is able to maximize the potential of a cyber physical space.

The objective of the efficient collaboration of cyber physical systems is to achieve an optimal decision making strategy so that as many tasks can be accomplished as possible by the cyber physical systems through collaboration. The collaboration problem of cyber physical systems poses several real-world challenges. First, a CPS has local knowledge instead of global knowledge. Second, a CPS has its own social network, i.e., a CPS has communication link to a limited number of other CPSs instead of all CPSs. Third, a CPS is smart enough to respond to a scenario, i.e., it is able to make a decision according to its current knowledge of the world and its capability. Therefore, given a task, a CPS communicates with accessible CPSs and makes a decision autonomously.

Service-oriented architecture (SOA) emerged as a solution for business and software integration by wrapping business processes as services with standard policies. The SOA-based methods provide solutions to the modeling, composition, and management of services. Their application in industry has proven their effectiveness in improving the interoperability between software applications. Recent advances on semantic web service techniques promote the usage of semantic information in automating services discovery and composition. These techniques may greatly help solve the collaboration problem in cyber physical space. Presenting cyber physical system functionalities as services helps modularize the CPS and deal with the CPS collaboration with the service composition approaches. However, SOA-based approaches are not readily applicable to the cyber physical space because of several distinctions in nature between the cyber physical space and the traditional business processes realized by software applications.

First, the existence of more than one CPS of the same model makes it common the existence of multiple CPS services with the same set of characteristics. This distinction calls for the idea of abstract services, a single description for multiple CPS services of the same kind but not grounded to any physical system. Second, the availability and performance of CPS service is highly dependent on the operational status, the resource usage, and the physical environment of its CPS provider. Such distinction demands the ontology of CPS, its operational status, and its properties, which complements the service ontology in facilitating service composition and CPS collaboration. The dynamic evaluation of CPS service availability and performance also requires the description of the context of CPS.

The problem of CPS service composition and coordination requires an appropriate model that is capable of presenting CPS functionalities as services as well as describing the context around CPSs. Without such model, a service oriented approach may not be properly applied in CPS. This chapter presents an extension of the SOA model. More specifically, the extension is based on the semantic web service model, OWL-S, which is a SOA model for describing the interfaces of services syntactically and semantically. The extension addresses the abstract service, resource contention, physical constraint, and context requirement issues. The difference between abstract services/processes, and concrete services/processes is that the former are not grounded to any CPS and the latter have a concrete CPS owner. Such differentiation is especially useful under the local knowledge and limited accessibility constraints. For example, a CPS that knows how to decompose a given tasks but does not know which concrete CPSs provide the required services is able to use the abstract service during the task decomposition and workflow development. Modeling the properties, context, and status of CPSs and automatic processing the model is a necessary step in the

SOA-based approach to dynamic CPS service composition.

In addition to the presentation of the extended OWL-S model, this chapter shows a case study that uses the extended OWL-S model to define physical services provided by CPSs. The case study illustrates the presentation of services provided by individual CPSs as atomic processes as well as the collaboration of multiple CPSs in solving a complex task as composite processes. It shows the service ontology, which organizes services along several dimensions as well as connects services with a number of relationships. It also explains the definition of communication network for concrete CPSs and definition of contextual requirements and effects for services. This chapter illustrates CPS collaboration mechanism by assigning a complex task to the cyber physical space and explaining how the possible solutions are calculated by different CPSs and how a final decision is made and agreed by all the CPSs.

BACKGROUND

This section introduces the background related to the work described in this chapter. It covers the introduction and literatures related to Service Oriented Architecture, Web Services, Cyber Physical Systems, Quality of Services, and context awareness.

Service Oriented Architecture

Service Oriented Architecture (SOA) (Erl, 2005) promotes to package software functionalities as interoperable services with their interfaces defined as protocols. The objective is to reduce coupling. There are a number of open standards that support SOA. The standards are normally based on Extensible Markup Language (XML) (XML, 2010). The XML provides a set of rules to encode information and standardizes the encoding. It is chosen as the standard message format because of its wide use

by major industrial corporations and open source development efforts. The Simple Object Access Protocol (SOAP) (SOAP, 2010) is an XML-based protocol for exchanging structured messages between Web services. The Web Service Definition Language (WSDL) (WSDL, 2010) represents the abstraction of software services by defining the supported operations as ports and data being processed as messages. The general definition of ports and messages, separated from their concrete instances, describes the public interface to the web service. The Universal Description Discovery and Integration (UDDI) (UDDI, 2010) protocol, a registry for web services, is also based on XML. It allows the businesses to publish their services by stating how the services interact with others. The registry allows the services to be discovered from worldwide. The above standards focus on the syntax of messages or services, but ignore their semantic meaning.

Service composition and interoperation involve the automatic selection, composition, and interoperation of Web services to perform some complex task, given a high-level description of an objective. As the traditional Web service standards ignore the semantic information, it is difficult for software programs to determine whether two Web services share the same application domain, thus makes the automatic Web service composition difficult. OWL-S (OWL-S, 2010) and WSMO (WSMO, 2010) are two prominent initiatives that address the service composition by considering the semantic information of Web services. Both languages are XML based.

OWL-S is a language to describe semantic Web service. It is derived from DARPA Agent Markup Language (DAML) (Sheila et al., 2001). It defines the ontology in three aspects, service profile, service process, and service grounding. The service profile defines the functionalities that the service provides, the service process defines how the service can be used, and the service grounding defines the necessary details about interaction protocols. In service process, service parameters, such as input, output, precondition, and effect are being defined. In addition, the usage of service is defined in the format of workflows. The workflow is able to describe service composition and data flow interactions. Such information is necessary to select and compose services. It could be manipulated to achieve the task of service selection and composition automatically.

Paolucci et al. proved that the web services could be searched and located on the basis of the capabilities that they provide instead of keywords (Paolucci et al., 2002). Their proof is based on DAML-S, a DAML-based language for service description. They have designed an algorithm to match the requests with the service advertisements both of which are described in DAML-S. They also showed that the DAML-S and an implemented version of the matching algorithm are able to provide capability/functionality matching to the UDDI registry.

An abstract service hierarchy has been proposed in (Dong et al., 2006, 2008) to model the common abstraction of services. Different levels of abstraction have been established to specify the relationships among the concrete services. The OWL-S has been extended to incorporate the abstract service concepts and abstract service hierarchy. In this chapter, we extend the abstraction from services to cyber-physical systems.

Cyber-Physical System

A cyber-physical system (CPS) is a combination of computational and physical elements with the elements integrated and coordinated between each other. A pre-cursor generation is often referred to as embedded systems, where the emphasis is more on the computational elements, and less on an intense link between the computational and physical elements. A full-fledged CPS is typically designed as a network of interacting elements instead of as standalone devices. The coordination, composition, and collaboration between CPSs have been a challenging issue for a long

time. It requires designing novel languages and models. The expectation is to achieve a network of autonomous, collaborative, and efficient CPSs.

Existing research on CPS modeling and composition is still preliminary and limited. Knowledge engineering has been applied in the CPS for system QoS composition in (Sha et al., 2009). However, there is no concrete model or approach. The abstraction of physical computational processes has been advocated by (Lee et al., 2006) who consider CPSs as integrations of computations with physical processes. Nevertheless, there is no concrete solution to resolve the mismatch between current abstractions and properties of physical processes. To deal with the heterogeneous data collected from diverse physical devices, a four-layer architecture of open data services is proposed in (Kang, 2008). This approach intends to provide a programming abstraction that enables efficient inter-operation and coordinated sharing of distributed and heterogeneous data. Lin et al. recognize the communication challenges posed by the heterogeneity and propose a data-oriented communication construct, cyber physical systems interconnection protocol (CPS-IP), to standardize the communication between cyber physical systems (Lin, 2008). In addition, they propose a framework to support CPS communication with CPS-IP at different levels. Their solution is designed to meet the special needs of the CPS and address the heterogeneity issue. To address the issue that cyber physical systems are under the physical constraints, Huang et al. (Huang, 2009) propose a context-sensitive resource-explicit service model. Their model helps to automate the dynamic composition of services provided by cyber physical systems that are under real-time constraints, physical resource constraints. The model allows them to use the AI planning algorithm, GraphPlan, to solve the resource scheduling problem in cyber physical systems, so that the usage of resources meets the physical constraints.

Quality of Service

The term Quality of service (QoS) originally refers to the technologies that manage network traffic. It is to guarantee a certain level of performance to a data flow by controlling resources reservation and setting priorities. Quality of service guarantees are especially important if the network capacity is insufficient. Ensuring QoS have been a very hot topic in the field of Web services (Menascé et al. 2002). It is also important in the CPS field. In the CPS collaboration problem, there are several tasks assigned to the cyber physical space. The quality of the collaboration is measured by the number of tasks accomplished. QoS in the CPS collaboration refers to the mechanism that guarantees as many tasks that can be accomplished as possible and the tasks are planned according to their criticality. Such mechanism is essential to achieve the maximum performance when the capacity of the space is insufficient.

Ran et al. proposed a new Web services discovery model, an extension to UDDI model, for service discovery. The model takes into account the functional and nonfunctional requirements (i.e. QoS). A new role is introduced into this framework – the Certifier(s). They verify the QoS claims from the Web service suppliers. They also proposed an extension to UDDI's data structure types that could be used for implementing the proposed UDDI model extension.

Zeng et al. (Zeng et al., 2004) present an approach to selecting Web services to maximize user satisfaction expressed as QoS attributes. Two selection approaches are presented, one based on local (task-level) selection of services and the other based on global allocation of tasks to services using integer programming Their effort includes defining service ontologies, specifying composite services using statecharts, and assigning services to the tasks of a composite service.

Erradi *et al*. (Erradi, 2006, 2007) introduces a service differentiation middleware, which prioritizes the requests and limits the number of requests being served. The middleware provide the QoS mechanism to make sure that most critical tasks are being responded. The goal is to increase conformance to negotiated service levels particularly in case of overloads such that the incurred penalties for violations are minimized.

Geihs et al. present a comprehensive modeling approach that facilitates the model-driven development of Context-aware adaptive applications. They made an effort to model concepts to align the description of services and their QoS-properties.

Context-Aware Services

Mokhtar et al. intended to realize an efficient, semantic, context- and QoS-aware service discovery approach (Mokhtar et al. 2008). They defined in OWL a language for semantic specification of functional and non-functional service properties. They also developed a set of conformance relations for matching service functional capabilities, which allows rating services with respect to their suitability for a specific request functionally and non-functionally.

Bellavista emphyasized the importance in including the user context in service discovery (Bellavista et al. 2006). He believes the user's context and personalized view are the key factors for the choice of service. For example, user preferences, access device capabilities, and environment conditions, and should exploit semantic technologies to allow flexible matching between requirements and capabilities in open and dynamic deployment scenarios. This chapter focuses on the cyber physical space and addresses the context of a cyber physical system, instead of the context of a user of web services.

(Broens et al. 2004) also discusses the approach to service discovery with the assistance of available contextual information about a particular user or service provider (e.g. user location or service opening times). In addition, it uses ontologies to semantically express user queries, service descriptions and the contextual information.

The approach also uses the concept lattices for clustering services with similar attributes, which provides a convenient way to order services by their relevancy for the user.

Keidl et al. present a context framework that facilitates the development and deployment of context-aware adaptable Web services. They also attempted to automate the processing of contextual information so that Web services are able to adapt to new environment themselves (Keidl et al. 2004).

Sudha et al. introduced a context-aware and co-ordination middleware framework for ubiquitous environment using ubiquitous semantic space, which uses ontologies to define semantics of various concepts to strengthen software agent understandability (Sudha et al. 2007).

(Chen et al. 2004) proposed a model to take advantage of the contextual information in Web services by providing a broker agent to maintain a shared model of context for all computing entities in the space and enforces the privacy policies defined by the users when sharing their contextual information.

Kranenburg et al. enabled context-aware services in distributed environments and developed a context management framework that is generic through hierarchic ordering of context sources and extensible with multiple reasoning realizations (Kranenburg 2006). Zimmermann et al (Zimmermann et al 2007) introduce a context definition that describes the appearance of context as well as characterizes the use of context and its dynamic behavior. (Chen et al. 2002) propose to collect, aggregate, and disseminate context information with a graph-based approach.

A pervasive service environment with its dynamic nature needs to take account of a user's context and preferences in determining which services to provide (Yang et al. 2006, Raverdy et al. 2006). Yang et al. present how services can be recomposed dynamically if the changes in context require it. Raverdy also presents a platform, which provides context-aware service discovery and access in pervasive environments. (Bottaro et al.

2007) saw the problem of service (re)composition problem in the pervasive environment where context evolves fast. They presented a computing infrastructure for the development of pervasive applications in the home domain.

EXTENDING SOA MODEL FOR CPS SERVICES

Modeling CPSs and CPS services according to the SOA model leverages SOA based technologies, which support the coordination, composition, and collaboration. This section discusses the differences between the CPS services and software services, which result in the insufficiency of the current SOA model in describing CPSs and CPS services. It also discusses the concepts identified during the CPS analysis and presents the extended model. Finally, it presents a case study, which demonstrates that the model is sufficient in modeling and facilitating the collaboration and dynamic composition.

CPS Services vs. Software Services

Cyber physical systems are defined as physical systems with computational power. This chapter uses the term CPS to refer to a broader range of systems. A system that physically exists, exhibits certain capabilities, stays in a network, and has the ability to analyze physical environments and make decisions is referred to as a CPS. For example, a human being plus a jeep equipped with communication devices is considered a cyber physical system. Such CPS is able to provide a number of services. For instance, it provides the transportation service. This service is can be used in a rescue service in a fire emergency scenario, and also be used to deliver first aid team to a spot with injured people. In this case, rescue and first aid are another two possible services provided by a CPS composed of a human being and a jeep.

Wrapping CPS functionalities as services helps modularize the CPSs and allows the possibilities to deal with the CPSs collaboration with the service composition approaches. SOA-based methods provide solutions to the modeling, composition, and management of Web services. For example, the OWL-S is capable of describing the functionalities, inputs and outputs, preconditions and effects of Web services. It is also able to describe the collaboration between Web services as workflows.

However, SOA-based methods may not be adequate for the modeling, composition, and management of CPS services. Cyber physical systems provide physical services, which are different from the services that are provided by software applications. They are different in the following aspects:

- **Physical Restrictions.** Software systems run in a virtual world and are free from physical restrictions. However, the availability of CPS services is highly dependent on the physical environment where the physical system stays. In certain environments, a service of a physical system may not be available. In other environments, a service may be executable but its performance may not be as good as it is in an ideal environment.

- **Service Instantiation Multiplicity.** Software services can have more than one instance at a time. A software system can be installed and execute on multiple machines. Thus, with the support of the hardware, a software service can have more than one instance at a time. Given that the hardware configurations are the same for all the machines that run the software, the performances of these software systems are the same. Even with only one machine, a software system can have multiple instance with the support of multithreading. Thus, requests from multiple clients can be processed at the same time by the same

system. To the client, the software service responses even if it at the mean time is responding to another client. On the other hand, physical services normally cannot have more than one instance at a time. A physical system can only be at one place physically. If it is responding to a request x at location A, it is not able to go to location B. It may only be able to respond to a different request y at location A, depending on the type of task it is performing and the resources it has. Figure 1 illustrates service instantiation multiplicity.

- **Service Provider Capability.** Software services are provided by software systems and physical services by cyber physical systems. Normally a physical system provides more than one service. Due to the physical constraints, once the resources of a physical system are occupied by one task, it cannot perform other tasks that require the same resources. In certain situations, even unused resources are suspended while it performs a task, making other services temporarily unavailable.

- **Service Description Scope.** The description of a web service includes information about how it could be accessed. With the software field, two software systems are different from each other. Functionalities provided by one system can be multiply instantiated at a time. A service description normally describes the functionality provided by one software system. On the other hand, one physical system can provide only one instance of a service, but there can be multiple physical systems of the same model. A description for a CPS service describes the functionality provided by CPSs of the same model. For example, consider a client requests a service provided by CPS m, consisting of an experienced firefighter and a jeep of a certain model/year, and fails. The client may be able to request the same service provided by CPS n, which involves another experienced firefighter and a jeep of the same model/year. CPSs of the same model are very likely to have similar general performance. When it comes to specific tasks, the performance varies depending on the specific context of that CPS.

- **Predictability of Results.** The results of software services are more predictable than those of physical services because software services have much less invocation parameters. Most of the time, the successfulness of the execution can be determined by the given inputs and the preconditions of the execution. If the inputs and preconditions satisfy the requirements, it has a very high possibility that the execution succeeds, i.e. generates the expected output and changes the state of the system (a closed world) to the expected state. Comparatively, physical services execute in real world/open world and it is impos-

sible and unrealistic to give every detail of the state of the world to the physical system which executes the service. Therefore, the successfulness of a physical service is sometimes unpredictable.

- **Performance Measurement.** The performance of a software service can be determined by the algorithm of the software application, the capability of the server where the service runs, and the bandwidth of the network where the messages are transformed. In other words, the performance of a software service can be calculated and stays most of the time the same. On the contrary, physical services have the unpredictability nature shown in their performance aspect. For example, the physical location of a physical system at run time determines how soon its services can be delivered to the clients at another physical location.

Figure 1. Service instance multiplicity

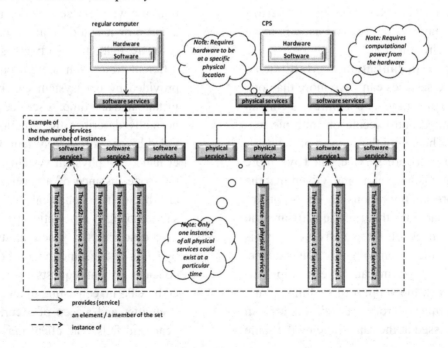

New Concepts for CPS Services

Due to the distinctive natures of CPS services compared to the traditional software service, the existing service oriented architecture frameworks, for example OWL-S, are incapable of describing the CPS services. On the contrary, they can be extended in order to address their special characteristics. This sub-section discusses the new concepts introduced specially for CPSs and CPS services.

Abstract CPS, Communication Network, and Context

As there are normally more than one physical systems of the same model, which typically provide the same set of services, we define the notation of abstract CPS to model all the individual systems to avoid duplication and abstract commonality when denoting service providers.

In real world, a CPS resides in an organizational structure. It does not have communication with every other CPS. The organizational structure describes from which CPSs it receives commands and to which it reports success or failure. There can also be CPS that is completely autonomous, i.e., it acts on its own. The communication network describes the communication links between CPSs, i.e., which CPSs a CPS knows and can communicate with. In this chapter, we define

the organizational structure and communication network as a mixture of both central control and p2p. Consider that the CPSs are organized into a B-Tree, as shown in Figure 2. The CPS nodes at any level of the tree have control over their decedents in the tree and thus have communication access too. CPSs within the same B-Tree node are able to communicate with each other, although not able to control each other. The organizational structure and communication network only include concrete CPSs but not abstract CPSs.

CPSs depend highly on their physical environment. If the environment is ideal for a service that a CPS provides, the service runs with the maximum performance. If the environment is not ideal, the service may still be able to run but with impaired performance. Sometimes the service is not able to run in certain environment that does not meet its requirement. Therefore, the environment is an important aspect in modeling CPS. The contextual information needs to be described from two perspectives. First, the contextual of a physical system is necessary. Second, the environmental requirements for the services to be executed have to be described. Common context attributes for cyber physical space include:

- Map, which includes locations of buildings, sites, etc;

Figure 2. Organizational structure and communication network

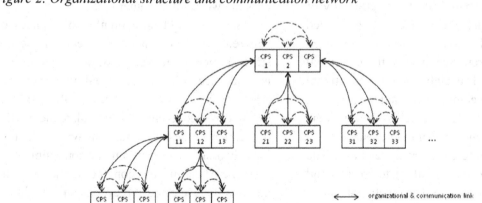

311

- Location of events; self and other physical systems, which affects the time cost of the physical service;
- Weather, which may affect the performance of certain services;
- Road condition, which may affect the performance of certain services.

In order to make a simulation that is close to the real-world life, we make assumptions regarding how the changes of context is being notified to/detected by CPS. Map changes whenever a road/route is being blocked by fire or cleared. The change of map and road condition is detected by the CPS itself. The location of a CPS is being tracked by the CPS itself. The information of location events and other CPSs are passed around by CPSs through communication links. The weather is being broadcasted to all CPS in a certain region.

Abstract Service and Service Hierarchy

It is inefficient to provide a description for a service provided by each physical systems of the same kind, because this ends up duplication that reduces the performance of dynamic service discovery and composition. Instead, it is more natural to provide the same descriptions for services provided by all physical systems of the same kind and the descriptions should not be bound or grounded to any particular concrete physical system.

This chapter promotes an intelligent searching method, which is based on the functionality of services and requires the services to be organized in a hierarchy. The services can be organized along three different dimensions, the functional generalization and specialization, the functional requirements and composition, and the provider. Such organization allows searching based on the functional requirements from the clients as well as the provider preferences from the clients. The hierarchy leads to functional related results and better search performance. The functional related results either have the same functionality, or one

service requires another service, or one service is a special (subclass) of another. The service hierarchy only includes the abstract services but not concrete services. Without the concrete services, the hierarchy turns out to be much simpler and easier to manage.

The abstract service hierarchy does not include concrete services. The concrete services are linked to the abstract services through the service instantiation relationship. During the dynamic service discovery and composition, the qualified abstract services are first found and the corresponding concrete services are then retrieved through such relationship.

Dynamic Service Composition with QoS Assurance

When a concrete CPS receives a task, which it is not able to accomplish on its own, it has to contact other concrete CPSs and request their help. First of all, it decomposes the task into subtasks and creates a procedure/workflow. If it knows one or more CPSs that provide the services it needs, it includes their concrete service in the workflow. However, if the CPSs that provide the required services are not directly accessible, the workflow is still definable/describable with the help of an abstract service. The CPS includes the abstract service in the workflow and passes the workflow to other CPSs, which may be able to replace the abstract service with concrete ones or otherwise pass the workflow to other CPSs.

As there could be a number of choices of concrete services as a replacement for the abstract service in the workflow, the final decision is made according to the Quality of Services (QoS) of each concrete service. In this case, all the involved concrete CPSs calculate the quality of their service and communicate with each other directly or indirectly through the communication network. At the end, one concrete service with the best quality is selected as the replacement. If there is more than one abstract service in the workflow, the above process repeats until the workflow has only concrete services. Finally, the workflow is sent back to the task initiator. The task initiator receives the task plan (the workflow) and informs the involved CPSs to execute their services. At this point, the CPSs in action suspend the occupied resources resulting in certain or all services being temporarily unavailable until the execution of current service is finished.

Extended Model for CPS Services

The extended model is shown in Figure 3. The model includes all the points discussed in the previous section. This section discusses the model in details.

First, it includes the Cyber Physical System (CPS) class, and the AbstractCPS class and the ConcreteCPS class, both of which are subclasses of the CPS class. An instance of the AbstractCPS class represents a model of a kind of CPSs; however, an instance of the ConcreteCPS class represents a specific CPS. Two kinds of relationships exist between the AbstractCPS and ConcreteCPS class, i.e. the instantiation relationship and the abstraction relationship. The former describes that a concrete CPS is an instance of an abstract CPS. The latter describes that an abstract CPS represents

the model for a concrete CPS. The model includes the Service class, which is a class defined by OWL-S. We extend the OWL-S with the addition of two subclasses of the Service class, i.e. the AbstractService class and the ConcreteService class. The AbstractService represents a service that is not grounded to any invocable or executable physical system.

Second, there are relationships, provide and providedBy, between the CPS class and the Service class. Such relationships exist between the AbstractCPS class and the AbstractService class, between the ConcreteCPS class and the AbstractService class, and between the ConcreteCPS class and the ConcreteService class. The multiplicities are *:* for all three combinations due to the following two reasons: (1) a service can be provided by more than one CPS or more than one kind of CPSs; (2) a CPS or a kind of CPSs can provide more than one service. Such relationships do not exist between the AbstractCPS class and the ConcreteService, since concrete services refer to the ones bounded to a concrete physical system. Note that the services discussed in this chapter are not software services. They may not have WSDL descriptions and do not necessarily need them. The providedBy relationship in the model helps the CPSs to know the providers of the ser-

Figure 3. Extended SOA model based on OWL-S

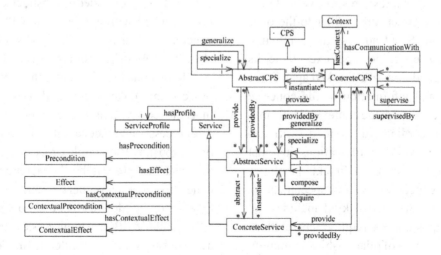

vices. With such information, the CPS is able to communicate with other CPSs about the assigned task. As the CPS service is different from software service, the grounding is not through WSDL. Service descriptions are stored in the memory of the CPS and served as the knowledge base for the communication, planning, and composition.

Third, this model includes the Context class, which represents the properties of the environment where a concrete CPS stays. Only instances of the ConcreteCPS have context, rather than those of the AbstractCPS. This is because abstract CPSs are models, they do not physically exist, and thus they do not have contexts. There is one relationship, called hasContext, from the ConcreteCPS class to the Context class. However, there is no relationship in the other direction. Such association has a multiplicity of *:1, since a concrete CPS can only be at one physical location at a specific time and there could be multiple concrete CPSs in the same location.

Fourth, as the contextual information has to be evaluated so as to determine whether a service is available, the required environmental properties should be defined for each service. Therefore, in addition to allowing the description of contextual information for concrete CPSs by introducing the Context class, the model includes the ContextualPrecondition class and ContextualEffect class, which describe the required context and the effects on the context, respectively. These precondition and effects are similar to the ones defined by OWL-S but address the contextual aspect. Before a service becomes executable, its contextual preconditions are checked against the current contextual information of the concrete CPS. After the execution, the contextual information is updated according to the contextual effects.

Fifth, there are two kinds of relationships exist between abstract services. The first kind includes the functional generalization and specialization relationships and the second kind includes the functional composition and requirement relationships. These two kinds of relationships are mainly designed to model service hierarchies. In this way, the services can be organized in two dimensions. The two-dimensional service hierarchies can also be viewed as a graph.

Sixth, there are also two kinds of relationships exist between the concrete CPSs. The first kind includes supervise and supervisedBy, which describe the organizational hierarchical structure of CPSs. The second kind includes hasCommunicationWith, which describes the communication network of CPSs.

Service Grounding and Service Process

In OWL-S top level service ontology, a service is described from three aspects, profile, process, and grounding. For traditional software services, the grounding defines where the service can be accessed. Normally the grounding describes the connection with the software service description in the WSDL format. CPSs do not have any descriptions in the WSDL format. Therefore, the grounding mechanism cannot be reused for CPS. However, the grounding has already been taken care of by the model we discussed in the previous section. The grounding is realized by the providedBy relationship. If an abstract service or a concrete service is providedBy a concrete CPS, such service is grounded to the concrete CPS. An abstract service can be providedBy abstract CPSs and is not grounded with any concrete CPS. However, concrete CPSs can still be found by following the abstract relationship from the abstract CPSs.

The extended service reuses the OWL-S service process and makes some modifications to better meet the requirements of the cyber physical space. The process of a service can either be simple, atomic, or composite. The simple process is used in this approach to represent the abstract process and the concrete process can either be atomic or composite. OWL-S model defines that a simple process can either be realizedBy an atomic process or expandsTo a composite process. The extended model interprets both realizedBy and expandsTo as the instantiate relationship. Since the interpretation of a model is done by a model reader, the way of interpretation can be realized by the implementation.

A service with an atomic process means the CPS accomplishes the task in a single step. The atomic process is performed by the CPS itself. A service with a composite process indicates that a number of services are performed in a certain sequence to accomplish the task. There are two situations for a composite process. First, a composite process only involves the atomic or composite processes provided by the CPS itself. Second, a composite process involves processes provided by itself as well as processes provided by other CPSs. The first case can be modeled as a normal composite process in OWL-S. In the second case, since a CPS does not have knowledge about how another CPS accomplish certain tasks and does not care to know, the composite process uses the simple process (abstract process) whenever an alien process is needed in the workflow description.

The above modification of the OWL-S process model, especially those on the simple and composite processes, allows the distribution of service/ process definition. In a cyber physical space, a CPS knows the procedure and how it performs certain tasks. It does not know and does not care to know the procedure of any other CPS and how it performs certain tasks. Therefore, a CPS has the detailed process definition for its own services. Such process definitions are kept to itself and unknown to others. On the other hand, it also has its service processes defined as simple processes which can be seen by other CPSs. In this way, when describing a service process that cannot accomplish on its own, simple (abstract) process can be used to refer to the required service process.

Case Study

This section employs a fire emergency handling scenario as a case study to show the solution. The scenario includes several kinds of CPSs,

police departments, fire departments, hospitals, and emergency medical technician (EMT). A police department has control over several jeeps and a number of helicopters. A fire department supervises fire jets and fire trucks. A hospital has doctors, nurses, and ambulances. During a fire emergency, all entities function as cyber physical systems by providing services, receiving commands from supervising entities, communicating with other entities, etc.

There are a number of services in this scenario, such as rescue service, fire extinguish service, transport service, and medical care service. A rescue service can be rescuing a group of people who are all in acceptable health condition or rescuing a group of people with injured ones among them. For fire extinguishing, there are two strategies, putting out fire with fire retardant and putting out fire by setting up controlled burns. The transport service has two different special services in this case, the transportation on the ground service and the transportation in the air service. The rescue service requires transport service. The rescue of injured people as a special case of the rescue requires not only the transport service, but also the medical care service.

The scenario is modeled according to the extended SOA model. The model is shown in Figure 4. In this model, all the services are modeled as the instances of the AbstractService class, and all the physical departments and devices are modeled as the instances of AbstractCPS class. There are relationships that organize the abstract services, such as the link between the RescueInjuredPeople service and the Rescue service, which is an example of the generalization relationship, and the link from the Rescue service and the Transport service, which is an example of the requirement/ composition relationship. Note that the figure does not show all details of the model for simplicity.

The services are connected with the service providers. For example, Helicopter provides the TransportInAir service and Jeep provides the TransportOnGround service. In this model, the

Figure 4. Model for abstract services and CPSs in the Fire emergency scenario

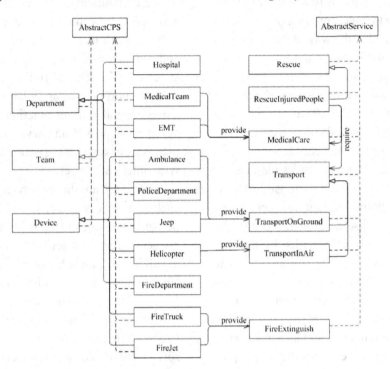

CPSs are connected to the most specialized service as a service provider. In other words, the Helicopter is connected to the TransportInAir service instead of being connected to the Transport service. This design makes the service of the helicopter searchable as a transport service and makes clear the special characteristics of such service.

A dynamic service discovery and composition decompose a task, search for the required services, and look up the capable CPSs. For example, the task of rescuing injured people can be decomposed to transportation and medical care according the requirement links in the model. The decomposition stops when there is no further require link that can be found. With the set of the smallest unit of services, the search continues by following the generalization/specialization link. For example, the transport service can be either transport in the air or on the ground. The sequence of following the requirement/composition link and the generalization/specialization link is interchangeable since both orders lead to the same result. The acquiring

of the decomposed and specialized services leads to the qualifying CPSs. For example, all helicopter, jeep, and ambulance are able to provide the transport service, and both medical teams from hospital and emergency medical technician (EMT) are able to provide the medical care service.

A jeep provides the transport service; thus, it has the potential of providing the rescue injured people service. During the dynamic service decomposition, the jeep creates a workflow for the rescue injured people service, which can be described as the diagram in Figure 5. This figure shows that the service is composed of a sequence with three steps. The first step is to move from its current location to the destination, where injured people are trapped. The second step is to treat the injured people. Since this medical treatment is not a service of its own, it is a simple process of an abstract service. The abstract service is not defined in its own service description file. Instead, it is defined in the upper ontology file (indicated by namespace *upper* ahead of the service name), which is shared by all CPSs. Such upper ontology file makes the CPSs know what services exist. Modifications can be made to the upper ontology file, so as to achieve a different level of accessibility. For example, the upper ontology can be divided into two pieces each of which is shared by a group of CPSs, so that only a group of CPSs know the existence of a service. The third step is again the transportation, moving from the current location to a safe place where injured people can be further taken care of. Note that in the diagram, the superscript after the name of the service shows the type of the process, *i.e.*, a represents atomic and s represents simple. The tables with columns "From" and "To" show the binding of the arguments of the composite process with those of the atomic processes.

Concrete CPSs in this scenario is modeled in Figure 6. The organizational structure can be seen clearly from the model. For example, there are one police department, two fire departments, one hospital, and two emergency medical technicians, all of which act on their own. There is one helicopter and two jeeps that belong to the police department and may receive commands from the department. There are fire trucks and fire jets that work for the fire departments. A medical team and an ambulance are under the supervision of the hospital.

Departments have direct or indirect communication channels among them. If a department does not have direct channel with another, they can only communicate through a third one, which has direct access with both of them. All devices have direct communication channels with their supervising departments. Some devices have direct communication channels with other devices either of the same kind or of different kinds under the same department. For example, the ambulance and the medical team can talk to each other. As another example, all fire trucks in a fire department are able to talk to each other, i.e., the communication network for these fire trucks is a complete graph. However, some do not directly talk to the devices of other kinds even though under the same departments due to some technical problem. For example, the helicopter and the jeep have difficulty talking to each other.

Following the previous discussion on jeep creating a workflow dynamically, here we assume that the discussion focuses on jeepA1. After realizing the need of a medical care service, the jeep sends the request to its supervisor, policeDeptA. policeDeptA further sends the request to its direct contacts, fireDeptA and hospitalA. Since fireDeptA does not provide the medical care service, it forwards the request to its direct contacts. Such procedure is continued until a provider is

Figure 5. Dynamic workflow for rescue injured people by Jeep

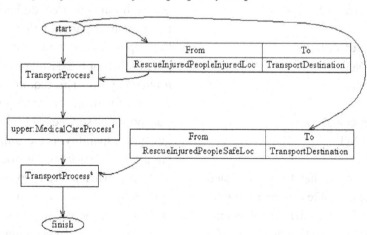

Figure 6. Model for concrete CPSs in the fire emergency scenario

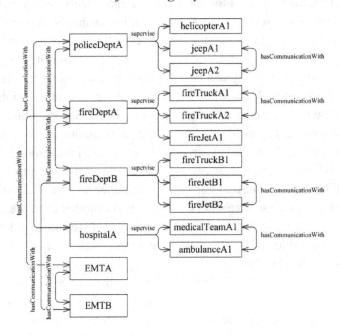

found for the service. Since hospitalA supervises medicalTeamA1, which provides the medical care service, it responds to the request if it currently available or forwards the request if it is currently unavailable. Once jeep gets responses from all request paths, it knows that it has the option to collaborate with medicalTeamA1, EMTA, and EMTB. It also knows the qualities of the services provided by the different CPSs.

As discussed in previous paragraphs, a rescue injured people task can be achieved by the following combinations of CPSs:

- Helicopter + medical team
- Helicopter + EMT
- Jeep + medical team
- Jeep + EMT
- Ambulance + medical team
- Ambulance + EMT

The quality of a service has to be evaluated during the final selection of the concrete services. The calculation of quality considers many factors, one of which is the communication overhead. The communication cost of the Ambulance + EMT combination is definitely higher than that of the Ambulance + medical team. Similarly, any pair without direct communication channel has greater communication cost and worse interoperability than the Ambulance + medical pair, since they work in the same department and have collaborated with each other a lot of times. Of course, other factors have to be considered in order to make a rational decision about the selection.

Figure 7 shows an example of contextual precondition and effect definition. The definition is for the transportation that jeep provided. Since the jeep moves on the ground, it requires that the road is clear or the destination location is not surrounded by fire. This requirement/precondition is also true for all other devices providing the ground transportation service but not having the fire extinguishing capability. For example, the ambulance has the same restriction, but the fire truck does not.

In case when injured people need to be rescued from a spot surrounded by fire, the contextual precondition for jeep or ambulance does not hold true. The contextual precondition being false means

Figure 7. Example contextual precondition-Model for Jeep transport service

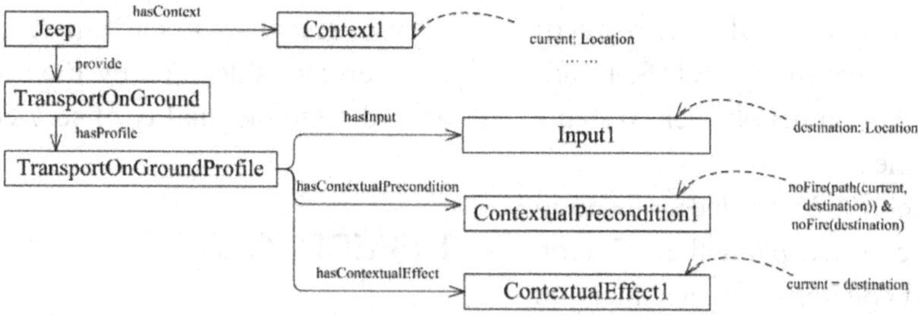

the service is incapable or unavailable. If this is the case, the only options for the transportation are helicopter + medical team and helicopter + EMT. The contextual precondition evaluation helps to eliminate certain options before the quality analysis is performed.

The mechanism of QoS guarantees the quality when the capacity of all CPSs in the cyber physical space is insufficient. There are several aspects of the mechanism. First, the collaboration framework makes sure that only necessary resources are being allocated for a task. There is no more than necessary resource being allocated but wasted. When there is a task that can be accomplished by more than one combination of CPSs, only one combination is selected. Second, when there is more than one combination of CPSs is able to accomplish a task, the most suitable one is being selected. The degree of suitability is being evaluated by calculating the response time, service cost, and the value of the return. The combination of CPSs with the best value is selected. Third, tasks assigned to the cyber physical space have their priorities. This makes the CPSs able to response to the most critical tasks in a queue first. Such approach normally yields the best overall performance, since it maximizes the value of the return.

FUTURE RESEARCH DIRECTIONS

The extended SOA model has been shown feasible and capable of modeling cyber physical systems with a case study. In the future, an algorithm will be implemented according to the collaboration mechanism with QoS assurance defined in this chapter. A simulation system for cyber physical system will be developed so that the service model and the algorithm can be evaluated. The simulation could demonstrate the adequacy of the extended model. It will be a better support for the research if more experiments can be done for the dynamic service discovery and composition. Complicated scenarios can be designed to test the model.

CONCLUSION

This chapter discusses the collaboration problem in the cyber physical system space with service oriented architectural models. Service oriented architectural models are employed to solve this problem because it has already been proven effective with web services and business applications. The semantic web service technologies facilitate the automation of service composition by providing semantic information that is understandable by software agents and helpful in making decisions. This chapter presents the approach to wrap physical system functionalities as services and solve the collaboration problem using semantic web services. It mainly focuses on presenting the model that is created especially for the cyber physical space. Such model is necessary because the cyber physical system differs from the traditional web service in many ways. This chapter discusses the differences and shows the insufficiency of the current SOA models in modeling the cyber physical systems. The differences lead to the extension of the SOA model, to be specific, OWL-S, to addresses the natures of the cyber physical systems and their functionalities.

This chapter presents the extended model to an appropriate level of detail. It explains the definition of CPS, abstract and concrete CPS, abstract and concrete Service, as well as a set of relationships that relate the concepts. It discusses the abstract service hierarchy and how it helps the analysis of service request and decision making. It elaborates the definition of context, and contextual precondition and contextual effect of services. It talks about what contextual information is important for CPS and how the change of context is notified to/detected by CPSs. It also explained how contextual information can be used to evaluate the availability of CPS services. In addition, this chapter discusses how the extended model deals with the three aspects of services, profile, process, and grounding. It discusses the modification of the service process model make it possible to represent CPS service processes in a distributed manner.

This chapter uses a case study, which focuses on the collaboration issue in a fire emergency scenario, to illustrate the modeling of CPS and CPS services using the extended model. It presents the model of abstract CPSs and abstract services, as well as the model of concrete CPSs. It uses an example to show the description of contextual information of services. It also explains the way the service processes are defined distributed with the simple process. This chapter covers the organizational structure and communication network of the cyber physical space and discusses how such relationships in real-life affects CPSs communication and collaboration ability. The case study shows the sufficiency of the model in defining different aspects of CPS. With the help of the model, a service request could be sent and forwarded along the communication links or down the organizational structure. Each

CPS will be able to know the physical service it provides and the quality of that service, and thus provide responses to the requestor. The selection of a service is decided by the service requestor according to the quality of services.

REFERENCES

Bellavista, P., Corradi, A., Montanari, R., & Toninelli, A. (2006). Context-aware semantic discovery for next generation mobile systems. *IEEE Communications Magazine*, *44*, 62–71. doi:10.1109/MCOM.2006.1705981

Bottaro, A., Bourcier, J., Escoffier, C., & Lalanda, P. (2007). Context-aware service composition in a home control gateway. *IEEE International Conference on Pervasive Services*, (pp. 223-231).

Broens, T., Pokraev, S., van Sinderen, M., Koolwaaij, J., & Dockhorn Costa, P. (2004). Context-aware, ontology-based service discovery. *Ambient Intelligence Conference*, (pp. 72-83).

Chen, G., & Kotz, D. (2002). Context aggregation and dissemination in ubiquitous computing systems. *Proceedings Fourth IEEE Workshop on Mobile Computing Systems and Applications*, (pp. 105-114).

Chen, H., Finin, T., & Joshi, A. (2004). Semantic Web in the context broker architecture. *Proceedings of the Second IEEE International Conference on Pervasive Computing and Communications* (PerCom'04), (p. 277).

Dong, J., Sun, Y., & Yang, S. (2006). OWL-S ontology framework extension for dynamic Web Service composition. In *Proceedings of the Eighteenth International Conference on Software Engineering and Knowledge Engineering (SEKE)*, (pp. 544-549). San Francisco Bay, California, USA, July 2006.

Dong, J., Sun, Y., & Zhao, Y. (2008). Hierarchical composition of OWL-S Web services. In *Proceedings of 6th International Conference on Software Engineering Research, Management and Applications (SERA)* (pp. 187-194). Czech Republic: IEEE CS Press.

Erl, T. (2005). *Service-oriented architecture: Concepts, technology, and design.* Upper Saddle River, NJ: Prentice Hall PTR.

Erradi, A., & Maheshwari, P. (2007). Enhancing Web Service performance using adaptive quality of service management. In Bentallah, B., Casati, F., & Georgakopolous, D. (Eds.), *Web Information Systems Engineering (WISE)* (pp. 349–360). Berlin, Germany: Springer. doi:10.1007/978-3-540-76993-4_29

Erradi, A., Padmanabhuni, S., & Varadharajan, N. (2006). Differential QoS support in Web Services management. In *Proceedings of the IEEE International Conference on Web Services* (pp. 781-788). Washington, DC: IEEE Computer Society.

Extensible Markup Language (XML). (2010). *Home.* Retrieved from http://www.w3.org/XML/

Geihs, K., Reichle, R., Wagner, M., & Khan, M. (2009). Modeling of context-aware self-adaptive applications in ubiquitous and service-oriented environments. *Software Engineering for Self-Adaptive Systems Conference,* (pp. 146-163).

Huang, J., Bastani, F., Yen, I.-L., & Jeng, J.-J. (2009). Toward a smart cyber-physical space: A context-sensitive resource-explicit service model. In *Proceedings of the 2009 33rd Annual IEEE International Computer Software and Applications Conference,* vol. 2 (pp. 122-127).

Junho, S. (2005). Roadmap for e-commerce standardization in Korea. *International Journal of IT Standards and Standardization Research, 3*(2), 1–4. doi:10.4018/jitsr.2005070101

Kang, K.-D., & Son, S. H. (2008). Real-time data services for cyber physical systems. In *Proceedings of the 2008 28th International Conference on Distributed Computing Systems (ICDCS) Workshops* (pp. 483-488). Washington, DC: IEEE Computer Society.

Keidl, M., & Kemper, A. (2004). Towards context-aware adaptable web services. Proceedings of the 13th International World Wide Web Conference on Alternate Track Papers and Posters, (pp. 55-65). New York, NY: ACM.

Lee, E., & Austin, T. (2006). *Cyber-physical systems - Are computing foundations adequate? WCPS: Research Motivation.* Techniques and Roadmap.

McIlraith, S. A., Son, T. C., & Zeng, H. (2001). Semantic Web services. *IEEE Intelligent Systems, 16*(2), 46–53. doi:10.1109/5254.920599

Menascé, D. A. (2002). QoS issues in Web Services. *IEEE Internet Computing, 6*(6), 72–75. doi:10.1109/MIC.2002.1067740

Mokhtar, S. B., Preuveneers, D., Georgantas, N., Issarny, V., & Berbers, Y. (2008). Easy: Efficient semantic service discovery in pervasive computing environments with QoS and context support. *Journal of Systems and Software, 81,* 785–808.

Mostefaoui, S., & Hirsbrunner, B. (2004). Context aware service provisioning. *IEEE/ACS International Conference on Pervasive Services* (ICPS), (pp. 71-80).

OWL-S. (2010). *Semantic markup for Web Services.* Retrieved from http://www.w3.org/Submission/OWL-S

Paolucci, M., Kawamura, T., Payne, T., & Sycara, K. (2002). *Semantic matching of Web Services capabilities* (pp. 333–347). The Semantic Web — ISWC.

Ran, S. (2003). A model for web services discovery with QoS. *ACM SIGecom Exchanges, 4*(1), 1–10. doi:10.1145/844357.844360

Raverdy, P., Riva, O., de La Chapelle, A., Chibout, R., & Issarny, V. (2006). *Efficient context-aware service discovery in multi-protocol pervasive environments*. 7th International Conference on Mobile Data Management (MDM), (p. 3).

Sawyer, S., & Tapia, A. (2005). The sociotechnical nature of mobile computing work: Evidence from a study of policing in the United States. *International Journal of Technology and Human Interaction, 1*(3), 1–14. doi:10.4018/jthi.2005070101

Service Oriented Architecture. (2010). *Wikipedia*. Retrieved from http://en.wikipedia.org/wiki/Service-oriented_architecture

Sha, L., Gopalakrishnan, S., Liu, X., & Wang, Q. (2009). *Cyber-physical systems: A new frontier. Machine Learning in Cyber Trust: Security* (pp. 3–13). Privacy, and Reliability.

Simple Object Access Protocol (SOAP). (2010). *Specifications*. Retrieved from http://www.w3.org/TR/soap

Sudha, R., Rajagopalan, M., Selvanayaki, M., & Selvi, S. (2007). Ubiquitous semantic space: A context-aware and coordination middleware for Ubiquitous Computing. *2nd International Conference on Communication Systems Software and Middleware* (COMSWARE), (pp. 1-7).

Universal Description, Discovery, and Integration (UDDI). (2010). Online community for the UDDI. Retrieved from http://uddi.xml.org/

van Kranenburg, H., Bargh, M., Iacob, S., & Peddemors, A. (2006). A context management framework for supporting context-aware distributed applications. *IEEE Communications Magazine, 44*, 67–74. doi:10.1109/MCOM.2006.1678112

Washington, DC: IEEE Computer Society.

Web Service Description Language (WSDL). (2010). *W3.org*. Retrieved from http://www.w3.org/TR/wsdl

Web Service Modeling Ontology (WSMO). (2010). Home. Retrieved from www.wsmo.org/

Yang, Y., Mahon, F., Williams, M., & Pfeifer, T. (2006). *Context-aware dynamic personalised service re-composition in a pervasive service environment* (pp. 724–735). Ubiquitous Intelligence and Computing.

Zeng, L., Benatallah, B., Ngu, A. H. H., Dumas, M., Kalagnanam, J., & Chang, H. (2004). QoS-aware middleware for Web Services composition. *IEEE Transactions on Software Engineering, 30*(5), 311–327. doi:10.1109/TSE.2004.11

Zimmermann, A., Lorenz, A., & Oppermann, R. (2007). *An operational definition of context* (pp. 558–571). Modeling and Using Context.

Glossary

Keywords	Definition or Descriptions
4I (Interface, Intelligence, Integration and Infrastructure)	4I is a service technology framework proposed by Institute for Information Industry (III) in Taiwan which includes interface technology, intelligence technology, integration technology and infrastructure technology. The 4I framework provides a reference to locate technology resources in a service design. From the front-end device machine, middle content analysis, back-end service to virtual service center, these four innovative system total solutions solve the technical problems in different layers.
6LoWPAN (IPv6 over Low power Wireless Personal Area Networks)	The 6LoWPAN working group of IETF (The Internet Engineering Task Force) has defined encapsulation and compression mechanisms to send and receive IPv6 packets over wireless networks with strong constraints on power consumption.
AOP (Aspect-Oriented Programming)	Aspect-Oriented Programming is a programming paradigm that emphasizes the idea of 'cross-cutting' to provide a way for managing separate parts of code which may belong to the same 'aspect'.
Apache Felix	Felix is a project of the Apache software foundation that provides an implementation of the OSGi service platform specification.
B2B (Business-to-business)	B2B describes commerce transactions between businesses, such as between a manufacturer and a wholesaler, or between a wholesaler and a retailer. B2B is also used in the context of communication and collaboration. Many businesses are now using social media to connect with their consumers (B2C).
BIMM (Business-IT-Mapping Model)	The Business-IT-Mapping Model defines a connection between a business process model and a service composition specification. Currently, this link is neither supported by business process modeling nor by CASE tools. In particular, BIMM allows storing and maintaining the complex dependencies between business process models and service composition specifications in a traceable way.
Bluetooth	Under the IEEE Std 802.15.1, Bluetooth, a Wireless Personal Area Network (PAN), is a wireless protocol for exchanging data over short distances via radio waves. It has been designed in order to replace data cables between fixed and mobile devices.
BPEL (Business Process Execution Language)	It is short for Web Services Business Process Execution Language (see BPEL4WS).
BPEL4People	BPEL4People is a BPEL extension for People. It extends BPEL in order to support the orchestration of role-based human activities.
BPEL4WS or WS-BPEL (Web Services Business Process Execution Language)	It is an OASIS standard executable language for specifying actions within business processes with web services. It extends the web services interaction model and enables it to support business transactions. WS-BPEL defines an interoperable integration model that should facilitate the expansion of automated process integration both within and between businesses. In BPEL, web service interactions can be described in two ways: executable business processes and abstract business processes. Executable business processes model the actual behavior of a participant in a business interaction; whereas abstract business processes are partially specified processes that are not intended to be executed.
Business Process	A business process serves a particular business goal (e.g., to handle customer orders, to deliver goods or to manage product changes) and it constitutes a recurring sequence of business functions whose execution has to meet certain rules. Furthermore, a business process model documents business requirements in respect to the process- and service-oriented information system to be designed. These business requirements are often elicited by interviewing end users as well as process owners. The graphical representation and documentation of business processes is usually supported by respective business process modeling (BPM) tools.

Keywords	Definition or Descriptions
Business-IT Alignment	Business-IT alignment targets at closing the gap between business processes and their IT implementations (e.g., service composition specifications). This goal can be achieved, for example, by improving the interactions between business and IT departments during the service development process as well as during service maintenance. Amongst others, this mapping model explicitly maintains the relationships between business process models and their implementation in a process- and service-oriented information system.
Case Base	It is a repository for storing cases, in which a case is a record that records a problem description and its solution learned from previous experience. It is used in a case-based reasoning approach. (see CBR)
CBR (Case-Based Reasoning)	CBR is a process of solving new problems based on the solutions of similar past problems. Case-based reasoning uses a four-step cycle, retrieve, reuse, revise, and retain, for providing solutions and learning process.
CBSE (Component-Based Software Engineering)	CBSE is a sub-discipline of software engineering based on the concept of separation of concerns where software systems are built as a composition of reusable components.
Cloud Computing	Cloud computing refers to anything that involves delivering services over the Internet. Such services can be divided in three categories: Infrastructure as a Service (IaaS), Platform as a Service (PaaS) and Software as a Service (SaaS). A Cloud service is available on demand and fully managed by the provider.
Component	A component is a central concept in CBSE. A software component can be defined as a unit of composition. A component is designed as a black box, i.e. its internal structure is not available to the public. Such design allows components to be easily substituted in a software system. (see CBSE)
Device	A device is an electronic entity which disposes of communication capabilities such as a computer, printer, router, mobile phone, PDA, etc.
DPWS (Devices Profile for Web Services)	DPWS is a specification fully aligned with Web Services technology which enables discovery and description of devices, as well as transmission of messages and events. Its objectives are similar to those of Universal Plug and Play (UPnP) but, in addition, DPWS is fully aligned with Web Services technology and includes numerous extension points allowing for seamless integration of device-provided services in enterprise-wide application scenarios.
Dynamic Testing Techniques	Dynamic testing techniques try to find bugs in a program (or part of it) by executing it. Typical techniques are test case generation, regression testing or stress testing. The advantages of such techniques are able to provide real-world results, easier to conduct testing, and simpler to automate the testing process. On the negative side, they may miss certain information that static testing techniques provide, so both are usually considered complementary.
EAI (Enterprise Application Integration)	EAI is an integration framework composed of a collection of technologies and services which form a middleware to enable integration of systems and applications across the enterprise. Typically, an enterprise has existing legacy applications and databases and wants to continue to use them while adding or migrating to a new set of applications that exploit the Internet, e-commerce, extranet, and other new technologies. EAI may involve developing a new total view of an enterprise's business and its applications, seeing how existing applications fit into the new view, and then devising ways to efficiently reuse what already exists while adding new applications and data.
EJB (Enterprise JavaBeans)	EJB is a component architecture written in the Java programming language for modular construction of enterprise applications.
Equilibrium	An equilibrium in an eco-system is a "steady state", where the competing forces balance each other out. Changes to an eco-system perturb these equilibria, but the system eventually settles into a new equilibrium that accommodates these changes. A service eco-system is in an equilibrium if all inter-service realization and consistency links are satisfied, and there is no alternative equilibrium that further minimizes change to the prior state of the service eco-system. Several key tasks in services engineering, including the implementation, deployment and life-cycle management of services require the computation of service eco-system equilibria.

Keywords	Definition or Descriptions
Equinox	Equinox is a project of the Eclipse consortium that provides an implementation of the OSGi service platform specification.
ESB (Enterprise Service Bus)	ESB is an architectural pattern to integrate and manage services. An ESB generally provides an abstraction layer on top of an implementation of an enterprise messaging system, which allows integration architects to exploit the value of messaging without writing code. Unlike the more classical enterprise application integration (EAI) approach of a monolithic stack in a hub and spoke architecture, an enterprise service bus builds on base functions broken up into their constituent parts, with distributed deployment where needed, working in harmony as necessary.
Extra-Functional Properties	Extra-functional properties are pieces of code which provide additional functionality to the system, where this functionality is not part of the main one or of the main concern approached by the system.
Fractal	Fractal, a project of the OW2 consortium, is a modular and extensible component model. Fractal aims to reduce the development, deployment and maintenance costs of software systems.
GENA (General Event Notification Architecture)	The GENA is a protocol that defines an HTTP notification architecture for the sending of notifications between resources.
Glassfish	Glassfish is an open-source implementation of the Java EE application server specification. Glassfish is a project of SUN Microsystems.
Goal Model	A goal model is a definition of user or system requirements in terms of the goal that the user wants the system to achieve. I is built hierarchically starting with the ultimate goal which is then supported by subgoals which must be achieved in order to satisfy the ultimate goal.
Goal-Driven Approach	A goal-driven approach uses goals in software analysis and design to represent user and system requirements
GSM (Global System for Mobile Communications)	GSM is a standard for mobile telephony systems. GSM is used by over 1.5 billion people (2010).
IDE (Integrated Development Environment)	An IDE is a system development environment providing tools for writing application logic and designing application user interfaces such as Eclipse, DevC++, Emacs, or Visual Studio, etc.
Intention	The target that a human user wants a software system to achieve. It is also the reason why the user issues a request to the system. (see Intention-aware system)
Intention-Aware System	A software system that can map service requests from users to a computer interpretable data structure and provide related actions to satisfy these requests based on user background.
Internet	Internet is the largest global network of interconnected computer networks that use the TCP/IP network protocols in order to transmit and exchange data between billions of user worldwide.
Intranet	A private computer network created using Internet protocols.
iPOJO	iPOJO is a service component model and runtime that specifically supports dynamically adaptable applications. iPOJO is part of the Apache Felix project.
Java EE (Java Enterprise Edition)	Java EE is a platform for server development in the Java programming language. It is broadly based on modular components such as EJB running on an application server. Those components provide functionalities to deploy fault-tolerant, distributed, multi-tier Java software. (see EJB)
JOnAS	JOnAS is an open-source implementation of the Java EE application server specification. JOnAS is a project of the OW2 consortium. (see OW2)
JSON (JavaScript Object Notation)	JSON is a text-based human-readable computer data interchange format. It allows for the representation of simple data structures and associative arrays, called objects.
JSON-RPC	JSON-RPC is a remote procedure call protocol encoded in JSON.
Knopflerfish	The Knopflerfish is a project that provides an implementation of the OSGi service platform specification.

Keywords	Definition or Descriptions
Loose Coupling	Loose coupling is a design goal to make the related modules having the minimum dependence. Loosely coupled systems provide many advantages including support for late or dynamically binding to other components while running and can mediate the difference in the component's structure, security model, protocols, and semantics, thus abstracting volatility. This is in contrast to compile-time or runtime binding, which requires binding the components at compile time or runtime (synchronous calls), respectively, and also requires that changes be designed into all components at the same time due to the dependencies.
MDA (Model-Driven Architecture)	MDA is a software design approach, which provides a set of guidelines for the development of software systems expressed as models. In this regard, model-driven development is a software development methodology which focuses on creating models of the systems, leaving implementation technologies for a later stage.
MEP (Message Exchange Pattern)	In software architecture, a messaging pattern is a network-oriented architectural pattern which describes how two different parts of a message passing system connect and communicate with each other. In telecommunications, a message exchange pattern (MEP) describes the pattern of messages required by a communications protocol to establish or use a communication channel. There are two major message exchange patterns: a request-response pattern, and a one-way pattern.
OSGi	OSGi is both a component-based platform and a service platform for the Java programming language. OSGi aims to facilitate the modularization of Java applications as well as the interoperability of such applications and services over various devices.
OW2	The OW2 consortium is a not-for-profit international consortium devoted to producing open-source middleware.
Paradigm Shift	Paradigm shift is the term used by Thomas Kuhn in his influential book "The Structure of Scientific Revolutions (1962)" to describe a change in basic assumptions within the ruling theory of science. It is in contrast to his idea of normal science. The term paradigm shift, as a change in a fundamental model of events, has since become widely applied to many other realms of human experience as well, even though Kuhn himself restricted the use of the term to the hard sciences.
Pervasive Computing	Pervasive or ubiquitous computing corresponds to an information processing model where the user interacts naturally with their environment. The model proposed by pervasive computing consists of using the objects in the environment as a means of interaction between users and computer systems.
PHR (Electronic personal Health Record)	PHR refers to electronically storing personal health related medical information records that generally provide purposes similar to Electronic Medical Record (EMR). It is typically a health record which is initiated and maintained by individual. A PHR provides health information for online accessing to one who has the rights to view the information.
Protocol	A set of formal rules describing how to transmit data, especially across a network. Low level protocols define the electrical and physical standards to be observed, bit- and byte-ordering and the transmission and error detection and correction of the bit stream. High level protocols deal with the data formatting, including the syntax of messages, the terminal to computer dialogue, character sets, sequencing of messages etc.
Publish/Scribe Messaging	In a publish-subscribe system, senders label each message with the name of a topic ("publish"), rather than addressing it to specific recipients. The messaging system then sends the message to all eligible systems that have asked to receive messages on that topic ("subscribe"). This form of asynchronous messaging is a far more scalable architecture than point-to-point alternatives such as message queuing, since message senders need only concern themselves with creating the original message, and can leave the task of servicing recipients to the messaging infrastructure. It is a very loosely coupled architecture, in which senders often do not even know who their subscribers are.
OASIS	OASIS is the abbreviation of "Organization for the Advancement of Structured Information Standards".
Quality Attributes	Quality attributes, such as response time, accuracy, security, reliability, are properties that affect the system as a whole. Most approaches deal with quality attributes separately from the functional requirements of a system.

Keywords	Definition or Descriptions
QoS (Quality of Services)	Quality of Service (QoS) is a set of technologies for managing network traffic in a cost effective manner to enhance user experiences for home and enterprise environments. QoS technologies concern with tasks to measure bandwidth, detect changing network conditions (such as congestion or availability of bandwidth), and prioritize or throttle traffic.
Replication	Replication refers to the use of redundant resources (also called "replica" or "failover" components), including software or hardware components, to improve availability, reliability, fault-tolerance, and performance.
REST (Representational State Transfer)	REST-style architectures consist of clients and servers. Clients initiate requests to servers, while servers process requests and return appropriate responses. Requests and responses are built around the transfer of representations of resources. A resource can be essentially any coherent and meaningful concept that may be addressed. A representation of a resource is typically a document that captures the current or intended state of a resource.
RFID (Radio Frequency Identification)	RFID is a wireless technology that allows for non contact reading. RFID is often used as an alternative to bar coding.
SaaS (Software as a Service)	SaaS is a delivery model for software whereby the vendor provides an application to customers for use as a service on demand. Customers pay for using the software rather than owning it. The software is hosted and maintained by the vendor. SaaS is an important feature of cloud computing.
Security Service	Security service is a processing or communication service that is provided by a system to give a specific kind of protection to resources, where said resources may reside with said system or reside with other systems, for example, an authentication service or a PKI-based document attribution and authentication service. Security services typically implement portions of security policies and are implemented via security mechanisms.
Semantic Web Services	The semantic web services, like conventional web services except for stressing the needs of meaning in the service description, are the server end of a client–server system for machine-to-machine interaction via the World Wide Web. Semantic services are a component of the semantic web because they use markup which makes data machine-readable in a detailed and sophisticated way (as compared with human-readable HTML which is usually not easily "understood" by computer programs).
Server Load Balancing	In order to achieve web server scalability, more servers need to be added to distribute the load among the group of servers, which is also known as a server cluster. The load distribution among these servers is known as load balancing. Load balancing applies to all types of servers (application server, database server), however, we will be devoting this section for load balancing of web servers (HTTP server) only. When multiple web servers are present in a server group, the HTTP traffic needs to be evenly distributed among the servers. In the process, these servers must appear as one web server to the web client, for example an internet browser. The load balancing mechanism used for spreading HTTP requests is known as IP Spraying.
Service	A service is an abstract resource that represents a capability of performing tasks that form a coherent functionality from the point of view of service providers and service requestors.
Service Availability	There are two interpretations for service availability: (1) service availability as the percentage that a Web service is available and functioning within its operational requirements; (2) service availability as the percentage of successful service invocations in all service invocations.
Service Broker	A software entity that collects a list of Web services advertisements from the service provider, accepts the service request from the requester, and helps to construct connections between them.
Service Composition	It is a way of creating a new service by combining existing services. Building enterprise solution typically requires combining multiple existing enterprise services. These composite services can be in turn recursively integrated with other services into higher level solutions. Such recursive service composition is one of the most important features of SOA, allowing to rapidly build new solutions based on the existing business services.

Keywords	Definition or Descriptions
Service Composition Schema	A service composition schema represents the technical and platform-specific specification of a business process. For the implementation of process- and service-oriented information systems, additional information which goes beyond the one from the respective business process model are required; e.g., technical specifications of data objects and data types, implemented services, user interfaces, business rules, and access control policies. The service composition schema has to meet a number of constraints in order to be executable by a service orchestration engine; e.g., specification of transition conditions, assurance of soundness or completeness of the specified data.
Service Provider	A software entity that is capable of and empowered to perform the actions associated with a service on behalf of its owner.
Service Requestor	A software entity that wishes to interact with a service provider in order to request that a task be performed on behalf of its owner.
Service-Oriented System	It is a software system that its implementation relies on a mesh of software services which comprise unassociated, loosely coupled units of functionality.
Smart Store	Smart Store integrates the information and communication technologies (ICT) and innovation of related services. It is based on a technological platform that offers the support for some attractive and efficient services for customers and administrative staff. Customers can obtain a new brand in a new experimental shopping environment from Smart Store.
SMS (Short Message Service)	SMS is a text communication service that allows the exchange of short text messages between mobile phones or land phones.
SMTP (Simple Mail Transfer Protocol)	SMTP is a text-based protocol for e-mail transmissions across the Internet.
Service Eco-System (or Service Ecosystem)	A Web service ecosystem is a logical collection of Web services whose exposure and access are subject to constraints characteristic of business service delivery. In these ecosystems, service consumers procure services through different distribution and delivery channels, outsourcing service delivery functions such as payment, authentication, and mediation to specialist intermediaries. Web service ecosystems make explicit the notion of service procurement, separating it from that of conventional service supply. (from A. P. Barros and M. Dumas "The rise of web service ecosystems", IT Professional, vol. 8, no. 5, 2006)
Servitization	Servitization is the process to partition software functionalities within an organizational context into a set of services. Servitization will consider multiple dimensions of viewpoints, such as manageability and utility, to package a combination of appropriate functionalities as a service.
SOA (Service-Oriented Architecture)	SOA is a flexible set of design principles used during the phases of systems development and integration in computing. A system based on SOA architecture will provide a loosely-coupled suite of services that can be used within multiple separated systems from several business domains. SOA defines how to integrate widely disparate applications for a Web-based environment and uses multiple implementation platforms. A specific implementation of SOA is the one based on Web services: modular applications, which are auto-descriptive (WSDL), that can be invoked through the Internet following some established standards (typically SOAP over HTTP).
SOAP (Simple Object Access Protocol)	SOAP is a protocol specification for exchanging structured information in the implementation of Web Services in computer networks. It relies on eXtensible Markup Language (XML) for its message format, and usually relies on other application layer protocols, most notably Remote Procedure Call (RPC) and Hypertext Transfer Protocol (HTTP), for message negotiation and transmission. SOAP can form the foundation layer of a web services protocol stack, providing a basic messaging framework upon which web services can be built.
SOC (Service-Oriented Computing)	SOC promotes the use of well-defined composition units – services – to support the rapid development of applications. The central objective of this approach is to reduce dependencies among composition units, where a unit is typically some remotely accessed by clients.

Keywords	Definition or Descriptions
Software Testing	Software testing comprises different techniques that aim to find bugs in a program or system. Depending on the kind of bugs, it can be functional testing (i.e., functional operation) or non-functional testing (e.g., usability, performance, etc.). If the tester is allowed to look into to the source code of the program it is a white-box testing approach;, otherwise it is black-box testing.
Software Verification and Validation (V&V)	Software verification and validation concerns with software quality in terms of correctness of code and user acceptance of a system. In particular, the software verification process verifies whether the resulting product meets requirement specifications, and the software validation one checks if resulting product satisfies the user's demands.
SSDP (Simple Service Discovery Protocol)	SSDP is a network communication protocol. It enables the discovery of available service on a network. SSDP uses UDP multicast or unicast in order to discover the services.
Static Testing Techniques	Static testing techniques try to find bugs in a program without executing it. This can be done by checking its development process (using code reviews, inspections, walk-throughs, etc.) or analyzing its source code (by means of model checking, Petri nets, pi-calculus, etc.). These techniques usually provide the most reliable results, but they are limited because of their complexity when compared to those of dynamic testing techniques, being complementary.
Test Case	A test case is a set of input values and expected results for an execution of a piece of software. A set of test cases is called a test suite. Test suites are usually produced to meet a certain adequacy criteria (e.g., executing all the instructions in the program at least once). When the expected results are missing, the test suite reduces to test data.
Ubiquitous Computing	See Pervasive Computing
UDDI (Universal Description Discovery and Integration)	UDDI is a platform-independent, Extensible Markup Language (XML)-based registry for businesses worldwide to list themselves on the Internet and a mechanism to register and locate web service applications. UDDI is an open industry initiative, sponsored by the OASIS enabling businesses to publish service listings and discover each other and define how the services or software applications interact over the Internet.
UPnP (Universal Plug And Play)	UPnP is a specification defined from an industrial initiative and is currently run by the UPnP Forum. The goal of this specification is to simplify connections between heterogeneous communicating devices and the construction of home networks.
Web Service	A web service is typically an application programming interface (API) or Web API that is accessed via Hypertext Transfer Protocol (HTTP) and executed on a remote system, hosting the requested service. The W3C defines a "web service" as a software system designed to support interoperable machine-to-machine interaction over a network. It has an interface described in a machine-processable format (specifically WSDL). Other systems interact with the web service in a manner prescribed by its description using SOAP messages, typically conveyed using HTTP with an XML serialization in conjunction with other Web-related standards.
Wi-Fi	Wi-Fi refers to a trademark that is commonly used to describe a set of standards enabling devices to be connected to the Internet through a wireless network.
WiMAX (Worldwide Interoperability for Microwave Access)	WiMAX (IEEE 802.16m) is a telecommunications protocol that provides fixed and mobile Internet access. WiMAX forum describes WiMAX as "a standards-based technology enabling the delivery of last mile wireless broadband access as an alternative to cable and DSL"
WSDL (Web Services Description Language)	The Web Services Description Language (WSDL) is an XML language for describing Web services as a set of network endpoints that can operate messages. It allows service descriptions in a standard format.
WS-HumanTask (Web Services Human Task)	WS-HumanTask is a BPEL extension which introduces the definition of human tasks and notifications. It is related to BPEL4People.
WS-I (Web Services Interoperability)	WS-I is an industry consortium chartered to promote interoperability amongst the stack of web services specifications.

Keywords	Definition or Descriptions
WS-Policy (Web Services Policy Framework)	WS-Policy defines a general-purpose XML-based model and syntax that may be used to describe and communicate the policies that inhere to any Web-based service. In other words, WS-Policy assertions express the capabilities and constraints that apply to some particular Web service to which they pertain.
WS-Security (Web Services Security)	WS-Security is a proposed IT industry standard that addresses security when data is exchanged as part of a web service. It is a member of the WS-* family of web service specifications and was published by OASIS. WS-Security specifies how integrity and confidentiality can be enforced on messages and allows the communication of various security token formats.
WSSG (Web Service Security Gateway)	WSSG is a high-performance software solution for Web Services Security Control & Management, powered by XML processing technology and built from the ground up with security in mind to be a security-enforcement point for XML and Web services transactions. It also helps provide comprehensive XML security and the high-speed performance needed for real-world applications.
WS-Transaction (Web Services Transaction)	The WS-Transaction defines what constitutes a transaction and what will determine when it has completed successfully. Each transaction is part of an overall set of activities that constitute a business process that is performed by cooperating Web services. WS-Transaction declares two coordination types: Atomic Transaction for individual operations and Business Activity for long running transactions. Developers can use either or both of these coordination types when building applications that require consistent agreement on the outcome of distributed activities.

About the Contributors

Jonathan Lee received his PhD degree from Texas A&M University in 1993, the year he joined the faculty of the Department of Computer Science and Information Engineering at National Central University (NCU) in Taiwan. His research interests include agent-based software engineering, service-oriented computing, and goal-driven software engineering. He is currently a Professor of CSIE and the Director of Computer Center at NCU. Dr. Jonathan Lee has published more than 100 refereed papers, three edited books and an authoring text book on Software Engineering in Chinese. He received a Distinguished University Professor award from Chinese Electrical Engineering Association (Taiwan) in 2008 and an Endowed Professor award from NCU in 2007. He is a senior member of the IEEE Computer Society and a member of the ACM.

Shang-Pin Ma received his PhD and BS degrees in Computer Science and Information Engineering from National Central University, Chungli, Taiwan, in 2007 and 1999, respectively. He has been an Assistant Professor of Computer Science and Engineering Department, National Taiwan Ocean University, Keelung, Taiwan, since 2008. His research interests include web-based software engineering, service-oriented computing and semantic web.

Alan Liu received the PhD degree in Electrical Engineering and Computer Science from the University of Illinois, Chicago, in 1994. He is currently a Professor with the Department of Electrical Engineering, National Chung Cheng University, Chiayi, Taiwan. His research interests in artificial intelligence and software engineering include knowledge acquisition, requirements analysis, intelligent agents, service computing, and applications in embedded systems and robotic systems. Dr. Liu is a member of IEEE, ACM, Taiwanese Association for Artificial Intelligence, Software Engineering Association of Taiwan, and Robotics Society of Taiwan.

***

Jonathan Bardin is a PhD candidate at the Laboratory of Informatics of Grenoble. His research interests include service-oriented components, especially based on OSGi, and resource distribution. He received his MSc in computer science from the University Joseph Fourier Grenoble.

Farokh B. Bastani received the BTech. degree in Electrical Engineering from the Indian Institute of Technology, Bombay, and the MS and PhD degrees in Computer Science from the University of California, Berkeley. He is currently a Professor of Computer Science at the University of Texas at Dallas. Dr. Bastani's research interests include various aspects of the ultrahigh dependable systems, especially automated software synthesis and testing, embedded real-time process-control and telecommunications systems, and high-assurance systems engineering. Dr. Bastani was the Editor-in-Chief of the IEEE Transactions on Knowledge and Data Engineering (IEEE-TKDE). He is currently an emeritus EIC of IEEE-TKDE and is on the Editorial Board of the *International Journal on Artificial Intelligence Tools, the International Journal of Knowledge and Information Systems, the International Journal of Semantic Computing,* and *the Springer-Verlag series on Knowledge and Information Management*. He was the Program Co-Chair of the 1997 IEEE Symposium on Reliable Distributed Systems, 1998 IEEE International Symposium on Software Reliability Engineering, 1999 IEEE Knowledge and Data Engineering Workshop, 1999 International Symposium on Autonomous Decentralized Systems, and the program chair of the 1995 IEEE International Conference on Tools with Artificial Intelligence. He has been on the Program and Steering Committees of several conferences and workshops and on the Editorial Boards of the *IEEE Transactions on Software Engineering, IEEE Transactions on Knowledge and Data Engineering,* and *the Oxford University Press High Integrity Systems Journal*.

Thomas Bauer is a senior Researcher at the Daimler Research Centre in Ulm where he is working in the area of process management. Before, he was a member of the Department Databases and Information Systems at the University of Ulm where he finished his PhD thesis on the efficient enactment of enterprise-wide workflows in 2001. Current research areas include business process and workflow management, process visualization, process variant management, and service-oriented computing.

M. Brian Blake is a Professor of Computer Science and Associate Dean for Research in the College of Engineering at the University of Notre Dame. Dr. Blake has published over 120 journal articles, book chapters, and refereed conference/workshop papers in the areas of service-oriented computing, intelligent agents and workflow, and web-based software engineering. His work has been awarded over $7 million in sponsored research from the federal and industry organizations. Dr. Blake has served on 4 National Academies' studies or committees and on the National Science Foundation's Advisory Committee for the CISE Directorate. He is currently the Associate Editor-in-Chief for IEEE Internet Computing and Associate Editor of IEEE Transactions on Service Computing. Dr. Blake is an ACM Distinguished Scientist and Senior Member of the IEEE. Dr. Blake received the BEE from Georgia Institute of Technology and PhD in Information and Software Engineering from George Mason University.

Behzad Bordbar has his BSc, MSc, and PhD in Mathematics (PhD from Sheffield, UK). Following his PhD, he worked as a researcher on a number of projects at University of Ghent, Belgium and University of Kent, UK. He is currently a Lecturer at the School of Computer Science, University of Birmingham, UK, where he teaches courses in Software Engineering and Distributed Systems. In recent years, he has had close collaborative research with various academic and industrial organizations, among them Ghent University, Osaka University, Colorado State University, BT, IBM, and HP research laboratories. His research activities are mostly aimed at using modelling to produce more dependable software and systems in shorter development cycles and at a lower cost. His current research projects are dealing with formal methods, model analysis, software tools, model driven development, and fault-tolerance in service oriented architectures.

Stephan Buchwald is a PhD student at the Daimler Research Centre in Ulm where he is working in the area of Enhanced Process Management through Service Orientation (Enproso). Before he started as a PhD student he was studying Computer Engineering and applied computer science at the University of Applied Science Ulm.

Ing-Yi Chen received a BSc degree in Physics from National Central University, Taiwan, in 1984, and MSc and PhD degrees in Electrical and Computer Engineering from the University of Arizona in 1989 and 1992, respectively. He is currently an Associate Professor in the Computer Science and Information Engineering Department at National Taipei University of Technology (NTUT) in Taiwan. In 2000 and 2001, prior to joining NTUT, he served as Chief Technology Officer for Chinatimes, with responsibility for the corporate strategic technology planning and for handling university relations. From 1992 to 2000 he was on the faculty of the Electronic Engineering Department at Chung Yuan Christian University (CYCU) in Taiwan. His research interests include various topics in SOA and solution frameworks for building service oriented applications. A member of the Phi Tau Phi scholastic honor society, he was a recipient of the IEEE/ACM Design Automation Scholarship Award in 1991, and the Distinguished Teaching Award at CYCU in 1996 and at NTUT in 2008.

Stéphanie Chollet is a post-doc fellow at the Laboratory of Informatics of Grenoble. She received her PhD from Grenoble University in 2009 under the direction of Prof. Lalanda. Her research interest is in heterogeneous service composition meeting non-functional properties, and in particular security.

Jing Dong received the BS degree in computer science from Peking University and the MMath and PhD degrees in Computer Science from the University of Waterloo. He has been on the faculty of the Department of Computer Science at the University of Texas at Dallas. He is currently with Hewlett Packard. His research interests include cloud computing, services computing, semantic web services, formal and automated methods for software engineering, design pattern, software modeling and design, ontology, and visualization. He is a senior member of the ACM and a senior member of the IEEE.

Didier Donsez is a Full Professor of Computer Science at the University Grenoble (France). His research is focused on service oriented architecture and component-based software engineering in the context of Machine-to-Machine applications. He had 8 years of experience in OSGi software engineering for J2ME to JavaEE runtimes. He was Chairman and Co-founder of the OSGi Users Group France. He contributes also to OSS communities (Apache, OW2 …) using OSGi. He earned his PhD in Computer Sciences (1994) at University Paris 6 and a HDR in Computer Sciences (2006) at University Grenoble.

Kiev Gama is currently a PhD student in Computer Science at the University of Grenoble, France. He holds B.Sc. and M.Sc. degrees in Computer Science from Universidade Catolica de Pernambuco (Brazil) and University of Grenoble, respectively. His research interests focus on enhancing dependability, monitoring, and management mechanisms for applications targeting dynamic component-based platforms and service-oriented architectures.

Aditya Ghose is Professor in the School of Computer Sc. and Software Engg. at the University of Wollongong, where he is Director of the Decision Systems Lab. He holds PhD and MSc degrees in Computing Science from the University of Alberta, Canada (he also spent parts of his PhD candidature at the Beckman Institute, University of Illinois at Urbana Champaign and the University of Tokyo) and a Bachelor of Engineering degree in Computer Science and Engineering from Jadavpur University, Kolkata, India. While at the University of Alberta, he received the Jeffrey Sampson Memorial Award. His research is (or has been) funded by the Australian Research Council, the Canadian Natural Sciences and Engineering Research Council, the Japanese Institute for Advanced Information Technology (AITEC) and various Australian government agencies as well as companies such as Bluescope Steel, CSC, Holocentric, and Pillar Administration. His research has been published in the top venues in service-oriented computing (SCC and ICSOC), software modelling (ER), software evolution (IWSSD, IWPSE) and AI (*Artificial Intelligence Journal*, AAAI, AAMAS and ECAI). He has been an invited speaker at the Schloss Dagstuhl Seminar Series in Germany and the Banff International Research Station in Canada. He has also been a keynote speaker at several conferences, and program/general chair of several others. He is a senior technical advisor to several companies in the areas of constraint programming and business process management, both in Australia and Canada. He reviews for well-regarded journals such as *Artificial Intelligence, the IBM Systems Journal,* and *the Journal of Autonomous Agents and Multi-Agent Systems*, serves as assessor (Ozreader) for the Australian Research Council and as an external reviewer for the Natural Sciences and Engineering Research Council (NSERC) of Canada and the Science Foundation of Ireland. Professor Ghose is a Research Leader in the Australian Cooperative Research Centre for Smart Services, Co-Director of the Centre for Oncology Informatics at the Illawarra Health and Medical Research Institute, Co-Leader of the University of Wollongong Carbon-Centric Computing Initiative, and Co-Convenor of the Australian Computer Society NSW SIG on Green ICT. He is also Vice-President of CORE, Australia's apex body for computing academics.

Jian Jason Huang received the BE degree in Automation Engineering from Tsinghua University, Beijing, in 2007. He is currently working towards his PhD degree in Computer Science at the University of Texas at Dallas. His research expertise includes software engineering, service-oriented architecture, Web technologies, and artificial intelligence. In particular, he is investigating Web Service composition problems in general contexts, such as cyber-physical worlds, using AI planning and Semantic Web techniques. He has collaborated on a research project with Codekko Software, Inc., on enhancing web server performance. In this research, he designed a prototype system that was later implemented by a group of professional software developers. He has also worked on a research project from the NSF Net-Centric Software and Systems (NCSS) I/UCRC in collaboration with researchers from Lockheed Martin Aero.

Tsung-Jen Huang was born on April 27, 1970 in Taipei, Taiwan. He received his BS and MS degrees in Information Engineering and Computer Science from Feng-Chia University, Taiwan, in 1992 and 1994, respectively. From 1994 to 2001, he was a PhD student in the Department of Computer Science from National Chiao Tung University, Hsinchu, Taiwan. Since 2001, he has been an engineer with Industrial Technology Research Institute, Hsinchu, Taiwan. Moreover he is a PhD student in Computer Science at National Taiwan Ocean University, Keelung, Taiwan. His current interests are in service oriented architecture (SOA), service composition, and clustering algorithms.

Philippe Lalanda is a Professor in Computer Science at Grenoble University. His research interests include software components and services, pervasive computing, and autonomic computing. He received his PhD in Computer Science in 1992 from Nancy University and worked several years as a R&D project leader at Thales Inc. and Schneider Electric.

Chiung-Hon Leon Lee received his PhD degree in Electronic Engineering from the National Chung Cheng University in Taiwan in 2006. He is an Assistant Professor at Department of Computer Science and Information Engineering, Nanhua University, Taiwan. His research interests are in agent-based software engineering, Web services, knowledge representation, and fuzzy time series. Dr. Lee is a member of IEEE, Taiwanese Association for Artificial Intelligence, and Software Engineering Association of Taiwan.

Rich C. Lee was the Enterprise Architect and Technical Consultant in New Convergent Billing System Development Project of Asia Pacific Telecom Group. He joined Foxconn USA, in early 2000 and brought new desktop assembly model for massive production, built up global logistic networks, and was in charge of manufacture business process design and SAP rollout. He was the initiator of Taiwan Supply Chain Project in 1999 and lead Mobile Operator Solution team in 1997 when he served Compaq. He also worked for DEC in 1995 before the merger by Compaq.

Shin-Jie Lee received his PhD in Computer Science and Information Engineering from National Central University (NCU) in Taiwan in 2007 and is currently a postdoctoral Fellow in Software Research Center at NCU. His research interests include agent-based software engineering, service-oriented computing, and object-oriented software engineering.

Yu-Ting Lin earned her Master's degree in Management Information System from National Chengchi University and is currently an Associate Engineer of IDEAS department at Institute for Information Industry in Taiwan. Her current research interests are in the areas of service science, human computer interface, and industry intelligence. Her paper has been published in 2011 Hawaii International Conference on System Sciences and several conference proceedings.

Guo-Kai Ni received his BS in Computer Science and Information Engineering from National Taipei University of Technology (NTUT) in 2005. Currently, he is working toward his PhD degree at NTUT. His areas of interest include software engineering and service-oriented architecture.

Guadalupe Ortiz completed her PhD in Computer Science at the University of Extremadura (Spain) in 2007. Since graduating in 2001 and for the following eight years, she worked as an Assistant Professor as well as a Research Engineer at the University of Extremadura's Computer Science Department. In 2009 she joined the University of Cádiz as Professor in the Computer Science Language and Systems Department. She has published numerous peer-reviewed papers in international journals, workshops, and conferences. She has been a member of various programme and organization committees of scientific workshops and conferences over the last years and acts as a reviewer for several journals. Her research interests embrace aspect-oriented techniques as a way to improve Web service development in various fields, with an emphasis on model-driven extra-functional properties and quality of service, as well as service context-awareness and their adaptation to mobile devices.

Manuel Palomo-Duarte was born in Spain in 1977. He has a PhD in Computer Science and works as Director to the Libre/Open-source Software and Open Knowledge Office of the University of Cádiz, and is Lecturer in the Department of Computer Languages and Systems. At the same university he is Socrates/Erasmus Program Coordinator for Computing degrees. He has taught different courses related to computer programming and operating systems administration using open source software. He is a member of the "Software Process Improvement and Formal Methods" research group. His fields of research are web services and e-learning, with a special focus on web service composition testing and technology-enhanced collaborative applications.

Manfred Reichert holds a PhD in Computer Science and a Diploma in Mathematics. Since January 2008 he has been appointed as Full Professor for Computer Science at the University of Ulm. Before that, he was working as Associate Professor at the University of Twente. His major research interests include next generation process management technology (e.g., adaptive & dynamic processes, data-driven processes), service-oriented computing (e.g., service interoperability, service evolution, mobile services), and advanced IT applications (e.g., e-health, automotive engineering). Manfred pioneered the work on the ADEPT process management technology, for which he received several awards (e.g., doIT Software Award, IFIP TC2 Manfred Paul Award). He has been participating in numerous research projects in the business process management (BPM) area and contributed numerous papers. Further, he has co-organized international and national conferences and workshops. Manfred was PC-Co-Chair of the BPM'08 Conference in Milan and the CoopIS'11 Conference in Crete, and General Co-Chair of the BPM'09 Conference in Ulm.

Walter Rudametkin is currently a PhD candidate at the Université de Grenoble. He obtained his B.Sc. from the Universidad Autónoma de Baja California, in his home town of Ensenada, Mexico. He later received his M.Sc. from Grenoble INP and the Joseph Fourier University in Grenoble while working on dynamic tracing in the Fractal component model. He is currently financed by an industrial CIFRE scholarship from Bull SAS, where he works part time validating his research on the open source Java EE application server JOnAS from OW2. His research interests include service-oriented computing, dynamic service platforms, adaptable middleware, and mechanisms to dynamically assemble applications.

Jun-Bin Shi was born on January 29, 1971, in Yunlin, Taiwan. He received MS degree of Information Engineering and Computer Science from Feng Chia University in 1998. He joined Information and Communications Research Laboratories (ICL) in 1999. ICL is one of the research laboratories in Industrial Technology Research Institute (ITRI). His research interests are in web services, service-oriented architecture, wireless sensor network, and digital rights management.

Arthur Shr received his MS and PhD degrees in Electrical Engineering from National Chung Cheng University, Chiayi, Taiwan, in 1997 and 2006, respectively. He received an award of Graduate Students Research Abroad Program sponsored by National Science Council, Taiwan to be a Visiting Researcher of Computer Science at Louisiana State University, USA from August 2003 to August 2005. Since September2006, he has been a Postdoctoral Researcher of Dr. Peter Chen's Research Group at Computer Science of Louisiana State University, USA. His research interests include knowledge representation, software engineering, service computing, and applications of planning and scheduling in semiconductor manufacturing. He is also a member of IEEE CS and ACM.

Index